Advancing Preservation *for* Archives *and* Manuscripts

ARCHIVAL FUNDAMENTALS SERIES III

Peter J. Wosh, Editor

1 **Leading and Managing Archives and Manuscripts Programs**
Peter Gottlieb and David W. Carmicheal, Editors

2 **Arranging and Describing Archives and Manuscripts**
Dennis Meissner

3 **Advocacy and Awareness for Archivists**
Kathleen D. Roe

4 **Reference and Access for Archives and Manuscripts**
Cheryl Oestreicher

5 **Advancing Preservation for Archives and Manuscripts**
Elizabeth Joffrion and Michèle V. Cloonan

6 **Selecting and Appraising Archives and Manuscripts**
Michelle Light and Margery Sly

7 **Introducing Archives and Manuscripts**
Peter J. Wosh

Advancing Preservation *for* Archives *and* Manuscripts

Elizabeth Joffrion &
Michèle V. Cloonan

CHICAGO

Society of American Archivists
www.archivists.org

Library of Congress Control Number: 2020941889

Printed in the United States of America.

ISBN: 978-1-945246-35-7 (paperback)
eISBN: 978-1-945246-36-4 (epub)
eISBN: 978-1-945246-37-1 (pdf)

Graphic design by Sweeney Design, kasween@sbcglobal.net.

Table of Contents

Table of Contents

FOREWORD

The Evolution of a Book Series

The Society of American Archivists (SAA) first conceived the notion of developing and publishing "manuals relating to major and basic archival functions" in the early 1970s. Charles Frederick Williams (popularly known as C. F. W.) Coker (1932–1983), a former US Marine Corps captain and North Carolina state archivist who recently had been appointed to head the Printed Documents Division of the National Archives and Records Services, edited the initial Basic Manual Series. The first five basic manuals, which appeared in 1977, illustrated the ways in which archivists defined and classified their core concepts at that historical moment:

- *Archives & Manuscripts: Appraisal & Accessioning* by Maynard J. Brichford
- *Archives & Manuscripts: Arrangement & Description* by David B. Gracy II
- *Archives & Manuscripts: Reference & Access* by Sue E. Holbert
- *Archives & Manuscripts: Security* by Timothy Walch
- *Archives & Manuscripts: Surveys* by John Fleckner

The entire series accounted for only 163 pages of text, which included numerous illustrations, graphics, sample forms, charts, and bibliographic insertions. Each 8.5" by 11" softbound pamphlet contained three holes, punched down the left side, for easy insertion into a loose-leaf binder that might be handily referenced at an archivist's desk. Individual volumes sold for $4, though SAA members received a $1 discount.

Archivists operated within a far different cultural, legal, and professional framework during the early and middle years of the 1970s. In 1973, the same year that SAA began work on the Basic Manual Series, IBM introduced the Correcting Selectric II typewriter as its major technological breakthrough, thereby eliminating the need for such popular tools as rubber erasers, correction fluid, and cover-up tape. This revolutionary product seemed destined to alter the nature of document creation forever. During this period, a few archivists had begun grappling with the challenges of something known as "machine-readable records," but a bibliographer who surveyed this puzzling development could still confidently conclude in a 1975 *American Archivist* article that "only a few archival establishments" appeared to be "developing programs for accessioning" such materials. Other momentous—and occasionally unsettling—changes appeared on the horizon. A new copyright law, which was enacted by Congress in 1976 and became effective on New Year's Day 1978, contained significant implications for how archivists would manage collections and serve researchers. Richard Nixon's resignation in 1974 prompted the promulgation of new legislation in 1978 that declared for the first time that presidential and vice presidential records are public documents. Professionally, the archival landscape seemed to be shifting as well. The Association of Canadian Archivists launched an exciting new journal, *Archivaria*, in winter 1975/1976, a development destined to deepen the discipline's intellectual discourse. Regional archival associations formed, became fruitful, and multiplied in the United States. In addition, a new era in archival education began as library schools and history departments inaugurated archives-based graduate programs in the late 1970s, ultimately resulting in a highly credentialed and formally trained corps of professional practitioners.

Such transformations, and many others too numerous to mention here, convinced the Society of American Archivists that only an active publications program that regularly refreshed the existing literature could provide its membership with easy access to rapidly changing trends and best practices. SAA accordingly published the Basic Manual Series II—a second set of five volumes—in the early 1980s:

- *Archives & Manuscripts: Exhibits* by Gail Farr Casterline
- *Archives & Manuscripts: Automated Access* by H. Thomas Hickerson
- *Archives & Manuscripts: Maps and Architectural Drawings* by Ralph E. Ehrenberg
- *Archives & Manuscripts: Public Programs* by Ann E. Pederson and Gail Farr Casterline
- *Archives & Manuscripts: Reprography* by Carolyn Hoover Sung

Over the years, SAA published scores of other titles, each illustrating the rich diversity of archival work: administration of photo collections, conservation, machine-readable records, law, management, a basic glossary, collections of readings on archival theory and practice, and books specific to archives in a variety of institutional settings (i.e., colleges and universities, businesses and corporations, religious and scientific institutions, museums, government agencies, historical societies, etc.). Even with the proliferation of publications, the bedrock of archival practice rested on the core knowledge represented in the basic manuals, which were reconceptualized and rechristened between 1990 and 1993 as the Archival Fundamentals Series:

- *Understanding Archives and Manuscripts* by James O'Toole
- *Arranging and Describing Archives and Manuscripts* by Fredric M. Miller
- *Managing Archival and Manuscript Repositories* by Thomas Wilsted and William Nolte
- *Selecting and Appraising Archives and Manuscripts* by F. Gerald Ham
- *Preserving Archives and Manuscripts* by Mary Lynn Ritzenthaler
- *Providing Reference Services for Archives and Manuscripts* by Mary Jo Pugh
- *The Glossary of Archivists, Manuscript Curators, and Records Managers* by Lynn Lady Bellardo and Lewis Bellardo

A second iteration of the seven books in this revamped series appeared roughly fifteen years later as the Archival Fundamentals Series II:

- *Understanding Archives and Manuscripts* by James O'Toole and Richard J. Cox
- *Arranging and Describing Archives and Manuscripts* by Kathleen D. Roe
- *Managing Archival and Manuscript Repositories* by Michael Kurtz
- *Selecting and Appraising Archives and Manuscripts* by Frank Boles
- *Preserving Archives and Manuscripts* by Mary Lynn Ritzenthaler
- *Providing Reference Services for Archives and Manuscripts* by Mary Jo Pugh
- *A Glossary of Archival and Records Terminology* by Richard Pearce-Moses

Mary Jo Pugh and Richard J. Cox edited these multivolume compilations, which almost instantaneously became required texts in archival education courses and necessary additions to archivists' bookshelves. The Archival Fundamentals Series I and II differed in scope and scale from the initial Basic Manual Series. For example, John Fleckner's comprehensive treatment of surveys did not appear in need of revision and dropped out of the series. Security became incorporated into a broader manual on preservation. SAA commissioned an introductory overview of the field, added a new book that focused on managerial issues, and developed a glossary with the goal of defining and historicizing key archival concepts. Beginning in the 1970s, both Archival Fundamentals Series I and II incorporated and delineated the evolving descriptive standards that defined professional practice, dissected the contentious debates surrounding appraisal and deaccessioning that enlivened archival discourse in the 1980s, and reflected the growing emphases on an expanding user base and more complex reference services that revolutionized reading rooms and repositories in the late twentieth century.

This third edition—Archival Fundamentals Series III—contains important continuities and significant departures from its predecessors:

- A new book, *Advocacy and Awareness for Archivists* by Kathleen D. Roe, reflects an increased understanding that these functions undergird all aspects of archival work.
- The management volume, *Leading and Managing Archives and Manuscripts Programs* edited by Peter Gottlieb and David W. Carmicheal, has been reconfigured to focus especially on leadership and to provide readers with opportunities to explore their individual managerial styles.
- *Advancing Preservation for Archives and Manuscripts* by Elizabeth Joffrion and Michèle V. Cloonan addresses digital challenges and focuses on such current issues as risk management, ethical considerations, and sustainability.
- *Arranging and Describing Archives and Manuscripts* by Dennis Meissner, *Reference and Access for Archives and Manuscripts* by Cheryl Oestreicher, and *Selecting and Appraising Archives and Manuscripts* by Michelle Light and Margery Sly may appear familiar topics to readers of the previous two series, but each book illustrates the innovations in thought and practice that have transformed these archival functions over the past fifteen years.
- A general overview volume that I am preparing, *Introducing Archives and Manuscripts*, provides a broad introduction to the historical, philosophical, and theoretical foundations of the profession.

One contribution that constituted a cornerstone of the previous series has been reformatted to maximize its currency and usability. Although not part of the Archival Fundamentals Series III, the *Dictionary of Archives Terminology* (dictionary.archivists.org) will replace *A Glossary of Archival and Records Terminology* and will be maintained and updated as a digital resource by SAA's Dictionary Working Group.

We hope that undergraduate and graduate students, new professionals, seasoned archival veterans, and others in the information science and public history fields will find the seven volumes in the Archival Fundamentals Series III helpful, provocative, and essential to both their intellectual life and their daily work. As Richard J. Cox observed in his preface to an earlier edition of the series, the time has long passed "when individuals entering the archival profession could read a few texts, peruse some journals, attend a workshop and institute or two, and walk away with a sense that they grasped the field's knowledge and discipline." This series provides an entry point and a synthetic distillation of a much broader literature that spans an impressive array of academic disciplines. We encourage you, of course, to do a deeper dive into each of the individual topics covered here. But we also remain confident that this series, like its predecessors, provides an honest and accurate snapshot of archival best practices at the beginning of the third decade of the twenty-first century.

The authors, of course, deserve full credit for their individual contributions. The Archival Fundamentals Series III itself, though, constitutes a collaborative enterprise that benefited from the work of SAA Publications Board members, editors, and interns throughout the past decade. These individuals helped to define the series parameters, reviewed proposals and manuscripts, and shepherded various projects to conclusion. Special shout-outs (in alphabetical order) are owed to: Bethany Anderson, Jessica Ballard, Roland Baumann, Cara Bertram, Mary Caldera, Amy Cooper Cary, Jessica Chapel, Paul Conway, J. Gordon Daines, Todd Daniels-Howell, Sarah Demb, Jody DeRidder, Keara Duggan, Margaret Fraser, Thomas J. Frusciano, Krista Gray, Gregory Hunter, Geoffrey Huth, Petrina Jackson, Joan Krizack, Christopher Lee, Donna McCrea, Jennifer Davis McDaid, Kathryn Michaelis, Nicole Milano, Lisa Mix, Tawny Nelb, Kevin Proffitt, Christopher Prom, Mary Jo Pugh, Aaron Purcell, Colleen Rademaker, Caryn Radick, Dennis Riley, Michael Shallcross, Mark Shelstad, Jennifer Thomas, Ciaran Trace, Anna Trammell, Joseph Turrini, Tywanna Whorley, and Deborah Wythe. Nancy Beaumont has been an inspirational executive director for SAA, as well as a brilliant editor in her own right. Abigail Christian, SAA's editorial and production coordinator, has skillfully shepherded design and layout. Teresa Brinati, keenly insightful and good-humored as always, remains the epitome of competent leadership and has transformed the SAA publications program into a model for professional associations. It has been a privilege and great fun to work with everyone on this project.

PETER J. WOSH
Editor, Archival Fundamentals Series III
Society of American Archivists

Section I

Preservation Frameworks

1

The Topography of Preservation Today

All things will eat themselves up.

—*Zuni saying*[1]

Introduction

The aim of this book is to complement—and augment—Mary Lynn Ritzenthaler's classic, *Preserving Archives & Manuscripts*, the second edition of which was published in 2010.[2] Ritzenthaler's book focuses on implementing preservation programs in archives, establishing a collections-friendly environment, storing and handling archival materials properly, copying and reformatting archives and records, and evaluating approaches to conservation and repair.

Advancing Preservation of Archives and Manuscripts covers topics not addressed by Ritzenthaler, including digital records, improved (and more rapid) access to records, the relationship between appraisal and preservation, risk management, sustainable preservation, the role of social networking and community archiving on preservation, and a consideration of who has the right to preserve and who decides *what* will be preserved. This book does not supersede Ritzenthaler's; most of the text of her book continues to be valuable to preservation managers. Rather, as the world around us has changed, we have attempted to provide a new context for preservation and to look at the opportunities and challenges that the digital world presents.

Our goals are to offer an overview of the current trends and challenges in archival preservation and to introduce our readers to the critical studies, standards, and guidelines that shape current preservation thinking. These principles and practices, central to the advancement of preservation, are a comprehensive review of preservation initiatives, protocols, or strategies; the aim here is to give students and professionals a holistic view of archival preservation, including an emphasis on the stewardship of digital resources as part of a comprehensive preservation management plan. This holistic approach distinguishes this book from previous works on archival preservation. The field of preservation has become increasingly bifurcated into foci on analog materials and digital resources, and distinctly lacking is literature that comprehensively addresses best practice and theory associated with the preservation and management of materials across these two realms. We hope that subsequent editions of the Society of American Archivists' Archival Fundamentals Series will continue to unite digital and analog preservation into an integrated set of practices that will inform future generations. This book is a beginning. We trust that our efforts focusing on theory and practice will spur additional research and writing that address the range of challenges associated with the preservation of cultural heritage, regardless of format.

Among the many subjects that we address are the history of archival preservation; trends and challenges in preservation management; the digital preservation landscape; new uses and users of records; the impact of More Product, Less Process (MPLP) on preservation practices; the similarities and differences in preservation practices among libraries, archives, and museums; risk management, community archiving; sustainability and the impact of climate change; cultural sensitivity; rapidly changing technology; and the future of archival preservation. We explore these topics in the context of a constantly changing social, educational, and political landscape.

This book is not intended to be a technical manual for archival preservation. Many excellent sources for that will be cited in the chapters that follow. Rather, we present here a context for preservation, and we look at standards and best practices. This book provides a framework for thinking about how preservation is practiced today and how it may be carried out in the future. Technology has transformed preservation. Increasingly, the challenge of digital preservation has created an artificial divide between professionals devoted to the "traditional" preservation of analog materials and those in digital preservation. At a basic level, the fundamental principles guiding archival preservation remain vital and relevant. However, to remain useful, archivists and other preservation professionals must envision a unified approach to our work and the principles that guide us. Digital preservation is in its infancy compared to the preservation of traditional types of objects, but the challenges associated with digital preservation have led to the development of new guidelines and standards, bringing preservation into a new era. The field will continue to develop new strategies to steward our collections and preserve our cultural heritage.

Our premise is that preservation, regardless of the format addressed, must be understood in a broad professional, social, and political context that shapes preservation programs. The infrastructures in which preservation programs exist are changing, but one thing remains constant—because archivists are stewards of cultural heritage, their role is to ensure that today's records will be accessible in the future. This book aims to advance archivists' knowledge and understanding of what it means to preserve our heritage.

The Topography

Preservation management emerged in this country as a distinct discipline in the 1960s and early 1970s. The field grew broadly in the late 1970s and throughout the 1980s, aided in part by federal funding and foundation grants from such institutions as the National Endowment for the Humanities, the Andrew W. Mellon Foundation, and, later, the Institute of Museum and Library Services. Preservation management was also spurred on by the establishment of such regional conservation centers as the Northeast Document Conservation Center (NEDCC) in 1973 and the Conservation Center for Art and Historic Artifacts (CCAHA) in 1977; by the opening of the graduate programs in preservation administration and conservation at Columbia University in 1981 and the subsequent creation of preservation courses in dozens of library, archives, and information science programs; the preservation activities of the Society of American Archivists, the American Library Association, and the American Institute for the Conservation of Historic and Artistic Works; and the considerable conservation and preservation outreach programs of the National Archives and Records Administration (NARA) and the Library of Congress (LC). Local and statewide preservation organizations were also founded. All in all, the environment for preservation was rich, and many archives and libraries established preservation programs and hired preservation managers.[3]

Many of the preservation infrastructures that were formed through the early 1990s are still in place, though others have shifted or disappeared. Some have attempted to address the dramatic changes wrought by technology. For example, the Council on Library Resources (CLR), now the Council on Library and Information Resources (CLIR) from its founding in 1956 was concerned with the preservation of collections and over the decades sponsored much research on this topic. In 1986, CLR created a program, the Commission on Preservation and Access, to advocate for preservation, particularly for the microfilming of brittle materials.

Computers have been transforming educational institutions for over fifty years. Automation made it possible to create online catalogs and extensive interlibrary loan programs, which led to the widespread (even global) sharing of information. An increasing number of digital information objects were created. By the 1990s, the collections in libraries and archives were increasingly born digital, thereby creating new preservation challenges. At the same time, it was possible to digitize analog collections. Digitization initiatives grew quickly with the rise of the internet and social media.

The internet has transformed the ways in which we learn, do research, and socialize. This has revolutionized education. Online education has led to new ways of collaborative learning and new expectations about long-term access and associated preservation of digital resources.

Access to massive amounts of data has altered research designs and strategies. Of course, the very ways we learn and play have changed as well. These changes dramatically affect libraries, archives, and museums, as the demand for online access to our collections—analog and digital—has grown. Yet, today, only a small percentage of our collections have been digitized.

However, the solution is not just to digitize more and more of our collections. Many new presentation platforms, including social media, live feeds, and streaming video have made information immediately accessible. Additional new technologies are being used, such as Geocaching and other mobile apps that lead the public to heritage collections and sites. And, in some institutions, exhibits may include immersive experiences with virtual reality. Each advance in technology leads to new preservation and security challenges. The maintenance and storage of these new formats is expensive and consumes considerable energy.

We have yet to achieve digital equity in the United States and in the world. Many people still lack access to the internet. Threats to net neutrality are ongoing. Personal privacy is disappearing. Cyber-crimes are proliferating. Trustworthiness is an issue, of which fake news is but one component.[4] Intellectual property issues continue to abound, and copyright reform is not likely for the foreseeable future. Ownership of much information is proprietary and inaccessible except through a pay wall. All of these challenges have an impact on our ability to preserve and access the information that we want and need.

New and Old Skills

With the tremendous changes facing the archival profession, new skills are required to meet the preservation challenges of the future. As we have established, the creation of digital records and digital publishing has significantly increased over the past two decades. Some genres, such as bound periodicals, have almost completely disappeared from libraries, archives, and museums. Common public areas for teaching and learning have replaced reference areas, periodical reading rooms, and other study spaces. Concurrently, many collections are being moved to off-site storage. In libraries, these newly opened spaces are used for research rooms, tutoring centers, coffee and food purveyors, and other patron-oriented services. Some museums are shutting their libraries down or moving them off-site and using the space for new exhibition galleries, staff offices, restaurants, or expanded museum stores.

Simultaneously, demand has increased for digital content that can be accessed by people who may never set foot in an archives, library, or museum—but who want to access resources from wherever they are. Hence, scholars who work remotely—and who desire full access to information from their homes or mobile devices—may be surprised to discover that they still need to go into a library or archives for some of their research needs.

To meet these needs, cultural heritage institutions are increasingly hiring professionals from the legal and IT fields, resulting in an interdisciplinary approach to information management in today's cultural heritage institutions. Moreover, some libraries and archives have established separate departments for digital initiatives. In these institutions, digital curators and preservation administrators may report to different units and will need to collaborate to ensure that preservation activities are efficiently and sustainably managed across the organization. In addition, a whole world of legal issues has emerged that will require access to attorneys as part of the larger preservation picture.

The next generation of information professionals will increasingly focus on the experience of users, and archivists have traditionally trained their professionals to preserve and protect collections while making them accessible. Today's graduates must be adept at creating new user experiences for analog and digital collections while ensuring their longevity. They must also be able to implement new technologies as they emerge. Computer scientists build systems, but librarians and archivists link people to information. People remain at the center of the work of the cultural heritage professional. Students entering these professions must understand how to fulfill their preservation responsibilities while simultaneously making cultural heritage collections accessible and user friendly. And, they must be prepared to become digital stewards of our growing virtual collections.

These opportunities and challenges impact preservation in important ways. Quite simply: how information is created and used will influence how archivists preserve it. At the same time, everything cannot be preserved, so archivists must decide what they can and should preserve. Do the changes in information creation influence preservation practices? What are the costs of sustaining our collections? As yet, no definitive answers exist.

As archives shift, so too must preservation. Archivists must facilitate the preservation of their institutional collections and lend their services to the communities that want these services. Examples include hosting community-based institutional repositories, providing advice on preservation strategies, and strategizing the repatriation of some of what resides in archives. Future archivists require training that will enable them to deal with new realities.

In this book, we touch on these topics, considering some in more than one chapter. Here is an overview.

Section 1

Chapters 1–4 focus on the context, theory, and historical development of archival preservation. As we have suggested in the present chapter, *preservation deals with the relationship between records and the environments in which they are created and maintained.* At its core, preservation manages heritage through local customs, professional practices and standards, education, the enactment of legislation, and international conventions and charters.

Records exist in many forms, including emerging formats that demand new approaches to preservation. Will the future involve one or two sets of professional practices?

In chapter 2, "History of Archival Preservation," we provide an overview of significant events in the development of preservation and conservation theory and consider the expanding societal responsibility of archives for the provision of responsible and sustainable preservation strategies. We explore the purpose of preservation and the rationales that have been used for preserving cultural heritage. We review the evolution of archival theory related to appraisal and the relationship between models such as More Product Less Process (MPLP) and preservation activities. And, we compare the life-cycle versus continuum models for preservation. We discuss the concept of cultural memory, authenticity, documentation, legal requirements, cultural differences in recordkeeping, and community value and use.

"Principles of Archival Preservation" are the focus of chapter 3. Here, we offer an overview of best practices, principles, and values for archival preservation, and we introduce core preservation concepts. We consider basic definitions and core archival principles such as the sanctity of evidence, original order, and hierarchical description. We acknowledge that preservation strategies may address an entire collection or selected documents or formats, or a recombination of the whole-to-part relationship, particularly in the digital realm.

In this chapter, we also consider in detail the challenges presented in a digital environment and describe the differences between digital curation, digital stewardship, and digital preservation. From there, we discuss archival ethics and preservation. We conclude the chapter with a consideration of archival preservation principles in the digital context.

Chapter 4, "The Context for Archival Preservation," compares and contrasts preservation management in a variety of cultural heritage institutions, with a focus on archives, libraries, and museums. We show that archival preservation must be practiced in institutional settings with a variety of missions. Professional training in the various cultural heritage subdisciplines (library and information science, archival science, museum studies, and conservation) may impact our approaches to preservation. We consider key studies central to an understanding of preservation practice, and we review significant preservation standards. We identify professional organizations that provide preservation leadership and advocacy.

Section 2

Chapters 5–8 focus on planning and implementing a holistic preservation management program that accounts for digital and analog content in a unified and balanced manner. Our discussion covers policy development, assessment, the prioritization of institutional preservation goals, and advocacy for needed resources. It looks at the steps required to establish a program, such as staff management, strategies to address the causes of deterioration and loss in collections, standards and best practices for maintaining stable storage environments and systems, and the use of digital and analog formats. Approaches to conservation are also considered. It concludes with a chapter on risk management.

In chapter 5, we cover the necessary aspects of developing a program such as mission, vision, and strategy, policy development, preservation assessments, budgeting for preservation, grant programs that support preservation, and program evaluation.

Once initial planning for a preservation program has been completed, implementation is the next stage. Chapter 6, "Administering a Preservation Program," discusses the implementation and ongoing evaluation of a program, as well as its sustainability. Staffing, outreach, risks to collections, environmental monitoring, facilities, and conservation are considered in an administrative context.

The focus of chapter 7 is "Preserving Analog and Digital Media." Here, we look at causes of deterioration, as well as frameworks and tools that can be used to organize the care of collections. The chapter also provides an overview of the formats most likely to be found in archives. The chapter suggests ways in which archivists can systematically approach the preservation of collections—regardless of their formats.

In chapter 8, "Risk Management: A Programmatic Approach," we consider several approaches to managing risk. The first is at the institutional level. Every institution must be able to protect its assets as well as ensure the continuity of services to its users. We show how risk management principles can be used to improve disaster planning and recovery. We then give examples of how risk management is used to assess building environments, security systems, IT systems, and digital assets. We show that risk management is a critical aspect of preservation.

Section 3

In chapters 9–10, we address the ethics and moral implications of contemporary preservation practices by focusing on two emerging areas: sustainability and ethical problems in preservation.

"Sustainable Preservation Practices" are considered in chapter 9. In an era of shrinking budgets and with the threat of climate change, cultural heritage institutions must become increasingly efficient stewards of the environment. We explore passive approaches to preservation and sustainable climate management, research on sustainable preservation practices, the impact of digital technology on the environment, and developing and administering green facilities. We conclude that sustainability is as much a behavioral hurdle as a technological one. Sustainability is a balancing act, much as is preservation itself.

Chapter 10, "The Right to Preserve: Who Decides?," considers ethical problems in archival preservation and access when archivists collaborate with underrepresented communities. What questions must archivists consider when they seek to collect and preserve documentation foundational to community identity? We reconsider ideas of cultural ownership and memory, and the role of digital archives, community archiving, and shared stewardship.

We conclude the book with chapter 11, "Final Remarks." In it, we offer final observations about emerging trends in preservation.

Terminology

We draw our definitions from several sources: *A Glossary of Archival and Records Terminology* (referred to in this book as the *SAA Glossary*), edited by Richard Pearce-Moses; his article on "Archival Preservation," in the *Encyclopedia of Archival Science*;[5] Ross Harvey and Martha R. Mahard, *The Preservation Management Handbook*;[6] and previous work by the authors of this volume.[7] We have used the terminology of the profession as consistently as possible, given that definitions are continually evolving and sources do not always use the terms consistently. We have endeavored to point out any inconsistencies.

The Future of Professional Practice

Enormous changes in technology will affect the future of archival preservation. Pressure on us to make our collections freely available and in a variety of formats will increase. Does the preservation and management of digital content constitute a paradigm shift for the archival profession? At the very least, digital stewardship will continue to impact preservation practices.

In her foreword to *Keepers of Our Digital Future: An Assessment of the National Digital Stewardship Residencies, 2013–16,* Abby Smith Rumsey observes,

> Today, librarians and archivists whose practices once embraced the wisdom of fixing knowledge permanently onto enduring formats in canonical forms—the photograph, the printed page—to ensure long-term access must be flexible, self-documenting, and transparent in their practices. While permanent solutions are elusive, incremental growth and ready response to the changes in the communities they serve are vital.[8]

Flexibility and transparency are, Rumsey suggests, two of the traits archivists must engage to advance preservation. These traits will continue to inform archival preservation theory and practice in the future.

NOTES

1 Zuni saying, quoted in Chip Colwell, *Plundered Skulls and Stolen Spirits: Inside the Fight to Reclaim Native America's Culture* (Chicago: University of Chicago Press, 2017), 52.

2 Mary Lynn Ritzenthaler, *Preserving Archives & Manuscripts*, 2nd ed. (Chicago: Society of American Archivists, 2010).

3 Michèle Valerie Cloonan and Patricia Norcott tracked the increase in preservation administration positions in libraries. See "The Evolution of Preservation Librarianship as Reflected in Job Descriptions from 1975 through 1987," *College & Research Libraries* 50, no. 6 (1989): 646–56, https://doi.org/10.5860/crl_50_06_646.

4 See "Most Americans—Especially Millennials—Say Libraries Can Help Them Find Reliable, Trustworthy Information," http://www.pewresearch.org/fact-tank/2017/08/30/most-americans-especially-millennials-say-libraries-can-help-them-find-reliable-trustworthy-information, captured at https://perma.cc/N6D7-4J6L.

5 Richard Pearce-Moses, *A Glossary of Archival and Records Terminology* (Chicago: Society of American Archivists, 2005), https://www2.archivists.org/glossary, and Richard Pearce-Moses, "Archival Preservation," in *Encyclopedia of Archival Science*, ed. Luciana Duranti and Patricia C. Franks (Lanham, MD: Rowman & Littlefield, 2015), 75–78.

6 Ross Harvey and Martha R. Mahard, *The Preservation Management Handbook: A 21st-Century Guide for Libraries, Archives, and Museums* (Lanham, MD: Rowman & Littlefield, 2014).

7 Michèle Valerie Cloonan, "Conservation and Preservation of Library and Archival Materials," in *Encyclopedia of Library and Information Sciences (ELIS)*, ed. Marcia J. Bates and Mary Niles Maack, 3rd ed. (CRC Press, Taylor & Francis Group, 2009); Michèle Valerie Cloonan, *Preserving Our Heritage: Perspectives from Antiquity to the Digital Age* (Chicago: ALA; London: Facet, 2015); Elizabeth Joffrion and Natalia Fernández, "Collaboration between Tribal and Nontribal Organizations: Suggested Best Practices for Sharing Expertise, Cultural Resources, and Knowledge," *American Archivist* 78, no. 1 (2015): 192–237, https://doi.org/10.17723/0360-9081.78.1.192.

8 Meridith Beck Mink, *Keepers of Our Digital Future: An Assessment of the National Digital Stewardship Residencies, 2013–16* (Washington, DC: Council on Library and Information Resources, December 2016), vii.

2

History of Archival Preservation

Introduction

For archivists, who are responsible for ensuring the reliability, authenticity, and usability of accumulations and collections of oral and written organizational and personal records and other documentary materials,[1] the creation and maintenance of such materials is closely linked to preservation management. The importance of preserving records has been recognized since the beginning of archives and recordkeeping. Records exist in many kinds of institutional and cultural settings. As the nature, use, and management of records and archives have evolved, so too have preservation practices. This chapter considers the development of archival preservation by looking at historical contexts, approaches, and settings of preservation as practiced in cultural heritage organizations, including community-based and volunteer organizations that the profession too often has marginalized. Archives are preserved in increasingly diverse communities, and nontraditional repositories play important roles in promoting community memory and social justice.[2] Indeed, a combination of traditional and emerging archival practices guides professionals today. Therefore, how preservation is carried out in a variety of settings, which we cover throughout this book, is worth exploring. Preservation has ancient roots, but motives and approaches have continually changed for archivists and other professionals in librarianship and museology. This chapter traces that evolution.

The Purpose of Preservation

Preservation activities are socially constructed and situational. That is to say, as the nature and use of records have evolved, so too have the ways in which archivists preserve them. As archivist and historian Lester Cappon once observed, an archivist is concerned with "the genuine origin and continuous preservation of the records."[3] The meaning of "continuous preservation" has necessarily evolved. The earliest known records were created in Mesopotamia and in China.

These records were closely held by those in power. Preservation meant storage and arrangement in a safe environment accessible to only a few people and often in highly durable formats such as stone, shell, and baked clay. Over time—and throughout many cultures—records became increasingly portable and also accessible to an ever-expanding number of literate users. The rise of printing, universities, nation-states, and learned societies made records and their descriptions increasingly available—at least to those who were educated or who had the means to travel to where the records resided. Today, archivists continue to preserve analog and digital materials for an increasingly wide audience as well as to support accountability, discoverability, and transparency. Unfortunately, this is not universally true. In countries with totalitarian governments, access to records continues to be limited. Wars and terrorism often result in the deliberate or collateral destruction of heritage, thus making continuous preservation impossible.

In an influential 2013 article, archival educator Terry Cook identified four archival "paradigms:" juridical legacy, cultural memory, societal engagement, and community archiving. Each paradigm provides additional context when one considers the purpose of preservation.[4] He discusses the evolving nature of the field since the end of World War II, an evolution that has come about for the following reasons: the dramatic increase in the number of records created; an interest among historians in the lives of ordinary people, rather than primarily in the notable or powerful; and a paradigmatic shift from archives-as-evidence to archives-as-memory. In this evolution, archivists have become mediators between dynamic collective memory—as reflected by the increasingly diverse holdings of archives—and an expanding stakeholder community. Archival theorists Anne J. Gilliland, Sue McKemmish, and Andrew J. Lau describe this shift as the "archival multiverse."[5] At the same time, information and communication technology has "disrupted" and expanded the field with new types of records, records creation, and transmission methods that have transformed preservation practices.

Cook views the archival field as transitioning to a new mode of archival thought in which archives are the locus of community sense-making and voice. Archivists have increasingly responded through active collaborations with communities to create more democratic, inclusive, and culturally responsive archives and archival practices. Although Cook never says so, this archival change affects preservation as well. Strategies for preserving and conserving records must now consider community stakeholders, as well as traditional decision-makers and audiences. And the community itself increasingly is defined broadly as anyone who creates information of any kind.

Even wealthy, democratic, and industrialized societies include the "information rich and the information poor." In the past, the term "digital divide" was geopolitical: it was assumed that wealthier countries had higher rates of internet use. In fact, in some countries, notably Japan, Korea, Norway, Sweden, Finland, Denmark, and the Netherlands, this has proven true.[6] However, studies have shown that, in the United States, access to information is severely restricted for those who do not have computers and lack online skills. Lack of access can sometimes be linked to social policies and economics. Public policy experts Karen Mossberger, Caroline J. Tolbert, and Mary Stansbury refer to this as "virtual inequality."[7] The potential end of net neutrality in the United States could intensify this digital divide because less information on the web will be available for free. Network management could become less transparent than it now is, and the paid prioritization of content could dramatically increase. The political implications of this are huge—and frightening. Governments, and therefore policies and laws, are typically controlled by those who control information.

A more subtle barrier to users of records also exists. As archival educator Kelvin White convincingly points out, "What many archivists fail to reflect upon is that during . . . appraisal, it is in their attempts to be impartial in preserving what is believed to have most value for society, that they perpetuate and privilege the values of the dominant group."[8]

The purpose and value of recordkeeping practices became increasingly formalized from the eighteenth century on, as did preservation activities. Only in the twentieth century, however, did preservation management, with its focus on the systematic and ongoing care of collections, develop as a field. The earliest preservation activities focused primarily on safe storage and the repair of damaged items. This gradually shifted as copying developed as a way of preserving information. Texts were copied from manuscript to manuscript, and later from manuscript to printed edition. The aims of copying were to preserve and transmit the content of documents.

Though archivists usually see preservation decisions as having to do with incoming materials, it is worth noting that archivist and historian Ernst Posner traces the practice of also retaining copies of outgoing letters. These copies were preserved in registers, thus, some people generated two sets of archives: original documents, received in the course of transactions, and registers.

The originals were stored in a "safe place," such as a church, public office, or archives. During the classical and medieval periods, a document's authenticity was inherent in its physical location. However, some unscrupulous people intentionally deposited forged documents into institutions to create the appearance of authenticity. Early historical scholars studied intrinsic and extrinsic evidence to determine authenticity. The evidence they used included the style of the script, the language, signatures, various markings, and seals. The resulting discipline came to be known as diplomatics. In 1681, Jean Mabillon published a treatise on the study of documents, *De Re Diplomatica*.[9] René-Prosper Tassin and Charles-François Toustain greatly expanded his work in the mid-eighteenth century.[10] Their writings paved the way for the use of diplomatics in the related disciplines of paleography, analytical bibliography, and textual criticism. Today, these traditional analytical techniques can be paired with new technologies to determine the age of the writing surfaces, inks, and other clues to document creation and authenticity of the records. Archival educator Luciana Duranti writes extensively about the origin and application of diplomatics in archival practice, arguing that diplomatic theory is essential to the interpretation and preservation of modern documents.[11]

In Europe, until the eighteenth century, few central depositories of archival materials existed. Records remained with the agencies that created them. Originals *and* copies were necessary. This early practice of copying archives presaged copying in modern times through xerography, photoreproduction, reformatting, and digitization. Copying has long been a preservation strategy that remains relevant in the management of digital formats.

Historic Landmarks in Preservation in Archives, Libraries, and Museums

To explain the development of preservation as a professional discipline requires acknowledging that preservation is not just for archivists. It is shared across cultural heritage and other professions, and it must be understood within the historical context in which each discipline developed. Libraries, archives, and museums have common roots. For many centuries, the disciplines were regarded as parallel and even interchangeable, although today most observers acknowledge that significant differences exist between them. The Latin term *museum* is derived from the Greek term *mouseion,* "place of study, library, or school of art and poetry," and originally "a seat or shrine of the Muses." The modern use of the museum as a "building to display objects" dates from the seventeenth and eighteenth centuries. The Latin terms *archivum* or *archiva* mean "written records." The French concept of archives, as "records or documents preserved as evidence" and as "a place where public records and historical documents are kept," dates from the sixteenth century. The term *library* derives from the Latin *librarium,* "book-case, chest for books," and *libraria,* "a bookseller's shop." Modern usage dates to the Renaissance, with *librarie* understood as "a place for books."[12]

The earliest libraries were composed of collections of texts that documented official religious and governmental activities. Little distinction was made in the common understanding of "a library" and "a museum" until the early modern period, when the development of typography and movable type led to a significant increase in the availability of texts, particularly in book form. Libraries emerged as places for collections of books and journals, and museums as places for the collection and display of objects.

In *Fiat Lux, Fiat Latebra,*[13] D. W. Krummel divides the history of librarianship into seven ages that roughly correspond to broad cultural and political shifts in Western civilization. This framework is also useful when we consider archival history. While today this schema appears limited because it does not account for the multiverse of records that have been created, though not necessarily preserved, by Indigenous and other marginalized groups, it is nonetheless a useful frame for thinking about the evolution of preservation. Temporal, geographical, and personal factors will always affect preservation.

The sixth age, which Krummel dubs "Democratic," coincides in part with the French Revolution and the founding of the Archives Nationales in 1789, as an office of the Assemblée Nationale. The archives became an official part of the French government in 1794.[14] Also, in that year, the Messidor Decree stated that archives must be accessible to the public. This edict further upheld the value of all records, even those of the "ancien régime" that were being destroyed.[15] Records destruction constitutes a familiar and perpetual historical problem in which new regimes set about to extinguish traces of an old order. Conquering armies frequently destroy the records of the conquered, though, on rare occasions, victors retain such records as evidence of the nefarious activities of their foes.[16] Clearly, the new French government was trying to systemize its recordkeeping while preserving as much of its patrimony as possible—with patrimony being the accurate description. This was one of many activities that led to the centralization and modernization of archives administration in France.

The French archives contained depositories of older materials as well as the new records of public agencies. Of special significance for preservationists is the fact that the creation of a national archives implied that a state would assume responsibility for the care of its documentary heritage

Occurring in the years beginning roughly:	A kind of institution emerged, the objectives of which may generally be characterized as:	The institutional objectives were to serve as a:	The library was sponsored by the:	The library's contents were seen as comprising mainly:
1. BC 3000	I. Quotidian	Working archive	Emerging civilization	Evidence of consensual understandings
2. BC 300	II. Academic	Center of culture	Society in search of authority	A supplement to discourse and dialogue
3. AD 500	III. Religious	Archival shrine	Monastery (Benedictine)	a. Service to God b. Tradition as authority
4. AD 1350	IV. Humanistic	Testimony to virtue	Renaissance prince	Munificence and beauty in content and form
5. AD 1600	V. Scientific	Basis for knowledge and study	Personal scholar or institution (university)	The record of the advancement of learning
6. AD 1700, 1850	VI. Democratic	Instrument for social betterment	Government, emanating from the (moral) policy	Public reading matter, in the interests of explicit values
7. AD 1910, 1945, 1970?	VII. Technocratic	Instrument for social change	Government, emanating from the authoritative (functional) policy	All communications media, in the interests of implicit values

FIGURE 2.1. The Seven Ages of Librarianship

Source: Donald W. Krummel, *Fiat Lux, Fiat Latebra: A Celebration of Historical Library Functions*, Occasional Papers (Champaign: Graduate School of Library and Information Science, University of Illinois, 1999), 2. Reproduced by permission of the iSchool, University of Illinois, Urbana-Champaign.

and carry out activities to ensure its perpetuation. In the nineteenth century, preservation was gradually included in the administrative practices of archives in many places around the world where records were in the custody of individuals, organizations, or the state. This raised a fundamental issue: is the preservation of archival materials inherently a state-sponsored activity, or should it be accomplished by organizations and other entities that create the information that needs to be preserved? Every information-generating entity, from the most grassroots to the most academic, from the poorest to the richest, needs to find a way to save the information it generates. What to save and how to do it, who does it, and for how long are just a few of the issues that make archival preservation tremendously complex.

Nineteenth-century "preservation" literature focused on the treatment of damaged paper.[17] According to Claire S. Marwick, the author of a historical study of document restoration methods, document repair began in earnest for archival records in 1837. Though early restoration techniques were not well documented, she was able to detail late-nineteenth-century document restoration practices at the Vatican, the Archives de France, and the manuscript division of the Library of Congress.[18]

Also, in the eighteenth and nineteenth centuries, a number of archival manuals were published in France, Prussia, the Netherlands, Spain, Italy, and elsewhere. These efforts helped to standardize and professionalize archival practices. This was also a period of great colonial expansion. Recordkeeping infrastructures were integral to many aspects of colonial administration, including communication and information management, financial accounting, and documenting and monitoring the colonized and their activities.[19] In particular, recordkeeping infrastructures were used in the colonial period to document activities such as land claims and slavery.[20] Slave ship records are some of the most horrific and gruesome documents to have survived. They endure primarily because of the commercial nature of slavery.

Important archival concepts to emerge during the eighteenth and nineteenth centuries were *respect des fonds,* the sanctity of original order, and the principle of provenance. Some scholars have pointed out that *respect des fonds* developed throughout Europe at around the same time, though it is often linked to France.[21] *Respect des fonds* and the principle of provenance created order and context for records; preservation activities were subsequently created around these principles. The so-called Dutch Manual,[22] Muller, Feith, and Fruin's work, was first published in 1898. The manual reifies the concept of original order and the principle of provenance and describes systematic organization. These archival practices were foundational to the future of archival preservation.

Sir Hilary Jenkinson's *Manual of Archive Administration*, first published in 1922, introduced these European archival concepts to Britain, as well as the rest of the English-speaking world. Jenkinson, a trained medievalist, incorporated two original interpretations into his theoretical framework that added significantly to an evolving body of archival theory. First, he saw the archivist as impartial custodian. He believed that archival appraisal, including the weeding-out and destruction of unimportant records, was not the responsibility of archivists, but of records creators, to be undertaken before the records were transferred to the archives. Second, Jenkinson believed that records exist organically in relation to other records from the point of creation through preservation. Thus, continual custody and control of archives was necessary to retain significance and authenticity, key components of current preservation practice.[23]

As modern governmental units developed and evolved, growing bureaucracies began to maintain official records separate from manuscripts, books, and artifacts. In the United States, two theoretical traditions emerged from this custom that would further define modern archival practice. The first, the historical manuscripts tradition, has its origins in the early republic when manuscript collections were accumulated by libraries and historical societies. The principles of librarianship informed the historical manuscripts tradition, emphasizing subject-based access, item-level description, and arrangement based on topical, geographic, and chronological classification schemes.

Waldo G. Leland introduced the second theoretical approach, the public archives tradition, at the 1909 meeting of the American Historical Association. Leland, secretary of the organization, studied at the École des Chartes and understood the importance of European concepts of provenance and hierarchal control that emerged in the nineteenth century. The introduction and acceptance of the public records tradition in the United States was essentially a transition away from the principles of librarianship to a practice that established the centralized archival recordkeeping authority and hierarchical control (based on provenance and original order) necessary for the preservation and management of modern—often large-scale—archival holdings.

As archival methods matured, historical societies and libraries began to move away from the acquisition of individual items to the collection of groups of records and manuscripts based on provenance. These large collections were similar in structure to public records, and historical societies and manuscript libraries began to adopt principles from the public-records tradition. This movement coincided with the origin of the National Archives and the Historical Records Survey of the Works Progress Administration, and with the formation of the Society of American Archivists (SAA) in the 1930s. Museums with archival collections, however, tended to maintain museum-based collection-management practices focused on item-level control. The methods associated with each tradition informed the scale of archival preservation undertaken, particularly in the context of arrangement, description, storage, and access.

Thus, archival practices in the United States were drawn from European traditions. Some archival theorists, however, such as Richard Pearce-Moses, outline clearer distinctions between practices in Europe and the United States.[24] The manuscripts tradition existed in the United States long before the existence of a national archives for the management of public records. Historical societies and other antiquarian organizations, as well as the Library of Congress, collected both private and government records. The records were collected individually and often lacked contextual relationships. Alexis de Tocqueville, French diplomat and political scientist, discerned the poor state of American recordkeeping while traveling in the United States in the 1830s as he attempted to gather the research for his *Democracy in America.* De Tocqueville observed that Americans were in danger of losing their history because "[n]o archives are assembled. . . . In America, society seems to live from day to day, like an army on the field."[25] Within the context of recordkeeping in the United States, the public records tradition, "grew out of efforts to ensure that government records were preserved for historic research."[26]

By the end of the nineteenth century, archives preservation consisted primarily of the proper arrangement and storage of records, along with the repair—and what was then called *restoration*—of paper-based documents. Preservation-minded archivists also worried about the fact that books and records were vulnerable to fires. The Library of Congress experienced three major fires in the nineteenth century: in 1814 (when the British set fire to the capital), in 1825, and 1851. In 1911, a fire at the State Library in Albany, New York, destroyed hundreds of thousands of books and documents. Efficient disaster mitigation practices, however, were not implemented until well into the twentieth century. In fact, not until the devastating floods of November 1966 in Florence, Italy, did the professional world develop systematic strategies for disaster prevention, recovery, and mitigation.

The archival principles developed in the nineteenth and twentieth centuries resulted in the acceptance and application of the concepts of provenance, original order, and appraisal in archival practice. Appraisal determines *what* is selected for acquisition and retention, and thus *what* will be preserved. Appraisal is critical to an understanding of archival preservation for it is, according to the definition in the Society of American Archivists' official glossary, "the process of determining whether records and other materials have permanent (archival) value."[27]

The framework for appraisal, originally articulated by archival theorist Theodore Schellenberg in the mid-twentieth century, formed a theoretical basis for archival selection and appraisal based on what was then considered a set of universal values. While rather record centric, these appraisal values defined and guided the practices and activities of archivists for several generations. Schellenberg's construction of legal, historical, evidential, and informational values confirmed the importance of the collection or the item selected for preservation and long-term access.[28]

Schellenberg's taxonomy divided the value of records into two types: primary and secondary. Primary values relate to the reasons the records were created and include administrative, legal, and fiscal values. Secondary values are divided into two additional broad categories, evidential and informational. The secondary value of records is considered in two ways: 1) the evidence they contain of the organization and functions of the organization or governmental body that produced them, and 2) the information they contain about persons, corporate bodies, things, problems, and conditions, with such information being considered worthy of saving for future use and thus central to the decision to preserve.

These values, taught to generations of archival students beginning in the 1950s, may seem dated in relation to current practice. Today, archivists recognize that selection considerations are driven by anticipated use, as well as by the need to fill the gaps in the historical record, find voice for the underrepresented, and allow for preservation across a range of formats.

Nonetheless, archival appraisal and selection offer a theoretical foundation that forms the basis for sound preservation decisions. These principles are grounded in a specialized body of knowledge regarding the nature of records and their use.

The archival profession in the nineteenth and twentieth centuries also witnessed the development of separate professional societies in the United States. The American Library Association formed in 1876, the American Association of Museums in 1906, and, in 1936, the Society of American Archivists.[29] The establishment of independent professional organizations, while a landmark for each discipline, solidified the understanding that each sector was engaged in aligned but distinctive activities, with each addressing archival materials in accordance with its own professional best practices.

Uniting Archival Theory and Preservation and Conservation Science

The diverse causes of the poor quality of paper manufactured from about 1870 were not recognized until the early 1900s. Paper can deteriorate for several reasons: poor manufacturing materials and techniques (often referred to as "inherent vice" because the deteriorating features are in the paper itself), storage in poor environments, air pollution, inadequate housing, or careless handling. The history of papermaking has been described by library administrator Verner Clapp as a series of developments that led to a "steady degradation through the increasing use of inferior raw materials and of short-cuts in manufacture—both made possible by advancing technology"[30] such as the introduction of wood pulp to paper manufacture. Wood pulp contains lignin, a brown organic polymer in the cell walls of trees that degrades paper.

The introduction of sulfites into papermaking also caused acidity. Yet a third cause of acidity was the use of alum-rosin sizing. Unfortunately, alum-rosin in combination as a sizing agent caused paper to become acidic because the by-product of the reaction between alum and rosin soap is free sulfuric acid. Aluminum sulfate—a cheap and concentrated source of aluminum compounds, was used for wood-pulp paper manufacture.

Air pollution, an external source of paper deterioration, precipitated acidity in paper and other organic materials such as leather. Archives were often stored in buildings without air conditioning. Heat accelerated the aging process. In the winter, coal heating introduced other pollutants. Unfortunately, not all of these causes of acidity in paper were understood. Nineteenth-century restorers did not study chemistry. Thus, archivists and librarians repaired the weak documents without knowing how to treat the paper itself. Two commonly used techniques were silking and lamination, though other methods were practiced as well.[31] Silking was a slow and expensive process. It left documents susceptible to insect damage, and the adhesives used to adhere the silk to the paper could dry out and discolor, leading the silk to separate from the document to which it is adhered. Silking is usually reversible, though it often leaves the original damaged. Lamination is not usually reversible. And, more important, while lamination may hold a document together, it does not reverse acidity.[32] A great deal of treatment trial-and-error ensued until conservators stopped using these techniques in the late twentieth century.

In the 1930s, William James Barrow developed a process for laminating documents with cellulose acetate film and heat. One problem with this process is that the treated documents continue to deteriorate even after they are laminated. Once Barrow realized this, he turned his attention to developing deacidification and alkalization treatments for acidic papers. However, he and others continued to laminate documents for decades. In 1976, Frazer Poole,[33] then assistant head of preservation at the Library of Congress (LC), wrote that LC would use lamination only in rare instances. And, when used, he cautioned, the documents would need to be deacidified and buffered first.

The American Institute for Conservation of Historic and Artistic Works (AIC), the professional association for conservators, has a "Code of Ethics and Guidelines for Practice." The document has been revised regularly since it was first developed in 1961. Reversibility is one of the many topics covered. As several conservators point out, there is really no such thing as reversibility because once treated, a document will never be the same. However, some treatment options are less intrusive than others. Today, conservators tend to minimize treatments when possible.[34]

Preservation management developed as a profession in the twentieth century and continued to build on the range of activities that constituted preservation during the nineteenth century. For example, Sir Hilary Jenkinson's *A Manual of Archive Administration* describes strategies for preventative care. In 1938, an "Archival Economy" course taught at Columbia University by Solon J. Buck included these aspects of preservation: "physical plant," "appraisal and disposal," "reproduction," and "exhibition." A section of the syllabus called "Protection or Preservation" included "cleaning, flattening, manuscript repair, binding, and restoration."[35]

Appraisal has continued to inform preservation decision-making. Archivists Hilary Kaplan and Brenda Banks observed in 1990 that "appraisal provides the mechanism to eliminate items that do not warrant preservation attention. By effectively applying standard appraisal practices, an archivist can narrow the field of items potentially requiring treatment. Many materials that may be difficult to maintain over time may, in fact, be of marginal value to the collection."[36]

This aspect of archival preservation is distinct from library preservation. Dutch archival theorist Eric Ketelaar observes that archives holding bureaucratic or organizational records differ from library collections "in that they are provenance-bound and have originated not artificially but organically."[37] Ketelaar also points out that (special) collections, similar to archives, are constructed by the creator and/or collector and by subsequent curators and users. Curators may assign *value* to the collection, which may then drive preservation decision-making. In an archives, value is determined through appraisal, which takes place at various moments, including when the archivist identifies what is created, what to keep, and what to keep preserving.

Archival practice expresses the meaning of *value* differently from the way preservation and conservation theory does. While it may not be possible to preserve everything, should archivists honor the premise that there "is nothing that is not useful in studying the past"? Bibliographer and textual critic G. Thomas Tanselle writes that

> Not only do editions differ from one another, but also copies within an edition (of any period) often vary within themselves; as a result, every copy is a potential source for new physical evidence, and no copy is superfluous for studying an edition's production history. Furthermore, since the shape, feel, designs, and illustrations of books have affected, and continue to affect, readers' responses . . . , access to the physical forms in which texts from the past have appeared is a fundamental part of informal reading and effective classroom teaching. The loss of any copy of an edition—from the earliest incunables to the latest paperback reprints diminishes the body of evidence on which historical understanding depends.[38]

His observations apply to manuscript as well as to published materials. Similarly, Paul Banks emphasizes in his *The Laws of Conservation* that "No one can have access to a document that no longer exists,"[39] so preservation of all documents should be weighed before any document is discarded.

Yet, today, when an increasing amount of our heritage is digital, recognition is near universal that saving everything is impossible. Thus, appraisal provides a systematic approach for determining what to preserve. And, a rapidly increasing body of digital materials makes it abundantly clear that only a tiny fraction of a percentage of newly produced information will be preserved. This puts a burden on those tasked with saving information to search widely and choose carefully to determine what they will preserve. It is a daunting task and a great responsibility.

Put into an archival context, Banks's and Tanselle's arguments are more Jenkinsonian than Schellenbergian. Jenkinson emphasized the importance of archives as evidence of the past. The contextual whole of archival collections requires preservation, not just individual items identified for conservation. He described this as the archivist's *duty* to the archives. Schellenberg did not wholly disagree with Jenkinson. Both believed in the principle of *respect des fonds.*

Schellenberg did carefully distinguish between modern and ancient archives, firmly believing that the sheer magnitude of modern records calls for new approaches. Owing to his influential status within the profession, selection and appraisal became key components of American archival practice and thus archival preservation.

Schellenberg wrote that one need not preserve something just because it was accumulated, but for other reasons such as reference and research use.[40] Comparisons between Jenkinson (UK Public Records Office) and Schellenberg (NARA) sometimes portray the former as wedded to historic notions of archives and the latter as a pragmatist who espoused modern records management. After all, at the National Archives, Schellenberg had to contend with the millions of cubic feet of records that the agency inherited upon its formation.

The traditional versus pragmatic approach to archives has a contemporary parallel in newspaper preservation. Beginning in the late 1970s, preservation managers in Europe and the United States began in earnest to address the needs of deteriorating newspapers. In Europe, the newspapers were either deacidified or microfilmed (today they are digitized). Whether filmed or digitized, the originals were maintained. In the United States, the opposite occurred: newspapers were microfilmed and then the originals were usually discarded. Significant funding for filming came from the US Newspaper Project, established by the National Endowment for the Humanities (NEH) and existing from 1982 to 2011. Every state received funding to microfilm, and/or later digitize, its newspapers. NEH funding covered selection, filming, and cataloging costs. But no funding existed for the rehousing of the originals. While some maintain that newspapers are not unique, in fact, many of the newspapers filmed were the last known copies. Nicholson Baker points out that use of black-and-white silver halide film, then the preservation standard for these projects, means that readers miss out on seeing how color was used in the newspapers. He particularly calls attention to the use of chromolithography in late-nineteenth-century newspapers.[41] Because the originals were usually discarded, important information was lost to the user. Yet, the scope of many large reformatting projects made it impossible for some institutions to preserve the originals and maintain the copies because of the expense of extra cataloging (the original and the reformatted versions) and the extra shelf space. Thus, the decision to discard the original newspapers is its own kind of appraisal, though librarians do not use that term.

As Elizabeth Kaplan and Brenda Banks note, appraisal takes care of some of the preservation decision-making. But more to the point, Schellenberg and Jenkinson express different reasons for preserving records and archives. For Jenkinson, archivists are the keepers of archives and, as such, must preserve everything in their collections. For Schellenberg, appraisal means that only records of value would need to be preserved. No matter which camp one supports, the preservation of archival materials has often been a function of needs versus capacities. And preservation was often a function of opinion—what one person deemed worth saving another might consider appropriate for the trash bin. Records that are "needed" should be preserved. But who decides what is needed? What does one do when so many records are determined to be needed that the cost or space to preserve them far exceeds the resources to do so? The need to save digital materials magnifies the problem and makes it considerably more complex than in the past. This includes items that were digitized from analog originals or from microform, and those documents born digital and perhaps only existing in that form. In fact, as digital materials proliferate at rates far greater than any institution's capacity to save them all, it is clear that archivists cannot save even a fraction of what is "out there." And, as we suggested, one person's pronouncement that we need to save archive "A" in its entirety may be challenged by someone who says that we need to save only 20 percent as a representative sample or perhaps discard the whole body of documentation. Add to this that we have not yet reached a point of true digital preservation, and the magnitude of the problem becomes clear.

Landmark Archival Models and Preservation: Life Cycle and Records Continuum

Preservation activities can be framed according to models that have developed to address theoretical and practical problems in archives. A predominant one in North America has been the life-cycle model, with its phases of a record's existence, from creation to final disposition. Schellenberg describes this approach in his *Modern Archives: Principles and Techniques.* The *SAA Glossary* says that "all [life-cycle] models include creation or receipt, use, and disposition. Some models distinguish between active and inactive use, and between destruction and archival preservation."[42] This model, often associated with analog formats, is based on the archival principle that a record is useful for as long as it has continuing value. At the end of the cycle, records are destroyed or transferred to an archival repository for permanent retention. These stages in recordkeeping require that records managers and archivists take responsibility for assigning value to records at various stages in their existence.[43] Once records have been appraised, they are placed in archival folders and boxes and stored under proper environmental conditions. If the records begin to deteriorate, they are repaired or deacidified. If the records have deteriorated enough to be no longer safe to use, they might be copied onto paper or film, or digitized. If their condition continues to worsen, they might be deaccessioned, depending on their perceived value. Thus, preservation activities follow the life cycle of the record. Implicit in this approach—and implicit also in the very term that describes it, "life cycle"—is that a *cycle* exists from birth to death. The implication is that at some point, *anything* in the archives could be discarded; it will have come to the end of its place in the cycle. But, clearly, this is a poor image because many, if not most, things in the archives are there to stay. Most things deemed worth preserving are worth saving until their usefulness ends, and that may be *never.*

With born-digital records, the life-cycle image proves a less effective model for the administration of modern archives and recordkeeping. To address the challenge of electronic records, preservation strategies need to be in place even before digital records are created. That means that institutions must create an infrastructure in which the records will remain reliable in digital form for as long as the records are needed. Therefore, digital preservation must ensure that digital documents of continuing and/or enduring value remain accessible and usable. As archival professionals grapple with the impediments to permanence that the digital world presents, a more appropriate framework for digital preservation can be found in the records continuum model developed in response to the challenges of managing and preserving digital records and archives. This model, created in Australia in the 1990s by theorists Frank Upward, Sue McKemmish, and Livia Iacovino, consists of four concepts expressed as overlapping rings, in contrast to the linear life-cycle model. It identifies four recordkeeping activities:

1. Create (a document is created and captured into a recordkeeping system).
2. Capture (records are captured into an information system).
3. Organize (records are organized in an archives as an indication that they have continuing value for the organization/group/community).
4. Pluralize (records demonstrate their ongoing value as collective memory by ensuring they are part of archival systems that carry records beyond the life of the organization).[44]

These activities can also be examined against these crossed axes: "transactionality," "evidentiality," and "identity." Preservation is not included as one of the activities, possibly because it is not a recordkeeping process. However, the model recognizes that records must be actively managed over time and in different spaces. This is exactly what is required to preserve digital records. In fact, the "pluralize" activity is consonant with the idea that preservation can facilitate social-justice activities.

The records continuum model emphasizes the importance of collaboration in the development of standards, tools, and sustainable software.[45] In the context of the records continuum, no clearly definable stages in recordkeeping exist.[46] Records are current and historical from the moment of creation. The records continuum model differs from traditional practice by requiring cooperation beyond the walls of a repository by including records creators along with archivists, records managers, curators, librarians, and other allied professionals. In this model, the creator has a clear role in determining preservation and use, and the distinction between the records manager and the archival professional is hardly relevant. This approach stresses the integration of creation, management, and preservation. Institutional commitment is critical for long-term sustainable preservation.

New and evolving archival approaches based on these models have resulted in a changing practice grounded in post-custodial and integrated approaches to the management of records, particularly those born digital. For example, in 2004, the Digital Curation Centre (DCC) emerged as a national center for meeting challenges in digital curation and data management that no single institution or discipline could effectively address. The DCC's Curation Lifecycle Model provides a graphical, high-level overview of the stages and actions required for successful curation and preservation of data from creation through the full curation cycle. The model emphasizes the importance of collaboration in the development of standards, tools, and sustainable software.[47]

The life-cycle and records continuum models may appear to perpetuate the divide between analog and digital preservation. But, actually, it is just a matter of perspective. As the DCC model indicates, the life-cycle model can be adapted to include preservation for all records, even before they are "born." All formats, if preserved long term, will require resources, appropriate storage systems, and institutional commitment.

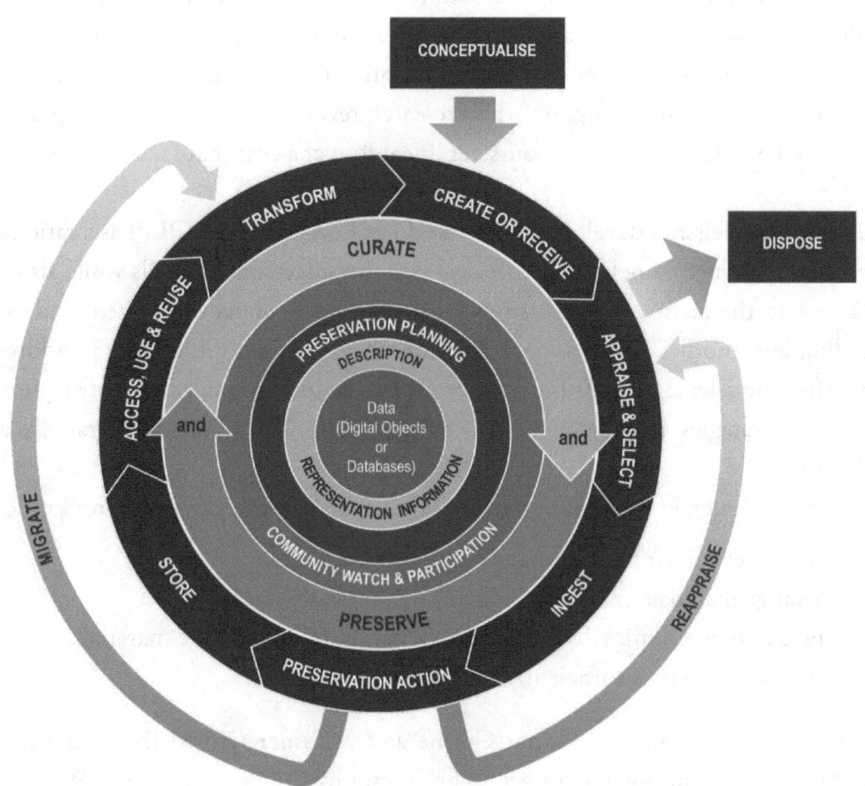

FIGURE 2.2. The Curation Lifecycle Model (DCC), 2004

Landmark Archival Models and Preservation: Minimal Processing

As mentioned previously, preservation activities should be understood in the context of archival theory and models for practice. No history of archival preservation would be complete without a consideration of the impact of the minimal processing model on archival practice and preservation strategies.

The establishment of large institutional repositories combined with the codification of appraisal values led to an explosion of archival processing backlogs in the late twentieth century. The major challenge to the archival profession during this period was the high cost of arrangement, description, preservation, and storage. Cultural heritage organizations continued to collect materials at an increasing rate as more and more materials are created; however, for most archivists, the resources required to preserve and provide access to collections have not kept pace with acquisition growth. Because most institutions have historically allocated limited resources for preservation, archivists needed new practical and theoretical approaches for preservation that limited cost and maximized efficiency.

In 2005, archivists Mark Greene and Dennis Meissner addressed this challenge in a seminal article, "More Product, Less Process: Revamping Traditional Archival Processing." In this and subsequent works, the authors call for archivists to rethink the way they process collections, warning that traditional, labor-intensive arrangement and description practices are no longer sustainable.[48] Greene and Meissner acknowledge that some "exceptional" collections might deserve meticulous, perhaps even item-level processing, but their research revealed that then-current practice resulted in processing rates as low as 24 to 40 hours per linear foot at a cost that far outweighed the benefits to users.[49]

Greene and Meissner developed More Product, Less Process (MPLP) as a rational decision-based approach designed to help archivists deal with unprocessed materials while also prioritizing prompt access to the archival record. In doing so, they articulated, validated, and sanctioned a long-standing but unofficial professional practice: using minimal processing to address looming backlogs. After the release of their publication, many cultural organizations struggling to implement practical strategies that increased processing rates and facilitated use rapidly and widely accepted MPLP.

MPLP was designed with four guidelines that have impacted archival preservation practice:

1. Get collections into users' hands faster than before.
2. Arrange materials enough to adequately meet user needs.
3. Take only the minimal steps necessary to physically preserve materials.
4. Describe materials sufficiently for use.

This framework emphasizes what Greene and Meissner termed the "Golden Minimum" or doing the least amount possible to get archival resources to potential users. With these central guidelines, the authors reinforced and prioritized the needs of the user over all other archival principles, including arrangement, description, and preservation.[50] According to Greene and Meissner,

> Arrangement, preservation, and description work should all occur in harmony, at a common level of detail—that is, if arrangement occurs only to the series level, so should description and preservation. However, there is no need for all series . . . to be processed with the same level of intensity, or to the same level of detail. Some series may warrant more than the minimum effort. Here, again, clearly demonstrable business reasons should apply.[51]

Many archivists welcomed the Greene and Meissner approach to processing; however, MPLP also met with criticism even from some early supporters. Tom Hyry, a promoter and advocate of minimal processing, acknowledges that trade-offs and compromises exist with MPLP. These include an increased burden of discovery on researchers, the risk of not identifying items of high value in a collection, and increased theft risk.[52] Other archivists question whether MPLP adequately deals with issues such as the management of electronic records and digitization practices, as well as privacy and confidentiality.[53] Ensuring the ethical management of culturally sensitive content that takes into account appropriate levels of access is another concern when employing MPLP.

In 2010, Mark Greene published an opinion piece in *American Archivist* that addressed many of the criticisms of MPLP. He acknowledged that the role of appraisal was missing in their initial consideration of the problem of backlogs.[54] He attempted to extend the application of MPLP to this, and other aspects of archival administration, including preservation, reference, electronic records, and digitization. In regard to preservation, he argued that effective preservation takes place at the holdings maintenance level and recommended that archivists spend their energy advocating for the creation of stable and secure storage environments. He also advised that "archivists should only engage in conservation and restoration measures in exceptional instances and that these decisions should be made in the aggregate rather than on an item by item basis."[55]

Also in 2010, Greene and Meissner further delineated the core elements of MPLP and addressed preservation more directly:

> To reduce it to bare essentials, MPLP is really advocating these fairly general things: 1. Make user access paramount: Get the most material available in a usable form in the briefest time possible. 2. Expend the greatest effort on the most deserving or needful materials. 3. Establish an acceptable minimum level of work, and make it the processing benchmark. 4. Embrace flexibility: Don't assume all collections, or all collection components, will be processed to the same level. 5. Don't allow preservation anxieties to trump user access and higher managerial values.[56]

In this piece, Greene and Meissner reinforced the notion that preservation activities should be minimized unless the archival materials are deemed highly valuable, especially for the large, unwieldy twentieth-century collections that have contributed to most processing backlogs.

For some archivists, this language constitutes a rejection of traditional practices associated with archival preservation. For its "antagonists," MPLP is particularly controversial because they feel it creates an unnecessary tension between two core archival principles: access and preservation. One of the first authors to challenge the assertion that preservation is an obstacle to access was Laura McCann of New York University, who claims that preservation is the foundation for sustainable access. She writes that MPLP relies too heavily on climate controls at the archival repository level that are not always achievable. She also states that the approach disregards key features of preventive conservation activities, such as disaster planning and integrated pest management, as well as standards for handling, storage, and use of materials that are critical to ensuring long-term access and use of archival materials.[57]

Archival preservationist Jessica Phillips offers a wide-ranging defense of preservation in the age of MPLP. She observes that "preservation is not the enemy of access; rather, it is its faithful companion."[58] She agrees that MPLP can be a tool for increasing the processing rate for many archival collections; however, she raises concerns about several of its core principles. First, she questions the dictate that processing a collection (or a portion thereof) must be done at a common level, asserting that this approach should not automatically extend to preservation or conservation. Instead, she asserts that preservation decisions should be based on the condition of the materials and the limitations of the storage environment, noting that, in most cases, at least a cursory item-level review is needed to achieve this goal. She also takes Greene and Meissner to task for their dismissal of archival preservation standards, condemning them to the realm of "micro-conservation." She suggests that the implementation of basic preservation activities, such as the removal of paper clips, refoldering, and photocopying, can produce significant benefits for the collections, particularly if, as is often the case, storage conditions are less than perfect. She says that we must "preserve now to avoid having to conserve later. To ignore the condition of materials is to allow them to fall into disrepair and is in opposition to SAA's Code of Ethics."[59]

Greene and Meissner responded to similar arguments by explaining that their approach is flexible and will vary depending on institutional capacity, mission, and the nature of the materials. They claim that MPLP relies on sound professional judgment to determine the appropriate level of arrangement, description, and preservation. Nonetheless, Greene and Meissner have consistently insisted that "the more enlightened, and cost-effective, path to physical preservation comes through steady environmental controls and not through remedial document repair."[60] While this may be true in some instances, it is not a universal truth; many institutions will never have the resources to significantly improve environmental conditions, and a wide range of valid preservation practices exists between these two extremes, as we address in detail in subsequent chapters.

Still, MPLP and its focus on access should not be perceived as antithetical to archival preservation. Its principles can inform appropriate preservation strategies when tied to sound appraisal decisions. Nonetheless, Greene and Meissner did not fully address the implications of MPLP for the long-term preservation of materials and the critical role of preventive care as a sustainable, cost-efficient strategy for analog and digital materials. In particular, their emphasis on establishing proper storage and climate control is not a sufficient answer to their critics, especially when we consider the complexities of digital preservation. Perhaps a more prudent approach would involve preservation programs that more fully embrace the interdependent relationship between preservation and access, where use drives strategic preservation decisions and processing is undertaken to maximize long-term preservation at the level most appropriate to the institutional resources and staffing. As an example, archival educator Robert S. Cox proposes a three-stage program for processing, beginning with a condition survey and continuing with minimal processing, while maintaining maximal processing as the end goal. Cox asserts that "the equation should be reversed from the minimal model: archivists should seek to maximize the physical and intellectual care of collections within the real and practical limits of the resources at their disposal.[61] The application of the MPLP framework to the appraisal of, preservation of, and access to electronic records is an emerging area of theory and practice. Shan Sutton explores how MPLP can inform digitization projects, noting that archivists should reconsider practices associated with selection, image capture, and metadata creation to increase productivity in ways that do not compromise future access.[62] Sophia Lafferty-Hess and Thu-Mai Christian apply MPLP to data curation, noting that the production of high-quality data requires skill, labor, and time achievable only at a high institutional cost.[63] Kevin Bradley acknowledges this concern in his investigation of digital sustainability.[64]

Archival backlogs will continue to grow exponentially (especially digital backlogs), and archivists must devise appraisal and processing policies and procedures that address the challenges of modern paper-based and digital collections. As Christopher Prom notes, "archivists should long since have been devoting considerable resources to administering born-digital records but have been stymied in part because of the still looming paper backlogs. The sooner we dispatch those backlogs the sooner we can begin the essential task of wrestling with digital collections."[65]

Preservation Today

Krummel's Seven Ages of Librarianship ends at 1970, yet, the past fifty years have been a period of great change for preservation, a possible indication that we are in the eighth age. The incredible growth of digital heritage, and the concomitant rise of social networking, are perhaps the most obvious changes. Archivists increasingly recognize the need to preserve not just the records, archives, and collections in institutions, but community archives as well. As Rebecka Sheffield puts it, "we can embed social justice within our core values by extending the definition of preservation to include a duty to steward . . . unexplored or marginalized histories."[66]

technological. **Networked.** social. **Open.** economics. social justice
communities. government. **Users.** public. **Diverse.**
computer scientists. librarians. archivists. curators
Preservation
information. evidence. values. **Collaborative.** aesthetics. stewardship
Recreational. Pluralistic.

FIGURE 2.3. Preservation today

How might we characterize our eighth age of librarianship and archival practice? The boldface words in Figure 2.3 are possible adjectives: *Networked, Users, Collaborative, Open. Recreational. Pluralistic.* All are appropriate ways to think about the context for archival preservation today.

Preservation, then, may seem like a simple concept, but it is in fact tremendously complex. The complexity may be seen in the following questions.

What does *preservation* mean? Is it time-based? That is, does the term *preservation* apply to items that will be discarded at some point, determined by some kind of retention schedule? If we determine that items of one particular kind are to be held onto for, say, three years after which they can be discarded, we have not really practiced *preservation* with them. Who is to decide what to preserve? On the basis of what? Can we formulate "best practices" and rules and regulations that will guide us to be fully responsible in our preservation? Probably not, because opinions, institutions, and materials differ—and even budgets differ. How is preservation a function of resources? Staff, physical space, and money all influence preservation decisions. Just what does "enduring value" mean, and who should determine it? What is the relationship between the condition of materials and plans for their preservation? How does preservation work with respect to conservation—especially when resources are scarce? Can appraisal be reconciled with preservation, especially because part of appraisal may include jettisoning materials?

Many other questions show the complex nature of preservation, which is an evolving concept. One person might ask, "Should we preserve this?" and the answer could be, "It depends." Once we figure out what "it depends" on, we can have a fuller grasp of what preservation is.

NOTES

1 We use the term *records* generically because, as Richard Pearce-Moses points out, "potentially *anything* can be a record, depending on its context." See Geoffrey Yeo, who defines it as the "persistent representation of activities, created by participants or observers or their authorized proxies," in his "Concepts of Record (1): Evidence, Information, and Persistent Representations," *American Archivist* 70, no. 2 (2007): 342, https://doi.org/10.17723/aarc.70.2.u327764v1036756q.

2 Rebecka T. Sheffield, "More than Acid-Free Folders: Extending the Concept of Preservation to Include the Stewardship of Unexplored Histories," *Library Trends* 64, no. 3 (2016): 572–84, https://perma.cc/M94J-N7CC.

3 Randall C. Jimerson, ed., *American Archival Studies: Readings in Theory and Practice* (Chicago: Society of American Archivists, 2000), 8.

4 Terry Cook, "Evidence, Memory, Identity, and Community: Four Shifting Archival Paradigms," *Archival Science* 13 (2013): 95–120, https://doi.org/10.1007/s10502-012-9180-7.

5 See Anne J. Gilliland, Sue McKemmish, and Andrew J. Lau, eds., *Research in the Archival Multiverse* (Clayton, Victoria: Monash University, 2017).

6 See, for example, "Internet World Stats" at www.internetworldstats.com. The United States ranked 29th on this list.

7 Karen Mossberger, Caroline J. Tolbert, and Mary Stansbury, *Virtual Inequality: Beyond the Digital Divide* (Washington, DC: Georgetown University Press, 2003). See also Patty Wong, Miguel Figueroa, and Melissa Cardenas-Bow, "Diversity, Equity of Access, and Social Justice," in *Information Services Today: An Introduction*, 2nd ed. (Lanham, MD: Rowman & Littlefield, 2018), 52–68; Richard E. Rubin, *Foundations of Library and Information Science*, 4th ed. (Chicago: American Library Association, 2016), 487–531.

8 Kelvin White, "Race and Culture: An Ethnic Studies Approach to Archival and Recordkeeping Research in the United States," in *Research in the Archival Multiverse*, 375.

9 Jean Mabillon, *De Re Diplomatica* (Luteciae Parisiorum, 1681).

10 René-Prosper Tassin and Charles-François Toustain, *Nouveau traité de diplomatique*, 1750–1765. See WorldCat for the many editions of this work.

11 Luciana Duranti, "Diplomatics: New Uses for an Old Science," *Archivaria* 28 (1989): 7–27, https://archivaria.ca/index.php/archivaria/article/view/11567/12513, captured at https://perma.cc/8UV7-CGVC.

12 *Online Etymology Dictionary* and *The Concise Oxford Dictionary of English Etymology*, ed. T. F. Hoad (Oxford or London, UK: Oxford University Press, 2003), s.vv. "museum," "mouseion," "archivum," "archiva," "library," "librarium," "libraria," "librarie."

13 Donald W. Krummel, *Fiat Lux, Fiat Latebra: A Celebration of Historical Library Functions,* Occasional Papers, Champaign: Graduate School of Library and Information Science, University of Illinois, 1999, p. [2].

14 Ernst Posner, "Some Aspects of Archival Development since the French Revolution," in *Archives and the Public Interest: Selected Essays by Ernst Posner*, ed. by Ken Munden (Chicago: Society of American Archivists, 2006), 25.

15 Krzysztof Pomian, "The Archives: From the *Trésor des chartes* to the CARAN," in *Rethinking France: Les Lieux de Mémoire,* ed. Pierre Nora and David P. Jordan, vol. 4, *Histories and Memories* (Chicago: University of Chicago Press, 2010), 47–49.

16 In the 1930s, the National Socialists in Germany displayed both phenomena, burning millions of books by and about the Jews while preserving their "degenerate" art. See Mark Glickman, *Stolen Words: The Nazi Plunder of Jewish Books* (Lincoln: University of Nebraska Press, 2016), and Henning Koch, *The Book Thieves: The Nazi Looting of Europe's Libraries and the Race to Return A Literary Inheritance*, trans. Anders Rydell (New York: Viking, 2017).

17 Back then, "restoration" was the standard word. "Preservation" and "conservation" became the proper—and differentiated—terms only in the twentieth century. Nonetheless, "preservation" was sometimes used in the nineteenth century.

18 Claire S. Marwick, "An Historic Study of Paper Document Restoration Methods," master's thesis, American University, Washington, DC, 1964.

19 Anne J. Gilliland, "Archival and Recordkeeping Traditions in the Multiverse and Their Importance for Researching Situations and Situating Research," in Anne Gilliland, Sue McKemmish, and Andrew J. Lau, *Research in the Archival Multiverse* (Clayton, Victoria: Monash University Publishing, 2017), 37.

20 Gilliland, 38.

21 Luciana Duranti and Giovanni Michetti, "The Archival Method," 84–85; Peter Horsman, "The Last Dance of the Phoenix, or the De-discovery of the Archival Fonds," *Archivaria* 54 (Fall 2002): 6, https://archivaria.ca/index.php/archivaria/article/view/12853; Jefferson Bailey, "Disrespect des Fonds: Rethinking Arrangement and Description in Born-Digital Archives," *Archive Journal* 3 (Summer 2013), https://www.archivejournal.net/essays/disrespect-des-fonds-rethinking-arrangement-and-description-in-born-digital-archives, captured at https://perma.cc/EKT5-QQ38.

22 Samuel Muller, J. A. Feith, and R. Fruin, *Handleiding voor het ordenen en beschrijven van archieven* (*Manual for the Description of Archives*); first published in Dutch, Haarlem, 1898. The 2nd edition was translated by Arthur Leavitt and published in New York by H.W. Wilson in 1940.

23 Sir Hilary Jenkinson, *Selected Writings of Sir Hilary Jenkinson*, ed. Roger H. Ellis and Peter Walne (Chicago: Society of American Archivists, 2003).

24 Richard Pearce-Moses, s.vv. "manuscripts tradition" and "public records tradition," in *Encyclopedia of Archival Science*, ed. Luciana Duranti and Patricia C. Franks (Lanham, MD: Rowman & Littlefield, 2015), 241–43 and 298–300.

25 Alexis de Tocqueville, *Democracy in America,* trans. Arthur Goldhammer, the Library of America, vol. 2 (New York: Literary Classics of the United States, 2004): 517–18.

26 Pearce-Moses, s.v. "public records tradition."

27 Pearce-Moses, *A Glossary of Archival Records and Terminology*, s.v. "appraisal," https://www2.archivists.org/glossary/terms/a/appraisal, captured at https://perma.cc/5BVX-JKPN.

28 Theodore Schellenberg, "The Appraisal of Modern Public Records," in *Modern Archives Reader: Basic Readings on Archival Theory and Practice*, ed. Maygene F. Daniels and Timothy Walch (Washington, DC: National Archives and Records Service, 1984), 57–70.

29 The American Association of Museums is now known as the American Alliance of Museums.

30 Verner W. Clapp, "The Story of Permanent/Durable Book Paper, 1115–1970," *Restaurator* supplement no. 3 (1972): 19.

31 Michèle Valerie Cloonan, "Conservation and Preservation of Library and Archival Materials,"in *Encyclopedia of Library and Information Sciences,* 3rd ed. (New York: Francis & Taylor), 5–6.

32 Andrew Oddy, "Does Reversibility Exist in Conservation?," in *Reversibility—Does It Exist?*, ed. Andrew Oddy and Sara Carroll, British Museum Occasional Paper, no. 135 (London, UK: British Museum Press, 1999), 1.

33 Frazer Poole, "Current Lamination Policies of the Library of Congress," *American Archivist* 39, no. 2 (1976): 157, https://doi.org/10.17723/aarc.39.2.vg627658l7421233.

34 For a full discussion of archival conservation, see Mary Lynn Ritzenthaler, *Preserving Archives & Manuscripts*, 2nd ed. (Chicago: Society of American Archivists, 2010), 331–69.

35 Michèle V. Cloonan, "The Pedagogy of Preservation," unpublished paper given at Society of American Archivists Annual Meeting, August 8, 2012. Note that "restoration" is still the term used in the late 1930s for treatment rather than "conservation."

36 Hilary A. Kaplan and Brenda S. Banks, "Archival Preservation: The Teaming of the Crew," *American Archivist* 53, no. 2 (1990): 270, https://doi.org/10.17723/aarc.53.2.q712w7522j55r524.

37 Eric Ketelaar, "Archival Turns and Returns," in *Research in the Archival Multiverse*, 230.

38 G. Thomas Tanselle, "Introduction: Statement on the Significance of Primary Records," in *Significance of Primary Records*, first published in *Profession 95* (New York: Modern Language Association, 1995), 28, https://apps.mla.org/pdf/spr_print.pdf, captured at https://perma.cc/MQ6H-HQGM.

39 Michèle Valerie Cloonan, *Preserving Our Heritage: Perspectives from Antiquity to the Digital Age* (Chicago: ALA; London: Facet, 2015), 328.

40 T. R. Schellenberg, *Modern Archives: Principles and Techniques* (Chicago: Society of American Archivists, 1956; rpt. 1975), 15.

41 Nicholson Baker, *Doublefold: Libraries and the Assault on Paper* (New York: Random House, 2001).

42 Pearce-Moses, s.v. "life cycle," *A Glossary*, https://www2.archivists.org/glossary/terms/l/life-cycle, captured at https://perma.cc/5R4S-3WYY.

[43] The idea of the life cycle of records, although originally developed for government records, can also be applied to many manuscript materials.

[44] Sue McKemmish, Frank Herbert Upward, and Barbara Reed, "Records Continuum Model," *Encyclopedia of Library and Information Sciences*, 3rd ed. (2010), 4447–48.

[45] Digital Curation Centre, "DCC Lifecycle Model," http://www.dcc.ac.uk/resources/curation-lifecycle-model, captured at https://perma.cc/Q23Z-SE4W.

[46] For more on the life-cycle and records continuum models, see Sarah J. A. Flynn, "The Records Continuum Model in Context and Its Implications for Archival Practice," *Journal of the Society of Archivists* 22, no. 1 (2001): 79–93, https://doi.org/10.1080/00379810120037522; Peter Marshall, "Life Cycle Versus Continuum—What's the Difference?," *Informational Quarterly* 16, no 2. (2000): 20–25; and the writings of Sue McKemmish and Frank Upward, who published extensively on the development of the continuum at the Australian Archives.

[47] Digital Curation Centre, "DCC Lifecycle Model."

[48] Mark A. Greene and Dennis Meissner, "More Product, Less Process: Revamping Traditional Archival Processing," *American Archivist* 68, no. 2 (2005): 208–63, https://doi.org/10.17723/aarc.68.2.c741823776k65863. See also Dennis Meissner and Mark A. Greene, "More Application While Less Appreciation: The Adopters and Antagonists of MPLP," *Journal of Archival Organization* 8, nos. 3–4 (2010): 174–226, https://doi.org/10.1080/15332748.2010.554069; Mark A. Greene, "MPLP: It's Not Just for Processing Anymore," *American Archivist* 73, no. 1 (2010):175–203, https://doi.org/10.17723/aarc.73.1.m577353w31675348.

[49] Greene and Meissner, "More Product, Less Process," 254.

[50] Greene and Meissner, "More Product, Less Process," 212–13.

[51] Greene and Meissner, "More Product, Less Process," 240.

[52] Thomas Hyry, "Reassessing Backlogs: Extensible Processing Is a Better Way to Make Materials Available," *Library Journal* 132, no. 7 (2007): S8. See also Thomas Hyry, "More for Less in Archives: The Greene/Meissner Approach at Work at Yale" (paper presented at RLG Members Forum: More Better, Faster, Cheaper: The Economic of Descriptive Practice, Washington, DC, August 8, 2006), http://www.worldcat.org/arcviewer/1/OCC/2007/08/08/0000070504/viewer/file209.pdf, captured at https://perma.cc/R392-W2M3; and Thomas Hyry, "More for Less in Archives," *Annotation* 33, no. 2 (2007): 7–10, https://www.archives.gov/files/nhprc/annotation/2007/2007-spring.pdf, captured at https://perma.cc/HF3G-VRTC.

[53] A summary of these concerns is in Greene, "MPLP: It's Not Just for Processing Anymore," 175–203.

[54] Greene, "MPLP," 175 and abstract.

[55] Greene, "MPLP," 181–82.

[56] Greene and Meissner, "More Application," 175–76.

[57] Laura McCann, "Preservation as Obstacle or Opportunity? Rethinking the Preservation-Access Model in the Age of MPLP," *Journal of Archival Organization* 11, nos. 1–2 (2013): 23–48, https://doi.org/10.1080/15332748.2013.871972.

[58] Jessica Phillips, "A Defense of Preservation in the Age of MPLP," *American Archivist* 78, no. 2 (2015): 473, https://americanarchivist.org/doi/abs/10.17723/0360-9081.78.2.470.

[59] Phillips, "A Defense," 475.

[60] Greene and Meissner, "More Application," 215.

[61] Robert S. Cox, "Maximal Processing, or, Archivist on a Pale Horse," *Journal of Archival Organization* 8, no. 2 (2010): 143, https://doi.org/10.1080/15332748.2010.526086.

[62] Shan C. Sutton, "Balancing Boutique-Level Quality and Large Scale Production: The Impact of 'More Product, Less Process' on Digitization in Archives and Special Collections," *RBM: A Journal of Rare Books, Manuscripts, & Cultural Heritage* 13, no. 1 (2012), https://doi.org/10.5860/rbm.13.1.369.

[63] Sophia Lafferty-Hess and Thu-Mai Christian, "More Data, Less Process? The Application of MPLP to Research Data," *IASSIST Quarterly* 40, no. 4 (2016), https://doi.org/10.29173/iq907.

[64] Kevin Bradley, "Defining Digital Sustainability," *Library Trends* 56, no. 1 (2007), http://hdl.handle.net/2142/3772.

[65] Christopher J. Prom, "Optimum Access? Processing in College and University Archives," *American Archivist* 73, no. 1 (2010): 146–74, https://doi.org/10.17723/aarc.73.1.519m6003k7110760.

[66] Sheffield, "More than Acid-Free Folders," 573.

3

Principles of Archival Preservation

Introduction

A discussion of archival principles must begin with the recognition that technology has transformed the field of preservation. Revolutionary advances in information technology have resulted in the creation of new formats, workflows, and storage environments, as well as the need for new skills and expertise to ensure preservation of the archival record. Dramatic and rapid changes to the information environment challenge the very definition of *preservation* and its place in archival practice, especially in the digital realm. With respect to these challenges, this chapter offers an overview of the practices, principles, and values defining archival preservation and introduces a series of core concepts that guide current practice. Increasingly, the challenge of digital preservation is creating an artificial divide between professionals devoted to the "traditional" handling of analog materials and those engaged in digital work. At a basic level, the fundamental principles guiding archival preservation practice remain vital and relevant. However, archivists and other professionals must envision a more unified approach to our work and the principles that guide us. Richard Pearce-Moses, a past president of the Society of American Archivists, observes that "the language of records is often tied to a paper realm, emphasizing physical qualities over functional characteristics. The challenge is to rearticulate the essential characteristics of those concepts in terms that make sense in a vastly different environment."[1] This reconceptualization of practice means that archivists and other information experts must expand our understanding of archival preservation to respond to the rapidly changing nature of the materials that archivists preserve.

Basic Definitions

This section introduces and defines basic concepts related to archival preservation, and, in some cases, reconsiders commonly accepted definitions to advance a holistic understanding of the record, documents, and documentation; analog, digital, and hybrid content; conservation; preservation; preservation storage; and digital preservation. Digital preservation is best understood as part of a comprehensive program, regardless of the format addressed or the activities, tools, or resources used in planning and management. The changing nature of preservation requires us to consider the broader rubric of *digital stewardship* and its relationship to digital curatorship in all institutions, regardless of size. Many of these concepts, as defined in the 2005 *SAA Glossary*, remain relevant today. Others provide an opportunity to add to a discussion of the synergies and divisions in current preservation practice. Many definitions remain fluid and can differ between disciplines.

Uniting the Record: Analog and Digital

Archivists preserve and provide access to a wide range of documentation and information. For most of history, these resources were considered "records" and understood as a written, graphic, or printed work that may be used as evidence or proof; a document. The traditional definition of a record, manuscript, or document focuses on its textual nature, especially text on a tangible support, typically paper. Over time, the concept of documents and records has expanded significantly to include written, graphic, and creative works intended for personal, professional, or other use in a range of media such as still and moving images, audio, artifacts, and electronic media. Also over time, the methods for creating and maintaining documentation have evolved, with more and more information in digital form. Thus, the historical concept of a record as a tangible object does not fully embrace the modern nature of documentation. For this book, the word "record" refers generically to the broad scope of materials that are (or will be) found in archival, manuscript, and digital collections, regardless of format or method of creation.

Hence, a record can be analog or digital, tangible or virtual, and a single or compound entity, while information is a collection of data, ideas, thoughts, or memories.[2] An electronic or digital record is data or information captured and fixed for storage and manipulation in an automated system and that requires the system (hardware and software) for access. Analog materials are best understood through the physical process that created them. They can be single objects or series of objects fixed on a tangible medium, and can include a range of formats, including printed materials, manuscripts, photographs, drawings, and audiovisual materials. Digital records represent information through a sequence of discrete units, typically binary code. Digital records can include graphic images, audio or video clips, images of text pages, and electronic transcriptions of text. Digital records can be born digital, or digital copies of analog materials, typically scanned or transformed into character data using optical character recognition or manual keyboarding. Born-digital resources are items created and managed in digital form.[3] Most archival repositories contain digital and analog materials. These hybrid collections challenge archivists at all points in the materials' life cycle, including creation, use, preservation, and accessioning or disposal.[4]

Establishing shared criteria to define a record in the digital realm is challenging, but whether the materials are tangible or virtual, most archivists agree that records reflect some aspect of a transaction or activity that merits retention and preservation for some period of time. Records and other archival documents have two fundamental qualities essential to preservation. First, records are fixed, and the information they contain is persistent. Ideally, someone who consults an archives today could see the same information a hundred years from now, regardless of format. Second, archival records have context, which supports a full understanding of their content and establishes their authenticity. Archival theorist Geoffrey Yeo defines records as "persistent representations of activities, created by participants or observers of those activities or by their authorized proxies."[5] Richard Pearce-Moses more recently stated that a record is "information in a fixed (persistent) format used as evidence of the past."[6] Applying these time-honored archival principles to digital content is challenging because today's archivist must accept that a fixed or persistent record in the digital realm will mean moving across formats and accepting a certain amount of loss over time.

Preservation, Conservation, Restoration, and Reformatting

The preservation of historical and cultural materials, in a range of forms and formats, is a cultural obligation and a central responsibility for archivists. As professionals, archivists must define archival preservation and develop and administer principles that support sustainable programs. The Society of American Archivists defines preservation as

> (1) The professional discipline of protecting materials by minimizing chemical and physical deterioration and damage to minimize the loss of information and to extend the life of cultural property. (2) The act of keeping from harm, injury, decay, or destruction, especially through noninvasive treatment. (3). LAW - The obligation to protect records and other materials potentially relevant to litigation and subject to discovery.[7]

In this legal context, embodied in public records law, the purpose of preservation is broadly an effort to distinguish records from non-records. Records warranting preservation, even for limited periods, are selected through established retention schedules.[8] Preservation in the legal sense means that no records should be destroyed that may be relevant to litigation or that have a reasonable likelihood of being used in legal proceedings.

Supplementing the theory and practice associated with archival preservation, allied organizations such as the American Institute for Conservation of Historic and Artistic Works (AIC) and the United Nations Educational, Scientific and Cultural Organization (UNESCO)[9] offer definitions of preservation that consider an object in the context of its environment, a critical factor that informs archival preservation. AIC considers preservation "the protection of cultural property through activities that minimize chemical and physical deterioration and damage and that prevent loss of informational content. The primary goal of preservation is to prolong the existence of cultural property." UNESCO states that the "aim of preservation is to obviate damage liable to be caused by environmental or accidental factors that pose a threat in the immediate surroundings of the object to be conserved. Accordingly, preventive methods and measures are not usually applied directly but are designed to control the microclimatic conditions of the environment with the aim of eradicating harmful agents or elements, which may have a temporary or permanent influence on the deterioration of the object."[10]

This concept of preventive care (also known as preventive conservation) is central to current preservation practice and involves the mitigation of deterioration and damage to cultural property through the formulation and implementation of policies and procedures for appropriate environmental conditions; handling and maintenance procedures for storage, exhibition, packing, transport, and use; integrated pest management; emergency preparedness and response; and reformatting/duplication. Each of these activities is central to a holistic approach to collections care.

In his 1990 survey of archival preservation practices, educator Paul Conway defined *archival preservation* as "the acquisition, organization, and distribution of resources (human, physical, monetary) to ensure adequate protection of historical information of enduring value for access by present and future generations." He noted that "archival preservation encompasses planning and implementing policies, procedures, and processes that together prevent further deterioration or renew the usability of selected groups of materials. Archival preservation management, when most effective, requires that planning precede implementation, and that preventive activities have priority over renewal activities."[11] Thus, in accordance with most accepted definitions of preservation, archival preservation management is a comprehensive approach that identifies needs, establishes priorities, and allocates resources in accordance with established institutional goals and objectives.

While preservation is a large-scale program of activities that protect whole collections or large parts of collections, *conservation* is a series of actions on individual objects or groups of objects intended to mitigate damage, deterioration, or loss. The aim of conservation is to extend the useful life of specific objects with treatments that preserve the information that inheres in them. Conservation may involve the repair or stabilization of materials through chemical or physical treatment.[12] Preservation and conservation focus on preventive care, though preservation is more concerned with the aggregate care of collections and with the implementation of institutional programs. Preservation programs establish policies and procedures for appropriate environmental conditions; facilities design, storage, handling, and maintenance; exhibition; packing; transport; use; integrated pest management; emergency preparedness and response; and reformatting and duplication.[13] Conservation does not always eliminate evidence of damage. This is particularly important in the digital realm as conservators grapple with the methods for managing digital resources. As a 2016 report by the Foundation of the American Institute for Conservation of Historic and Artistic Works notes, "the digital landscape—the digital information, technologies, support infrastructures and behaviors that conservation professionals rely on to conduct their work—is complicated, [and] the field's capacity to harness the potential of this environment is poorly understood."[14] This problem is often compounded by a lack of shared practices for working with digital resources and the exclusion of conservation departments from information technology management.[15]

Restoration is the process of rehabilitating an item to return it as nearly as possible to its original condition, or to a known previous condition. In many instances, restoration is cosmetic, aimed at hiding all signs of damage. It may include the fabrication of missing parts with modern materials and using processes and techniques similar to those originally used to create the item. Restoration, in the archival context, is more of a historic term and not typically applied to current archival conservation and preservation practices, which focus more on stabilization and access to information. Many archives contain documents restored in the nineteenth or early twentieth century. Today, digital restoration is a technique typically used to address fragile or damaged photographs, moving images, and documents so that they can be handled or displayed. In this context, digital restoration may allow for the creation of an enhanced digital copy or an exact copy of the original with no alteration. Restoration of any sort is unethical when carried out simply to enhance monetary value.

When an item or series of items is reformatted, a new copy is created with a format, medium, or structure different from that of the original, typically for preservation or access. In digital and analog reformatting, the process involves the migration of information from one carrier to another. In principle, an item can be reformatted without any effect on its content. For example, a nitrate negative can be reformatted by making a duplicate on safety film. However, Marshall McLuhan's prescient observation that "the medium is the message" is a reminder that physical characteristics influence meaning. In the case of a reformatted photograph, some information embedded in the material of the original will be lost in the reproduction. For example, a modern copy print of a nineteenth-century cabinet print will almost certainly use a different process to create the image. Furthermore, the reformatted copy may not be the same size or include information found on the verso, such as a caption, photographer, and date, which can help scholars identify the original.[16]

Similarly, data files are commonly reformatted to render them intelligible by programs different from those of the original; they may also be reformatted to counter technology obsolescence, as may also be done for analog materials. Reformatting may result in the loss of characteristics or significant properties associated with the original object. As this example shows, definitions commonly applied to analog materials can be modified to embrace digital technologies because digital copies may not have perfect fidelity to the original.[17] The Library of Congress defines *digital preservation* as the active management of digital content over time to ensure ongoing access.[18] It can include the use of digital technology to restore an item that has been damaged. This definition is fully aligned with the concepts and ethical considerations associated with the preservation of analog materials.

Thus, a holistic definition of digital preservation, and by extension, preservation, is needed to encompass digital and analog materials. This definition should consider the theories and practices associated with restoration, conservation, reformatting, and duplication. For this book, *preservation* (of all formats) is defined as a series of actions and interventions that ensure continued and reliable use of and access to authentic digital or analog objects for as long as they are valuable and useful. This definition encompasses technical and physical activities, and also all of the strategic and organizational considerations related to the survival and management of digital and analog materials. For digital preservation, this includes capturing the most accurate rendering possible of authentic content over time, while retaining as much as possible all of the information that an item contains.

Defining Preservation Storage Frameworks: Digital Curation, Digital Stewardship, and Digital Preservation

Archival records and manuscripts should be stored in environments designed to limit degradation regardless of format. These environments protect materials from hazards such as theft, fire, flood, particulates, pests, or vandalism, and from extremes or fluctuations in temperature, relative humidity, or light. The preservation of digital content requires suitable storage technology (including usable hardware and software), as well as proper storage environments based on established procedures that ensure the longevity of documentation, including back-up and redundant copies.

Concepts such as migration, emulation, and conversion will be discussed in detail in subsequent chapters, but it is important to acknowledge that each requires a suitable, planned, and managed environment for preservation.

Curation and stewardship have long been the work of archivists, librarians, and museum professionals. These activities involve the proper care and control of cultural heritage materials, including ensuring adequate preservation, proper custody, and reasonable access. With respect to digital content, the terms "digital curation" and "digital stewardship" are often used interchangeably, though there are important distinctions. Digital curation involves maintaining, preserving, and adding value to digital research data throughout its life cycle.[19] It involves selection and appraisal by creators and archivists; evolving provisions for intellectual access; redundant storage; data transformations; and, for some materials, a commitment to long-term preservation.[20]

"Digital stewardship" is a broader term than either digital curation or digital preservation. Library and archival educators Ross Harvey and Martha R. Mahard offer an excellent hierarchical structure for considering concepts such as preservation, curation, and stewardship. They suggest that digital stewardship is an institutional responsibility: "its practice encompasses the full range of preservation activities applied by information professionals, who have the obligation of keeping collections, and the objects in them, in trust for future generations." In their model, digital stewardship encompasses digital curation, which involves "maintaining and adding value to a trusted body of information for current and future use." Digital curation encompasses digital preservation, "a technical process involved in maintaining digital information over time."[21] All of these activities are intrinsic to the goals and objectives of sustainable preservation management, regardless of format.

Defining Principles: Archival Values and Ethics

Two central documents guide archivists: the *Society of American Archivists' Core Values Statement* and the *Society of American Archivists' Code of Ethics*. These professional standards address a range of issues central to the archival endeavor, including access and use, accountability, custody, selection, authenticity, privacy, trust, and the importance of preserving a diverse archival record.[22] The documents also provide guidance in matters of social responsibility, judgment, professionalism, and service. Together, SAA values and ethics statements provide a theoretical foundation for the archival profession based on a set of universal principles that define and guide the practices of archivists, and offer important context for archival preservation.

Archival Values and Preservation

The preamble to the SAA *Core Values Statement* says that these "values embody what a profession stands for and should form the basis for the behavior of its members."[23] The values provide direction on institutional and professional obligations, and on the responsibilities inherent in maintaining the documentary record. While all of the SAA core values are relevant to a discussion of archival preservation, three core SAA statements must be emphasized.

First is the relationship between archives, history, and memory. Archivists recognize that primary sources enable people to examine the past and thereby gain insight into the human experience. Archival materials support human memory individually and collectively, and, when properly maintained, they contain evidence against which individual and social memory can be tested. Archivists preserve primary sources to enable us to comprehend the past, understand the present, and prepare for the future.

Second is the centrality of selection. Archivists make choices about which materials to preserve based on a wide range of criteria, including the needs of potential users. Understanding that because of the cost of long-term retention and the challenges of accessibility most of the documents and records created in modern society cannot be kept permanently, archivists must seek the advice of other stakeholders in deciding what to retain. They acknowledge and accept the responsibility of shaping and interpreting documents that they select to preserve.

The third core SAA concept concerns the value of preservation to the archival endeavor. Archivists preserve a wide variety of primary sources for future generations. Preserving materials is a means to an end, not an end in itself. Within prescribed law and best-practice standards, archivists may determine that the original documents themselves must be preserved, while, at other times, copying the information that they contain to alternate media may be sufficient. Archivists thus preserve materials for the benefit of the future more than for the concerns of the past.[24]

Thus, preservation is a core archival value fundamental to other archival activities. The archival record is saved because it contains valuable evidence. The resources needed for archival preservation are justified because society values all kinds of records, regardless of format. Under this ethical mandate, archivists follow accepted standards to select appropriate documents for long-term access and apply preservation practices to ensure maximum longevity of records and the information they hold. These values and definitions entail a number of assumptions. First, the ultimate goal of preservation is use. Second, preservation is the responsibility of all professionals charged with caring for historical and cultural materials. Third, preservation decisions are based on many factors, and there may be no perfect preservation solution. Add to this that no two institutions are alike, and it appears inevitable that the preservation mandates and practices of some organizations will differ from those of others. Finally, the decision to preserve selected information, regardless of format, is based on an appraisal of its historical or informational value. The theoretical framework for appraisal, originally articulated by Theodore Schellenberg, is grounded in a specialized body of knowledge regarding the nature of records and their use that form the foundation for sound preservation decisions. In other words, the appraisal of a record's value ultimately justifies the resources that will be required for long-term preservation.

Archival Ethics and Preservation

The *Code of Ethics for Archivists*, approved by SAA Council in 2005 and revised in 2012, is a set of principles for archivists to consider as they select, manage, preserve, and administer cultural materials. The code provides guidance in several areas relevant to archival preservation. While some of these ethical issues address preservation directly, they are also devoted to related topics such as professional relationships, judgment, authenticity, security and protection, access and use, privacy, and trust. The following four ethical principles, in particular, are relevant to preservation and are taken directly from the *Code of Ethics for Archivists*.[25]

First is the idea that archivists must exercise professional judgment in acquiring, appraising, and processing materials to ensure the preservation, authenticity, diversity, and lasting cultural and historical value of their collections. Archivists should carefully document their collections-related decisions and activities to make their role in the selection, retention, or creation of the historical record transparent to their institutions, donors, and users. Archivists are encouraged to consult with colleagues, relevant professionals, and communities of interest to ensure that diverse perspectives inform their actions and decisions.

Second, archivists should ensure the authenticity and continuing usability of records in their care. They must document and protect the unique characteristics of records and strive to protect the records' intellectual and physical integrity from tampering or corruption. Archivists may not willfully alter, manipulate, or destroy data or records to conceal facts or distort evidence. They should thoroughly document any actions that may cause changes to the records in their care or raise questions about the records' authenticity.

Third, archivists must provide security and protection for all materials for which they are responsible, minimize the physical deterioration of records, and implement specific security measures to protect all records—analog and digital. Archivists must guard all records against accidental damage, vandalism, and theft and should have well-formulated plans to respond to any disasters that threaten records. Archivists must cooperate actively with colleagues and law enforcement agencies to apprehend and prosecute vandals and thieves.

And, fourth is the universal archival commitment to access and use. Archivists must recognize that use is the fundamental reason for keeping archives, and they must actively promote open and equitable access to the records in their care within the context of their institutions' missions and users. They must minimize restrictions and maximize ease of access, as well as facilitate the implementation of institutional access policies while encouraging responsible use. They must work with donors and originating agencies to ensure that any restrictions are appropriate, legal, well documented, and equitably enforced. When repositories require restrictions to protect confidential and proprietary information, such restrictions should be implemented in an impartial manner. In all questions of access, archivists should seek practical solutions that balance competing principles and interests.

Sherri Berger, a digital programs administrator, reveals the difficulty in implementing these ethical principles. She observes that preservation is based on two fundamental truths: 1) information artifacts will always deteriorate, and the process will be accelerated with use; and 2) no adequate resources or storage spaces exist to take the fullest preservation measures or to save every item. Therefore, archival preservation is an ethical challenge. To make ethical preservation decisions, archivists must understand how preservation relates to selection and appraisal. Selection is also relevant to conservation and reformatting decisions, both of which may entail significant resources and the possibility of sacrificing some characteristic of the object for the greater preservation good.[26] For this reason, as Mary Lynn Rizenthaler notes, current archival conservation aims for minimal intervention through methods such as mending, filling, or flattening documents. When archivists reformat items, they create a different set or version of items, and they should strive to retain as much of the items' original information as possible, assuming that it still exists.[27]

Preservation is a cultural obligation and a central responsibility of archivists. It is an ethical concern grounded in accepted values, and it assists archivists with critical issues: *why* we must save the cultural record, *who* is responsible, *what* is selected, and *how* it is done. Central to archival ethics and values is the concept of appraisal, which determines *what* content or artifact is valued enough to be preserved and made accessible, and therefore, what should not be preserved, based on cultural and legal considerations.

Allied Fields and Preservation Principles

Over the past several decades, museum and library preservation professionals have also codified values, ethics, and principles relevant to their disciplines and organizations. Thus, a comparison across professional disciplines is useful for developing a holistic framework for archival preservation principles. The American Library Association (ALA), the American Alliance of Museums (AAM), the American Institute for Conservation of Historic and Artistic Works (AIC), and the American Association for State and Local History (AASLH) have ethics statements that address preservation to varying degrees. Like SAA, ALA's code of ethics is a framework for decision-making and focuses on equitable access, privacy, confidentiality, and professional behavior. ALA's code of ethics does not include a specific statement on preservation, but instead acknowledges that library professionals can "significantly influence or control the selection, organization, preservation, and dissemination of information," further noting that "in a political system grounded in an informed citizenry, we are members of a profession explicitly committed to intellectual freedom and the freedom of access to information. We have a special obligation to ensure the free flow of information and ideas to present and future generations."[28]

The *Code of Ethics of the American Alliance of Museums* addresses three primary concerns: governance, collections, and programming. Within these broader issues, it considers exhibitions, research, scholarship, publications, and educational activities. The section devoted to collections offers several key principles relevant to archival preservation. The AAM code acknowledges that collecting materials is a public trust responsibility. This trust implies that collecting institutions will ensure that collections are protected, secure, and preserved, and that all collections activities should be documented. The AAM *Code of Ethics*, unlike that of SAA, also acknowledges that the special nature of culturally sacred objects should inform all collection decisions, including preservation.

The *Statement of Professional Standards and Ethics of the American Association for State and Local History* emphasizes the need to develop policy and documentation for the proper care and management of collections. The code notes that "access to history resources is what gives preservation activities their meaning" while acknowledging the importance of interpretation and accurate representation of history through sound research and scholarship. Two statements are worthy of additional consideration. The first recognizes that historical collections include objects with significant monetary value. As a result, if collection-based resources are sold, proceeds from the sale of those objects should support the direct care and preservation of existing collections. Second, historical institutions must respect other legal, ethical, and cultural standards regarding sensitive cultural materials and respect the rights and authority of cultures and people who had no voice in the disposition of collections related to them.[29]

The preamble to the *American Institute for Conservation of Historic and Artistic Works Code of Ethics and Guidelines for Practice* states that "The primary goal of conservation professionals is the preservation of cultural property." The AIC guidelines offer several principles useful for, and different from, principles underlying archival preservation. These include the mandate to attain the highest possible standards in all aspects of conservation, including preventive conservation, examination, documentation, treatment, research, and education. The AIC places a high priority on preventive conservation by endeavoring to limit damage or deterioration to cultural property, providing guidelines for continuing use and care, recommending appropriate environmental conditions for storage and exhibition, and encouraging proper procedures for handling, packing, and transport. Similar to AAM's and AASLH's codes, the AIC code emphasizes that conservation must be governed by respect for cultural property, its unique character and significance, and the people or person who created it. The AIC code further stipulates that conservation professionals should practice within the limits of personal competence and education and institutional capacity, and use methods and materials that do not adversely affect future use or treatment of cultural property. And, finally, it stipulates that all preservation activities should be documented with permanent records and reports.[30]

Interestingly, these guidelines and ethical statements do not address digital content or digital preservation directly, although many of the principles can be broadly applied to preservation in the digital realm.

Those engaged in digital preservation have inherited much from archivists, librarians, and museum professionals. While digital resources often differ fundamentally from their analog counterparts in creation and management, and while they may demonstrate different preservation needs, they still adhere to the same ethical principles applied to analog materials. To date, a code of ethics for digital preservation remains to be defined and broadly accepted, and cultural heritage professions are in great need of integrating ethical frameworks for the care and management of digital materials. Perhaps the many difficulties inherent in preserving digital content have hindered the development of shared standards. True digital preservation may be years, if not decades, in the future. Only once this has been achieved might we see a useful document that delineates a practicable set of ethical guidelines for this purpose.

Toward Some Basic Principles for Archival Preservation

Based on conclusions proposed in the previous discussion, this section offers a set of core preservation principles grounded in ethics, standards, values, and practice associated with archives and its allied disciplines.[31] It is important to note that emerging standards and practices, technological change, and other challenges will continue to shape and define these principles.

Principles of Archival Preservation

1. Archival materials are collected and preserved to be used. All preservation actions should consider the needs of the user and how information is accessed and used.
2. Archives should be arranged, described, and preserved in a timely manner to facilitate use.
3. Preservation involves a series of ongoing strategies and actions over time.
4. The provenance of collection content must be preserved to demonstrate authenticity.
5. After appraisal, archival records should be preserved as completely and coherently as possible with critical information about context and intellectual connections maintained.

6. Preservation strategies should embrace preventive conservation measures that are sustainable and that balance effectiveness, cost, and environmental impact.
7. Preservation decisions should respect differing cultural perspectives and be based on partnerships in which knowledge, expertise, and community input are equally valued and shared.
8. Preservation is the responsibility of the creator, the archives, and the user and spans the full life cycle of the record or object.
9. Responsible stewardship, regular auditing, and planned preventive care reduce the need for future preservation actions.
10. Preservation actions should be documented.
11. Determining and maintaining authenticity of an object must be a key consideration in any preservation action.
12. Preservation actions should not harm any object.
13. Metadata standards will ensure long-term preservation and should be recorded and accessible to document preservation activities.
14. Understanding the structure of archival materials and/or the systems that created them is central to determining optimum preservation actions and how materials may be used.
15. Distinguishing between the preservation of objects or formats and the preservation of information or content they convey is necessary.
16. Preservation that addresses large quantities of material rather than individual objects is preferred to treatment of single objects, though both are part of a wider preservation program.
17. The preservation professional should maintain and implement plans based on a holistic understanding of the collections.
18. Preservation requires active managed care. Collections should be regularly monitored for condition and facilities for preservation risks.
19. Preservation master copies of digitized collections must be maintained along with the original to minimize loss.
20. Preservation actions should adhere to broader professional ethical considerations.

The Problem of Digital Preservation

The preservation principles defined in the previous section consider analog and digital materials; however, the preservation of digital materials clearly presents an exceptional challenge that must be considered in detail. For some people, "digital preservation" is an oxymoron; if a resource is digital, it cannot be preserved long term, owing to a number of factors related to the creation and long-term maintenance of digital objects. In 2010, an OCLC Research report, *Taking Our Pulse,* described the management of born-digital materials as the third biggest challenge facing libraries, special collections, and archives, after space and digitization.[32] Central to this challenge is the recognition that all digital objects will cease to be accessible without active management and intervention. While this notion may apply to some analog materials, the differences in long-term preservation for and access to digital resources are notable. According to the Digital Preservation Coalition, these challenges are as follows:

- **Machine Dependency.** Digital materials all require specific hardware and software for access and use.
- **Rapid Pace of Technological Change.** Preservation actions must be undertaken more rapidly for digital formats than for paper. This time frame for action is measured in a few years, as opposed to the decades or even centuries that we associate with the preservation of traditional materials.
- **Technological Obsolescence.** The rapid evolution of technology (specifically with respect to hardware and software) is generally regarded as the greatest threat to ensuring continued access to digital material.[33]

Archival educator Margaret Hedstrom writes extensively on the challenge of digital preservation. She acknowledges the numerous technical, organizational, legal, and economic barriers to a comprehensive infrastructure for protecting and preserving digital assets.[34] She notes that the relative instability and short life of most digital storage media and software have always challenged efforts to preserve digital information. Although technological improvements have ameliorated this situation in recent years, no "permanent" digital storage medium exists that meets the standards of longevity and durability established for analog materials, such as acid-free paper or archival microfilm. To be preserved, digital media must be copied or reformatted. Yet, she observes, even if digital objects are copied perfectly and transferred to new storage media, "it may be impossible to retrieve, render, or interpret these objects because of incompatibilities between the systems used to create them originally and the current generation of systems used to retrieve these objects."[35] Furthermore, such emulation, migration, or other means of updating digital files will last only as long as the technology continues to evolve. This "preservation" strategy will need to be done again and again until a truly permanent solution is found. To be sure, the biggest challenge to the long-term accessibility of digital objects is the rapid pace of technological change and the continual development of new computing hardware and software. One engine driving this change is the need to create and store ever-larger amounts of data. As data needs grow, technology that was once cutting-edge is rapidly superseded and must be discarded. A second problem is the reality that technology is created by commercial entities intent on continuing to reap profits. If technology providers stop creating new software and hardware, the older versions will suffice and consumers will stop buying their products. For companies to remain profitable, they must continue to make sure that their current products become obsolete. This obsolescence is built into the business model, and it threatens the longevity of access to digital materials. Clearly, technology companies stay profitable by forcing consumers to respond to constant requirements to upgrade their devices.

To complicate matters further, most digital files or formats remain dependent upon the originating computing system for accurate representation of their content. As explained in a 2006 Joint Information Systems Committee (JISC) briefing paper, any change to the computing environment can alter the representation of a resource or eliminate access completely. "The severity and impact of the change varies considerably between objects or environments and can often have a detrimental effect on the authenticity and integrity of a resource. This in turn affects its reliability, trustworthiness, and capacity for subsequent reuse. Planned and tested strategies to counter these risks are therefore vital."[36] Because digital content relies on a complex set of systems for creation, transmission, access, and storage, finding a solution to the problem of digital preservation is extremely challenging. A practicable and sustainable solution will require a significant allocation of resources at the institutional, governmental, and corporate levels.

Further thwarting the quest for true digital preservation are the vast numbers of stakeholders who are working independently to solve this problem, rendering it difficult, if not impossible, to pool their knowledge and operations. In fact, the basic issues may be so idiosyncratic that a solution that works for one professional sector or institution may not work for another. Ultimately, a range of solutions may be necessary, and digital preservation may need to take countless forms. Advocacy and global cooperation are needed to arrive at a common set of universally accepted international standards and preservation requirements. More important, to achieve true digital preservation, the technology industry must be committed partners in support of digital preservation by changing their business practices. This partnership implies that all manufacturers of hardware and software would agree to slow down the rate of evolution of their products for the "public good." Is it really possible for the technology industry to value the preservation of digital materials when it may affect its ability to continue to reap profits? Obviously, reaching a point of true digital preservation is a monumental challenge. And, because of the issues raised here, a true solution may always be out of reach.

Can Traditional Archival Preservation Principles Remain Valid?

Archivists have developed effective methods for preserving the content of most well-established formats and genres. These techniques and processes include reformatting, rehousing, secure storage, modern conservation practices, infrastructure for preventive care, staff resourcing, and training, all of which are typically performed at the institutional level. However, our current preservation methods are strained or inadequate to address problems associated with new and emergent documentation, particularly digital technologies. The cost of digitizing and providing the ongoing maintenance and auditing required for sustainable long-term access to digitized and born-digital materials is significant, and archivists are challenged to stay abreast of technological change and its financial implications. In 2006, the Digital Preservation Coalition commissioned a study that concluded that most organizations do not have control over their electronic holdings, nor do they have the training, knowledge, or resources to effectively plan and implement preservation strategies at their institutions. It recommended advocacy at all levels, and especially with software and hardware developers for the use of open-file formats that support appropriate preservation efforts.[37] As with the issues that Margaret Hedstrom raised, these concerns, though more than a decade old, are still with us. As the scope and scale of born-digital collections continue to grow and expand, it is increasingly likely that no individual library, archives, or museum will be able to provide affordable, sustainable preservation, but will need to rely on a distributed and decentralized approach to the custody of digital content.

In the analog world, practicable methods of preservation have been with us for more than half a century. Microfilming and photocopying onto archival substrates yield hundreds of years of stable access, and untold quantities of texts are available in these proven preservation formats. We are not advocating going back to these means of preservation, but a blended approach may be practical until a proven digital form of preservation is developed. In the meantime, digital texts allow for access beyond anything that the analog world could provide, so digitization should continue as a supreme enabler of access.

The digital realm is complicated, but the basic principles that guide preservation remain valid, as long as archivists remain nimble in responding to a rapidly evolving landscape of information technologies, infrastructures, and behaviors.

NOTES

1 Richard Pearce-Moses, *A Glossary of Archival and Records Terminology* (Chicago: Society of American Archivists, 2005), xiv, http://files.archivists.org/pubs/free/SAA-Glossary-2005.pdf, captured at https://perma.cc/9RAQ-36E4.

2 Pearce-Moses, s.vv. "record," "electronic record," "information, "*A Glossary*.

3 Ricky Erway, "Defining 'Born Digital': An Essay" (Dublin, OH: Online Computer Library Center, 2010), http://www.oclc.org/content/dam/research/activities/hiddencollections/borndigital.pdf, captured at https://perma.cc/TZ8A-HYYT.

4 Ian Anderson, "Archival Digitization: Breaking Out of the Strong Box," in *Record Keeping in a Hybrid Environment: Managing the Creation, Use, Preservation and Disposal of Unpublished Information Objects in Context*, ed. Alistair Tough and Michael Moss (Oxford, UK: Chandos, 2006), 203–26.

5 Geoffrey Yeo, "Concept of Record (1): Evidence, Information, and Persistent Representations," *American Archivist* 70, no. 2 (2007): 315–43, https://doi.org/10.17723/aarc.70.2.u327764v1036756q.

6 Richard Pearce-Moses, conversation with Elizabeth Joffrion, August 18, 2017.

7 Pearce-Moses, s.v. "preservation," *A Glossary*.

8 Pearce-Moses, s.v. "record," *A Glossary*.

9 The American Institute for Conservation is a national membership association for conservators and allied professionals who preserve cultural heritage. UNESCO focuses on the promotion of peace through international cooperation in education, the sciences, and culture.

10 United Nations Educational, Scientific and Cultural Organization, s.v. "preservation," *Glossary*, http://uis.unesco.org/en/glossary.

11 Paul Conway, "Archival Preservation Practice in a Nationwide Context," *American Archivist* 53, no. 2 (1990): 204–22, https://doi.org/10.17723/aarc.53.2.d0gt78p562832655.

12 Pearce-Moses, s.vv. "preservation," "conservation," "restoration," *A Glossary*.

13 Pearce-Moses, s.v. "preventive care," *A Glossary*.

14 Diane M. Zorich, *Charting the Digital Landscape of the Conservation Profession: A Report to the Profession* (Washington, DC: Foundation of the American Institute for Conservation of Historic and Artistic Works, 2016), 1, https://www.culturalheritage.org/docs/default-source/publications/reports/digital-landscape-report.pdf?sfvrsn=4, captured at https://perma.cc/X2QY-T548.

15 Zorich, *Charting the Digital Landscape*, 1.

16 Pearce-Moses, s.vv. "reformat," "preservation," *A Glossary*.

17 For more on the limits of preservation in the digital realm, see Colin Webb, David Pearson, and Paul Koerbin, "'Oh, You Wanted Us to Preserve That?!': Statements of Preservation Intent for the National Library of Australia's Digital Collections," *D-Lib Magazine* 19, nos. 1–2 (2013), doi:10.1045/january2013-webb.

18 Library of Congress, "About: What Is Digital Preservation," http://www.digitalpreservation.gov/about.

19 Digital Curation Centre, "What Is Digital Curation?," http://www.dcc.ac.uk/digital-curation/what-digital-curation, captured at https://perma.cc/A97K-EAAH.

20 Christopher A. Lee and Helen R. Tibbo, "Digital Curation and Trusted Repositories: Steps toward Success," *Journal of Digital Information* 8, no. 2 (2007), https://journals.tdl.org/jodi/index.php/jodi/article/view/229/183.

21 Ross Harvey and Martha R. Mahard, *The Preservation Management Handbook: A 21st-Century Guide for Libraries, Archives and Museums* (Lanham, MD: Rowman & Littlefield, 2014), 9.

22 Society of American Archivists, "SAA Core Values Statement and Code of Ethics, Society of American Archivists," https://www2.archivists.org/statements/saa-core-values-statement-and-code-of-ethics, captured at https://perma.cc/BF9K-HSJR.

23 SAA, "Core Values."

24 SAA, "Core Values."

25 "SAA "Core Values."

26 Sherri Berger, "The Evolving Ethics of Preservation: Redefining Practices and Responsibilities in the 21st Century," *The Serials Librarian* 57, nos. 1–2 (2009): 57–68, https://doi.org/10.1080/03615260802669086.

27 Mary Lynn Ritzenthaler, email correspondence with Elizabeth Joffrion, March 9, 2018.

28 American Library Association Committee on Professional Ethics, American Library Association, "Professional Ethics," http://www.ala.org/tools/ethics, captured at https://perma.cc/9YEQ-42YT.

29 The American Association for State and Local History (AASLH), "Statement of Professional Standards and Ethics," https://d221a1e908576484595f-1f424f9e28cc684c8a6264aa2ad33a9d.ssl.cf2.rackcdn.com/aaslh_f3b127c7bc6e406a8ae1829095a08c49.pdf, captured at https://perma.cc/Y9T7-96P3.

30 The American Institute for Conservation of Historic and Artistic Works (AIC), "Code of Ethics and Guidelines for Practice," Ethics and Standards Committee, www.conservation-us.org/ethics, captured at https://perma.cc/VF85-38SD.

31 Richard Cox and James M. O'Toole, *Understanding Archives & Manuscripts*, Archival Fundamentals Series II (Chicago: Society of American Archivists, 2006); Harvey and Mahard, *The Preservation Management Handbook*, 17–19; and Maureen Pennock, "The Twelve Principles of Digital Preservation (and a Cartridge in a Repository . . .)," *Collection Care* (blog), British Library, http://blogs.bl.uk/collectioncare/2013/09/the-twelve-principles-of-digital-preservation.html, captured at https://perma.cc/2V76-BJS9.

32 Jackie M. Dooley and Katherine Luce, *Taking Our Pulse: The OCLC Research Survey of Special Collections and Archives,* Report of OCLC Research (Dublin, Ohio: OCLC, 2010), http://www.oclc.org/research/publications/library/2010/2010-11.pdf, captured at https://perma.cc/8Q9E-BQEZ.

33 Neil Beagrie, Maggie Jones, and the Digital Preservation Center, *Preservation Management of Digital Materials: The Handbook* (Glasgow, 2008), 32.

34 Margaret Hedstrom, *Digital Preservation: Problems and Prospects* (Ann Arbor: School of Information, University of Michigan, 2001), http://www.dl.slis.tsukuba.ac.jp/DLjournal/No_20/1-hedstrom/1-hedstrom.html, captured at https://perma.cc/U568-NV3X. See also Margaret Hedstrom, "Digital Preservation: A Time Bomb for Digital Libraries," *Computers and the Humanities* 31, no. 3 (1997): 189–202, https://www.jstor.org/stable/30200423; and Margaret Hedstrom and Sheon Montgomery, *Digital Preservation Needs and Requirements in RLG Member Institutions* (study commissioned by the Research Libraries Group, Mountain View, CA, 1998).

35 Hedstrom, *Digital Preservation: Problems and Prospects*, 1.

36 Maureen Pennock, *Digital Preservation: Continued Access to Authentic Digital Assets* (Edinburgh: ISC Digital Curation Centre, 2006).

37 Martin Waller and Robert Sharpe, *Mind the Gap: Assessing Digital Preservation Needs in the UK* (York, UK: Digital Preservation Coalition, 2006).

4

Context for Archival Preservation

Introduction

Archival preservation is not just for archivists. It occurs in a range of institutional settings that support archival and manuscript collections, including academic, special, and public libraries; government agencies; nonprofit and corporate institutions; historical societies, athenaeums, and museums; and even in the commercial world of law practices and hospitals. While the missions of these organizations commonly align with the broad objectives of cultural heritage, a great deal of variation exists in practice across these sectors that can impact preservation. These differences include organizational size, governance structures, funding and resource allocation, staff levels and expertise, collection management standards and best practices, emphasis on education and outreach, and user communities. A common theme across these institutional settings is preservation, and each type of institution brings its practices and standards to that endeavor.

An understanding of archival context depends on a knowledge of the sources of the materials to be preserved: Who created them? For whom? When were they created? What cultural value do they have? And, what is the rationale for maintaining them? To understand preservation within this context, archivists and other cultural heritage professionals must be familiar with the key studies, standards, and guidelines that informed and shaped past and current preservation practice.

This chapter will compare and contrast preservation practices and standards in a range of institutions and the implications for the preservation of digital collections in each model. It will also examine the influence of professional organizations and national institutions, such as the Society of American Archivists, the Library of Congress, and the National Standards Organization, in advocating for preservation standards and practice.

Archival Preservation Is Not Just for Archivists: Preservation Management in Libraries, Archives, and Museums

The public sees libraries, archives, and museums as managing and preserving collections as well as offering distinctive user experiences. Nonetheless, the three kinds of institutions share several characteristics. Each selects and develops collections of cultural resources, preserves them for use, and makes them accessible to various constituencies. Despite collaborative efforts to advance common preservation standards across these institutions, many archivists, librarians, and museum professionals differ practically and philosophically about the nature of the materials they manage and preserve. The books, journals, and other resources in libraries are made available to the public with little staff mediation, and preservation efforts are employed to extend the life and use of materials for as long as they remain useful and relevant. The use of the original materials in archives has traditionally required extensive mediation, and care is taken to preserve the integrity and authenticity of the documentation, some of which will be preserved in perpetuity. While libraries and museums consider integrity and authenticity important, they do not emphasize these values as archives do, nor do museums focus on research value as do libraries and archives. Historically, the objects and artifacts collected by and maintained in museums were intended for education and exhibition, with individual research access not typically considered a core mission. Current digitization efforts have motivated museums to adopt technologies and standards that are historically more aligned with library and archival practices in regard to access. Libraries, archives, and museums also differ in how they see the permanence of their collections and therefore the purpose of preservation. Archivists follow appraisal guidelines and records retention schedules and dispose of materials during processing. Librarians weed collections and dispose of outdated or duplicate materials. Museums deaccession items to varying degrees, and some follow the guidelines of the American Alliance of Museums.[1]

Preservation management is also practiced in a variety of contexts in libraries, archives, and museums (LAMs). In most cultural heritage organizations, preservation is a shared responsibility, often distributed across the organization, and the size of an institution impacts the scale and operations of a preservation program. "Preservation managers" can rarely be found outside the largest organizations. Rather, in most organizations, preservation responsibilities are part of the duties of librarians, archivists, conservators, object preparators, processing staff, technical support personnel, registrars, curators, facilities employees, security staff, people in the shipping department, and any others responsible for the handling, safety, and well-being of objects or collections. For this reason, preservation programs in most cultural heritage institutions are small and decentralized, and collection managers must have a broad expertise to support preservation. Conservation work, digitization, and other reformatting projects are likely to be contracted to outside vendors, and thus staff must be savvy about preservation services. The smallest archives and libraries may only support a lone arranger, curator, or collections manager. That individual may also be responsible for all preservation activities and may work only part time as a preservation professional. Collaboration is a key component of a successful preservation program in these institutions.

Large libraries, archives, and museums may support a preservation manager, also known as a preservation officer or administrator, with responsibilities for developing a preservation program and a disaster preparedness and recovery plan, and for overseeing such functions as environmental monitoring, repair, conservation, and reformatting. Large museums may maintain separate conservation labs specializing in paintings, paper, textiles, furniture, and other kinds of objects. The largest institutions are likely to have digital curators, intellectual property attorneys, and other information professionals with preservation responsibilities. A preservation manager may coordinate all or some of these activities.

Preservation programs in such institutions are large and complex. Conservation and digitization will often be done in-house, and several staff members might undertake preservation responsibilities. These institutions may partner with one another for storage or large-scale aggregations of digital content. The preservation portfolio in such institutions is likely to be more far reaching than it would be in smaller institutions. And, in general, large institutions can more easily obtain external funding than can small, understaffed ones. Preservation managers must be attuned to organization-wide activities, such as digital initiatives and digital humanities projects that may impact preservation programs by creating new demands on archives and special collections departments. In larger institutions, support for research and scholarship increasingly depends on networked computing, including cyber-scholarship, e-research, online databases, and social media. Therefore, the creation, management, and use and reuse of large bodies of data must be central to preservation programs. This information environment exists predominantly in large-scale research or government organizations; however, these programs sometimes collaborate with smaller institutions through regional networks and other alliances. One example, the Internet Archive, founded by Brewster Kahle in 1996, is a nonprofit organization dedicated to the preservation of and access to born-digital materials across a variety of media.[2] Another is the HathiTrust, established in 2008 to promote online access to aggregated library content.[3]

Many—though not all—of the largest preservation and conservation programs in the United States and Canada exist in large academic institutions. "Research 1" universities are the 124 institutions in the United States and Canada designated in the Carnegie Classification of Institutions of Higher Education as having the "Highest Research Activities."[4] Many of these institutions support campus libraries, museums, and archives engaged in the research and development needed to advance preservation. The research publications and standards developed by these organizations support preservation and conservation at organizations of all sizes. State and federal institutions such as the National Archives, the Library of Congress, and the Smithsonian Institution also sponsor research on conservation, preservation, and digitization. The Library of Congress features online access to the publications of its preservation and conservation specialists from 1980 to the present.[5] Furthermore, privately funded institutions such as the Getty Conservation Institute conduct conservation and preservation research. A number of research libraries and art museums also feature preservation programs and activities. For example, the Boston Museum of Fine Arts, in partnership with other institutions, created CAMEO: Conservation and Art Materials Encyclopedia Online.[6]

Regardless of type or size, libraries, archives, and museums are responding to growing user expectations for digital access, which have profoundly impacted the cost and scale of preservation. The adoption of new and evolving information and communication technology across libraries, archives, and museums has generated a common need for new digital competencies, standards, and best practices that can be adequately addressed only through cooperation across sectors. A recent white paper by the Coalition to Advance Learning in Archives, Libraries and Museums notes that cultural organizations, such as libraries, archives, and museums, are inherently cross-sector, with shared affinities and needs, even though practitioners tend to retreat to their own disciplines for answers to professional questions. In other words, while these organizations face many of the same challenges, they are often isolated in the application of professional practices.[7] The report further acknowledges that coordinated advocacy at the national, local, and institutional levels should be a high strategic priority across sectors.[8]

This convergence of practice across disciplines has begun to blur traditional boundaries and has created new opportunities for collaboration, including the development of shared standards necessary for preservation.[9] The future of preservation depends, in part, on how traditional and philosophical differences across LAMs are managed—and how professionals across cultural sectors find consensus in, and advocate for, shared standards and best practices related to preservation, especially in the digital realm.

Key Studies and Standards in Preservation

This section introduces several critical studies, standards, and guidelines that have shaped the current preservation realm. The recommendations and principles delineated here, central to the advancement of preservation, constitute only some of the initiatives, protocols, or strategies that professionals employ. Additional information is provided on standards and best practices throughout the book. In addition to introducing several key studies on past and current practice, this section will introduce key reports and guidelines associated with digital preservation. These recommendations and standards for the creation and management of digital content are inherently cross-sector, impacting libraries, archives, and museums. Current initiatives focus increasingly on digital preservation, while those relating to analog formats are declining due to limited interest by funders and other key advocates. The amount of literature about analog materials may be declining because a great many reliable sources are already available, and publishers and practitioners believe that new source materials are not needed to advance a field already replete with information. This, to us, seems shortsighted because analog formats are not going away, nor are they being produced in diminishing quantities.

The Surveys

The systematic collection of data documenting the preservation of cultural heritage is critical to understanding and articulating budget, staffing, and resource needs. In addition to tracking internal activities, preservation programs in libraries, archives, and museums rely on local and national data to guide preservation decisions and to advocate for programs at the institutional and national levels. Academic libraries were the first to launch systematic surveys documenting preservation conditions. One of the first, Gay Walker's massive 1985 survey of the physical condition of book collections at Yale, assisted libraries nationwide in identifying their preservation needs and in developing appropriate programs.[10] During the same period, the Association of Research Libraries (ARL) launched a national pilot project to measure the preservation efforts of ARL member libraries. Walker's article and the concurrent ARL survey, which both appeared in print the same year, increased awareness of the poor condition of our collections and set the stage for an annual ARL preservation statistics program conducted from 1984 to 2008.

Also in 1985, while serving on SAA's Task Force on Institutional Evaluation, Paul Conway designed and administered the first comprehensive survey of archival repositories in the United States. His study evaluated resources, responsibilities, and activities in federal, state, local, academic, religious, business, special subject, and museum organizations.[11] Responding to the report's recommendation for additional studies, including an analysis of the state of preservation activities in these institutions, the Society of American Archivists, with the assistance of the National Endowment for the Humanities (NEH), carried out the first nationwide study of archival preservation practices.[12] In addition to establishing a framework and methodology for the assessment of archival practice, Conway's study determined that

- Archivists understood the significance of preservation and its techniques, but archival preservation management was not fully integrated into professional practice.
- Archival institutions should develop and implement systematic strategies for selecting materials from among their holdings for preservation action and for using preservation methods appropriate to the value of selected materials.
- Archival programs are isolated from their parent organizations and should be fully integrated into the institutions that support them.
- The archival profession must develop a collaborative framework that provides archivists, institutions, service organizations, funding agencies, and professional associations with a clear statement of archival preservation goals and objectives.

In 1986, the National Association of Government Archives and Records Administrators (NAGARA) and the Society of American Archivists sponsored a survey entitled *Preservation Needs in State Archives* that focused on the nature and dimension of preservation programs in all fifty state government archives in the United States. The report concluded that none of the state archives was meeting its preservation challenges and called for a national strategy to address funding and resource issues.[13]

These early surveys, conducted in the 1980s, also determined the extent of the "brittle book" problem in libraries. Most books and documents created from the third quarter of the nineteenth century to the mid-twentieth century were printed on wood-pulp papers sized with alum-rosin. If the paper's pH became low enough, paper eventually became brittle. The Yale survey and other investigation results were sufficiently startling that the National Endowment for the Humanities (NEH) Division of Preservation and Access and other agencies and foundations funded large-scale preservation microfilming projects. Later critics, such as Nicholson Baker, lamented that, in some cases, unique materials, newspapers, and periodicals were discarded once they were filmed. He claimed microfilm could be inadequate for a variety of reasons and therefore needed to be checked against the originals for completeness and legibility.[14] For this reason, he felt that the discarding of original materials was shortsighted. This argument is also relevant to the disposal of analog materials once they are digitized.

However, preservation microfilming resulted in important and positive outcomes. For example, the NEH-sponsored US newspaper microfilming project saved many periodicals. Newsprint is particularly unstable, and many newspapers would have deteriorated enough to seriously diminish their use if they had not been filmed. Today, with support from NEH and the Library of Congress, newspapers from that long-running project are being digitized as part of the National Digital Newspaper project. Its public interface, Chronicling America: Historic American Newspapers, provides access to newspapers from nearly all fifty states dating from 1836 to 1922.[15]

The 2005 Heritage Health Index (HHI) offered the first comprehensive survey of the condition of US cultural heritage collections across professional sectors. The study, conducted by Heritage Preservation in partnership with the Institute of Museum and Library Services (IMLS), revealed new and startling data on the preservation needs of analog and digital materials and recommended that immediate action be taken to save millions of resources in over 30,000 archives, historical societies, libraries, museums, and other research organizations. The published findings contain recommendations applicable to all types of collections and formats, and include information about the condition of digital content in a wide range of institutions across the United States.[16]

According to staff involved in the survey, "the goal of the Heritage Health Index was to cross professional boundaries to look at collections in a wide variety of institutions, large and small, and to assess the condition of the full range of collections." The Heritage Health Index asked institutions to report on all aspects of conservation and preservation and to estimate the quantity and condition of the collections for which they had a preservation responsibility. As a result, important baseline data now exist on the condition and preservation needs of materials at archives, libraries, historical societies, museums, and scientific and archaeological research organizations.[17]

The Heritage Health Index survey revealed empirical data indicating that a large percentage of the nation's collections existed in suboptimal environmental conditions and that at least a quarter were poorly cataloged. While planners of the survey were not certain how many institutions in the United States were actively involved in digital preservation, they anticipated that the documentation collected by the Heritage Health Index could provide valuable initial data regarding the extent of digital holdings and what issues institutions faced regarding their care. The findings supported the idea that digital preservation should be linked to the conservation and preservation missions at the organizational level. The report made four general recommendations:

1. Institutions must give priority to providing safe conditions for the collections they hold in trust.
2. Every collecting institution should develop an emergency plan to protect its collections.
3. Every institution should assign responsibility for caring for collections to members of its staff.
4. Individuals at all levels of government and in the private sector should assume responsibility for providing the support that will allow these collections to survive.[18]

The Heritage Health Index addressed the condition and preservation needs of collections and institutions at a scale previously unknown. With these findings, the HHI did more to advance the cause of preservation than any initiative that preceded or followed. The information gathered across sectors identified preservation priorities for the nation and set the stage for subsequent work, including plans for the collection of comparative data and assessment every ten years.

In 2012, several years after the loss of the ARL preservation statistics program, the American Library Association (ALA) committed to a second national preservation metrics effort, the Preservation Statistics Survey. ALA's Preservation and Reformatting Section and the Association of Library Collections and Technical Services (ALCTS) coordinated this program. In their 2015 Preservation Statistics Survey report, Annie Peterson, Holly Robertson, and Nick Szydlowski note that the survey aimed "to document the state of preservation activities in this digital era via quantitative data that facilitates peer comparison and a better understanding of trends in the preservation and conservation fields over time" while acknowledging it did not receive the anticipated respondent rate.[19] In a subsequent analysis of national survey projects, the authors point out the importance of documenting current preservation trends and challenges but also note the substantial cost in developing this data.[20] ALCTS continued to issue the survey in subsequent years, but without a strong commitment from funders, professional organizations, and the reporting institutions who gain the most from the analysis, the future accumulation of national preservation statistics remains uncertain.

Since the early 1990s, the challenge of digital preservation has intensified in importance and magnitude. Preserving our digital assets assures the continuity of records. Digital preservation programs involve a number of stakeholders, including public, industry, and heritage organizations. Collaboration is also central to these efforts and will continue to be so, particularly in the area of standards and best practices.

Metadata and Digitization Standards for Preservation

Metadata is structured data that describes information objects and entities. It is primarily created to organize and retrieve digitized content over time. Metadata standards are traditionally associated with the discovery, longevity, and interoperability of digitized content or digitized information about content. But, metadata also exists in analog form as inventories, card catalogs, and other indexes. Generally, metadata falls into three principle categories, all critical to long-term digital preservation and used across all LAM sectors:[21]

1. "Descriptive metadata" describes a resource for purposes such as discovery and identification. It can include elements such as title, abstract, author, and keywords.
2. "Structural metadata" indicates how compound objects are arranged and related, for example, how pages are ordered to form chapters.
3. "Administrative metadata" provides information that assists in managing a resource, such as file type and other technical information, explanations about when and how the resource was created, and instructions about who can access it. Several subsets of administrative data are sometimes listed as separate metadata types:
    - "Rights management metadata" addresses intellectual property rights.
    - "Preservation metadata" records the provenance of digital objects and provides information to archive and preserve a resource and ensure access over time, including preservation activities such as migration or emulation.
    - "Technical metadata" provides information necessary for rendering files.

Another category of metadata, mark-up language, specifies code for the processing and presentation of text. An example is XML, the language used for Encoded Archival Description (EAD) that determines the formatting layout and style within an EAD text file. XML, like PDF and HTML, is static and thus relevant in the context of preservation because these languages can be read using a variety of hardware and software programs.

A more thorough description of key tools, concepts, and issues associated with using metadata and metadata elements, standards, and schemas, such as Dublin Core, is beyond the scope of this book and is covered more fully in other volumes associated with the Archival Fundamentals Series III. Instead, our discussion of metadata will focus on standards intrinsic to the creation of a "preservation friendly" digital information object. According to Ross Harvey and Martha R. Mahard in their 2014 publication, *Preservation Management Handbook*, a preservation-friendly object "is an object that has a better chance of being accessible and usable in the future because it has been created with longevity in mind."[22] Creating preservation-friendly objects is not a new concept. For example, records creators frequently generate documents on acid-free paper to enhance the longevity of content. However, as the authors note, approaches to long-term preservation have assumed greater importance in recent decades due to the fragility of digital objects. Metadata is necessary to build authoritative, reliable, and useful (preservation-friendly) digital resources. Technical, descriptive, and preservation metadata document how a digital information object was created and maintained, and how it operates in relation to other information objects. They ensure that digital information objects can exist independent of the current system used to store and retrieve them, as well as survive migration through consecutive generations of computer hardware and software and the transfer to new delivery systems. For information objects to remain accessible and intelligible over time, it is essential to preserve and migrate metadata with the object it describes.[23] Two key standards for the application of metadata in the context of digital preservation are METS—Metadata Encoding and Transmission Standard—a structure for encoding descriptive, administrative, and structural metadata, and PREMIS—Preservation Metadata: Implementation Strategies.

In 2003, OCLC and the Research Libraries Group (RLG) jointly sponsored the formation of the PREMIS Working Group, comprised of international experts in the use of metadata, to support digital preservation activities. The group's charge, in part, was to develop a core set of implementable preservation metadata, broadly applicable across a wide range of digital preservation contexts. Its work was intended to comply with Open Archival Information Systems (OAIS) guidelines and recommendations for the creation, management, and use of digital objects. In May 2005, the working group released its *Data Dictionary for Preservation Metadata: Final Report of the PREMIS Working Group*. In addition to defining a data dictionary for preservation metadata, the report also includes a set of XML schemas to support implementation of the data dictionary in digital preservation systems. The report defines preservation metadata as "the information a repository uses to support the digital preservation process." The PREMIS data dictionary further defines core preservation metadata across a number of categories, including administrative (including rights and permissions), technical, and structural. The dictionary pays particular attention to the documentation of digital provenance (the history of an object) and to the documentation of relationships, especially relationships among different objects in the preservation repository.[24] The data dictionary has been updated several times, with the current version, PREMIS 3.0, published in 2015.[25]

In 2009, with the support of the Library of Congress, Priscilla Caplan published an important overview of the PREMIS preservation metadata standard entitled *Understanding PREMIS*.[26] The work, revised in 2017, aims to be a user-friendly introduction to the complex PREMIS data dictionary. According to Caplan,

> If you think of all of the metadata needed by an organization managing a preservation repository, PREMIS can be seen as defining a subset in the center. On the one hand, it is not concerned with discovery and access, and on the other, it does not attempt to define detailed format-specific metadata. It defines only that metadata commonly needed to perform preservation functions on all materials.[27]

Thus, the primary and intended use of PREMIS focuses on repository design, evaluation, and information. In this sense, PREMIS is a guideline to support long-term digital preservation by maintaining information about the provenance, the intellectual property rights, and the technical and descriptive environments of a digital object archived in a repository system.[28]

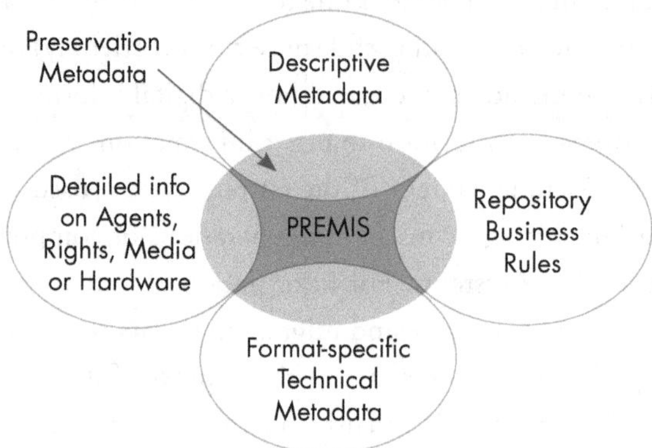

FIGURE 4.1. PREMIS as a subset of all preservation metadata. Library of Congress, 2017.

Internationally, other preservation initiatives are developing important metadata models for digital preservation systems. One of the more influential is the National Library of New Zealand's *Metadata Standards Framework—Preservation Metadata.*[29] More broadly, several organizations have developed important guidelines for understanding metadata standards and best practices, including how they support preservation. The National Information Standards Organization (NISO) published a primer on metadata basics entitled *Understanding Metadata.*[30] The Library of Congress provides online access to all of the current standards associated with metadata and other descriptive standards.[31] The Getty Trust has created several tools and resources, including a crosswalk that examines metadata use across various schemas used by libraries, archives, and museums.[32]

In addition to the PREMIS data dictionary, which establishes the metadata needed to support the long-term preservation of digital materials, several free tools are designed to meet the fundamental requirement of digital repositories to identify the precise format of all stored digital objects. Examples of tools that capture technical and other preservation metadata include DROID, JHOVE, and the National Library of New Zealand's Metadata Extractor.[33]

Standards and Guidelines for Digital Object Creation and Management

To maintain preservation-friendly objects, archivists must follow best practices and standards designed for consistency and interoperability from the point of creation and throughout the life cycle of the object. Many standards and guidelines exist regarding digital content creation, including the Research Library Group publication *Moving Theory into Practice: Digital Imaging for Libraries and Archives*, the *NINCH Guide to Good Practice in the Digital Representation and Management of Cultural Heritage Materials*, and the Northeast Document Conservation Center's *Handbook for Digital Projects: A Management Tool for Preservation and Access*.[34] The NARA *Technical Guidelines for Digitizing Archival Materials for Electronic Access* defines procedures used by NARA laboratories for digitizing archival records and the creation of master image files. The Federal Agencies Digital Guidelines Initiative (FADGI) is a collaborative effort started in 2007 by federal agencies to articulate common sustainable practices and guidelines for digitized and born-digital content specific to two major areas: still images and audiovisual materials.[35] And finally, the Council on Library and Information Resources regularly publishes reports on preservation, digital libraries, information use, international developments, and the changing role of the library.[36]

Standards for Repository Architecture and System Development

OAIS

In 1994, the Consultative Committee for Space Data Systems (CCSDS) began developing a reference model for long-term storage and archiving of digital data. The project, led by the National Aeronautics and Space Administration (NASA) to preserve data from the space community, was open to other interested disciplines and intended to be a high-level model for managing the functions and responsibilities for archiving digital data in a range of contexts. The model, known as the Open Archival Information System (OAIS), now an ISO standard (ISO 14721), is widely accepted by digital preservationists and vendors for managing digital repositories.[37] The CCSDS maintains these standards and practices, and they are reviewed every five years, with the current version published in 2012 (ISO 14721:2012). The OAIS Model, the standardization of best practices for long-term storage of digital objects, represents the first comprehensive and consistent framework for describing and analyzing digital preservation issues. The model describes a core set of mechanisms by which an OAIS-based archives meets its mission to preserve information and make it available in the long term. These functional requirements collectively define the OAIS preservation and access operations, and include date of ingestion, archival storage, administration, preservation planning, and access. Furthermore, the model identifies six mandatory responsibilities that a system must address:

1. Negotiating for and acceptance of information
2. Obtaining sufficient control for preservation
3. Determining the designated community (end-users)
4. Ensuring that information is independently understandable
5. Following established preservation policies and procedures
6. Making information available

The model also describes a conceptual framework for the long-term preservation of data, known as the "information package." The package consists of the digital object and the metadata needed to support the object all bound into a single entity. To be functional, a system must ingest and accept three varieties of information packages. These are the

1. **Submission information package (SIP)**, which includes the information provided by the creator or producer
2. **Archival information package (AIP)**, the version of the information package held and maintained by the repository over time
3. **Dissemination information package (DIP)**, the information package provided to a consumer in response to an access request

In addition, the OAIS model describes the necessary components to preserve a digital object over time. The construction of the AIP includes information about the content data object that is the focus of preservation, as well as any representation data, including preservation description information (PDI), packaging information (PI), and descriptive information (DI), that support the discovery of the object.[38]

Since its inception, OAIS has provided the foundation for numerous architectures, standards, and protocols that influence system design, metadata requirements, certification, and other issues central to digital preservation. To assist archivists, librarians, and others in understanding and applying OAIS at the institutional level, Brian Lavoie and the Digital Preservation Coalition published an excellent overview of OAIS that describes the core principles and functional elements, as well as how the model supports long-term preservation, access, and understandability of data.[39]

TRAC, TDR, and ISO 16363

One of the most important contributions of the OAIS model was the development of a common vocabulary for digital preservation. In addition, the model established the groundwork for the development of auditing requirements needed to support trusted digital repositories. In 1996, the Task Force on Archival Digital Information, convened by the Commission on Preservation and Access and the Research Libraries Group (RLG), published a report that identified the need for trusted digital repositories capable of providing reliable, long-term access to digital resources.[40] In 2002, an initiative sponsored by OCLC and RLG identified the attributes of a trusted digital repository necessary for the responsible management of a full range of digital content and formats.[41] The report acknowledged that institutions are not capable of certifying themselves as trusted stewards of digital content, but it stopped short of establishing specific criteria for a certification process. This challenge was undertaken in 2003 by the Task Force on Digital Repository Certification sponsored by RLG and the National Archives (NARA). The 2007 report issued by the task force, *Trustworthy Repositories Audit and Certification: Criteria and Checklist*, is commonly known as TRAC.[42] The report extended the attributes identified in earlier reports and the OAIS model into a checklist that could be used to support certification. In 2011, the CCSDS published the *Audit and Certification of Trustworthy Repositories: Recommended Practice* (TDR), also known as the Magenta Book.[43] TRAC and TDR adhere to the OAIS Reference Model and are intricately tied to the development and philosophy of trusted repositories. Collectively, these efforts provided the basis for ISO 16363:2012-*Audit and Certification of Trustworthy Digital Repositories,* the international standard that superseded TRAC.

Several other important certification efforts should be noted. The European Framework for the Audit and Certification of Digital Repositories designates three levels of trustworthiness (basic, extended, and formal) based on the understanding that many institutions do not have the funding or other resources to provide for full external audit and certification of their digital preservation systems. To receive the designation of an extended or formal trusted repository, an organization must receive a seal of approval based on ISO 1616363 or DIN 31644 (a similar German standard).[44] The National Digital Stewardship Alliance (NDSA) developed a similar approach, known as the "Levels of Digital Preservation," a tiered set of recommendations guiding organizations in building or enhancing their digital preservation activities at four levels.[45] And, finally, DRAMBORA is a methodology and toolkit developed by the Digital Curation Centre and Digital Preservation Europe designed to facilitate internal audits and help organizations identify the strengths and weaknesses of their digital repositories and how to deal with them. Currently, the Center for Research Libraries provides assessment and audit oversight for certification, for example, certifying HathiTrust as a trustworthy repository in 2010.

According to Sheila McAlister, "trustworthy" repositories are committed to providing reliable, long-term access to digital resources for a specific community of users. For a repository to be "trusted," it must meet several system requirements, including financial security and sustainability; standards-based methods for the ongoing management, access, and security of deposited materials; and auditability and procedures for systems evaluation. Critical responsibilities include ingesting, controlling, and maintaining data and their accompanying metadata; following well-documented policies and procedures for collections development, access control, storage, and updating of procedures over time; providing access to the community of users; and encouraging content providers to follow current best practices for digital object creation.[46] An example is the Electronic Records Archives (ERA) managed by the National Archives. The ERA system ingests and stores electronic records from the White House, Congress, and agencies across the federal government. ERA 2.0 is a modernization of the existing ERA system based on OAIS standards and cloud-based architecture designed to manage electronic records throughout their life cycles, from upload by a producing federal agency, through processing, preservation, and production of access versions for the National Archives Catalog.[47]

Blue Ribbon Task Force on Sustainable Digital Preservation and Access

The Blue Ribbon Task Force on Sustainable Digital Preservation and Access was launched in late 2007 by the National Science Foundation and the Andrew W. Mellon Foundation, in partnership with the Library of Congress, the Joint Information Systems Committee of the United Kingdom, the Council on Library and Information Resources, and the National Archives and Records Administration. The task force was commissioned to explore the economic sustainability challenges associated with digital preservation and access. Its final report evaluates four categories of content: scholarly discourse (books, journals, etc.); research data; commercially copyrighted materials; and web content.[48]

The report recommends three imperatives for sustainable digital preservation: articulating a compelling value proposition for preservation; offering clear incentives to preserve in the public interest; and defining roles and responsibilities among stakeholders for the allocation of resources throughout the digital life cycle.[49] A key contribution of the report is the identification of five conditions necessary for digital preservation sustainability:

1. Recognition of the benefits of preservation by decision makers
2. Selection of materials with long-term value
3. Incentives for decision makers to act in the public interest
4. Appropriate organization and governance of preservation activities
5. Ongoing and efficient allocation of resources to preservation

These values are consistent with ethical mandates associated with archival preservation. The first condition is directed to resource allocators who have responsibility for digital objects appraised as being valuable. These values can be articulated as administrative, legal, and historical and are justified by the legal and research implications if the materials are lost. Selection for long-term value acknowledges that all digital content cannot be saved and emphasizes that what is saved should be based on identified criteria. The report concludes by warning that preservation, like other societal challenges, is a balancing act, weighing the needs and desires of the present day with those of the future. All stakeholders must provide leadership and accept responsibility for the development of a common digital preservation infrastructure that is sustainable in the long term, and this involves advocacy and leadership across generations and professional disciplines.[50]

Preservation Leadership and Advocacy

The reports, guidelines, and recommendations discussed in the previous section underscore the importance of collaborating with, and advocating for, preservation among the stakeholders and resource allocators associated with preservation programs in libraries, archives, and museums. For most cultural heritage organizations, resources are finite, and advocacy at the national and local levels is critical. Professional organizations, consortia, and preservation-focused nonprofits play a central role at a time when advocating for sustainable preservation is critical. Most archives students and professionals are introduced to these organizations in informal ways and often fail to understand their connections and the context in which they function to advance preservation. This section identifies key professional organizations and their missions and how these missions impact preservation practices. It is not an exhaustive list.

The Professional Organizations

The Society of American Archivists (SAA), established 1936, is North America's oldest and largest national professional association dedicated to the needs and interests of archives and archivists. SAA represents more than 6,200 professional archivists employed by governments, universities, businesses, libraries, museums, religious institutions, and historical organizations.[51] The society supports its members and the archival profession through its publications, educational programs, and annual meetings. SAA publishes a semi-annual refereed scholarly journal, *American Archivist*, as well as newsletters, books, manuals, and other resources addressing all aspects of the profession. SAA also supports continuing and graduate education, certificate programs, and workshops that address current archival training needs, such as instruction in metadata and description standards, the digitization of archival materials, and the preservation and conservation of materials. The society advocates for the profession by publishing position statements on public policy, promoting standards and best practices, and advancing public awareness of issues impacting the profession. SAA supports many component groups, including sections, committees, task forces, and working groups representing specialized functions and interests of the profession. Currently, SAA sponsors forty-six sections, including the Preservation Section, the Electronic Records Section, the Metadata and Digital Objects Section, and the Security Section, all involved in advancing and advocating for archival preservation. The Preservation Section promotes the preservation of archives and manuscript collections. Its mission is to raise awareness of and disseminate information about the preservation of archival materials regardless of format. The section sponsors an annual preservation publication award, special interest sessions at the annual meeting, and access to selected preservation resources.[52]

The American Library Association (ALA), founded in 1876, is the oldest and largest library association in the world. The mission of ALA is "to provide leadership for the development, promotion and improvement of library and information services and the profession of librarianship in order to enhance learning and ensure access to information for all."[53] From its beginnings, ALA has incorporated specialized sections, roundtables, and divisions, including college and reference librarians (1889), trustees (1890), and catalogers (1900). Currently, ALA sponsors eleven membership divisions, representing specific library types, such as academic, public, and school libraries, or a library function or specialization, such as reference/user services, information technology, and management. ALA divisions publish journals, books, newsletters, and other materials; offer continuing education; bestow awards and scholarships; sponsor institutes and conferences; and maintain networks of affiliates, chapters, and other collaborative relationships. In particular, two divisions of ALA support archival preservation activities. The Association of College and Research Libraries (ACRL) represents academic and research librarians and library personnel working in college, university, and research libraries.[54] ACRL, the largest ALA division with over 11,000 members, supports several communities of practice through sections, committees, discussion groups, editorial boards, interest groups, and chapter affiliates. Currently, ACRL sponsors sixteen sections, including the Rare Books and Manuscripts Section, which is charged with exercising leadership in the local, national, and international special collections communities to represent and promote concerns related to rare books, manuscripts, and other special collections. RBMS does not currently support a committee devoted to preservation activities, but it does sponsor a committee on digital collections, a Curators and Conservators Discussion Group, and various task forces devoted to preservation-related issues, such as security standards.

The Association for Library Collection and Technical Services (ALCTS) is the national association for information providers who work in collections and technical services, such as acquisitions, cataloging, metadata, collection management, preservation, and electronic resources.[55] ALCTS supports several sections, including the Preservation and Reformatting Section (PARS).[56] This section of ALCTS focuses on preserving and reformatting of library materials in all kinds of institutions and applying new technology to ensure continued access to library collections. In addition to sponsoring Preservation Week and several preservation-related awards and publications, PARS promotes appropriate methods and materials for preserving all formats of library materials; identifies relevant information regarding standards, recommended practices, and technical reports;

and coordinates similar activities inside and outside of PARS. Currently, six interest groups are associated with PARS:

- Book and Paper Interest Group
- Digital Conversion Interest Group
- Digital Preservation Interest Group
- Preservation Administration Interest Group
- Preservation Metadata Interest Group
- Promoting Preservation Interest Group

These groups have distinct charges, they promote accepted standards and best practices, and they advocate for preservation. They advance the understanding of preservation principles and objectives and the development of preservation skills, and they cultivate preservation funding sources.

The American Alliance of Museums (AAM), formerly the American Association of Museums, was founded in 1906, and currently represents more than 35,000 museum professionals and volunteers from a range of museum types, including art, history, science, military, maritime, and youth, as well as public aquariums, zoos, botanical gardens, arboretums, historic sites, and science and technology centers, with many of these organizations holding important archival collections.[57] AAM provides professional education, information exchange, accreditation services, and information about standards and best practices; develops publications and educational programs; bestows grants and awards; and advocates on issues of concern to the museum community. It publishes the bimonthly magazine *Museum* and *Adviso,* a monthly newsletter that occasionally addresses preservation issues. The organization supports Museum Advocacy Day, the Museum Assessment Program (MAP), and several professional networks organized around job responsibilities and areas of common interest, such as collections care and security. Two examples are PIC Green, a group devoted to sustainable energy-efficient museums, and the Media & Technology (M&T) professional network for the production of media resources, standards, database development, and the creation and maintenance of technologies used by museums, with a specialized focus on audiovisual formats.[58]

The American Institute for Conservation of Historic and Artistic Works (AIC) is a national membership organization supporting conservation professionals in the preservation of cultural heritage. Incorporated in 1972, AIC began as the American offshoot of an international group of conservators, the International Institute for Conservation of Historic and Artistic Works (IIC). AIC and IIC are dedicated to upholding professional standards, promoting research and publications, providing educational opportunities, and fostering information exchange among conservators, allied professionals, and the public.[59] The organization consists of several committees and groups relevant to archives and archival preservation, including Books and Paper, Electronic Media, Photographic Materials, and the Sustainability Committee. Each of these groups organizes annual meetings and sponsors publications and other resources in its area of interest. AIC's disaster response and recovery efforts include coordinating the National Heritage Responders (NHR) and creating numerous guides and manuals supporting disaster prevention and emergency response, including *The Field Guide to Emergency Response* and *The Emergency Response and Salvage Wheel* with instruction and assistance on how to respond to specific disasters and emergencies. These two resources were originally created by Heritage Preservation, which was dissolved in 2015 and which also sponsored the Health Heritage Index discussed previously in this chapter. AIC also hosts Conservation Online (CoOL), a free online collaborative resource for information about the conservation and preservation of cultural heritage.[60] Its 2016 report, *Charting the Digital Landscape of the Conservation Profession*, notes that the current digital environment "fails to meet the growing needs of the conservation profession and the audiences it serves" due to poor leadership, policy, training, digital content and resources, and the low visibility of the profession and its practitioners.[61]

In addition to these four major national organizations, several state, regional, national, and international professional organizations devoted to library, archives, and museum practice also provide leadership and advocacy for archival preservation. At the international level, the International Federation of Library Associations and Institutions (IFLA) is the leading international body representing the interests of library and information services and their users.[62] It maintains several divisions, including the Library Collections Division that sponsors the Committee on Standards and Preservation and Conservation (PAC). It also maintains sections devoted to issues in rare books and special collections, and another in preservation and conservation that works closely with PAC. At the national level, the Council of State Archivists (COSA), the National Association of Government Archives and Records Administrators (NAGARA), and the American Association for State and Local History (AASLH) hold annual meetings and create publications relevant to archival preservation in state archives, local historical societies, archives, libraries, and museums.

At the regional level, some of the larger archival professional organizations include the Midwest Archives Conference (MAC), the Mid-Atlantic Archival Conference (MARAC), the New England Archivists, the Southwest Archivists, and the Northwest Archivists, Inc. The Association of Moving Image Archivists (AMIA) and the Association of Recorded Sound Collections (ARSC) provide important preservation support and information regarding audiovisual collections. The Society of American Archivists publishes a directory of archival organizations in the United States and Canada that provides a current listing of many of these organizations.[63]

The National Cultural Heritage Institutions

The National Archives, the Library of Congress, and the Smithsonian Institution support important preservation and conservation programs designed to promote preservation nationwide. NARA's preservation and conservation programs offer guidance to the National Archives, federal records centers, presidential libraries, and affiliated archives to ensure that government records are appropriately preserved and available for use. The preservation program conducts research, provides input on national standards, and publishes technical information, such as *Digitizing Archival Records for Electronic Access: Technical Guidelines*.[64] The program also provides assistance to the public in preserving family archives, and offers practical information on a variety of materials: photographs, negatives, and film; paper and parchment; books and scrapbooks; digital and electronic media; audio and video tapes, and motion pictures.[65] In 2017, beginning with the papers of the Barack Obama administration, NARA's preservation program announced a new model for managing presidential records that no longer involves administering a museum or a traditional "presidential library." It instead focuses on preserving and making accessible presidential papers in digital format.[66]

The Library of Congress, Preservation Directorate, is responsible for ensuring long-term access to the world's largest library collection through a broad range of activities distributed across the Library of Congress.[67] These activities include conservation, library binding, mass deacidification, reformatting, materials analysis and testing, collections emergency management, and conservation of general and special collections; collections storage and environmental management; integrated pest management; collections rehousing and stabilization for transport and relocation; care and handling training; development of preservation standards; and preservation science research. Preservation Directorate staff promote access by supporting online and in-house exhibitions as well as loans. The directorate also sponsors public programs such as the Topics in Preservation Series (TOPS) lectures that advance important issues and research in preservation.

The Smithsonian's Museum Conservation Institute (MCI) is the center for conservation and scientific analysis for all of the Smithsonian's collections and museums. With access to state-of-the-art instrumentation and scientific techniques, the MCI advances preservation through its programs in conservation research, technical studies, and consultation.[68] MCI staff operate and maintain a large number of analytical resources and tools, including spectroscopy, X-ray, and spectrometry instruments that support their research, conservation, and outreach programs. In addition to requests for consultations from within the Smithsonian, the MCI responds to requests from affiliates and outside organizations, including federal, museum, and academic organizations. The MCI also sponsors a professional-development program with formal coursework in preservation science.

The National Standards Organizations

Hundreds of standards-developing organizations (SDO) are estimated to operate in the United States today. These SDOs are independent organizations typically focused on market and business needs, but their impact can be significant in the development of standards supporting appropriate preservation activities. The American National Standards Institute (ANSI) oversees the creation, promulgation, and use of norms and guidelines across a wide range of organizations and acts as a clearinghouse for the accreditation of emerging standards. Founded in 1918, it relies on its user communities to cooperatively develop voluntary national consensus for standards. Accreditation by ANSI signifies that the procedures promoted by the standards body meet the institute's essential requirements for openness, balance, consensus, and due process.[69]

The nonprofit National Information Standards Organization (NISO) is accredited by ANSI to identify, develop, maintain, and publish technical standards, today focusing on the management of digital information. Founded in 1939, it draws its support from publishing, libraries, IT, and media.[70] NISO standards apply to traditional and new technologies and to information across its life cycle, from creation through documentation, use, repurposing, storage, metadata, and preservation. ANSI designates NISO to represent US interests on the Technical Advisory Group to the International Organization for Standardization's (ISO) Technical Committee 46 on Information and Documentation, the group responsible for developing interoperable standards and compatible information systems for libraries, archives, and museums.[71] NISO also offers programming on emerging topics that often lead to the formation of committees to develop new standards. The International Organization for Standardization (ISO) is an international standard-setting body composed of representatives from various national standards organizations. Founded in 1947, the organization promotes worldwide proprietary, industrial, and commercial standards.[72] The ISO Technical Committee focuses on interoperable standards and compatible information systems for libraries, archives, and museums.

While numerous SDOs operate in the United States, two others deserve special mention for their impact on archival preservation. The American Society for Testing and Materials (ASTM) creates technical standards related to materials, products, systems, and services, including standards supporting architectural and document conservation.[73] The Association for Information and Image Management (AIIM) is a nonprofit organization focused on the management of documents, content, records, and business processes. AIIM's Standards Program develops and promotes standards and recommended practices, and it produces technical reports and industry specifications. Originally focused on microfilm and micrographics, AIIM is now involved in the development of standards for digital imaging.[74]

The Preservation Consortia and Other Organizations

The Regional Alliance for Preservation (RAP) is a national network of nonprofit organizations with expertise in conservation and preservation. Through coordinated outreach, educational programs, and publications, RAP organizations advocate for and foster awareness of preservation concerns across a range of cultural heritage institutions in the United States. RAP members present training programs, provide conservation and preservation services, create publications to assist institutions in caring for their collections, and provide free technical advice to collecting institutions across the country. Specifically, these regional field service programs support preservation through surveys, workshops, and seminars, and offer disaster assistance and information services to the staff of museums, historical organizations, libraries, and archives.[75] RAP currently has fourteen members, including the Balboa Art Conservation Center in San Diego, the Midwest Art Conservation Center in Minneapolis, and the Williamstown Art Conservation Center in Williamstown, Massachusetts. The three largest RAP member organizations are LYRASIS (in Atlanta), the Conservation Center for Art and Historic Artifacts (CCAHA), and the Northeast Document Conservation Center (NEDCC).

LYRASIS is the nation's largest regional nonprofit membership organization serving member libraries, archives, museums, and other cultural heritage organizations. Its specialized unit LYRASIS Digital supports digitization, allowing member organizations to create, host, manage, and share their unique collections. LYRASIS also hosts the archival collection management system ArchivesSpace. The current organization was formed in 2009 by the merger of several smaller regional associations, including PALINET, SOLINET, and NELINET.

The Conservation Center for Art and Historic Artifacts was established in Philadelphia in 1977. It serves cultural, educational, and research institutions; government agencies; corporations; private organizations; and collectors. NEDCC, founded in 1973 in Massachusetts, was the first independent conservation laboratory in the nation to specialize exclusively in treating collections made of paper or parchment, such as works of art, photographs, books, maps, and manuscripts. The center offers conservation treatment, digital imaging, and audio preservation services, as well as training, consultations, and disaster advice. NEDCC publishes the Preservation Leaflets Series with information on a wide variety of preservation topics and resources.[76]

The regional preservation programs have been providing services to cultural institutions with significant grant support from the National Endowment for the Humanities, Division of Preservation and Access, and other national funding organizations. This funding initially supported traditional preservation practices, such as disaster planning and preventive preservation, and now increasingly provides support and training for digitization and digital preservation, often to smaller institutions.

Several other nonprofit organizations and consortia include preservation in their research and advocacy. OCLC Research, formally known as the Research Libraries Group (RLG), is one of the world's leading centers devoted to information technology and its impact on libraries and archives. Its mission is to advance libraries and librarianship through research in five areas of support for research collections, library systems, data science, user studies, and learning. It is a community resource for shared research and advocacy. Its publications and reports frequently address key issues in the preservation of cultural heritage.[77]

The National Digital Stewardship Alliance (NDSA) is a consortium of organizations committed to the long-term preservation of digital information. The mission of the NDSA is to establish, maintain, and advance the nation's means of preserving its digital resources. NDSA, a membership organization, was launched in July 2010 as an initiative of the National Digital Information Infrastructure and Preservation Program of the Library of Congress, where it remained for it first four years. In 2016, the Digital Library Federation (DLF) at the Council of Library and Information Resources (CLIR) became NDSA's institutional home. NDSA publishes reports and guidelines that advance digital preservation. The organization has also developed standards, resources, and tools, such as "Digital Preservation in a Box," and it sponsors an annual meeting focused on digital preservation.[78] As referenced earlier, CLIR, founded in 1956 as the Council on Library Resources, is an independent nonprofit that forges strategies to enhance research, teaching, and learning in cultural heritage institutions. Its first president, Verner Clapp, spearheaded many preservation initiatives, and, today, CLIR continues this vision through the regular publication of reports on topics relating to preservation and digital libraries.[79]

The Digital Preservation Coalition and the Digital Curation Centre, both based in the United Kingdom, are collaborative membership organizations devoted to advancing digital preservation. The Digital Preservation Coalition published a useful online resource entitled the *Digital Preservation Handbook*.[80] The Digital Curation Centre has advanced digital preservation by promoting the concept of a digital curation life cycle grounded in the archival principles of selection and appraisal.[81] This introduction to preservation organizations focuses on those in the United States and the United Kingdom. Of course, others throughout the world have contributed significantly to preservation research, standards, and advocacy.[82]

Conclusion

Archival collections are housed in a variety of institutions. Preservation strategies and actions necessarily vary from institution to institution. The steady development of professional associations since the nineteenth century has led to the maturation of the preservation field and to the creation and adoption of shared best practices. Over the past twenty years, international metadata and digitization standards for preserving digital content have brought us closer and closer to true digital preservation, even as digital systems evolve and change. For example, the OAIS Model provides a common framework for describing the architecture and operation of a digital archives. While standards associated with the preservation of digital content are in their infancy compared to those of traditional types of objects, the development of these new guidelines and standards have ushered in a new era of preservation. Adoption of these strategies will enhance our capacity to be responsible stewards of our digital heritage.

NOTES

1 American Alliance of Museums, "Deaccessioning Activity," https://www.aam-us.org/wp-content/uploads/2018/01/deaccessioning-activity.pdf, captured at https://perma.cc/2EA7-EDC2.

2 Internet Archive, https://archive.org.

3 HathiTrust, https://www.hathitrust.org.

4 Carnegie Classification of Institutions of Higher Education, "News and Announcements," Indiana University Center for Postsecondary Research, http://carnegieclassifications.iu.edu, captured at https://perma.cc/28GU-XLRW.

5 Library of Congress, "Publications by Preservation Directorate Staff," https://www.loc.gov/preservation/resources/staffpubs/index.html, captured at https://perma.cc/26AT-NXUY.

6 Museum of Fine Arts Boston "Conservation and Art Materials Encyclopedia Online (CAMEO)," http://cameo.mfa.org/wiki/Main_Page, captured at https://perma.cc/YM7D-2E3S.

7 Stephanie Allen et al., *Collective Wisdom: An Exploration of Library, Archives and Museum Cultures* (Dublin, OH: OCLC Research, 2017), http://www.oclc.org/content/dam/research/publications/2017/collective-wisdom-white-paper.pdf, captured at https://perma.cc/A54X-D7EY.

8 Allen et al., *Collective Wisdom.*

9 For more on LAM collaboration, see Alexandra Yarrow, Barbara Clubb, and Jennifer-Lynn Draper, *Public Libraries, Archives and Museums: Trends in Collaboration and Cooperation*, IFLA Professional Reports, no. 108 (The Hague: International Federation of Library Associations and Institutions, 2008); Diane Zorich, Günter Waibel, and Ricky Erway, *Beyond the Silos of the LAMs: Collaboration among Libraries, Archives and Museums* (OCLC Programs and Research, 2008); Günter Waibel and Ricky Erway, "Think Global, Act Local—Library, Archive and Museum Collaboration," *Museum Management and Curatorship* 24, no. 4 (2009): 323–35, https://doi.org/10.1080/09647770903314704; Deanna Marcum, "Libraries, Archives and Museums, Coming Back Together?," *Information & Culture: A Journal of History* 49, no. 1 (2014): 74–89, https://doi.org/10.1353/lac.2014.0001; Paul F. Marty, "An Introduction to Digital Convergence: Libraries, Archives, and Museums in the Information Age," *Library Quarterly* 80, no. 1 (2010), https://doi.org/10.1086/648549; "Libraries, Archives and Museums, Intersecting Missions and Converging Futures," special issue, *RBM: A Journal of Rare Books, Manuscripts and Cultural Heritage* 8, no. 1 (2007), https://doi.org/10.5860/rbm.8.1.281; and Paul F. Marty, "Digital Convergence and the Information Profession in Cultural Heritage Organizations: Reconciling Internal and External Demands," *Library Trends* 62, no. 3 (2014): 613–27, https://www.ideals.illinois.edu/bitstream/handle/2142/89728/62.3.marty.pdf.

10 Gay Walker, Jane Greenfield, John Fox, and Jeffrey Simonoff, "The Yale Survey: A Large Scale Study of Book Deterioration in the Yale University Library," *College & Research Libraries* 46 (1985): 111–32, https://doi.org/10.5860/crl_46_02_111. Randy Silverman has recently provided a critique of surveys and their flaws. He maintains that Yale's survey was skewed by its choice of the American Studies collection in Sterling Memorial Library, which contains largely nineteenth- and twentieth-century imprints. Also, Yale did not study the impact of the lack of air conditioning in the library at the time of the study. See Randy Silverman, "Surely, We'll Need Backups," *Preservation, Digital Technology & Culture* 45, no. 3 (2016): 102–21, https://doi.org/10.1515/pdtc-2016-0013.

11 Paul Conway, "Perspectives on Archival Resources: The 1985 Census of Archival Institutions," *American Archivist* 50, no. 2 (1987): 174–91, https://doi.org/10.17723/aarc.50.2.l211240g46238078.

12 Paul Conway, "Archival Preservation Practice in a Nationwide Context," *American Archivist* 53, no. 2 (1990): 204–22, https://doi.org/10.17723/aarc.53.2.d0gt78p562832655.

13 National Association of Government Archives and Records Administrators, *Preservation Needs in State Archives* (Albany: NAGARA, 1986.)

14 Nicholson Baker, *Double Fold: Libraries and the Assault on Paper* (New York: Random House, 2001).

15 Library of Congress, "Chronicling America," https://chroniclingamerica.loc.gov.

16 Heritage Preservation and the Institute of Museum and Library Services, *A Public Trust at Risk: The Heritage Health Index Report on the State of America's Collections* (Washington, DC: Heritage Preservation, 2005).

17 Kristen Overbeck Laise, "The Heritage Health Index Findings on Digital Collections," *First Monday* 12, no. 7 (2007), http://dx.doi.org/10.5210/fm.v12i7.1920.

[18] Heritage Preservation, *A Public Trust at Risk,* 2.

[19] Annie Peterson, Holly Robertson, Nick Szydlowski, and Joshua Ranger, *Preservation Statistics Survey: FY2015 Report* (Preservation and Reformatting Section, Association of Library Collections and Technical Services, American Library Association, December 2016), http://www.ala.org/alcts/sites/ala.org.alcts/files/content/resources/preserv/presstats/FY2015/FY2015PreservationStatistics.pdf, captured at https://perma.cc/MNQ4-JGW4.

[20] Annie Peterson et al., "Do You Count? The Revitalization of a National Preservation Statistics Survey," *Library Resources and Technical Services* 60, no. 1 (2016), https://doi.org/10.5860/lrts.60n1.38.

[21] Jenn Riley, *Understanding Metadata* (Baltimore: National Information Standards Organization, 2004). Other excellent sources on the history, development, and categorization of metadata standards and frameworks include Murtha Baca, ed., *Introduction to Metadata,* 3rd ed. (Los Angeles: Getty Publications, 2016), http://www.getty.edu/publications/intrometadata; Priscilla Caplan, *Metadata Fundamentals for All Librarians* (Chicago: American Library Association, 2003); Zorana Ercegovac, ed., "Integrating Multiple Overlapping Metadata Standards, A Special Topic Issue," special issue, *Journal of the American Society for Information Science* 50, no. 13 (1999); and Marcia Lei Zeng and Jian Qin, *Metadata* (New York: Neal-Schuman, 2008).

[22] Ross Harvey and Martha R. Mahard, *The Preservation Management Handbook: A 21st-Century Guide for Libraries, Archives and Museums* (Lanham, MD: Rowman & Littlefield, 2014), 109.

[23] For an introduction to the function and purpose of metadata, see Anne J. Gilliland, "Setting the Stage," in *Introduction to Metadata.*

[24] PREMIS Working Group, *Data Dictionary for Preservation Metadata: Final Report of the PREMIS Working Group* (Dublin, OH: OCLC and RLG, May 2005), http://www.oclc.org/research/projects/pmwg/premis-final.pdf, captured at https://perma.cc/G5K9-EQNT.

[25] PREMIS Editorial Committee, *Data Dictionary for Preservation Metadata,* rev. ed. 3.0 (Dublin, OH: OCLC and RLG, 2015), http://www.loc.gov/standards/premis/v3/premis-3-0-final.pdf, captured at https://perma.cc/T5JU-SXRB.

[26] Priscilla Caplan, *Understanding PREMIS* (Washington, DC: Library of Congress, 2017), http://www.loc.gov/standards/premis/understanding-premis-rev2017.pdf, captured at https://perma.cc/ZE8E-GFQJ.

[27] Caplan, *Understanding PREMIS,* 3.

[28] For more on preservation metadata, see Brian Lavoie and Richard Gartner, *Preservation Metadata,* 2nd ed., DPC Technology Watch Report No. 13-03 (Digital Preservation Coalition, May 2013), https://doi:10.7207/twr13-03. For detailed and updated information about PREMIS, see the LOC PREMIS Maintenance Activity website, www.loc.gov/standards/premis and LOC "PREMIS Resources" (bibliography), https://www.loc.gov/standards/premis/bibliography.html, captured at https://perma.cc/YZ9V-GJV7. For more on implementation of PREMIS, see Paul Conway and Devan Ray Donaldson, "Implementing PREMIS: A Case Study at the Florida Digital Archive," *Library Hi Tech* 28, no. 2 (2010): 273–89, https://doi:10.1108/07378831011047677; Devan Ray Donaldson and Elizabeth Yakel, "Secondary Adoption of Technical Standards: The Case of PREMIS," *Archival Science* 13, no. 1 (2013): 55–83, http://hdl.handle.net/2022/22472; "Digital Preservation Metadata for Practitioners, Implementing PREMIS," ed. Angela Dappert, Rebecca Squire Guenther, Sébastien Peyrard (Switzerland: Springer, 2016), https://doi:10.1007/978-3-319-43763-7; and Deborah Woodyard-Robinson, *Implementing the PREMIS Data Dictionary: A Survey of Approaches* (Washington DC: Library of Congress, June 2007), http://www.loc.gov/standards/premis/implementation-report-woodyard.pdf, captured at https://perma.cc/7FUT-VZ6D.

[29] The National Library of New Zealand, *Metadata Standards Framework—Preservation Metadata,* rev. (Wellington: National Library of New Zealand, June 2003), https://ndhadeliver.natlib.govt.nz/delivery/DeliveryManagerServlet?dps_pid=IE753269, captured at https://perma.cc/NJ2U-2XPP.

[30] Jenn Riley, *Understanding Metadata, What Is Metadata, and What Is It For? A Primer Publication of the National Information Standards Organization,* NISO Primer Series (2017), https://www.niso.org/publications/understanding-metadata-2017, captured at https://perma.cc/8SYL-QU5L.

[31] Library of Congress, "Standards," https://www.loc.gov/librarians/standards.

[32] Patricia Harping, "Metadata Standards Crosswalk," Getty Vocabulary Program, Getty Research Institute, last modified October 24, 2017, http://www.getty.edu/research/publications/electronic_publications/intrometadata/crosswalks.html, captured at https://perma.cc/26QT-TKV9. See also Baca, ed., *Introduction to Metadata.*

[33] DROID, created by the National Archives in the United Kingdom, identifies file formats through a batch process; see http://www.nationalarchives.gov.uk/information-management/manage-information/preserving-digital-records/droid. JHOVE identifies, validates, and characterizes file formats, see https://jhove.openpreservation.org/. The Metadata Extraction Tool extracts preservation-related metadata from digital files and outputs it in XML, see https://sourceforge.net/projects/meta-extractor/files/.

[34] Anne R. Kenney and Oya Y. Rieger, *Moving Theory into Practice: Digital Imaging for Libraries and Archives* (Mountain View, CA: Research Libraries Group, 2000); Humanities Advanced Technology Information Institute, *The NINCH Guide to Good Practice in the Digital Representation and Management of Cultural Heritage Materials* (Washington, DC: National Initiative for a Networked Cultural Heritage, 2002); Maxine K. Sitts, *Handbook for Digital Projects: A Management Tool for Preservation and Access* (Andover, MA: Northeast Document Conservation Center, 2000).

35 Federal Agencies Digital Guidelines Initiative, "FADGI Guidelines," http://www.digitizationguidelines.gov.

36 Council on Library and Information Resources, "CLIR Reports," https://www.clir.org/pubs/reports.

37 Consultative Committee for Space and Data Systems (CCSDS*), Reference Model for an Open Archival Information System (OAIS): Recommended Practice CCSDS 650.0M-2: Recommendation for Space Data System Practices*, Magenta Book, Recommended Practice 2 (Washington, DC: CCSDS Secretariat, June 2012), 1–9, https://public.ccsds.org/pubs/650x0m2.pdf, captured at https://perma.cc/9S3L-Y83M.

38 Edward M. Corrado and Heather Moulaison Sandy, *Digital Preservation for Libraries Archives and Museums*, 2nd ed., (Lanham, MD: Rowman & Littlefield, 2017), 56–62. For an overview of the components of OAIS information packages, see Brian Lavoie and Digital Preservation Coalition, *The Open Archival Information System (OAIS) Reference Model: Introductory Guide*, 2nd ed., DPC Technology Watch Report 14-02 (2014), 14–18.

39 Lavoie, *The Open Archival Information System (OAIS) Reference Model*, 14–18.

40 Task Force on the Archiving of Digital Information, *Report of the Task Force on Archiving Digital Information* (Commission for Preservation and Access and Research Libraries Group, 1996), https://www.clir.org/pubs/reports/pub63/, captured at https://perma.cc/Q7BY-KJFL.

41 Anne Kenney et al., *Trusted Digital Repositories: Attributes and Responsibilities* (Mountain View, CA: Research Libraries Group, May 2002), http://www.oclc.org/content/dam/research/activities/trustedrep/repositories.pdf, captured at https://perma.cc/45U5-3ALK.

42 RLG NARA Task Force on Digital Repository, *Trustworthy Repositories Audit and Certification: Criteria and Checklist* (Chicago: Center for Research Libraries, February 2007), https://www.crl.edu/sites/default/files/attachments/pages/trac_0.pdf, captured at https://perma.cc/9PK6-N6YU.

43 Consultative Committee for Space and Data Systems (CCSDS*), Audit and Certification of Trustworthy Digital Repositories: Recommended Practice, CCSDS 652.0-M-1, Recommendation for Space Data System Practices*, Magenta Book (Washington, DC: CCSDS Secretariat, September 2011), https://public.ccsds.org/pubs/652x0m1.pdf, captured at https://perma.cc/L52U-RXFG. Note that the CCSDS reports are often referred to by the color of their cover reflecting the stage of development of the recommendation. Blue books are recommended standards. Magenta books are current practices. Red and pink books are draft revisions.

44 European Framework for Audit and Certification of Digital Repositories, "Welcome to the Trusted Digital Repository," http://www.trusteddigitalrepository.eu/Welcome.html.

45 National Digital Stewardship Alliance (NDSA), "Levels of Digital Preservation," http://ndsa.org/activities/levels-of-digital-preservation, captured at https://perma.cc/CTB6-ZPDS. See also Megan Phillips, Jefferson Bailey, Andrea Goethals, and Trevor Owens, "The NDSA Levels of Digital Preservation: An Explanation and Uses," *Proceedings of the Archiving (IS&T) Conference* (Washington, DC: NDSA, April 2013), http://ndsa.org/documents/NDSA_Levels_Archiving_2013.pdf, captured at https://perma.cc/QKX8-M62K.

46 Sheila McAlister, "Designing a Preservation Survey: The Digital Library of Georgia," *Provenance, Journal of the Society of Georgia Archivists* 25, no. 1 (2007), http://digitalcommons.kennesaw.edu/provenance/vol25/iss1/3.

47 National Archives and Records Administration (NARA), "National Archives Electronic Records Archives (ERA)," https://www.archives.gov/era.

48 Blue Ribbon Task Force on Sustainable Digital Preservation and Access, *Sustainable Economics for a Digital Planet: Ensuring Access to Long-term Digital Information*, Final Report (La Jolla, CA: OCLC, February 2010). The work of the Blue Ribbon Task Force built on the findings of an earlier report, *Sustaining the Digital Investment: Issues and Challenges of Economically Sustainable Digital Preservation*, which evaluated digital preservation as an economic activity and identified the necessary ongoing resource allocations required to meet long-term goals for digital preservation.

49 Blue Ribbon Task Force on Sustainable Digital Preservation and Access, *Sustainable Economics for a Digital Planet.* See also Corrado and Sandy, *Digital Preservation for Libraries, Archives and Museums*, 124.

50 Blue Ribbon Task Force on Sustainable Digital Preservation and Access, *Sustainable Economics for a Digital Planet,* 81.

51 Society of American Archivists (SAA), https://www2.archivists.org.

52 Society of American Archivists (SAA), "Preservation Section," https://www2.archivists.org/groups/preservation-section.

53 American Library Association (ALA), http://www.ala.org.

54 American Library Association, Association of Colleges & Research Libraries (ACRL), http://www.ala.org/acrl.

55 American Library Association (ALA), Association for Library Collections & Technical Services (ALCTS), http://www.ala.org/alcts.

56 American Library Association (ALA), "Preservation & Reformatting Section (PARS)," http://www.ala.org/alcts/mgrps/pars.

57 American Alliance of Museums (AAM), http://www.aam-us.org.

58 American Alliance of Museums (AAM), "Media & Technology Network," http://www.aam-us.org/resources/professional-networks/media-technology.

59 American Institute for Conservation of Historic and Artistic Works (AIC), http://www.conservation-us.org.

[60] Conservation Online (CoOL), http://cool.conservation-us.org/index.html.

[61] Diane M. Zorich, *Charting the Digital Landscape of the Conservation Profession: A Report to the Profession*, rev. ed., (Washington, DC: American Institute for the Conservation of Historic and Artistic Works, 2016), 22.

[62] International Federation of Library Associations and Institutions (IFLA), https://www.ifla.org. For a full listing of the IFLA Library Collections Division groups, see https://www.ifla.org/library-collections.

[63] Society of American Archivists (SAA), "Directory of Archival Organizations in the United States and Canada," https://www2.archivists.org/assoc-orgs/directory.

[64] National Archives (NARA), "Specifications and Research," https://www.archives.gov/preservation/technical.

[65] National Archives (NARA), "Preservation," https://www.archives.gov/preservation.

[66] National Archives (NARA), "National Archives Announces a New Model for the Preservation and Accessibility of Presidential Records," press release, May 3, 2017, https://www.archives.gov/press/press-releases/2017/nr17-54, captured at https://perma.cc/6DQW-VTTK.

[67] Library of Congress, "Preservation Directorate," http://www.loc.gov/preservation.

[68] Smithsonian Instiution, "Museum Conservation Institute," https://www.si.edu/mci/english/research/index.html.

[69] American National Standards Institute (ANSI), https://www.ansi.org.

[70] National Information Standards Organization (NISO), http://www.niso.org.

[71] International Organization for Standardization (ISO), "Technical Committee 46: Information and Documentation," https://www.iso.org/committee/48750.html.

[72] International Organization for Standardization (ISO), https://www.iso.org/home.html.

[73] The American Society for Testing and Materials International (ASTM), https://www.astm.org.

[74] Association for Information and Image Management (AIIM), http://www.aiim.org.

[75] Regional Alliance for Preservation (RAP), http://www.rap-arcc.org.

[76] This series is available at its website at https://www.nedcc.org/free-resources/preservation-leaflets/overview.

[77] Online Computer Library Center (OCLC), "Research," http://www.oclc.org/research.html.

[78] National Digital Stewardship Alliance (NDSA), http://ndsa.org.

[79] Council on Library and Information Resources (CLIR), https://www.clir.org.

[80] Digital Preservation Coalition, *Digital Preservation Handbook*, 2nd ed., (2015), https://www.dpconline.org/handbook.

[81] Digital Curation Centre, "What Is Digital Curation?," http://www.dcc.ac.uk/digital-curation/what-digital-curation, captured at https://perma.cc/A97K-EAAH.

[82] Conservation Online (CoOL) maintains an international list of educational opportunities in museum, library, and archives conservation and preservation, see http://cool.conservation-us.org/bytopic/education/#international.

Section II

Implementing and Managing a Preservation Program

5

Planning and Developing a Preservation Program

Introduction

Archival preservation management identifies programmatic objectives, establishes strategic priorities, and allocates resources to meet planning goals. The preservation of collections, whether analog or digital, requires sufficient staffing, funding, and a comprehensive long-term plan closely linked to mission, goals, and broader organizational objectives. The success of a preservation program requires resource allocators to understand that organizational support for preservation is fundamental to providing sustainable access to collections and to meeting user expectations over time, or for as long as collections are needed. These goals are accomplished by developing and implementing organizational policies and plans that incorporate long-term administrative, technical, and financial strategies for the preservation of all formats of cultural heritage materials.

According to conservator and author Sherelyn Ogden, preservation planning is "a process by which the general and specific needs for the care of collections are determined, priorities are established, and resources for implementation are identified. Its main purpose is to define a course of action that will allow an institution to set its present and future preservation agendas."[1] Though the specific tasks may vary between analog and digital materials, many of the considerations and actions necessary for a successful analog preservation program are applicable to both realms. Thus, logically, a comprehensive preservation plan requires an integrated curatorial approach to analog and digital content.

This chapter will discuss policy, strategy, and planning for preservation programs across a variety of formats, including digitized, reformatted, and born-digital content. This discussion is not intended to outline step-by-step procedures for preservation planning and management; instead, it considers the creation and implementation of successful preservation program planning at the institutional level.

Planning and Managing a Preservation Program: The Big Picture

Successful preservation management requires sophisticated infrastructures, staff expertise, planning, and institutional support. Historically, archives and library preservation management programs were undertaken at the institutional level and focused on the management of analog materials. Numerous sources exist for the planning and implementation of a traditional local preservation program. For example, "The Preservation Program Blueprint," written by librarians Barbra Buckner Higginbotham and Judith W. Wild, is a foundational source that offers guidance about key programmatic activities, including administration, facilities management, storage, and reference services.[2] As archiving digital content becomes increasingly commonplace in institutions, a sustainable approach to digital preservation must also be a high-level management concern. Ideally, the preservation of all content regardless of format should be considered—in practical and theoretical respects—in a fully integrated preservation program. Moreover, as responsibility for born-digital content is distributed increasingly across organizational departments, considering the specific skills, roles, and actions needed to optimize preservation activities for all formats is important. In the development and implementation of a preservation program, planning for the stewardship of digital and analog content should be considered comprehensively, and preservation planning should address all stages of the life cycle, from acquisition through maintenance and use. Nevertheless, when addressing the longevity of digital content, preservation professionals typically consider digital objects in isolation, rather than as part of a comprehensive preservation program. The Digital Preservation Management Workshop and Tutorial Series supports a balanced conceptual approach to digital preservation imagined much like a three-legged stool.[3] This model suggests that a fully implemented and practicable preservation program must successfully address three areas that represent the stool: organizational issues, technological concerns, and resource needs.[4] Edward M. Corrado and Heather Moulaison Sandy expand on this with their own schematic triad of management, technology, and content. The management component includes the policies and resources that provide the rationale for preserving cultural documentation; technology refers to the structures, systems, and standards that support digital preservation; and the concern with content emphasizes the value of a repository's service to the public.[5]

When considering the preservation of digital objects, archivists Erin O'Meara and Kate Stratton offer five recommendations that could apply equally to the preservation of all materials in archival collections:[6]

1. Identify the components that contribute to the preservability of objects, including metadata for file formats, context of creation, and preservation actions taken.
2. Understand core principles, practices, and standards from the archive and digital preservation community.
3. Research the tools and systems available to facilitate metadata creation, preservation activities, and management of objects.

4. Develop and document local implementation of standards and processes for acquiring, packaging, ingesting, managing, migrating, and monitoring of objects. Project and plan for preservation improvements, adding incrementally to capabilities.
5. Evaluate and audit the health of digital objects and the systems that hold them.

As these recommendations show, programs for the preservation of digital content build on many of the principles used for the preservation and conservation of physical items, with a few differences and caveats. As we established previously, preservation is defined as a series of managed actions and interventions required to ensure continued access to authentic digital or analog objects for as long as they are of value. The goal of digital preservation is the most accurate rendering possible of authenticated digital content over time. In addition to the elements of a preservation program described here, digital preservation includes the following considerations:

- Digital preservation of archival collections is most effective when considered in the context of established preservation programs.
- Creation and management of digital content and associated metadata must be aligned with current standards, including PREMIS, OAIS, and the audits and checklists must be established in support of trusted digital repositories.[7]
- Storage technology and systems must be monitored and risks assessed on a timely and regular basis to ensure strategic approaches to the migration, emulation, upgrades, or maintenance of digital objects.

Conservation and copyright are two additional areas in which practices may differ across formats. The *SAA Glossary* defines *conservation* as "the repair or stabilization of materials through chemical or physical treatment to ensure that they survive in their original form as long as possible."[8] Previously, we have defined *conservation* as "a series of actions on individual objects intended to mitigate damage, deterioration, or loss." Yet, as Trevor Owens acknowledges, these understandings of conservation are not relevant when dealing with digital media because the preservation of digital content focuses on creating new copies and migrating these materials onto new platforms and systems.[9] And, procedures such as media conversion or reformatting, designed to maintain the intellectual content, may also permanently alter the digital object or result in loss.

Digital preservation may involve the creation of preservation copies that are a form of intellectual property. Consideration of copyright is critical when additional or altered copies of a work are generated for preservation. Analog materials are relatively stable with well-established legal frameworks for preservation.[10] The legal structure surrounding the preservation of digital materials is still evolving, and the laws supporting current digital preservation will change over time.[11]

Despite these caveats and differences, we seek a unified and balanced approach to the management of digital and analog content. This goal requires planning, policy development, assessment, and strategic prioritization of institutional preservation goals combined with advocacy for needed resources. Based on our discussion, we can identify a set of high-level requirements for preservation program planning and management (regardless of the format under consideration):

- Alignment with institutional mission and strategic goals
- Compliance with best practices and standards
- Administrative approval and financial sustainability
- Staffing support

- Environmental and system security
- Documentation and procedural accountability
- Risk management and disaster plans
- Regular program assessment

As with any program, preservation management should be tailored to the size and needs of the organization, and the scale of the program may vary depending on institutional capacity and resources. In addition to these high-level requirements, we have identified additional essential components of a holistic preservation program that will be addressed in this and subsequent chapters:[12]

- A mission statement and policies that explain the purpose of preservation activities
- An assessment of preservation conditions that forms the basis for future planning
- A preservation plan that addresses needs and priorities
- Staff training and development
- Monitoring of systems and environmental conditions
- Storage and maintenance control
- Availability of duplicating and reformatting equipment and resources to accomplish these functions
- Fully developed plans for risk management, emergency response, and disaster mitigation and recovery
- Administrative and fiscal support for conservation and collections maintenance
- Mechanisms to review the preservation program over time

Mission and Policy Development

As we have established, preservation is an integral part of a cultural institution's mission, and preservation planning should be part of its overall strategic plan. It is not possible to develop a successful preservation program without a clear mission statement and a comprehensive collection policy. Thus, the first step in any strategic planning process is the development, or in some cases, the evaluation and revision, of an institutional or organizational mission statement. The mission statement outlines the general administrative scope of the archives and its parent organization, and states the purpose of the archival program. It establishes the basis for subsequent program goals and policies.

The archival collection management policy is a core document that further defines the purpose of the organization and outlines a structure for daily operations. It can be an institutional document of which the archives, digital or special collection, is one section, or it can be written specifically to address the unit responsible for these collections. The collection policy provides guidance for all collection responsibilities and actions, including collecting scope and priorities, selection and acquisition procedures, methods of documentation, access and use of collections, duplication and reformatting, deaccession and disposal, preservation, risk management, security, storage, loans, exhibition, and outreach. Administrative sanction to develop a collection management policy implies that an institution is capable of maintaining consistent procedures for the stewardship, oversight, and management of collections through institutional and staff changes. Such a policy reduces the possibility of legal, administrative, and ethical problems, clarifies authority and staff responsibility, and can facilitate communication and collaboration across departments. As an example, Yale University Library, Manuscripts and Archives, offers a useful overview of the purpose of and rationale for its collection development policies. (See Appendix A.)

As preservation expert Margaret Child notes, collection policies are vital in helping personnel make sound preservation decisions. Such considerations must inform a collection policy if it is to be a reliable guide to the development and management of collections. At each stage of managing collections, all staff, and especially those directly involved in collection development and management, should understand the preservation implications of their decisions and actions.[13]

Thus, mission statements, collection policies, and other strategic-planning documents provide the foundation for the development and implementation of a preservation policy. However, an important distinction must be made between a preservation plan and other higher-level policies that are developed to administer and regulate strategies and resource allocations across an organization. A preservation policy is an official expression of the operating principles that direct the long-term preservation of materials in the archivists' care. A preservation policy lays out clearly and succinctly the purpose of the preservation program and the appropriate scope and duration of all preservation activities. It articulates for administrative bodies, governing boards, trustees, staff, donors, and volunteers the aims and objectives of the preservation program and delineates a responsible use of resources, the establishment of priorities, and areas where additional funding is required. It establishes the framework for practice, accountability, and assessment. The preservation policy is often the first step in comprehensive planning and development.[14] According to Mirjam Foot, a typical preservation policy should address[15]

- The aims and objectives of the library or archive
- The functions and activities of the library or archive
- Storage and access needs and requirements
- Lending exhibitions and reprographic services
- Resource needs

As an example, the University of Texas Library's Preservation Policy addresses the preservation programs in a range of departments, including archives and manuscripts.[16] (See Appendix B.)

Furthermore, as we have indicated, preservation polices should also be endorsed by senior management, shared widely, reviewed at regular intervals, and supported by appropriate resource commitments. These policy objectives are also relevant in the management of digital content; however, for most cultural institutions, the development and implementation of policies for digital preservation are in their infancy. Nonetheless, several studies and resources regarding digital preservation are worth mentioning that could be incorporated into a holistic preservation policy at the institutional or consortium level.

In 2008, the Northeast Document Conservation Center (NEDCC) created two useful digital preservation tools supporting policy development: the Digital Stewardship Questionnaire and a Digital Preservation Policy Template.[17] The questionnaire is intended to help an institution assess the current status of its digital collections care and will be discussed in more detail in the next section. The policy template is intended to guide the user through the steps required to write a preservation policy. Also in 2008, the Joint Information Systems Committee (since 2012 known simply as "JISC") funded a study to analyze the role of digital preservation in higher education institutions with the goal of outlining a model for digital preservation policies. The study

Access and Use	Preservation Model/ Strategy
Accessioning and Ingest	Preservation Planning
Audit	Rights and Restriction Management
Bibliography	Roles and Responsibilities
Collaboration	Security Management
Content Scope	Selection/Appraisal
Glossary/Terminology	Staff Training/Education
Mandates	Storage, Duplication, and Backup
Metadata or Documentation	Sustainability Planning
Policy/Strategy Review	

FIGURE 5.1. National Digital Information Infrastructure and Preservation Program, Digital Preservation Policies Taxonomy

concludes that digital preservation policies were a relatively new concept at that time and that only a few organizations were creating and implementing strategic and procedural policies. The report also stresses that a digital preservation policy must be framed in terms of the key business drivers and strategies of the institution.[18]

In 2010, the PLANETS (Preservation and Long-term Access through Networked Services) project published a report entitled *The Digital Divide. Assessing Organisations' Preparations for Digital Preservation.* PLANETS was a four-year project funded by the European Union that surveyed over 200 organizations to examine core digital preservation challenges and to help them create a rationale for establishing digital preservation programs.[19] According to the PLANETS report,

> a digital preservation policy should outline the high-level objectives, the philosophy behind the policy and the benefits that digital preservation will bring. In particular, it should set out the roles and responsibilities of the staff involved, the remit for appraisal and acquisition, and guidance on retention. In addition, it should specify the standards for storing, managing and accessing digital materials. This should include the metadata needed for each object, the practices for refreshing storage media, the procedures for assessing the risks involved with different file formats and how to handle obsolete formats.[20]

The report notes that organizations with a digital preservation policy are more likely to include digital preservation in their operational, business continuity, and financial planning, and were three times more likely to have secured a budget for digital preservation. As a result, more institutions are developing these policies to advance their strategic preservation goals. As an example, the Indiana University Libraries Digital Preservation Policy offers a useful overview of the components of such a policy. (See Appendix C.)

In 2013, the National Digital Information Infrastructure and Preservation Program (NDIIPP) engaged in an analysis of digital preservation policy documents for cultural heritage organizations. The researchers were able to locate and evaluate thirty-three digital preservation polices published between 2008 and 2013.[21] The policies and strategies analyzed primarily represented archives and libraries, with two policies developed by museums. About half of the policies were from US institutions, with the rest primarily from Western Europe.[22] In North America, most digital preservation policies were developed by academic institutions and state governments, while preservation policies in Europe, Australia, and New Zealand typically originated from national-level government bodies. At the time, Australia was the only nation to have published a comprehensive digital preservation strategy for its national archives, library, and museum.[23] The most important contribution of the report is a taxonomy of the topics and issues represented across the policies, as shown in Figure 5.1.[24]

The report found that the rate of inclusion for each of these topics was inconsistent across institutional types, year of origin, and geographic location. Archives tended to have a high inclusion rate for topics such as terminology, security management, storage, duplication and backup, policy or strategy review, and rights and restriction management. Libraries more typically addressed collaboration, bibliographies, sustainability planning, and metadata and other documentation. While additional research is needed in this area, the authors rightly conclude that institutional digital preservation policies are still in early development. "Given that many more than 33 institutions around the world are likely responsible for digital stewardship, it seems safe to say that most are still considering how best to define and document their policies."[25]

The Canadian Heritage Information Network (CHIN) has published *The Digital Preservation Policy Framework: Development Guidelines*, developed by preservation expert and former SAA president Nancy Y. McGovern.[26] The framework's components reflect the basic standard of the digital preservation community, "Trusted Digital Repositories: Attributes and Responsibilities" and include the following requirements:

- **OAIS Compliance:** explicit statement of the intent of the digital preservation program to comply with the Open Archival Information System (OAIS).
- **Administrative Responsibility:** establishes an institutional commitment to digital preservation and to compliance with prevailing standards and practice; makes explicit the intentions of an institution and defines the essential role a digital preservation program plays in fulfilling the mission to protect the organization's digital assets.
- **Organizational Viability:** addresses the legal status as well as human and other resources needed to establish and maintain a digital preservation program; it deals with organizational principles, roles and responsibilities, selection and acquisition, access and use, and challenges and risks.
- **Financial Stability:** documents the tangible basis for sustaining the digital preservation program and confirms and synthesizes the support for the program and the resources available to sustain the digital preservation program.
- **Technical and Procedural Suitability:** summarizes the approaches, strategies and techniques that are employed by the digital preservation program to achieve stated objectives.
- **System Security:** specifies the organization's commitment and approach to ensuring the accuracy, completeness, authenticity, integrity, and long-term protection of the organization's digital assets.
- **Procedural Accountability:** summarizes the preservation approach, strategies and techniques that are employed by the digital preservation program to implement and maintain the framework, and acknowledges the need for and stipulates the means for ensuring the transparency and accountability of the digital preservation program's policies and operations.[27]

Another effort by the Inter-University Consortium for Political and Social Research (ICPSR), *Digital Preservation Policy Framework*, defines high-level factors for digital preservation policies with an emphasis on making the institutional commitment explicit.[28] Like other efforts, its proposed framework also addresses the basic standard of the digital preservation community, "Trusted Digital Repositories: Attributes and Responsibilities."[29] The organization of the framework also incorporates the seven attributes of a trusted digital repository, themes that underscore most policy development recommendations for digital preservation.

As these frameworks have shown, digital preservation is a complex, technical problem that cannot be resolved with simple storage solutions, such as backing up data in institutional repositories or relying on cloud-based storage systems. While techniques for addressing the preservation needs of digital and analog content may differ, planning and policy development are central to the success of any program, as is adherence to appropriate standards, including OAIS and trusted repositories.

Planning: Institutional Surveys and Needs Assessments

As we have established, a preservation policy provides the high-level foundation for planning an institutional preservation program. Typically, this begins with a preservation needs assessment, involving an evaluation of the condition of collections and the physical or technical environment in which they are housed. This assessment is often conducted in the form of a survey. A needs assessment survey allows the staff to reexamine the current preservation program and environment and to generate the baseline data needed to develop a strategic vision for preservation.

As Sherelyn Ogden explains,

> A survey must evaluate the policies, practices, and conditions in an institution that affect the preservation of all the collections. It must address the general state of all the collections, what is needed to improve that state, and the long-term preservation of collections. It must identify specific preservation needs, recommend actions to meet those needs, and prioritize the recommended actions.[30]

NEDCC offers some of the most comprehensive resources for preservation planning and policy development.[31] These include a wealth of information in its free resources library and its Preservation Leaflet Series, including Ogden's "The Needs Assessment Survey," in which she observes that "a needs survey should address the entire building in which collections are housed. The survey should identify threats to collections, considering such factors as environment, storage, security and access, housekeeping, conservation treatment, policies and practices."[32] She recommends that information acquired in the survey should be recorded in a formal report, which then serves as a primary tool for drafting a larger preservation plan. Institutions with qualified staff may conduct their surveys internally, otherwise, most organizations choose to contract with an outside consultant with appropriate skills. Both approaches have advantages and disadvantages that should be considered before a decision is made to hire an outside surveyor or to begin the process in-house.

One additional important planning and assessment tool is the *Collection's Trust: Benchmarks in Collections Care for Museums, Archives and Libraries. 2.1.* This self-assessment tool assists organizations in achieving individual benchmarks drawn from sector performance standards regarding policy, environment, facilities, storage and handling, reformatting, conservation, and emergency response.[33] Another useful resource, the Preservation Self-Assessment Program (PSAP) is a free online tool that helps collections managers prioritize efforts to improve conditions of collections. Through guided evaluation of materials, storage/exhibit environments, and institutional policies, the PSAP produces reports on the factors that impact the health of materials and defines the points from which to begin care. In particular, it supports targeted preservation assessments of paper documents, books, photographs, audiovisual materials, and objects.[34] Similarly, the Philadelphia Area Consortium of Special Collections Libraries (PACSCL) developed a survey instrument to assess formats in archival collections and applicable cross-institutionally in many kinds of institutions. The model deals with planning and prioritization for collections in individual institutions and across consortia to improve access to unprocessed and underprocessed collections.[35]

Another resource developed for NEDCC is "Assessing Preservation Needs: A Self-Survey Guide." This tool, created by archivist Beth Patkus, provides a step-by-step guide to surveying institutional collections. It is also designed to address analog collections in small-to-medium-sized institutions with limited budgets and minimal preservation knowledge.[36] Her work details methods for surveying building environments, collection condition, handling, and the protection of collections from loss. The Patkus survey and other assessment tools and guidelines referenced here focus on preservation practices for analog collections and do not address needs assessment for digital preservation. However, a few assessment guidelines and frameworks addressing digital and analog preservation exist for developing comprehensive preservation planning programs. As early as 2007, digital library expert Sheila McAlister adapted Patkus's NEDCC guidelines to create a survey of the digital projects supported by the Digital Library of Georgia. She says that "many of the elements of preservation planning for digital objects mirror those of more traditional library materials, (e.g. security, disaster planning, environmental controls, etc.). Issues related to ownership, mutability, and the speed of technological change make planning all the more important."[37] She further notes that institutions must balance resources and technological capacity, and develop a policy framework that adequately addresses long-term stewardship of digital objects: "A preservation needs-assessment is a critical piece in benchmarking a repository's readiness for preservation activities and its primary areas of concern."[38] To further these goals, McAlister offers a modified version of the Patkus preservation needs-assessment questionnaire that identifies which aspects of the original survey are still valid in the digital environment and additional or revised questions regarding specific activities. These additions include security and access, creation of digital objects, file formats, and metadata.[39]

A growing number of resources specifically assess digital preservation programs. Frameworks and tools for assessing digital preservation programs range from basic checklists to rigorous audits applied in different ways based on an organization's size and expertise. These approaches include self-assessments, peer review, and assessments by third parties and external auditors. One of the first digital assessment tools was developed in 2004 by NEDCC, in partnership with Heritage Preservation, the American Institute for Conservation, the Museum Computer Network, and the Center for Research Libraries. In 2005, NEDCC conducted an online survey to gather data about the state of digital preservation readiness in cultural organizations. This survey showed that many organizations were digitizing content without policies in place to deal with long-term preservation of those resources. With this information, NEDCC developed several tools designed to help institutions understand their preservation needs and plan for digital preservation. These include

"Planning for Digital Preservation: A Self-Assessment Tool" and *Planning for Digital Preservation: 20 Questions for Providers of Digital Storage Services*. The "Self-Assessment Tool," developed by Liz Bishoff, lists key areas for the assessment of digital content and programs. This tool can be the foundation for further planning and policy development for digital preservation.[40] The areas of focus are

- Mission and goals
- Policies and procedures
- Staffing
- Finances
- Digital content
- Technology
- Access and metadata
- Digital preservation
- Rights management

The *20 Questions for Providers of Digital Storage Services* (see Figure 5.2) developed by Bernard Reilly focuses on issues that institutions should raise when evaluating or selecting digital storage providers, including topics such as security, file types, quality control, and cost management.[41] The questions are based on "Trustworthy Repositories Audit & Certification (TRAC) Criteria and Checklist," version 1.0 and metrics developed by the Center for Research Libraries for trusted digital repositories.

The *Institutional Readiness Survey* developed by Digital Preservation Management Workshops is another example of a self-assessment tool designed to assist smaller organizations to understand and implement a digital preservation program. The survey is based on the concept of the three-legged stool of digital preservation developed by this group. The mutually supporting legs of the stool consist of organizational infrastructure, technological infrastructure, and resource concerns.[42] The survey provides a checklist of questions to evaluate digital assets in terms of mission, policies, collection scope, storage, OAIS compliance, funding, staffing, and other resource needs.[43]

The *Digital Preservation Handbook* also provides a useful approach for assessing the extent and significance of an organization's digital collections. The authors recommend creating a digital asset register to explain to staff the nature and extent of digital collections, identify priorities, and plan for preservation actions.[44] This high-level assessment can assist archivists in planning, especially when a comprehensive and detailed audit is not feasible. The tool focuses on simple straightforward questions such as

- What is the subject of the collection?
- Where does it come from and what is its function?
- Where is it stored and what kinds of media are used?
- Why is it being retained?
- Who is responsible for it; who are the users; who are the subjects of the data?
- How is the data accessed?
- How is the data likely to change and grow in the near future?

For a more detailed assessment, the Digital Preservation Coalition has also developed the Interactive Assessment Decision Tree for the Selection of Digital Materials for Long-term Retention,

1. What is the current museum, library, and/or archives client base of the provider? The provider should be able to supply references.
2. What types of content files does the provider accept and store? The provider should be able to present examples.
3. What protections does the repository have in place to prevent unauthorized access to, and/or use of, archived content?
4. What kinds of uses, if any, will the repository make or allow others to make of archived content? What rights must the content owner grant to the provider for such uses?
5. What services and/or features does the repository provide that increase the functionality or value of the content archived? Some repositories make tools, services, and other features available that can be useful to content owners.
6. What costs connected with the storage, management, migration, and preservation of content and metadata is the content owner expected to bear?
7. What documentation of the repository's systems, procedures, and policies is available for examination?
8. What metadata standards are observed and maintained for content files accepted and stored by the provider?
9. What characteristics or traits of the content that is accepted and stored are designated for preservation?
10. Does the provider modify content in any way to optimize the repository's processes? If "normalization" is part of the ingest process, what traits or functionalities of the content are lost?
11. How and how often does the provider check archived content (Archival Information Packages [AIPs]) against the content originally submitted (Submission Information Packages [SIPs])? Such comparisons are a way to detect corruption or loss of content.
12. What kinds of reports of such checks does the provider generate, and how frequently are those reports issued?
13. Does the provider offer content owners direct access to their archived content? Some repositories make online searching and verification of the presence of archived content available to content owners through a web interface.
14. What provisions has the provider made for the migration of archived content to new software and hardware platforms when the current platform is obsolete? Has the repository completed a successful migration of content in the past?
15. Has the provider's repository undergone an IT audit against ISO standard 27001? Or against other industry standards? Has there been any independent party verification of the repository's services? Providers should be able to furnish certification or audit reports for these controls.
16. What level of systems redundancy does the repository have in place? The provider should be able to indicate the number and location(s) of sites where multiple copies of the archived content are hosted.
17. In the case of primary system failure or catastrophic natural or manmade disaster, how soon can the provider bring the backup system fully online? How will this recovery be funded? The provider should be able to reference a written disaster plan.
18. What additional backup provisions does the repository have against content loss or corruption?
19. What level and form of indemnification is provided to the content owner against loss or corruption of digital content?
20. How is the return of content to owners handled? The provider should be able to indicate in detail how, and in what form, files and metadata will be returned and how their removal from the repository system will be documented.

FIGURE 5.2. From *Planning for Digital Preservation: 20 Questions for Providers of Digital Storage Services*, by Bernard Reilly, President, Center for Research Libraries. © 2007 Northeast Document Conservation Center and Center for Research Libraries. Reproduced with their permission.

which involves a series of detailed questions that must be answered before the planner moves to the next section of the decision tree.[45] This schema focuses on three distinct areas of assessment:

- Selection of content and version
- Rights and responsibilities
- Technical concerns and cost

Several assessment frameworks exist in the digital preservation community, and the number is likely to increase. The examples discussed here introduce this growing area of assessment. However, the increasing number of options can make it difficult for practitioners to compare and select a framework that fits their organizations' needs. According to Emily Maemura, Nathan Moles, and Christoph Becker, digital preservation assessment might be approached through three categories that align with different organizational goals and levels of readiness. First, organizations starting a new digital preservation initiative can benefit from frameworks that facilitate *initial planning*. Second, organizations with existing processes and workflows can benefit from assessments that support *improvement* by identifying specific areas for organizational investment and development. Third, experienced organizations with documented and formalized processes can undertake assessment for external *certification* to recognize compliance with standards, such as OAIS.[46]

Establishing Preservation Priorities and Decision-Making

Prioritizing is the process of deciding which actions will have the most significant impact, which are the most important, and which are the most feasible.[47] The Digital Preservation Coalition's Decision Tree and other such tools are used in the assessment of digital collections, and for establishing priorities and making preservation decisions across all types of formats. Most institutions have ongoing preservation concerns that can be resolved by a range of actions.

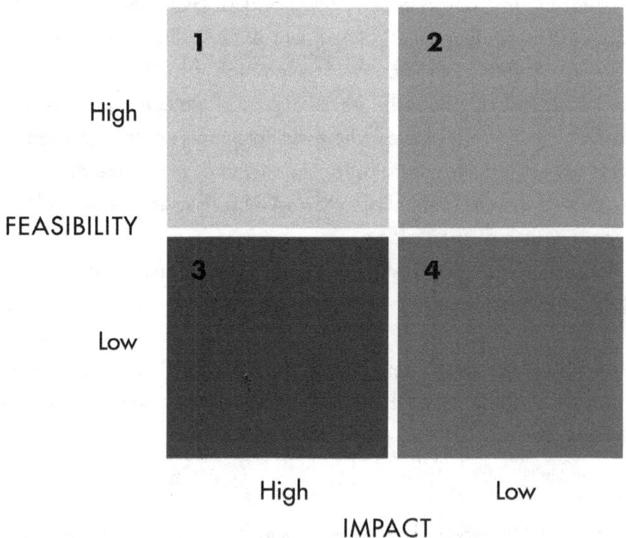

FIGURE 5.3. NEDCC Preservation Leaflet Series: Impact and Feasibility Grid

However, most have limited resources to enable these actions. Thus, preservation activities must be prioritized in the context of short- and long-term planning. And, ultimately, organizations will decide their priorities based on their strategic plans. When developing priorities, an organization must consider the cost of potential actions, required staff time and expertise, and necessary resources and infrastructure. This information is weighed against the benefit of the activity and the risk of not undertaking the action. This analysis of need, risk, impact, and available resources makes it possible for staff to identify reasonable solutions and eliminate or revise unrealistic or overly ambitious activities.

To identify high-level preservation priorities, the archivist might find it useful to consider the criteria of impact and feasibility for each proposed action. Pamela Darling suggests that high-impact actions are "those that will result in dramatic improvement in the present condition of materials, substantial decrease in the rate of deterioration, substantial increase in efficiency of current preservation activities, or considerable savings of time, energy or money."[48] She developed a device for evaluating the impact and feasibility of each action that can be plotted on a grid, modified in Figure 5.3 from the NEDCC Preservation Leaflet Series.[49]

High-impact actions that can be implemented with some or little difficulty (boxes 1 and 3) are typically the highest priority, while those that are difficult to implement and have little impact can be eliminated or postponed until they become more important to implement (boxes 4 and 2). (Impact and feasibility actions, such as improvements to climate control systems, are discussed in further detail in chapter 6). To supplement this type of analysis, NEDCC has developed a useful priority checklist that outlines a range of necessary actions commonly identified by a preservation planning survey. Topical areas include building maintenance, storage, climate and energy efficiency, security, and protection from a range of threats, such as fire and flooding.[50]

The long-term management and preservation of digital materials is an expensive, ongoing, and complex series of activities that require an evaluation of feasibility, risk, impact, and cost. As discussed in this and previous chapters, the Open Archival Information Systems (OAIS) model and corresponding criteria for trustworthy repositories (TRAC) specify requirements that inform this process, but neither model provides concrete guidance on prioritization and decision-making. Christoph Becker, director of the Digital Curation Institute at the University of Toronto, has conducted extensive research on scalable decision support for digital preservation, including the EU-funded project SCAPE: Scalable Preservation Environment Framework, an open-source decision-making tool for the planning and implementation of preservation strategies.[51] Becker's work shows that prioritization and assessment in digital preservation has increased markedly over time, but most research focuses on developing new assessment models rather than on rigorous evaluation and validation of existing frameworks. Significant gaps exist in the application of conceptual foundations and design methods, and in the level of evidence available to enable the evaluation and validation of assessment models. The design of assessment models in digital preservation should be studied in theory and practice, and the development of future models will benefit from applying existing methods, processes, and principles for model design.[52]

Another example is "Keeping Research Data Safe (KRDS)," a series of cost/benefit studies, tools, and methodologies that focus on the challenges of curation and preservation of research data. The KRDS Digital Preservation Benefits Analysis Toolkit is intended to help an organization identify, assess, and communicate the benefits of investing resources in the curation and long-term preservation of research data.[53] Although the resource focuses on research data, it applies to other areas of digital preservation. These tools and frameworks are typically funded by international organizations and designed to further research in high-level planning and evaluation that consider complex technological and business models for digital preservation. At the center of this issue is making the case for the benefits that digital preservation investments could generate.

Budgeting for Preservation and Advocating for Resources

Building and maintaining sustainable preservation programs involves advocacy and careful financial planning. A budget reflects an organization's priorities because it determines how scarce resources are distributed and used. As archival educator Paul Conway explains, "the essence of preservation management is resource allocation. People, money, and materials must be acquired, organized, and put to work to ensure that information sources are given adequate protection."[54] In an era when archives, libraries, and other institutions are building complex digital collections and infrastructure, it is imperative that adequate resources are allocated for preservation. In most institutions, that effort is articulated through planning and budgeting.

Making the case for funding sustainable preservation requires a compelling argument for the value of collections, the impact of preservation, the risks to an organization for failing to act, and defining roles, responsibilities, and the costs of preservation across organizational boundaries.

According to archivist Michael J. Kurtz, "accurate, realistic budget projections provide an aura of legitimacy for an archival program in the competition for resources within a larger organization or from an appropriating body. In addition, the budget is a key element in effective internal management."[55] Kurtz also points out that "financial management is critical to any effort to expand, grow, or even escape from the archival cycle of poverty."[56] Thus, budgeting provides a crucial opportunity to articulate and advocate for resource needs that is especially critical for the success of archival preservation.

Carefully prepared, well-thought-out budgets ensure that an organization performs fundamental functions of management, including planning, coordination, and control, and encourage strategic approaches to preservation. Organizations must justify their budgets to three primary audiences. The first is a legal or higher authority that typically allocates funds, such as a state legislature. The second is an institutional authority, such as a university budget office or a nonprofit organization's board of directors. The third is an organizational manager, such as a state archivist, a university archivist, a library dean, or a head of special collections. Budgets are subject to audit and review at the internal, state, and national levels, including audit by the Internal Revenue Service. Most organizational budgets fall into two categories. The first is the operating budget that provides a formal statement of the requirements to operate a program for a defined period of time. The second, a capital budget, is a statement of requirements for a large-scale and long-term project such as building construction, the purchase of major equipment, or the implementation of a system or infrastructure.[57] Most organizations develop operating budgets based on projected income and expenditures, typically annually or biannually.

Allocations for preservation are usually drawn from an operating budget. There are two primary approaches to the distribution of operating funds. "Consolidated budgeting" assigns income and expenditures to specific lines that are distributed across an entire organization. These dedicated budget lines are predictable organization-wide expenses such as salary and commonly used materials and services. "Program budgeting" allocates costs and expenditures such as salary, benefits, materials, and maintenance to a specific program.[58] Ideally, an organization supports a preservation program through both of these approaches, covering common needs and salaries at the organizational level, supplemented by an annual program budget adequate to meet preservation goals and objectives. In tight years, this approach can also be risky if the purchase authority for necessary line items is redistributed to programs without additional allocations. Unfortunately, in many organizations, preservation activities are neither dedicated line-items nor specific program budget areas. In these instances, advocacy for preservation becomes particularly critical, and seeking outside funding becomes necessary.

Fundraising and Grant Programs

Few organizations are able to meet all of their needs through the internal budget process, and most have had to look elsewhere for money to finance many of their core activities, including preservation. Most large institutions have established foundations, advisory groups, or development teams responsible for acquiring funds in support of operations not fully covered by budget allocations. The success of many archivists depends on competing successfully for internal and external funds to support preservation and access, training, and public programming. Most projects will be funded through the reallocation of internal resources; through external support, such as grants, endowments, or capital campaigns; or simply by an interested donor. Funding requests for preservation may not be fully understood by external parties, who may see this work as an institutional responsibility or an internal management issue, rather than as a high-profile objective in need of support.

Thus, as with all planning, fundraising must align with the organization's mission, goals, and strategic objectives, and be fully understood by management and potential funders. Before seeking funding for preservation, the archivist must plan and justify the goals, activities, and costs. Funding requests can focus on a specific project or activity or long-term, line-item funding for a preservation program, including salary, space, supplies, and equipment. Regardless of scale, planning for fundraising should include the following activities:

- Identify a specific project that aligns with organization goals.
- Investigate available funding sources.
- Obtain guidelines from potential funders.
- Organize an advisory project team to discuss resource needs.
- Develop a high-level plan of work and share this plan with others for their input.
- Determine if the project is suited for internal or external funding.
- Develop a project budget.
- Write a proposal for funding.
- Discuss the proposal with a board or with management and gain approval.

Grant organizations, such as government agencies and private foundations, offer funding in support of archival preservation. These include the National Endowment for the Humanities (NEH), the Institute of Museum and Library Services (IMLS), the Council on Library and Information Resources (CLIR), the National Historical Publications and Records Commission

(NHPRC), and numerous private foundations such as the Andrew W. Mellon Foundation, the Bill and Melinda Gates Foundation, and the Getty Foundation. In addition, some states support preservation grant programs; two examples are the Minnesota Heritage Preservation Grants and the New York State Discretionary Grant Program for the Conservation and Preservation of Library Research Materials.

Before pursuing grant funding, the archivist must articulate project ideas, priorities, and needs and then investigate relevant funding opportunities. Proposals that come across simply as responses to a funding announcement are rarely competitive. On the other hand, conducting extensive research on the landscape of relevant grant programs can inspire creative thinking and set in motion collaborations and partnerships, within and outside an institution.[59]

For the first-time applicant, starting with a local or small private foundation can be a good option, rather than approaching large and more competitive national funding organizations. This can also raise the profile of an institution and its needs in the local community. When applying for funding, the archivist should keep up with changing guidelines and strategic goals of the funder. Regardless of size or mission, most grant agencies evaluate and change their programs to address areas of critical need. Historically, funding support for key preservation activities has addressed

- Improved preservation and access, through cataloging, metadata development, arrangement, and description
- Development and improvement to buildings and other infrastructure
- Planning and assessments for care of collections and facilities
- Improvement to environmental controls and storage
- Conservation treatment
- Reformatting and digitizing collections
- Education and training
- Research and development
- Public programs and outreach

Many sources exist for assistance in finding and developing grants, including workshops offered by the Society of American Archivists and state and regional professional organizations, as well as online tools and classes provided by nonprofit organizations such as NEDCC and LYRASIS.[60] Most of these organizations publicize their grant opportunities and deadlines. The most important and valuable assistance is the information provided by the granting agencies themselves and the advice offered by their staff. Most successful grant proposals have a few things in common. These applicants have matched their project ideas with a grant opportunity designed to support their goals, and they have confirmed that all of the proposed activities are eligible. Most granting agencies offer the opportunity to discuss proposals by phone or email—or even in person—and some will read an initial draft and provide advice on improving the application. Contacting a program officer at a granting agency is the most effective way to increase the competitiveness of any proposal. Most large organizations support a central grants office that can help the fundraiser with finding the best opportunity, as well as assisting with writing, calculating budget costs—and for a federal grant—ensuring that the organization is registered to apply to the granting agency.

In writing the grant, it is important to address all information required by the guidelines. Requirements typically include a reasonable case for the impact or significance of the project, a practicable plan of work, staffing levels, and a realistic budget that addresses all grant activities.

Many agencies have priorities for funding, such as collaboration, innovation, and project outcomes that will offer a benefit to the larger profession. Most grants are reviewed through a peer process or by an advisory board appointed by the funding organization. In the development of the grant application, the archivist should consider the nature of the review process and the criteria used to evaluate the proposal. Most agencies include these criteria in the guidelines or other documentation associated with the grant program. Due to the limited budgets of most granting institutions, most applications don't receive funding. In fact, many agencies have a 20 percent or less funding ratio. If a grant proposal is not successful the first time, it is usually possible to apply several times, perhaps over multiple years. Many agencies will share the reviewer comments and suggestions, which can significantly assist the applicant in strengthening a future submission.

Budgeting, fund development, and grant writing are not key elements in the training of many staff engaged in preservation, and advocating for resources may seem daunting and unrelated to their regular responsibilities. Recognizing this gap, NEDCC has developed resources targeted to the preservation community in support of budget planning, including methods for effective advocacy, sources of funding, budget development, and cost analysis.[61] Many sources of information are also available to assist with fundraising and budget advocacy. For example, the American Library Association has developed many useful tools including its Frontline Fundraising Toolkit.[62] In addition to the previously mentioned workshops offered by preservation and other organizations, several clearinghouse resources exist for finding grants, including the *Foundation Directory Online*, the *National Directory of Corporate Giving*, the *Guide to US Foundations*, and the *Guide to Funding for Library and Information Services.*

Many larger organizations have subscriptions to aggregated databases of sponsored funding opportunities, such as the database SPIN. Operated by InfoED Global, SPIN data can be customized to target specific needs though the SPIN Matching and Research Transmittal Service (SMARTS) that provides access to information about a wide range of small or local grant opportunities that could be overlooked.

Conclusion

Planning for a preservation program involves many moving and interrelated parts. These include defining the purpose of the preservation program, developing policies and procedures, assessing and prioritizing objectives, and finding and advocating for resources. Whether a small or large organization is seeking financial assistance, planning for preservation offers several benefits. Planning defines program goals and objectives as they relate to preservation, and it assists in justifying resource needs to stakeholders. The development of policy and other planning documentation helps managers to maintain direction and control over preservation, and to respond to unexpected challenges. And, most important, planning provides a framework for accountability and long-term sustainability. Planning and administering a preservation program requires careful decision-making. Organizations with limited staff and expertise may need to seek professional assistance from a consultant to formulate priorities and strategies and develop an overall plan for preservation. As with all planning efforts, preservation plans, policies, procedures, and resource needs should be reviewed and revised to ensure that the program is aligned with broader organizational objectives and to stay abreast of the changing technological landscape impacting archival preservation.

NOTES

1 Sherelyn Ogden, *Preservation Planning: Guidelines for Writing a Long-Range Plan*, Professional Practice Series (Washington, DC: American Association of Museums; Andover, MA, Northeast Document Conservation Center, 1997), 2. Also online at Northeast Document Conservation Center, see Preservation Leaflet Series 1.1, "What Is Preservation Planning?," https://www.nedcc.org/free-resources/preservation-leaflets/1.-planning-and-prioritizing/1.1-what-is-preservation-planning, captured at https://perma.cc/65KB-XWAB.

2 Barbra Buckner Higginbotham and Judith W. Wild, "The Preservation Program Blueprint" (Chicago: American Library Association, 2001).

3 "Digital Preservation Management: Implementing Short-Term Strategies for Long-Term Solutions," online tutorial developed for the Digital Preservation Management Workshop, developed by Cornell University Library, 2003–2006, extended and maintained by ICPSR, 2007–2012, and now extended and maintained by MIT Libraries, 2012, https://dpworkshop.org/dpm-eng/conclusion.html, captured at https://perma.cc/WGY3-M42C.

4 *Digital Preservation Management Workshop*, "Implementing Short-term Strategies for Long-term Problems: Where to Begin," https://dpworkshop.org/dpm-eng/index.html, captured at https://perma.cc/BBM9-9M4X. See also Anne R. Kenney and Nancy Y. McGovern, "The Five Organizational Stages of Digital Preservation," in *Digital Libraries: A Vision for the Twenty-first Century*, a *festschrift* to honor Wendy Lougee, 2003, available from the University of Michigan Scholarly Monograph Series website, https://quod.lib.umich.edu/s/spobooks/bbv9812.0001.001/1:3/-digital-libraries-a-vision-for-the-21st-century?rgn=div1;view=fulltext, captured at https://perma.cc/J46J-WSWW.

5 Edward M. Corrado and Heather Moulaison Sandy, *Digital Preservation for Libraries, Archives, and Museums*, 2nd ed. (London, UK: Rowman & Littlefield, 2017), 17–18.

6 Erin O'Meara and Kate Stratton, *Module 12: Preserving Digital Objects*, in *Digital Preservation Essentials*, ed. Christopher J. Prom (Chicago: Society of American Archivists, 2016), 38.

7 See Steve Marks, *Module 8: Becoming a Trusted Digital Repository*, in *Digital Preservation Essentials*, ed. Christopher J. Prom, (Chicago: Society of American Archivists, 2015).

8 Richard Pearce-Moses, *A Glossary of Archival and Records Terminology*, s.v. "conservation" (Chicago: Society of American Archivists, 2005).

9 Trevor Owens, *The Theory and Craft of Digital Preservation* (Johns Hopkins University Press, 2018), 56–57.

10 There are many good sources for investigating legal issues and copyright for analog and digital content. See Tomas A. Lipinski, *The Librarian's Legal Companion for Licensing and Information Resources and Services* (New York: Neal Shuman, 2012); Mary Minow and Tomas A. Lipinski, *The Legal Answers Book* (Chicago: American Library Association, 2003); Peter Hirtle, *Copyright Term and the Public Domain in the United States* (Ithaca, NY: Cornell University Library, 2018), https://copyright.cornell.edu/sites/default/files/2018-01/copyright_term_and_the_public_domain2018.pdf, captured at https://perma.cc/5BCH-CX75; Heather Briston, "Understanding Copyright Law," in *Rights in the Digital Era*, Module 4 in the Trends in Archives Practice series (Chicago: Society of American Archivists, 2015), https://www2.archivists.org/sites/all/files/Module_4_CaseStudy_HeatherBriston.pdf, captured at https://perma.cc/DCF9-HHQE; and Library of Congress, "Section 108 Study Group Report (2008), http://www.section108.gov/docs/Sec108StudyGroupReport.pdf, captured at https://perma.cc/4Y2R-MS42.

11 *Digital Preservation Handbook*, 2nd ed. (Digital Preservation Coalition, 2015), 37–38, https://www.dpconline.org/handbook.

12 Liz Bishoff, "Digital Preservation Plan: Ensuring Long-Term Access and Authenticity of Digital Collections," *Information and Standards Quarterly* 22, no. 2 (2010): 21–22, https://doi.org/10.3789/isqv22n2.2010.03; and Mary Lynn Ritzenthaler, *Preserving Archives & Manuscripts*, 2nd ed. (Chicago: Society of American Archivists, 2010), 10.

13 Margaret Child, "Planning and Prioritizing. 1.5 Collection Policies and Preservation," Preservation Leaflet Series (Andover, MA: NEDCC), https://www.nedcc.org/free-resources/preservation-leaflets/1.-planning-and-prioritizing/1.5-collections-policies-and-preservation, captured at https://perma.cc/2U58-7BDY.

14 Ross Harvey and Martha R. Mahard, *The Preservation Management Handbook: A 21st-Century Guide for Libraries, Archives and Museums* (Lanham, MD: Rowman & Littlefield, 2014), 37–38.

15 Mirjam M. Foot, "Preservation Policy and Planning," in *Preservation Management for Libraries, Archives and Museums*, ed. G. E. Gorman and Sydney J. Shep (London, UK: Facet Publishing, 2006), 21–27.

16 University of Texas at Austin, University Libraries, Preservation Policy, 2019, https://www.lib.utexas.edu/about/policies/preservation-policy, captured at https://perma.cc/J2AH-EGXZ.

17 Northeast Document Conservation Center (NEDCC), "Digital Preservation," https://www.nedcc.org/free-resources/digital-preservation, captured at https://perma.cc/B4VH-RBY5.

18 Neil Beagrie, Najla Semple, Peter Williams, and Richard Wright, *Digital Preservation Policies Study*, Technical Report (Charles Beagrie Limited, October 2008), 52.

19 Pauline Sinclair, *The Digital Divide: Assessing Organisations' Preparations for Digital Preservation* (Planets, March 2010), http://www.planets-project.eu/docs/reports/planets-market-survey-white-paper.pdf, captured at https://perma.cc/4RJC-88GS. See also A. Adam Farquhar and Helen Hockx-Yu, "Planets: Integrated Services for Digital Preservation," *International Journal of Digital Curation* 2, no. 2 (2007), 88–99.

20 Sinclair, *The Digital Divide.*

21 Madeline Sheldon, "Analysis of Current Digital Preservation Policies: Archives, Libraries and Museums," *The Signal* (blog), Library of Congress, August 2013, https://blogs.loc.gov/thesignal/2013/08/analysis-of-current-digital-preservation-policies-archives-libraries-and-museums, captured at https://perma.cc/KNE2-JNS5. For the full report, see Madeline Sheldon, "Analysis of Current Digital Preservation Policies: Archives, Libraries and Museums" (National Digital Information Infrastructure Program, 2013), http://www.digitalpreservation.gov/documents/Analysis%20of%20Current%20Digital%20Preservation%20Policies.pdf?loclr=blogsig, captured at https://perma.cc/QN6S-3T9S.

22 Sheldon, "Analysis of Current Digital Preservation Policies," 11.

23 Sheldon, "Analysis of Current Digital Preservation Policies," Appendix A, provides a list of digital preservation polices. See also SCAPE Public Wiki, "Published Preservation Policies," http://wiki.opf-(labs.org/display/SP/Published+Preservation+Policies, captured at https://perma.cc/GP9W-U45U.

24 Sheldon, "Analysis of Current Digital Preservation Policies."

25 Sheldon, "Analysis of Current Digital Preservation Policies."

26 Government of Canada, *Digital Preservation Policy Framework: Development Guidelines*, version 2.1, October 2012. https://www.canada.ca/en/heritage-information-network/services/digital-preservation/policy-framework-development-guideline.html#a1, captured at https://perma.cc/ZB7D-HUHF.

27 Government of Canada, *Digital Preservation Policy Framework.*

28 Inter-university Consortium for Political and Social Research (ICPSR), "Digital Policy Preservation Framework," version 4 (2018), https://www.icpsr.umich.edu/icpsrweb/content/datamanagement/preservation/policies/dpp-framework.html, captured at https://perma.cc/X3H6-LGQC.

29 Research Libraries Group and OCLC, "Trusted Digital Repositories, Attributes and Responsibilities," http://www.oclc.org/content/dam/research/activities/trustedrep/repositories.pdf, captured at https://perma.cc/U4CR-J375.

30 Sherelyn Ogden, "1.1 What Is Preservation Planning?," NEDCC Preservation Leaflet Series, https://www.nedcc.org/free-resources/preservation-leaflets/1.- planning-and-prioritizing/1.1-what-is-preservation-planning, captured at https://perma.cc/65KB-XWAB.

31 Northeast Document Conservation Center (NEDCC), "NEDCC Preservation Leaflets," https://www.nedcc.org/free-resources/preservation-leaflets/overview, captured at https://perma.cc/B4VH-RBY5.

32 Sherelyn Ogden, "1.3 The Needs Assessment Survey," NEDCC Preservation Leaflet Series, https://www.nedcc.org/free-resources/preservation-leaflets/1.-planning-and-prioritizing/1.3-the-needs-assessment-survey, captured at https://perma.cc/N926-78C5.

33 Alex Dawson and Nick Poole, eds., *Benchmarks in Collection Care for Museums, Archives and Libraries* (Collections Trust, 2018), https://326gtd123dbk1xdkdm489u1q-wpengine.netdna-ssl.com/wp-content/uploads/2016/09/Benchmarks-in-Collections-Care-2.1-1.pdf, captured at https://perma.cc/ARZ7-5G6Q.

34 University of Illinois at Champaign-Urbana, Preservation Self-Assessment Program (2016), https://psap.library.illinois.edu.

35 Philadelphia Area Consortium of Special Collections Libraries (PACSL), Consortial Survey Initiative, "About the Project" (2006), http://archive.pacscl.org/pacsclsurvey/about.html.

36 Beth Patkus, "Assessing Preservation Needs: A Self-Survey Guide" (Andover, MA: Northeast Document Conservation Center, https://www.nedcc.org/assets/media/documents/apnssg.pdf, captured at https://perma.cc/Y998-SBHC.

37 Sheila McAlister, "Designing a Preservation Survey: The Digital Library of Georgia," *Provenance, Journal of the Society of Georgia Archivists* 25, no. 1 (2007): 29–20, http://digitalcommons.kennesaw.edu/provenance/vol25/iss1/3.

38 McAlister, "Designing a Preservation Survey," 29–30.

39 McAlister, "Designing a Preservation Survey," 31–34.

40 Liz Bischoff and Erin Rhodes, Northeast Document Conservation Center, "Planning for Digital Preservation: A Self-Assessment Tool," https://www.nedcc.org/assets/media/documents/DigitalPreservationSelfAssessmentfinal.pdf, captured at https://perma.cc/RP4S-MY4G.

[41] Bernard Reilly, "Planning for Digital Preservation: 20 Questions for Providers of Digital Storage Services," Northeast Document Conservation Center, https://www.nedcc.org/assets/media/documents/QuestionstoAskProvidersofDigitalStoragefinal.pdf, captured at https://perma.cc/5BHE-FLR5.

[42] Digital Preservation Management Workshops, "Implementing Short-term Strategies for Long-term Problems," https://dpworkshop.org/dpm-eng/conclusion.html.

[43] Digital Preservation Management Workshops, "Implementing Short-term Strategies for Long-term Problems.

[44] *Digital Preservation Handbook*, "Getting Started," 2nd ed. (Digital Preservation Coalition, 2015), http://www.dpconline.org/handbook/getting-started.

[45] *Digital Preservation Handbook*, "Decision Tree," http://www.dpconline.org/handbook/organisational-activities/decision-tree, captured at https://perma.cc/8LZT-Q8AX.

[46] Emily Maemura, Nathan Moles, and Christoph Becker, "Organizational Assessment Frameworks for Digital Preservation: A Literature Review and Mapping," *Journal of the Association for Information Science and Technology* 68 (2017), 1619–37, https://doi.org/10.1002/asi.23807.

[47] Sherelyn Ogden, "1.4 Considerations for Prioritizing," NEDCC Preservation Leaflet Series, https://www.nedcc.org/free-resources/preservation-leaflets/1.-planning-and-prioritizing/1.4-considerations-for-prioritizing, captured at https://perma.cc/7KSR-TTNP.

[48] Pamela W. Darling with Duane E. Webster, *Preservation Planning Program: An Assisted Self-Study Manual for Libraries*, expanded 1987 edition (Washington, DC: Association of Research Libraries, Office of Management Studies, 1987), 29.

[49] Ogden, "1.4 Considerations for Prioritizing."

[50] Northeast Document Conservation Center, NEDCC Preservation Leaflet Series, "1.6 Priority Actions for Preservation," https://www.nedcc.org/free-resources/preservation-leaflets/1.-planning-and-prioritizing/1.6-priority-actions-for-preservation, captured at https://perma.cc/8PKU-AA73.

[51] SCAPE, "Scalable Preservation Environments," http://scape-project.eu.

[52] Emily Maemura et al., "Organizational Assessment Frameworks for Digital Preservation"; see also, Christoph Becker, Luis Faria, and Kresimir Duretec, "Scalable Decision Support for Digital Preservation: An Assessment," *OCLC Systems & Services: International Digital Library Perspectives* 31, no. 1 (2015): 11–34, http://dx.doi.org/10.1108/OCLC-06-2014-0026; and Christoph Becker et al., "Systematic Planning for Digital Preservation: Evaluating Potential Strategies and Building Preservation Plans," *International Journal of Digital Libraries* 10 (2009): 133–57, https://doi.org/10.1007/s00799-009-0057-1.

[53] Charles Beagrie Limited, "Keeping Research Data Safe (KRDS)" (2011), https://www.beagrie.com/krds.php and "KRDS/I2S2 Digital Preservation Benefit Analysis Tools Project," https://beagrie.com/krds-i2s2.php.

[54] Paul Conway, "Preservation in the Digital World," Council of Library and Information Resources (March 1996), https://www.clir.org/pubs/reports/conway2/index, captured at https://perma.cc/M35S-CRN6.

[55] Michael J. Kurtz, "Archival Management," in *Managing Archives and Archival Institutions*, ed. James Gregory Bradsher (Chicago: University of Chicago Press, 1988), 248.

[56] Michael J. Kurtz, *Managing Archival & Manuscript Repositories* (Chicago: Society of American Archivists, 2004), 185.

[57] Gregory S. Hunter, *Developing and Maintaining Practical Archives: A How-To Manual* (New York: Neal Schuman, 2003), 343–44.

[58] Hunter, *Developing and Maintaining Practical Archives*, 343–44.

[59] Elizabeth Joffrion et al., "Advice for Grant Seeking in Cultural Heritage Communities," Council on Library and Information Resources (2012), https://www.clir.org/hiddencollections/applicants/advice-for-grant-seekers-in-the-cultural-heritage-communities.

[60] Northeast Document Conservation Center (NEDCC), "Funding Opportunities," https://www.nedcc.org/free-resources/funding-opportunities/overview.

[61] Northeast Document Conservation Center (NEDCC), "Preservation 101 Session 9, Building a Preservation Program: Program Funding," https://www.nedcc.org/preservation101/session-9/9program-funding, captured at https://perma.cc/G75X-WLMT.

[62] American Library Association (ALA), "Frontline Fundraising Toolkit" (April 5, 2011).

6

Administering a Preservation Program

Introduction

The previous chapter stressed the importance of developing a preservation plan that aligns with an archives' mission, vision, and strategy. The mission provides a framework for the archives—and for its preservation planning and policies. This chapter considers how to execute the plan by covering the basics of administering a program. The first consideration is how to start a program. Next, is an examination of an important aspect of archival preservation: the components of a program designed to mitigate risks to all collections—analog and digital. This includes determining

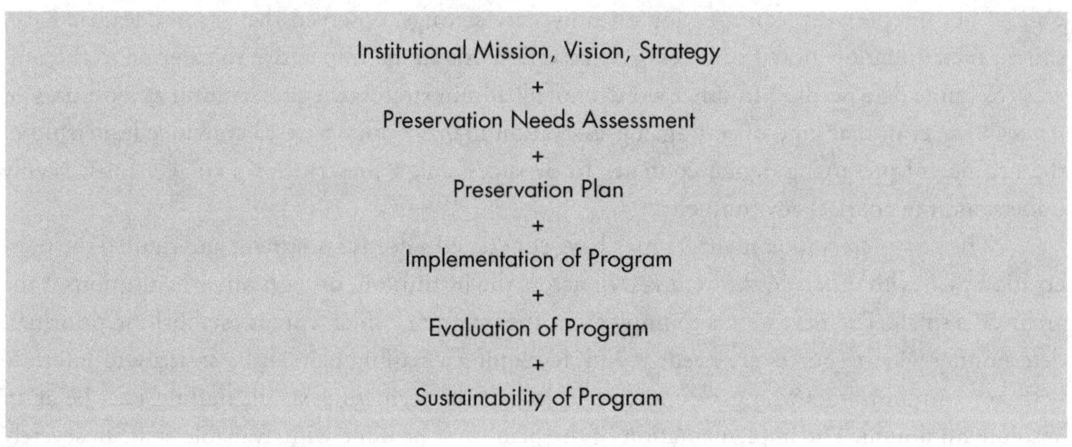

FIGURE 6.1. Creating and maintaining a preservation program

preservation needs; the ongoing monitoring of the environment, security systems, and storage conditions; the careful handling and use of materials; the physical treatment of items; copying and reformatting; and digital archiving. The chapter concludes with a consideration of how to sustain a preservation program.

Prelude: Change and Ambiguity

Digital collections have grown significantly over the past thirty years. As has been outlined in previous chapters, this growth has led to the formation of digital preservation organizations such as the National Digital Stewardship Alliance (NDSA); the development of preservation strategies (refreshing, migration, and emulation); the creation of standards (the OAIS Reference Model and PREMIS); new tools (ArchiveSpace, Archive-It, Preservica); and the emergence of new preservation positions (digital archivists, digital curators). Yet, this expansion of the preservation function sometimes results in the fragmentation of preservation activities and personnel in archives and libraries. Instead of centralizing all preservation activities, responsibilities may now be spread across many units: information technology (IT), special collections, and new digital initiatives units, to provide a few examples. Distributing preservation activities across an institution can lead to competition for resources rather than the coordination of efforts. The premise of this book is that preservation programs must be responsible for collections in all media and work with all relevant stakeholders. This chapter offers approaches to implementing a comprehensive program, whether centralized or decentralized.

Getting to Know Your Community

When undertaking a preservation program, it is critical to fully understand the institution and its needs. Beyond the mission and vision of the archives, what are its current challenges? What is the commitment of senior leadership to preservation? Preservation scholar Oya Y. Rieger interviewed twenty-one experts and thought leaders for her 2018 report on the state of digital preservation. One of her interviewees, commenting on university settings, observed that "[some leaders have] shifted their attention away from seeing preservation as a moral imperative to catering to the university's immediate needs."[1] In other words, not all administrators see preservation as a primary or strategic issue. In that kind of setting, a preservation manager may have to convince leadership of the urgency of preserving digital content. To be successful, a preservation manager must keenly understand the political environment.

The new preservation manager may have conducted a needs assessment and drafted the preservation plan with others in the archives, or across the institution, or with other institutions if the archives is small. The next step is to implement the program, which entails establishing priorities, determining what resources are needed, and developing a staffing plan and a strategy to interface with key administrators who can fund the project. If the archives is small, staffing may be at an absolute minimum. The implementation of the plan must be done with available staff. In severely understaffed institutions, a careful distribution of responsibilities is necessary. Regardless of the size of the staff, an effective program must be established with the resources available. If the existing budget cannot cover new or special projects, finding additional institutional resources may be necessary, but, more likely, funds will need to be raised from external sources. Some states and local communities have grant programs that support preservation assessment, planning, and implementation for small institutions.

Preservation management is collaborative, depending on close and sustained partnerships with people inside and outside the organization. These include other organizational units such as the IT department, the maintenance/facilities unit, and development staff. External partners may include donors and funders, vendors, and consultants. Successfully advocating for preservation resources depends on the ability to keep the "bigger picture" of the institution—and indeed the profession—in mind. A central underlying principle is that the preservation program advances the institution in many ways. Archivists must practice constant advocacy so that stakeholders understand the value of preservation in supporting organizational goals.

If the archives is in a university, preservation staff will work with people across the campus. One complex activity—disaster planning and recovery—illustrates how collaboration can work. As part of the preservation plan, an archives should create a disaster recovery plan, a key component of risk management. To evaluate risks, the archivist may invite the fire marshal to visit the archives, check the fire extinguishers, identify possible fire hazards, and explain to staff the role of the fire department in a fire or other emergency. The fire department and other emergency responders routinely take charge of a site once a disaster has taken place. Only they, or other emergency responders, have the authority to determine when it is safe to return to a damaged building. Thus, preservation staff should develop a relationship with the fire department and other appropriate agencies, and it is wise to have emergency personnel visit the facility regularly. This benefits all parties: the more first responders know about the layout of a facility, the more effective they will be in fighting a fire or dealing with a similar catastrophe. They may also offer sound advice about changes that staff can make to the facility to simplify the fire department's job if they need to access the archive. Another typical component of a disaster recovery plan is the use of on-site freezers to stabilize wet documents damaged by broken pipes or flooding. Freezing documents prevents subsequent mold and decay. Thus, the preservation department should know the staff in food services, or other departments with freezers. They should also develop relationships with police and others involved with safety and security.

One typical example illustrates the point. Perhaps when staffers arrive at work on a Monday morning, they discover a large puddle of water on the floor caused by a leak that occurred over the weekend when the building was unattended. The logical response would be to contact the facilities staff who might determine that the water spill resulted from an ongoing problem with the pipes. Because the preservation unit has established a relationship with physical plant personnel, they will now regularly check for water or other problems in that area.

These are but a few examples of the need to engage personnel outside the archives for assistance. The preservation unit might collaborate with many other people, including vendors, contractors, and donors. In a university setting, preservation staff might work with the development office, contracts and grants, campus police, insurance personnel, custodial services, and specialists such as entomologists.

In a small institution, or in any setting with a single archivist and no support staff, it might be necessary to find external preservation partners. Sometimes, small institutions work collaboratively with one another to create "mutual aid pacts." Archivists might share supplies or other resources, such as staff. Sometimes, programs or departments share specialists like conservators. These collaborations can occur among institutions in relatively close proximity—which can be advantageous if a disaster occurs. Institutions might also partner with one another for projects, such as digitization, or the storage of digital records. Sometimes these partnerships exist within consortia.

Universities or other nonprofit consortia can share cloud-based and other data-management services. Universities are under pressure to regularize and centralize their services to protect vital records and other sensitive materials. Non-profits can benefit tremendously by sharing their IT costs. Some shared activities relate directly to digital preservation, such as software development and support for digital preservation services. For a preservation program to be successful, archivists must be aware of all consortial programs that will impact the long-term preservation of an institution's digital assets.

In an archives, almost every unit or function has an interest in preservation: acquisitions, appraisal, processing, arrangement and description, IT, and those responsible for intellectual property and copyright matters, not to mention those who created the collections in the first place. To have a successful program, a preservation manager must establish several relationships—and quickly. A plan cannot be properly implemented unless key relationships have been developed from the outset of the program.

It is important to form a preservation advisory committee. Including colleagues involved in earlier preservation planning and policy development can be effective. And it is wise to include people with responsibility for institution-wide matters such as technology, intellectual property, fundraising, and risk management. Big-picture perspectives will always benefit preservation programs. The greater the number of people who feel connected to the preservation program, the more successful it will be. This is a form of *outreach* and *advocacy*, which are at the heart of a successful preservation program.

Developing a collaborative network also requires gathering a tremendous amount of information to support the preservation program. This includes an assessment of all the buildings in which collections are stored, on-site and off. It is also necessary to review the contracts for any existing preservation-related services. Understanding previous preservation practices across the institution is equally important to decide which to continue and which to modify.

This documentation should be maintained in a shared database with information about all key personnel, offices, and vendors who have contributed to the program and who might provide support in the event of a disaster. The database should be maintained on a computer—and backed up to the network or the cloud. It should be accessible from a portable tablet or smart phone—and also, in paper form—in case an institution's communication systems become inaccessible. A list of key personnel, also known as a "telephone tree," should have the staff to call or text arranged in order of importance. In some institutions, key staff members keep copies at home because disasters can strike at any time of the day, weekend, or holiday. And this database should be updated regularly (at least annually).

Implementation of the Program

Organizational Structure

Mary Lynn Ritzenthaler, a senior conservator at the National Archives, observes that "preservation is a core function of archives management."[2] As such, it may be situated in any number of units in an archives. In fact, an archives may itself exist in any number of institutions: library special collections department, historical society, government agency, corporation, public relations office, or another service area. Where the preservation program is located and the institution's reporting structure will have an impact on the design and success of the program. In general, the fewer levels between the preservation manager and the director of the institution, the easier it will be for a new program to function successfully. If the preservation program reports up through several levels, obtaining approvals for initiatives will take longer than if it reports to those who make fiscal decisions.

Preservation programs themselves may be in acquisitions, processing, or special collections, or they may reside with the director. The important point is that regardless of where the program is situated, preservation concerns must be considered throughout the institution—and beyond if items are to be lent to other institutions, digitized, and/or conserved by outside specialists. Once again, collaboration is key to the implementation of a successful program and the archivist must partner with all those whose work dovetails with the preservation activities of the archives.

Wherever the program is situated, the most important aspect of developing a preservation program is setting achievable goals and then implementing and regularly reviewing them. Several models exist for doing this work. Chapter 5 discussed the feasibility/impact grid that Pamela Darling created in the 1980s to measure goals and their impacts.[3] When moving from planning to implementation, expanding her grid into levels of difficulty, levels of impact, and cost is useful.

The levels of difficulty to achieve are **easy-to-do, medium-hard-to-do, difficult-to-do**. These can then be paired with the impact of these activities on the preservation program: **low impact, medium impact, high impact**. It makes sense to promote a new preservation program with easy-to-do activities that will have a high impact, like placing UV sleeves on fluorescent bulbs. An easy-to-do, medium-impact project might be to take archival boxes off floors, which offers both aesthetic benefits and constitutes an important disaster mitigation action. A medium-hard-to-do but high-impact action could involve replacing light switches with timers in areas where collections are stored. A difficult-to-do but high impact activity might involve installing or replacing a heating, ventilation, air-conditioning (HVAC) system.

Ease and difficulty frequently correlate directly with expense level. Thus, a third element of the grid should be cost: inexpensive, moderately expensive, expensive, and aspirational. Aspirational goals might include such things as building renovations, installation of HVAC systems, or the creation of a preservation endowment. Maintaining such a list is important because preservation staff might be asked to share project ideas with potential donors or an institution's capital campaign.

Another approach is to create a timeline for key preservation activities. A practical method would be to divide the timeline into three categories: short term (within six months), medium term (one to two years), and long term (over two years).

These approaches should be developed with other colleagues as appropriate to the preservation goal. When implementing a new program, it can be effective to accomplish as many easy-to-do projects as possible within the first year to build momentum for the program, because more challenging and complex projects may take years to accomplish.

The Impact of Institutional Functions

To collaborate effectively, it is imperative to learn about all of the functions, programs, and practices in the organization that will have an impact on preservation activities and to assess preservation programs at other institutions. This will assist in formulating a workable program and also in discerning whether collaborations at other institutions appear feasible. The nature of the collections and clientèle will determine the nature of the preservation needs. Are the collections old? New? Analog? Digital? Lightly used? Heavily used? Are they in good condition—or poor? Are they located in a facility with good preservation conditions or not? Is the archives primarily a research collection? Are typical users local or remote? If primarily distant, does a constant demand exist for the reproduction of items? These questions can help the archivist to understand the life of the record: its history, creation, acquisition, appraisal, condition, exhibition, use, and storage. It may also be useful to factor in the intellectual and monetary value of items in the collection. Each unit should be able to delineate items of greatest value for prioritizing preservation activities during and after a disaster. Each of these functions will have an impact on a collection's longevity and may influence elements of the preservation program.

Preservation problems are identified, and response takes place, at different stages of records' existence. Immediate problems are often identified during the accessioning and appraisal process. For example, a collection might contain unidentifiable formats or damaged paper documents. If the preservation problems are serious enough, an archivist might decide to decline a collection or to mark it for high-priority conservation treatment. During arrangement and description, still other problems might emerge. Digital records might have viruses; paper documents might suffer from insect damage or mold. Once a collection has been processed, it might later be damaged during a flood, fire, or other disaster. All of these issues underscore the fact that a preservation consciousness must permeate every archival function from appraisal through reference. Ideally, preservationists should be involved with collections from the earliest contact with donors.

Today, with the increase in born-digital collections, archivists must anticipate the preservation needs of records even before they are created or accessioned to provide for continuous access to resources. In the life-cycle model of preservation, which was established for analog collections, treatment decisions are made largely in response to the physical deterioration of items. Preservation of born-digital records is only possible when an infrastructure is in place to preserve them from their creation or acquisition until they are no longer needed and can be discarded. And, of course, some records should never be discarded. Because of the permanent value of some digital records, it is necessary to address the obsolescence of software, deterioration of hardware, discontinued computer drives, and deterioration or damage to storage media. This involves identifying the best strategies for preservation. Is it better to migrate some records and emulate others? How will they stored? If cloud-based systems are the chosen storage strategy, who owns the cloud and what is their commitment to preservation? What is the back-up plan if the cloud provider goes out of business? or if critical hardware or software become obsolete? Is there personnel with responsibility for monitoring the accessibility of digital materials and the currency of hardware and software? Is there a plan if responsible personnel leave the institution or are not available? No matter the size or resources of an institution, all digital initiatives need to be thoughtfully managed.

Once again, the preservation manager will need to work with IT and anyone else in the institution who creates, manages, or funds digital projects. While the myth persists that only large institutions can fund digital preservation initiatives, affordable tools and services are available, as well as external funding, for institutions of all sizes.

Strategies for Preservation Management

A basic few strategies exist for preserving documents and other formats: benign neglect, improving environmental conditions, periodic inspections of collection storage areas, the processing of collections, careful handling and use, education programs for staff and users, conservation treatment, and reformatting. A robust preservation program will incorporate several strategies, along with risk management, which will be taken up in more detail in subsequent chapters. In short, risk management evaluates the vulnerability of collections to a variety of risks, including natural and human caused disasters, theft, damage, and loss.

Benign Neglect/Minimal Attention

Benign neglect is the least expensive, simplest method for managing collection resources. It involves letting things alone, allowing them to reside in storage untouched. The curious term has been in use since 1899.[4] The *Merriam-Webster Dictionary* (on the web) and the *American Heritage Dictionary* (5th ed.) define it as an attitude or *policy* of ignoring a situation rather than assuming responsibility for improving it. On its face, creating a policy to ignore something seems oxymoronic. However, in a library, archives, or museum, benign neglect means to give minimal attention to something rather than to ignore it. Considering the rapidly changing nature of information, is this an acceptable preservation management strategy?

The term unfortunately includes the word "neglect," which is, of course, not accurate because *neglect* means paying *no attention* to an item, and this has a pejorative connotation. If "benign neglect" can be understood as "minimal attention," then it can be considered an acceptable preservation management approach. For example, a preservation program usually includes environmental monitoring and upgrading, as well as building maintenance. These actions slow down the deterioration of archival materials. Benign neglect/minimal attention might mean no additional actions would be taken to preserve the paper *or* that the actions taken might be minimal. Perhaps, for example, a small institution cannot afford an HVAC system. One approach might be to minimize temperature fluctuations by shading all the windows, using timers to reduce the length of time that rooms are lighted, using fans during the hottest months, and employing any other strategy to decrease fluctuations in temperature or humidity that damage organic materials. In fact, a bibliographic search for "benign neglect" shows it often used in articles about environmental monitoring. The so-called neglect is acceptable if a program of regular monitoring that will lead to action is in place, even if the action is by necessity minimal.

Benign neglect usually refers to paper-based collections. Interestingly, Ross Harvey and Martha R. Mahard write in their preservation management manual that evidence suggests that the benign neglect of some digital objects might not be disastrous. They cite David Pearson's work at the National Archives of Australia as an example. Pearson has shown that it is possible to recover files from digital storage media from 1970 onward if the media have been kept in high-quality storage. Benign neglect, or minimal attention, may be a more-acceptable principle for digital media than has previously been thought.[5]

Environmental Monitoring

The purpose of environmental monitoring is to manage the conditions under which collections are stored. Over the past couple of decades, our thinking about environmental standards has evolved. At one time, preservationists emphasized establishing strict ranges of temperature and humidity levels, or setpoints. However, such levels are not easy to maintain, and they can also be expensive and environmentally wasteful. Also, setpoints are sometimes too demanding on heating, ventilation, and air-conditioning systems in climates that have cold winters and hot, humid summers.

Of course, archives are housed in many types of buildings and in institutions with a variety of functions, as well as in a variety of climates ranging from arid to tropical. Standards need to be flexible, considering a variety of building sizes and types, in a wide range of geographic locations, and with different volumes of employees and visitors. Buildings are not always sensibly designed for the environment in which they reside, despite Vitruvius's admonition of some 2,000 years ago that buildings "will be properly designed if one has first taken into account which of the world's regions and climes they are being built in."[6] For some buildings, or in humid climates, running HVAC systems continually can waste money and energy. These differences are yet another reason that preservation practices must be situational.

Although Vitruvius identified a fundamental architectural problem—ignoring the external environment in which the building is situated—it is equally important to focus on the needs of stored materials. In fact, the two issues are obviously interdependent. Most preservation practices adhere to commonly accepted ranges for temperature and relative humidity (RH) and their fluctuations. It is generally recommended that temperatures be maintained at no higher than 72 degrees, and that RH be kept between 30% and 50%. Variation in these ranges is reported in the literature and on the web. Part of the reason is that acceptable ranges vary by type of material.

Light is a form of energy that generates heat; its levels must be monitored and adjustments made to windows and sources of indoor lighting. If light levels are too high—or ultraviolet wavelengths too short—materials will fade and their physical structures will become damaged. Light damage can occur because of the intensity of the light and/or the amount of time that materials are exposed to it; damage is cumulative. Fifty lux (5 foot-candles) is a recommended level for light-sensitive materials. Two-hundred lux (20 foot-candles) is recommended for most items. If materials with different light sensitivities are stored together, the archives should maintain the levels appropriate for the most sensitive materials. UV (ultraviolet) radiation must also be monitored. Ideally, UV levels will not exceed 75 microwatts per lumen. Common methods for reducing UV include placing light shields on fluorescent tubes, placing protective film on windows, or installing UV window shades. Temperature, RH, and light levels can all be monitored using proper equipment.

Temperature and humidity are not the only factors in the deterioration of archives. Airborne and/or gaseous pollutants and particulate matter such as dust also contribute to their decline. Extremes of temperature and humidity can lead to mold outbreaks. Open windows or food in the archives can promote insect infestation. Furthermore, an archives may acquire collections that have moldy or insect-infested materials. New acquisitions must be inspected and monitored, or placed in a freezer facility or isolated until they can be appraised and processed.

Staff at the Library of Congress have written that "improving environmental storage conditions, regardless of whether the item can be deacidified, will also significantly slow the rate of degradation and extend the useful life of paper items."[7] In other words, maintaining a stable environment benefits all collections. It will never be possible to conserve everything that requires treatment, and even if it were, the aggregate collections still need to be well stored and cared for.

James M. Reilly and others at the Image Permanence Institute (IPI) in Rochester, New York, have shown that rigid adherence to a narrow range of temperature and humidity levels is not necessary to ensure the longevity of collections. At the same time, archivists must understand the conditions under which the collections in their care are stored and improve them when necessary and possible.

Archivists can understand the conditions only by recording, analyzing, and using the data that they collect to maintain or improve a preservation-quality environment. Among the various tools that IPI has created for these purposes are the Preservation Environment Monitors (PEM and PEM2), also called digital data-loggers. Unlike the old hygrothermographs, which simply recorded temperature and humidity on flat sheets of stiff paper, data from a PEM can be organized variously and downloaded into spreadsheets where they can be presented in any number of ways and stored in digital form.

THE BRITISH LIBRARY HAS DEVELOPED USEFUL DEFINITIONS FOR ADDRESSING THE AMBIENT CONDITIONS IN COLLECTIONS STORAGE:

- **Environment:** the qualities of the atmosphere in which collections are housed.
- **Environmental conditions:** a range of factors such as temperature, humidity, light, and pollution that contribute to the overall environment.
- **Environmental damage:** the damage that can be caused by incorrect humidity or temperature and by light, pollution or a pest infestation that results from a poor environment.
- **Environmental monitoring:** the process of capturing evidence about environmental conditions. Monitoring can be carried out on a continuous basis or as spot readings. A wide range of instruments is available to monitor different environmental factors.
- **Environmental records:** the outputs from monitoring activity that take the form of handwritten lists, charts or databases.
- **Stewardship:** a wide range of practices used to ensure the well-being of a collection including the management of environmental conditions and general collection care but also activities such as documentation and security.[8]

However, some practitioners point out that IPI's PEM data-loggers are expensive and difficult to recalibrate. Many other monitoring products exist on the market at a range of prices.

Educators Monica G. Maceli and Anthony Cocciolo have experimented with the use of single-board computers for monitoring.[9] More in-house approaches are on the horizon. An ideal system records the data, stores the information for as long as needed, and allows archivists to analyze the data by enabling their manipulation into various kinds of charts.

A by-product of regular and careful monitoring involves the opportunity to systematically inspect building(s) for damage, leaks, or infestation. Integrated Pest Management (IPM) focuses on long-term prevention of pests through a combination of techniques such as good housekeeping, appropriate landscaping, and modification of staff and user practices. The idea behind this approach is to avoid using pesticides whenever possible. Many kinds of modifications might be introduced to minimize the risks of insects and rodents. Bushes and plants can be pruned away from buildings; garbage can be moved away from loading docks; leaks and cracks in buildings can be repaired; holes can be plugged to deter rodents from getting inside; food and liquids can be prohibited in the building, or at least in close proximity to archival materials; and trash can be removed daily.

In summary, to minimize the decay of collections, archivists should keep their buildings cool with moderate RH levels. If collections and people are colocated, a balance has to be achieved between temperatures that are comfortable for people and good for collections. In the summer, dew points should be kept as low as possible, and, in the winter, dew points should not drop too low. It is important to set achievable targets and to avoid major fluctuations in temperature and RH. Archivists should regularly monitor collections and find attainable ways to fix problems.

Storage, Handling, and Use

Collections can be damaged through improper storage, handling, and use. Several standard practices should be implemented in most archives to combat these problems, including the following rules and procedures. Archival boxes and books should be shelved on units that are the correct size. Shelves should not be overcrowded. Nothing should be stored on the floor or in the aisles. Oversized volumes, maps, or plans should be stored flat with only a few per shelf. When items are paged, they should not be crowded onto book trucks. In the reading room, book cradles and other devices should be available so patrons can use items with minimal handling. For special collections, only pencils should be allowed. Patrons should be permitted to use only a few items at a time. Opinions vary as to whether users should wear white cotton gloves when handling special collections materials. As mentioned in chapter 4, practices may differ in libraries, archives, and museums. Handling some materials, such as certain types of photographs or metals, with bare hands may leave permanent grease marks.

Archival storage furniture, including storage racks, flat files, cabinets, and shelving, should meet standards appropriate for the preservation of collections. Furniture made from wood or wood composites such as chip board, plywood, particle board, or Masonite may contain peroxide or formaldehyde, which may off-gas. Depending on how it is manufactured, metal furniture can also emit fumes, so it is important for archivists to determine which types of furniture are safe for collections storage. Several relevant standards exist for the storage of archives and library materials. The most important place to start is with accepted storage standards, such as *Information and Documentation—Storage Requirements for Archive and Library Materials*.[10] Of the guidelines for storage, handling, and use, one especially useful source is the Northeast Document Conservation Center's "Storage Methods and Handling Practices."[11]

For digital records, "collections storage" has two meanings: the medium on which information is stored and the managed environment required to ensure that access to digital materials is maintained. Archivists manage digital content to prevent media failure or technological change. According to computer scientist and LOCKSS cofounder David Rosenthal, digital files, and their associated metadata, warrant three particular approaches: "1) the more copies, the safer; 2) the more independent [different storage technologies] the copies, the safer; and 3) the more frequently the copies are audited, the safer."[12] Secure and durable storage is a critical component of digital preservation. The National Archives of Australia summarizes the primary ways in which digital information can be stored:

- Online storage, whether locally on an agency server, or hosted such as cloud storage. Online storage is characterized by quick access to the information.
- Offline storage, from which data can be quickly retrieved through an external storage system and brought online for access. The offline storage is typically a tape library. This is also known as "near-online" or "near-line" storage.
- Transferable media such as magnetic tapes, CDs, DVDs, memory cards, flash drives (USB sticks). These "offline" storage devices are not usually directly accessible.[13]

The preservation manager must determine how and where an institution's digital assets should be stored. There are many approaches to storage, and the solutions will depend on the size and complexity of the organization, as well as its budget. Some institutions may opt to use a storage provider such as Preservica, which has developed cloud-hosted preservation software that meets the OAIS ISO 14721 standard.[14] Other options exist, as well, and the preservation manager is responsible for being well informed about them. One excellent source is *The Signal*, a blog published by the Library of Congress. It has a useful subject index, and regular posts cover preservation issues.[15] Regardless of the storage solutions selected, the process must be actively managed.

Proper storage is critical to the longevity of collections. Increasingly, libraries and archives store large parts of their collections in off-site facilities, some of which might be purpose-built with appropriate shelving, environment, and storage units for a variety of materials. Literature on off-site storage is increasing, though most focuses on libraries.[16] These facilities may also have state-of-the-art HVAC systems, proper air filtration, and appropriate light levels. In some instances, a facility might be a warehouse space that must be retrofitted for the collections. Regardless of type, all buildings need to be monitored regularly. Temperature, humidity, light levels, and air quality must be checked, as well as pipes, windows, sprinkler systems, security systems, and any other aspect of the building that could impact the collections. Therefore, staff time for monitoring all buildings in which collections are stored should be allocated.

Off-site facilities might be owned or leased by one institution, shared by several institutions, or constitute commercial vendors. Whatever the situation, there must be a plan for monitoring the building.

Security is always a preservation issue, and off-site storage could pose a security problem. The off-site facility must have the same level of high security the archives has, with the same kind of connectivity to security personnel (police, private security company). If the institution does not own the off-site facility, it should have a long-term lease. Moving collections subjects them to damage.

Processing Collections

As is covered in chapter 2, Mark A. Greene and Dennis Meissner point out that minimal (MPLP) processing in archives will reduce backlogs and provide access to collections much more quickly than slower traditional processes involving more intensive preservation activities.[17] MPLP has been widely adopted throughout the profession but, as the authors acknowledge, it does not apply to all archival situations. Preservation typically follows local policies and practices. Most repositories can effectively balance preservation *and* access. An effective preservation program must constantly weigh ideal preservation practices against the resources available, but with access to information always in mind. Most archives place their primary emphasis on controlling environmental conditions, because improving the environment will benefit *all* collections. Proper archival preservation requires a budget for and access to resources necessary to protect individual collections with specific needs as the process of arrangement and description moves forward. This might include specialized housing for analog resources or server space for digital collections.

Prior to undertaking any archival processing activities, procedures must be in place to ensure that any new collection that enters the archives is inspected for mold, pests, or any other serious problems that may affect the well-being of the new collection and migrate to nearby materials within the repository. To avoid the contamination of collections, some institutions choose to maintain "holding areas" where new acquisitions can be inspected before being brought into spaces where collections reside. Some archives maintain equipment, such as freezers, that can house collections until they are deemed safe for general storage. Collection-condition surveys can also be carried out with spot checks of boxes and folders.

If the collection is a gift, the preservation manager may be able to convince the donor to contribute to processing and/or preservation funds. Archival materials for housing can be expensive and will need to be included in the preservation supply budget.

Conservation

Preservation deals with collections globally. That is, these activities help archivists to preserve the collections as a whole, or address large areas of them. Using data-loggers to monitor the environment, placing UV filtering sleeves on fluorescent bulbs and similar filtering sheets over window panes, and practicing integrated pest management protects the collections as a whole. Complementing preservation is conservation, the care and treatment of individual items (and sometimes collections). Conservation educator Caroline K. Keck writes that conservation is "experience, experiments and observations."[18] Before preservation was established as a distinct field in the 1970s, conservators were in charge of preservation and conservation, and, in some archives, that relationship remains in force. There is one important distinction, however. While conservators can carry out preservation functions, preservationists usually cannot perform conservation treatments, unless they have had formal training in conservation as well as a graduate degree in library, archives, and/or information studies.

Preservation managers may work with in-house conservators or be responsible for contracted conservation services. In either case, preservationists should be familiar with the basics of conservation practices, materials, and ethical guidelines. A preservationist may not be trained to undertake some aspects of conservation work, but anyone engaged in preservation activities should understand all the possibilities for treatment, how patrons use materials, and the ethical issues inherent in conservation. By the same token, scholars must understand what is possible, practicable, and affordable, and conservators must be enlightened about budgeting and time constraints.

Furthermore, a preservation manager should keep up with conservation research and literature. If a trained conservator is needed for the treatment, the consulting conservator should provide a comprehensive treatment plan for approval by the preservation manager before the work begins. A signed contract is also imperative.

Conservation treatment is recommended for items with artifactual value, those that are important to the history of the institution, or those that will be exhibited. In 1989, preservation expert Barclay Ogden wrote a piece discussing the range of options for preserving deteriorating artifacts, from full treatment to reformatting. He also considered the many reasons why originals are preserved, including authenticity, evidence, and aesthetic characteristics of the original, that remain relevant today.[19]

Most scholars continue to stress the importance of using original materials rather than surrogates in their research. If they truly need access to damaged documents, conservators may need to treat them to extend their useful life. At the same time, the trend is now toward minimal treatments to preserve bibliographic or historic evidence. For example, the cleaning of documents used to be standard practice; now even mechanical cleaning might not be recommended because it might compromise physical evidence. Scholars are interested in the materiality of objects. Furthermore, science that can link DNA evidence to documents is in the early stages of development. Our thinking about conservation continues to evolve.

Digital preservation expert Trevor Owens connects principles of conservation to the digital realm by recognizing the importance of understanding the structure and nature of digital information and media. He points out that digital information is best understood "as existing in and through a nested set of platforms."[20] Thus, the digital is always material, and there are elements of conservation and preservation in the management of digital objects. The conservation aspect relates to levels in digital objects, such as files in the file system, rendered files, subfile information, bitstreams, and compound or complex objects. Understanding the physical nature of digital objects makes it possible to interpret and preserve the objects.

At the same time, the notion of digital conservation has inherent limitations. An artifactual conservation approach can be taken to computing machines, but it is more commonly used for preserving digital art than digital records. Still, thinking about digital conservation may help us to create a unified approach to maintaining all of our collections. And, as Owens illustrates, there are parallels between conservation science and computer science.[21] This suggests that, just as preservation managers must rely on the knowledge of conservators, they must also work closely with computer scientists.

Training

An important component of a preservation program is the training of staff, volunteers, and users in the proper care, handling, and use of all archival materials, whether analog or digital. The Northeast Document Conservation Center has produced ten preservation leaflets about storage and handling, and five concerning photographs.[22] The leaflets are excellent training tools. The Library of Congress and NARA websites also offer a wealth of information on preservation suitable for training. Webinars, often sponsored by professional organizations, are becoming popular training tools for novices as well as for those who seek continuing education.

Training is also important for holdings protection and security. Theft is a major threat to collections, and now stolen goods are easily sold online through huge internet marketplaces such as eBay. Threats to collection security exist inside and outside an institution. Therefore, policies and procedures must be in place to deter all types of theft. Additionally, thieves often target more than one archives. So, if possible, materials should be marked with visible and invisible identification. It is critical for institutions to share information and to work closely with law enforcement agencies. SAA and ALA have both published guidelines about security and theft that are worth consulting.[23] Preservation security expert Shelby Sanett and her colleagues at the National Archives and Records Administration provide an excellent overview of training approaches, physical security options, and procedures to minimize theft in *The Preservation Management Handbook*.[24]

Constant staff turnover, new users of the collections, and changing institutional policies and procedures all point to the need for ongoing training programs in archives.

Conclusion

A preservation program may exist as a freestanding department, or it might have only one full-time (or even part-time) employee. If preservation constitutes a department, it likely contains several units including collections care, conservation, reformatting, and digitization. The preservation department also may have primary responsibility for born-digital assets, or, if not, preservation staff must play an advisory role. This means that preservation staff will need to establish good working relationships with everyone in the institution responsible for digital records. Regardless of whether the preservation unit is small or large, many other people in the archives, such as digital curators and intellectual property specialists, will be responsible for key components of preservation.

Therefore, as stated at the beginning of this chapter, a successful program relies on the work of many people across the organization as well as outside it. A preservation administrator must manage throughout the institution and beyond.

At the core of every successful program are mechanisms for its sustainability. This chapter offered techniques for setting and reviewing goals. Annual and long-term goals should be reassessed each year. What has been accomplished? What still needs to be? Are there new goals that supersede old ones? If the goals have been set with the assistance of an advisory committee, it should play an ongoing role in the review along with other collaborators in the preservation network. No matter what the resources of the institution are, an effective plan coupled with energetic advocacy of it should guarantee the success of a preservation program.

NOTES

1 Oya Y. Rieger, "The State of Digital Preservation in 2018: A Snapshot of Challenges and Gaps," Issue Brief (Ithaka S&R: October 29, 2018), 7, https:doi.org/10.18665/sr.310626.

2 Mary Lynn Ritzenthaler, *Preserving Archives & Manuscripts,* 2nd ed. (Chicago: Society of American Archivists, 2010), 9.

3 NEDCC's Preservation Leaflet "1.4, Considerations for Prioritizing" describes the grid that Pamela Darling designed for implementing preservation priorities. See https://www.nedcc.org/free-resources/preservation-leaflets/1.-planning-and-prioritizing/1.4-considerations-for-prioritizing, captured at https://perma.cc/7KSR-TTNP.

4 *Merriam-Webster*, s.v. "benign neglect," https://www.merriam-webster.com/dictionary/benign%20neglect, captured at https://perma.cc/75TW-XN5Q.

5 Ross Harvey and Martha R. Mahard, *The Preservation Management Handbook: A 21st-Century Guide for Libraries, Archives, and Museums* (Lanham, MD: Rowman & Littlefield, 2014), 17.

6 Marcus Vitruvius Pollio, "De Architectura," in *Preserving Our Heritage: Perspectives from Antiquity to the Digital Age*, ed. Michèle Valerie Cloonan (Chicago: American Library Association, 2015), 6.

7 Library of Congress, "The Deterioration and Preservation of Paper," loc.gov/preservation/care/deterioratebrochure.html, captured at https://perma.cc/RDG8-WN8P.

8 Jane Henderson, *Environment* (London, UK: British Library, 2007; rev. June 2013), library-archive-environment-preservation-guide.pdf.

9 Monica G. Maceli and Anthony Cocciolo, "Monitoring Environmental Conditions with Low-Cost Single-Board Computers," *Preservation, Digital Technology & Culture,* 46, no. 4 (2017): 124–31, https://doi.org/10.1515/pdtc-2017-0008.

10 This is commonly referred to as ISO 11799:2003.

11 Northeast Document Conservation Center (NEDCC), "4.1 Storage Methods and Handling Practices," Preservation Leaflet series, https://www.nedcc.org/free-resources/preservation-leaflets/4.-storage-and-handling/4.1-storage-methods-and-handling-practices, captured at https://perma.cc/8Y54-3XGJ.

12 David Rosenthal, as quoted in Harvey and Mahard, *The Preservation Management Handbook*, 311.

13 National Archives of Australia, "Storing Digital Information," https://www.naa.gov.au/information-management/store-and-preserve-information/storing-information, captured at https://perma.cc/L9LA-NDZQ.

14 Preservica, https://preservica.com/about.

15 *The Signal*, https://blogs.loc.gov.

16 Lizanne Payne, *Library Storage Facilities and the Future of Print Collections in North America* (Dublin, OH: OCLC, 2007), https://www.oclc.org/content/dam/research/publications/library/2007/2007-01.pdf, captured at https://perma.cc/VR8Q-LEVB; and Charlotte Priddle and Laura McCann, "Off-Site Storage and Special Collections: A Study in Use and Impact in ARL Libraries in the United States," *College & Research Libraries* 76, no 5 (2015): 652–70, doi:10.5860/crl.76.5.652.

17 Mark A. Greene and Dennis Meissner, "More Product, Less Process: Revamping Traditional Archival Processing," *American Archivist* 68, no. 2 (2005): 208–63, https://doi.org/10.17723/aarc.68.2.c741823776k65863.

18 Quoted from Michèle Valerie Cloonan, ed., *Preserving Our Heritage: Perspectives from Antiquity to the Digital Age* (Chicago: American Library Association, 2015), 323.

19 See also, Barclay Ogden, *On the Preservation of Books and Documents in Archival Form* (Washington, DC: Commission on Preservation and Access, 1989); Phyllis Franklin, "Scholars, Librarians, and the Future of Primary Records," *College & Research Libraries* 54 (September 1993): 397–406, http://hdl.handle.net/2142/41619; Stephen G. Nichols and Abby Smith, *The Evidence in Hand: Report of the Task Force on the Artifact in Library Collections. Optimizing Collections and Services for Scholarly Use* (Washington, DC: CLIR, 2001); and Robert Bee, "The Importance of Preserving Paper-Based Artifacts in a Digital Age," *The Library Quarterly* 78, no. 2 (2008): 179–94, https://doi.org/10.1086/528888.

20 Trevor Owens, *The Theory and Craft of Digital Preservation*, chapter 2, "Understanding Digital Objects" (Baltimore: Johns Hopkins University Press, 2018), 34.

21 Owens, *The Theory and Craft of Digital Preservation*, 56.

22 See NEDCC's website, https://www.nedcc.org.

23 The American Library Association, Association of College and Research Libraries, Rare Books and Manuscripts Section "ACRL/RBMS Guidelines Regarding Security and Theft in Special Collections" (revised January 2019), http://www.ala.org/acrl/standards/security_theft, captured at https://perma.cc/N7GA-639X. The Society of American Archivists has two relevant publications, *Libraries and Archives: An Overview of Risk and Loss Prevention* (1994) and *Protecting Your Collections: A Manual of Archival Security* (1995).

24 Shelby Sanett et al., "Holdings Protection," in Harvey and Mahard, *The Preservation Management Handbook*, 133–46.

7

Preserving Analog and Digital Media

Introduction

Archivists must care for—and make accessible—collections in a variety of analog and digital formats. This chapter examines causes of deterioration as well as methods that can be used to care for collections. It is not possible to describe every format, though this chapter looks at the ones most commonly found in archives. The focus is on developing systematic approaches for taking care of all collections. For new media, archivists must strike a balance between preserving and reformatting objects, so as to make them accessible.

Why Do Collections Deteriorate?

Records are composed of organic materials, synthetic materials, and/or bits and bytes. This chapter examines some of the causes of deterioration. Over thousands of years, archives have contained a host of media. The challenge for archivists is to make sure that records in their care—regardless of medium—are preserved and made accessible. Some types of records require more active preservation and ongoing management than do other types. For example, the longevity of paper-based records may depend only on appropriate protective housing and storage in a controlled environment, while digital records may need to be regularly backed up, reformatted, or migrated. Much of this chapter will focus on newer records such as time-based digital media.

The preservation of digital objects has materiality. Archivists may need to preserve legacy computers, microcontrollers, LED panels, software libraries, hard drives, floppy discs, proprietary discs, disc images, videos, magnetic tape, tape recorders, and record players. Materiality is also a component of preserving literary scholarship, especially personal digital papers and personal digital archives. Digital theorist Matthew Kirschenbaum observes that such writers as David Foster Wallace and John Updike left as part of their legacies electronic records as well as traditional manuscript materials. Therefore, the computers and the digital environments of these authors' archives must be saved as well as their papers.

Kirschenbaum credits a conversation with British librarian and author Richard Ovenden as contributing to his use of the phrase "the digital materiality of digital culture" to describe the blend of physical and ethereal aspects of contemporary collections.[1]

Storage is another challenging component of digital collections for archivists. An extensive physical infrastructure, including hardware, wiring, platters, and buildings, permeates digital culture. Describing the material aspects of digital files, media preservation experts Crystal Sanchez and Lauren Sorensen maintain that "how a file is constructed and how it tells us how it needs to be opened, played, or understood" are important considerations for conservators,[2] who must understand how files are transferred and how they are handled at each stage of their moves. Additionally, archivists must ponder the physical aspects of storage and determine which they must understand. The preservation of digital media depends on storage, integrity, and security. This all constitutes part of the *digital ecosystem.*

For responsible preservation, all media—analog, digitized, and born digital—must be surveyed, appraised, and described or cataloged. Conservation centers and companies recapture old formats and digitize them, though this can be expensive. Therefore, assessment is an important component of preserving new media. If archivists determine that the media are central to the archives' collections, resources must be found to reformat and/or digitize the media or to preserve them in some other way.

Former New York state archivist Christine Ward points out that, in addition to the variety of physical formats and media that exist in repositories, the "different formats are often scattered throughout the archives, sometimes mixed within series; and the numerous ways in which archival materials are, or could be, used are all factors that make it impossible to find a single strategy to preserve archival records."[3] For example, in one archival collection, a single box could contain a vellum document, a paper pamphlet, two kinds of photographs, and even a floppy disc and a thumb drive, making it often impracticable in large collections to identify preservation problems that might exist in every box. The same is true for digital collections, so it is incumbent upon preservation professionals to create systems for managing digital objects that mitigate the risk of losing content.

This chapter focuses on the most common formats that exist in archives: paper-based records and objects, photographs, moving images, sound recordings, email, websites, tweets, and other new forms of communication.[4] The content may be analog, digitized, or born digital. In considering various media, we focus on challenges, best practices, and research and/or resources. This chapter is an overview and an introduction; many comprehensive works are available for further reference.[5]

How Do Archivists Preserve Collections?

Preserving the many formats in our collections can be difficult because their complexity makes the provision of access difficult, and infrequent use may be misperceived as low research value.

This can lead archivists to simply ignore them, often to the items' detriment. The grids described in chapters 5 and 6 are a useful starting point for prioritizing preservation actions. Archivists can begin with the easy-to-do actions, such as placing items in secure boxes and removing them from the floor, at the same time, making whatever improvements are possible to the environment. As time and resources allow, archivists can conduct a survey and address the specific preservation needs of individual collections.

Another fairly easy-to-do strategy is "pre-transfer appraisal"—collaborating with the creators of the digital materials whenever possible to address technology issues before collections enter the archives. Digital records archivist Matthew Farrell describes this approach in an article he wrote about email management. In his example, Duke University arranged for annual transfers of selected emails from the writer Stephanie Strickland, who uses agreed-upon tags to indicate which emails should be transferred to the archives.[6]

Surveys

As discussed in chapter 5, preservation surveys continue to be an important preservation tool. To address preservation needs across formats, archivists and preservationists must determine the extent and scale of existing preservation concerns. Documentation of formats, their condition, and storage environments is a critical component of a survey. In recent years, some institutions have focused on surveying vulnerable or at-risk collections. The Andrew W. Mellon Foundation funded programs at the Library of Congress, Yale University, and Harvard University to allow these institutions to comprehensively survey photographs in their collections. The Smithsonian Institution Archives partnered with seven institutional units to conduct a thorough survey of audiovisual collections consisting of analog film, audio, and video. As explained on the Smithsonian's website, the project provides an opportunity to develop institution-wide guidelines for preserving these materials by collecting comprehensive data on the condition and storage environments in which they are housed.[7]

Frameworks and Tools

Many authors, beginning with Pamela Darling in the 1970s and, more recently, Ross Harvey and Martha R. Mahard in 2014, have observed that preservation relies primarily on effective administration because collections require "active, managed care."[8] Managed care is the intersection of people, policies, processes, and technology that, taken together, can ensure the longevity of collections. That care varies somewhat for analog and digital media, but the goal is the same: to prolong the life of a collection for as long as it is needed and to mitigate the possibility of loss.

Technology consultant and educator Caryn Anderson created a framework for investigating, discussing, and understanding technology that is also useful for preservation decision-making. The framework is a checklist of things to consider for diagnosing technology problems and developing a strategy for preservation. As Anderson describes it, "Technology tools should advance the primary purpose or mission of the organization and solve a clearly defined problem or meet a justifiable need."[9] The problem here is the long-term preservation of archival collections in a variety of media. Anderson's framework (Figure 7.1) has been slightly modified for this book.

DESCRIPTION		
Area	**Element**	**Questions to Ask**
Components	Hardware	What hardware is necessary or involved in this technology? (or specifications for hardware)
	Operating system	What type of OS is needed or involved? What adjustments to the OS might be needed?
	Application software	What type of program(s) is(are) necessary or involved in this technology?
Agents	Data	What data are involved in this technology? Specific formats? Types of content?
	Standards	What standards are involved? International? Organizational?
	Action	What types of actions are performed by this technology? (exchange, storage, transformation, creation, reading, updating, deleting) What kind of interaction occurs with data in other systems?
Filters	Access	What controls are there over access to the data? (authentication issues, permissions/protection, selection, data views, backups/history)
	Organization	How is the organization of the information affected by the data or the system? Is a certain type of organization of the data or system important to the functioning of the technology?
	Presentation	How does the presentation of data affect their usability? What options are available for how things look?
People	Creators	Who built the technology? Is it proprietary? Is it open source? Is it maintained by a third party? Who will maintain it and provide help?
	Users	Who will use the technology? What is their function or role? What are their proficiencies and preferences for interacting with information? Are there resources to enhance the discovery of and access to collections?
	Beneficiaries	Who benefits from the technology? Do they need the output/benefit in a certain form? (e.g., reports for senior leadership) Are there the resources to maintain the collections for as long as they are needed?
Costs	Cash	What are the direct cash outlays for the technology? Future costs? Costs to implement? Updates? Technical assistance? Training?
	Labor	What labor costs are associated with the technology?
	Auxiliary	What hidden costs are there? (e.g., climate controlled rooms? cloud storage? plug-ins? reformatting?)
Implementation	Steps	What are the key stages of implementation? (e.g., testing, promotion)
	Challenges	What problems might be expected during implementation? What ways are available to avoid or overcome these problems?
	Maintenance	What problems might arise or be overlooked in regard to maintenance? Other systems in place already? Old data stores to be integrated?
Evaluation	Measures	What measures will be used to evaluate the success of the technology—and its preservation? (quantifiable, achievable)
	Plan	What would be an effective plan for evaluating these measures? What obstacles might there be to executing the plan? Are resources needed?
	Results	What constitutes "good" results and how should the evaluation results be used?

FIGURE 7.1. Technology 7 Framework

An additional tool that can help preservationists cope with digital information is the Digital POWRR Tool Grid, developed by the Preserving Digital Objects With Restricted Resources (Digital POWRR) Project. Funded by the National Endowment for the Humanities and the Institute of Museum and Library Services, the project was established in 2012 with the goal of making digital preservation accessible to a wide range of institutions. The tool complies with the OAIS Reference Model and has been tested with related systems such as Archivematica, Curator's Workbench, DuraCloud, Internet Archive, MetaArchive, and Preservica. The tool makes it possible to assess the steps needed for digital preservation and storage, and it indicates which products accomplish particular objectives. POWRR no longer maintains the grid. Instead, it has developed a wiki, called the Community Owned Digital Preservation Tool Registry (COPTR), which is updated daily.[10] There are also tools for determining the costs of preservation. For example, the Royal Danish Library and the Danish National Archives developed a cost-modeling tool for migration based on the OAIS Reference Model.[11] According to the authors, their model addresses "the cost of manpower-intensive migration projects, while it reinstates an often underestimated cost, which is the cost of developing migration software."[12] While the model focuses on migration, components of it could be worked into other preservation program initiatives.

As the foregoing discussion indicates, so many planning tools are freely available now that it is no longer necessary to start from scratch to organize preservation initiatives. Part of the implementation of a preservation program is to compare tools and adapt them as needed.

Frameworks for Digital Collections

Certain preservation practices apply to all categories of objects. As conservator and educator Paul N. Banks once observed, "providing a suitable environment is the most fundamental means of preserving library and archive collections."[13] However, the preservation of digital collections is complex and requires additional frameworks that address these specialized concerns. Four issues of particular relevance are:

1. Archivists manage assets over their life cycles—which are necessarily different for analog and digital media. Records must be managed within the broad framework of archival functions: creation, selection and appraisal, description, use and reuse, authenticity, trustworthiness, and permanence. Other relevant archival functions include policy development, cyberinfrastructure, repository management, and intellectual property. All of these have an impact on preservation practices.
2. Most media types discussed here require technology to view them, so their preservation will eventually necessitate reformatting and maintenance, updating, or replacing hardware or software.
3. Maintaining the authenticity of records is a key component of preservation. The definition put forth by the international preservation project InterPARES[14] for digital records is useful: "the quality of being authentic, or *entitled to acceptance*. As being authoritative *or duly authorized*, as being what it professes in origin or authorship, as being genuine."[15]
4. The rights to reproduce records can be complex for new media and must be well documented.

Preservation Strategies across Formats

Description of the most common formats in archives follows. Books and articles have been written about each one; the endnotes and bibliography point to additional resources. The intention here is to provide succinct overviews. Archivists should develop strategies for addressing preservation concerns for all formats in their collections.

Paper

Background and Challenges

Most records in archival collections were created on paper. These include manuscripts, books and pamphlets, letters, architectural reproductions, maps and charts, prints and drawings, scrapbooks, photographs, and albums. Paper is one of the most remarkable materials ever invented; when manufactured well and stored under stable conditions, it can last for well over a thousand years. It was invented in China around the 2nd century BC, which is also the date of the earliest extant specimen, though many sources still incorrectly give the date as AD 105.[16] Papermaking spread from Asia to the West via the trading routes along the Silk Road. By the twelfth century, papermaking was practiced in Europe, though the techniques and materials had changed from those used in Asia.

Paper is made from matted fibers, usually from plants. The fibers are beaten and combined with water. In Asia, small shrubs are used. In the West, cotton, flax, and hemp have been used for papermaking. In the nineteenth century, wood pulp and pulp made from other fibrous materials were introduced. This "innovation" enabled the mass production of paper and led to the widespread decline in paper quality. Replacing rags with trees solved the shortage of paper, but quality became an issue. Unfortunately, wood pulp contains lignin, a brown organic polymer in the cell walls of trees, which degrades paper. While lignin can be removed through chemical processes, it is not removed from mechanical wood pulp, used for the manufacture of newsprint and other papers. Chemical wood pulp introduced acid into papers because it is made by using acids to break down fibers. By the end of the nineteenth century, many wood-pulp papers were noticeably acidic.

The combination of lignin in the pulp and acidic alum-rosin sizing also led to the degradation of paper. Papers thus manufactured deteriorated in a matter of decades instead of lasting for many centuries, as earlier papers did. Widespread processes for manufacturing permanent, durable wood-pulp papers were not developed until the mid-twentieth century.

Once the pulp, consisting of macerated fibers floating in water, was created, the papermaker dipped the mold into the vat and formed sheets of paper. In Western papermaking, the newly formed sheets were pressed onto felts alternated one with the other; the sheets and felts were pressed to remove as much water as the pressure allowed, then the sheets were removed from the felts, pressed again, and dried in the air. Once dry, the sheets were sized using a variety of methods. Without sizing, ink feathers into paper. Blotter and newsprint are examples of unsized paper; newspapers are printed with quick-drying inks, so the ink dries before it has a chance to feather. One determinant of strength in paper is fiber length; long and strong fibers result in papers that are inherently more durable than those with short fibers. Japanese plants (kozo, gampi, and mitsumata) have long fibers, and these papers are often used in conservation treatments of Western papers.

Paper can deteriorate for several reasons: poor manufacturing techniques, acidic materials in the paper (often referred to as "inherent vice" because the deteriorating features are in the paper itself), storage in poor environments, inadequate housing, or careless handling. The ANSI/NISO Standard Z39.48 for the *Permanence of Paper for Publications and Documents in Libraries and Archives* was created in 1984; its most recent revision was in 2009. The standard establishes criteria for coated and uncoated paper "that will last several hundred years without significant deterioration under normal use and storage conditions in libraries and archives."[17] The scope of the standard is for papers used in scholarly publications, reference works, government documents, original documents, records and forms, original art and art reproductions, and titles that are "not appropriate for transfer to other formats."[18]

The ANSI/NISO standard complements other standards on paper manufacture, including the ASTM D 4988-89 *Standard Test Method for Determination of Calcium Carbonate Content of Paper*, and TAPPI T592 on-88, *Surface pH Measurement of Paper.* The ANSI Z39.48 contains specifications for pH (minimum of 7.5), tear resistance, alkaline reserve, and paper stock (no more than 1% lignin by weight of fiber content of the paper), as well as other technical standards. It is often easy to tell whether publishers use papers that meet these standards: the verso of a book's title page will contain an infinity sign (∞) followed by this statement: "The paper used in this publication meets the minimum requirements of American National Standard for Information Sciences—Permanence of Paper for Printed Library Materials, ANSI/NISO Z39.48-1992." However, no such equivalent pertains to unpublished materials. Archivists can use a pH pen or pH strips to do a surface test of the paper to determine its level of acidity. While surface readings are not precise, they are accurate enough to determine whether a piece of paper is acidic.

Pressure on publishers to use papers that contain 50% to 100% recycled fiber content is increasing. The Green Press Initiative[19] recommends that the recycled fiber be either unbleached or bleached using chlorine-free processes. Unfortunately, the ANSI/NISO standard does not cover recycled papers. Unless published materials mention the Z39.48 and show the infinity symbol, archivists cannot be sure of the longevity of paper they are responsible for maintaining.

Best Practices

Archivists can increase the longevity of paper in three ways: monitoring the use of the records, placing records in permanent/durable enclosures, and storing records on proper shelving in a building with good environmental controls. Many preservation scientists no longer advocate that items be stored under rigidly controlled temperature and humidity levels. In fact, research has shown that while the monitoring of collections is essential, acceptable ranges are wider than those promulgated as recently as twenty years ago. Other factors also need to be weighed, such as regional climate conditions.[20] Chapter 9 addresses conditions that will assure the long-term preservation of records and remain sustainable from an environmental perspective.

Analog Photographs

Archives include three categories of images: analog (or traditional photographs), digitally printed images, and digital file formats. Each deserves special consideration.

Background and Challenges

The history of photography has roots in antiquity, but the development of the camera obscura during the Renaissance led to new techniques for capturing and reproducing images. The commercial production of photographs dates from 1839. Two methods were developed almost simultaneously, one by Louis Daguerre (daguerreotypes) and the other by William Henry Fox Talbot (calotype, talbotype). Daguerre's images were exposed in the camera, and therefore no negatives were produced; each image was one-of-a-kind. Fox Talbot's process included the creation of negatives, which made it possible to make copies of the images. Photographs have also been printed on a variety of support materials, including uncoated and coated papers, glass, metals, plastics, and textiles—and even on wood. Images are captured or recorded with a camera, which is an optical instrument. The images may be still photographs or sequences, such as videos or movies. Proper identification is critical to understanding their care and preservation.

From 1840 until the end of the twentieth century, photographers and manufacturers experimented with many materials, processes, and formats. As a result, archival collections may contain any number of types of photographs, including ambrotypes and tintypes; those on cellulose nitrate film; Cibachrome, Polaroid, and chromogenic color slides; and chromogenic (or C) prints, to name but a few. Some of these were used for many decades, while others for just a few years. The age of the collection in which a photograph resides may also offer clues, but such an identification might not be accurate because some processes continued in common use past the generally accepted dates. Sometimes, only an expert can identify the photographic process and its probable date. Several excellent resources for the identification of photographs are available, including Monique Fischer's, "A Short Guide to Film Base Photographic Materials,"[21] the American Institute for Conservation of Historic and Artistic Works (AIC) wiki, "Photographic Processes,"[22] and the Image Permanence Institute's *Graphics Atlas*.[23] The Image Permanence Institute offers "Photographic Process Identification Webinars" for those who wish to become more familiar with processes and techniques.[24]

Best Practices

Determining the types of photographs in a collection is important because most variants require different handling, storage, and salvage treatments. Care must be taken when handling photographs as their surfaces can scratch easily. The support materials may also be fragile. For example, glass may crack, break, or chip. Photographs should not be marked, nor should they be clipped or rubber-banded. Many institutions require staff and patrons to wear gloves when handling photographs. Practices differ depending on the nature and use of the collections.

Storing photographs in appropriate protective enclosures is critical for the safety of the images. As mentioned, the use of gloves is not always necessary, but, when appropriate, nitrile gloves are preferred with most prints.[25] Photos should be housed in mats, folders, sleeves, or envelopes. Either buffered or unbuffered paper can be used for most photographs. Horizontal storage is preferred for oversized prints and photographs.

Traditional standards suggest maintaining temperatures at 70 degrees or below. Relative humidity should be maintained at between 30% and 50%, and fluctuations should be minimized. Photographs kept in cold storage should be placed in a closed container and be allowed to acclimatize to room conditions before they are used.[26] Black-and-white photographs benefit from cool

(54 degrees F), or cold (40 degrees F) storage, while color photographs may benefit from frozen (less than 32 degrees F) storage conditions.[27]

Photographs are sensitive to heat and light, so they must not be stored where there is exposure to direct or intense light, or near radiators or other types of heating systems. Ongoing exposure to light can cause photographs to yellow, fade, or become brittle. Direct sunlight is particularly damaging, though indoor lighting needs to be controlled as well. Fluorescent tubes should be sleeved and external windows coated to minimize the photographs' exposure to ultraviolet light. If photographs are exhibited, light levels should be kept as low as possible, and exhibits should be of short duration. If a photograph is particularly rare or fragile, it might be preferable to display a facsimile. Air pollution and dust also contribute to the deterioration of photographs. Dust and other particulate matter can abrade their surfaces, possibly causing permanent damage.

Digitally Printed Photographs

Background and Challenges

Many printing technologies are used to generate output from computers. Research scientist Daniel Burge focuses on three: inkjet; digital electrophotography, including laser prints and processes in which LEDs are the light source; and dye sublimation.[28] Some digitally printed photographs deteriorate rapidly because they are sensitive to light and/or abrasion. Some inkjet dyes bleed when exposed to high humidity. Other visible deterioration includes fading, yellowing, and embrittlement. IPI has determined that cold storage significantly reduces deterioration caused by aging and pollution, particularly for inkjet prints.[29]

Best Practices

As with traditional photographs, digitally printed images are best stored in cold or frozen conditions. Of course, such cold conditions, while adding to the longevity of the prints, create another complication. To be used, the photographs must be brought into an environment congenial to human beings. This means that items must be slowly acclimatized so that there is no condensation on them by the time they are warm enough to be given to the user.

Digital Photographs

Background and Challenges

The Society of American Archivists' *Glossary* defines a digital photograph as "an image produced using a digital camera and stored as an electronic file; or, an image originally produced using a digital camera and rendered for viewing as a virtual image or on film or paper; also called [a] digital print."[30] In 2007, digital cameras were added to cell phones. Archives may now expect to acquire phones or computers that contain individual images and/or image files.

A digital photograph can be represented by more than one data object. One created with a digital camera can be stored in TIFF (Tagged Image File Format), JPEG (Joint Photographic Experts Group), or other formats. These are manifestations or representations of the object.

Best Practices

Several image format tools make it possible to convert, verify, or check image files. Digital preservation experts Edward M. Corrado and Heather Moulaison Sandy describe three: ImageMagick, ImageVerifier, and DPF Manager.[31] However, products are constantly evolving, and archivists responsible for digital preservation must stay abreast of the changes. Some useful sources include publications of the Photographic Materials Group (PMG) published by the American Institute for Conservation of Historic and Artistic Works,[32] as well as numerous resources developed by the Image Permanence Institute at the Rochester Institute of Technology[33] and the Northeast Document Conservation Center.

One of the preservation dilemmas in this postfilm era is the failure to save images when acquiring new devices. Alternately, content may be saved to a cloud service that may not preserve the images for the long term. In some instances, donors may "save" them only to social media sites, such as Facebook, which then controls the content.[34] It is important for archivists to educate potential donors about appropriate preservation practices, such as backing up files and addressing rights management issues.

Film and Moving Images

Background and Challenges

The term "moving images" refers to motion picture film, magnetic videotape, and digital moving images. Although each of these technologies is distinct, the term "film preservation" is often used to refer to the care of all of them. Film has many precursors; in other words, there were many ways to create moving images. These include shadowography (hand shadows), shadow puppetry, magic lanterns, and persistence-of-motion (also known as persistence-of-visual-memory) devices such as the zoetrope and the thaumatrope. But the products of most of these media—the actual moving images—were not preservable because these methods of showing movement were not recordable on any analog device or medium.

Film has been manufactured since the early 1890s and exists in many formats including nitrate (1891–1951); diacetate (early safety film; 1909–late 1940s); other acetate safety stocks (1930s–1948); triacetate film (1948–present); polyester film (ca. 1960–present).[35] Nitrate, the first type of film produced, was in common use in the United States until 1951 (later in other countries).

Nitrate film, held by many archives, is unstable. Cellulose nitrate decomposition causes the film base to shrink and yellow. The base can become brittle and sticky, often leading to complete disintegration. Furthermore, elevated temperature and humidity levels will cause the film to deteriorate quickly. As the film breaks down, it gives off nitric acid and can self-ignite at temperatures around 100 degrees F.[36] Even more alarming, if the film is maintained in a tightly closed container and the gases cannot escape, spontaneous combustion can occur. These flames cannot be extinguished once ignited, which creates a serious fire hazard. Nitrate film therefore must be stored in a cool or cold environment, in ventilated storage containers.[37] The National Fire Protection Association (NFPA) has a standard for the storage and handling of nitrate film.[38]

Cellulose triacetate (CTA), introduced in 1948, was considered safer than nitrate film because it is less flammable. However, acetate-based film is prone to "vinegar syndrome," when acetic acid is emitted from the base of the film as it begins to deteriorate. Partially degraded CTA is common. Acetic acid is a component of vinegar, thus the smell produced by this deteriorating film is somewhat vinegar-like. Acetate film can also shrink, cup, and become brittle. A-D strips—dye-coated paper strips that measure the level of acetate decay—can be used to determine acetic acid levels. Molecular sieves, also known as zeolites, can be placed in film cans or boxes to adsorb moisture and acetic acid. Deteriorating films should be stored away from other films.

Polyester film stock is the most recent of the film types listed here, originating in the 1950s. It is durable and so it became the standard for reformatting acetate and nitrate films. One type of reformatting is known as film-to-film transfer. Polyester film does not deteriorate in the manner of nitrate and acetate, and therefore is considered an archival storage medium.

Dozens of color processes have been used from the beginning of filmmaking. During the silent film era, films were tinted. Later, additive and subtractive processes were developed for colorizing film. The most common preservation problem with color film involves fading. Proper storage can minimize, though not eliminate, this concern.

The Edison Company created the Kinetoscope in 1891, and, by 1895, the Lumière Brothers in Paris were showing films to audiences. Film studios were operating by the end of that decade in France and the United States. Early films were shown in music halls or any venue where a screen could be set up and a room darkened. The first films were only a few minutes long. However, filmmaking developed quickly after the 1890s. By 1914, film industries were operating in the United States and Europe. From an early date, people experimented with creating color film, though consistent processes were not in place until the 1930s. Sound was introduced in the 1920s. *The Jazz Singer* (1927) is credited as the earliest feature-length film with synchronized sound.

Motion picture film is produced on rolls in a variety of formats, which are referred to with respect to the width of the film stock. The most common are 8mm, Super 8mm, 16mm, 35mm, and 70mm.

Magnetic videotape was introduced in the mid-1950s by the Ampex Corporation for broadcast television. Until the 1980s, television broadcasters used the Quad (Quadruplex) system, in which imagery was recorded onto 2-inch open-reel magnetic tape, to record live programs for delayed rebroadcast in different time zones.[39] Many other formats were developed; Betamax and VHS videocassettes were two of the formats developed for consumer use. They are often referred to as *home videos*. Beginning in the 1970s, theatrical films were released on magnetic videos, which led to a home video and video rental boom. From the 1980s to the early 2000s, a number of video cameras were developed for amateur and home use.

Digital moving images are also referred to as digital cinematography. The first digitally filmed and post-produced movie was released in 1996.[40] Tellingly, the film was transferred to 35mm film for release in theaters. It took over a decade for most theaters to exchange their film projectors for digital equipment. By 2014, however, 80 percent of movie theaters in the United States had digital projectors and digital playback systems.[41] Digital moving images are captured using digital image sensors rather than film stock. This is now the dominant "film" technology. Movies produced in this manner are digitally distributed and exhibited and sent to theaters on hard drives, or Digital Cinema Packages (DCP).

Archives have collected various moving image formats since the early twentieth century. The Library of Congress collected films for copyright purposes almost as soon as they were commercially produced. The National Archives and Records Administration contains many moving image collections as well, including those comprising corporate and government films.

One of the first film libraries in the United States was started at the Museum of Modern Art in New York City in 1935. Soon after, as more institutions began systematically collecting film, it became apparent to the curatorial community that film was disintegrating—beginning with nitrate film, which can begin to deteriorate at 70 degrees Fahrenheit. Not only was nitrate film an ongoing problem, but ironically, the later so-called acetate safety film used to replace nitrate began showing the symptoms of vinegar syndrome.

Today, as archives broaden their acquisition strategies to accession more home movies and film orphans, new challenges have arisen. "Orphan films" lack either clear copyright holders or commercial potential to pay for their preservation.[42] The term can also refer to any neglected film, whether the neglect is physical (a deteriorated print), cultural (a censored film), or commercial (an unreleased film). Whenever possible, archivists should try to obtain as much informational metadata as possible about the moving images from the donor, such as maker, date, title, format used, and brand and/or manufacturer of the film or video. If possible, archivists should also endeavor to obtain intellectual property rights.

Best Practices

The guidelines for the handling and use of film are similar to those for other formats, with a few differences:

- Have clean hands and use a new pair of nitrile gloves (using clean cotton gloves is better than having fingerprints on the film, but cotton fibers are abrasive and can scratch the emulsion).
- Store and handle film in a clean environment; minimize exposure to dust and airborne particulates.
- Keep food and drink away from film.
- Do not touch the face of the film, including the emulsion; if film must be directly handled, handle it only by the edge.
- Keep playback equipment clean and well maintained.
- Use duplicate films for access when possible, and outfit the projector with a low-heat bulb.
- Allow materials from cool storage to acclimatize to room temperature over a period of at least twenty-four hours before use.[43]

It is important to store films in containers to protect them from water, air pollution, and dust. However, the cans should provide ventilation, which is particularly important for nitrate films. Original film canisters should be kept if they are in good condition. Any labels, brand information, and/or other important metadata should be retained if the film is rehoused. If the canister is damaged or rusted, it should be discarded, or, if important in some way, stored elsewhere. New film canisters used for storage should be vented. Acetate film should be stored in a separate area from other films to minimize the effects of off-gassing from acetic acid decomposition. Freezing is recommended for nitrate film.

Films should be stacked horizontally, in film canisters and on an inert plastic core. Films should never be stacked on reels without a film canister. Enameled steel, stainless steel, or anodized aluminum are the preferred materials for cabinets and shelves. Wood should be avoided.

Maintaining a stable environment with low temperature, light, and RH is recommended. The air should be as dust-free as possible.

Nitrate and acetate film can be reformatted onto polyester film if the originals are not too deteriorated. A former reformatting practice was to copy films onto videotapes. Archives still contain these "preservation videotapes," but today films are more commonly digitized than reformatted to analog because film projectors are becoming scarce and digitized films can be viewed on a variety of devices. Digitization is particularly recommended for nitrate films. Unless an institution specifically collects nitrate films and can meet NFPA standards for storage and exhibition, such films are preferably discarded. If an item is unique, perhaps it can be donated to a film archives that can provide safe storage. Digital versions, it should be noted, also require careful monitoring.

It is also important to note that the creation and ownership of many films cannot be attributed. For example, an orphan film, as mentioned previously, is a work abandoned by its owner or copyright holder. Archives may also contain films or film fragments with no identifying information. They have not been intentionally abandoned, but no way may exist to identify the owner or determine the property rights of the film. Thus, rights management is critical to the proper stewardship of film and moving image collections.

The preservation of magnetic tape is complicated because this format usually comprises two layers: a magnetic material that stores the recorded signal and a base layer that supports the magnetic material. The magnetic material contains particles suspended in a polymer binder that disperses them evenly across the tape surface. The mixture may also include additives or preservatives; processes differed from manufacturer to manufacturer.

While poorly manufactured tapes can deteriorate, the improper storage and use of magnetic media will also cause decline. For example, if reel-to-reel machines and cassette players are not well maintained, they can abrade or break tapes. Also, excessive temperature and humidity can harm them. High humidity, for example, can cause binder hydrolysis, which may make the tape soft and sticky. High humidity can facilitate mold growth; high temperatures accelerate aging.

To enhance its longevity, magnetic tape should be stored vertically and away from fluorescent and natural light. Moreover, this format should be stored on sturdy shelves that have been electrically grounded. If possible, the tapes should be rewound prior to storage to avoid deformation of the tape base.[44] Open-reel tapes should be wound onto reels made from noncorrosive metal or inert plastic. Enclosures consisting of sturdy, chemically inert materials such as polypropylene should protect the tapes from light, water, heat, and dust. Any important information that exists on or in the original enclosures should be preserved.

As with other formats, low temperature and humidity are recommended. High humidity (above 65% RH) can be particularly damaging to magnetic tape, resulting in "sticky-shed" syndrome, where the magnetic layer pulls away from the base. As with film, good air quality and cleanliness are important because dust and other particulate matter can abrade tapes. Magnetic media should be handled carefully and with clean, dry hands. Lint-free cotton gloves may be worn.[45] Patrons should never eat, drink, or smoke near the tapes. Reformatting and digitization of magnetic tape is a primary preservation practice for this format. Preservationists at one time recommended recopying magnetic media every five years.[46] Now, such collections are more likely to be digitized for the same reason as is film: playback equipment is disappearing. Digitization allows for dissemination and repurposing of the media.

Film that is properly stored and cared for can last for at least a century. Digital film constitutes another issue. At present, there is no guarantee that digitally stored "texts" will be preserved for as long as archivists project they will need these materials. Storing digital masters is more expensive than storing film masters. But, even as storage costs come down, other expenses remain, including the costs of preserving source materials for a movie and for maintaining accessibility to the digital work as file formats, hardware, and software evolve. Because digital media can deteriorate and playback equipment can become obsolete, the recommended practice is to migrate digital films and videos and store them in trusted digital repositories.

Several important resources contain additional information. The National Film Preservation Foundation is the nonprofit organization created by the US Congress to save America's film heritage. It supports activities nationwide that preserve American films and improve film access for study, education, and exhibition. The Moving Image Research Center, Motion Picture, Broadcasting, and Recorded Sound Division, at the Library of Congress has many resources on its website.[47] Several professional organizations concern themselves with film, including the Association of Moving Image Archivists (AMIA) and the International Federation of Film Archives (FIAF). These associations have active publications programs. AMIA publishes the journal *The Moving Image: The Journal of the Association of Moving Image Archivists*; FIAF publishes the *Journal of Film Preservation.*

Sound Recordings

Background and Challenges

As with moving images, many early devices created movement and sound. Devices that could emit sound included musical clocks, mechanical bells, and music boxes. Modern sound recordings date from the late nineteenth century. Thomas Edison patented a tinfoil cylinder in 1877, which led to the commercial wax cylinder produced by the American Phonograph Company in 1889. Gramophone disc systems were developed in the 1880s by Emile Berliner as well as by Alexander Graham Bell. Many new recording devices followed, including electrical recordings and magnetic tape. In 1898, Valdemar Poulsen invented the wire recorder, and the resulting devices, commercially available in the 1920s and 1930s, were still in use in the 1950s. Magnetic tape was developed as a recording medium before World War II, and, by the end of the 1940s, Ampex produced the first tape recordings in the United States. In 1954, it introduced the first multitrack audio recorder derived from multitrack data-recording technology. The company developed the first magnetic theater sound system, made for Todd/AO CinemaScope.[48] Other major recording formats evolved on platforms such as foil, wax, wire, magnetic tape, and "vinyl," or in more traditional terms, "records" or "LPs." LPs, short for long-playing, have been around since 1948, and, for the past decade have been made popular again in a "vinyl revival."[49] Archives might acquire some of these discs and may need to acquire turntables, which have also made a modest comeback.

Cassette tapes (also known as "compact cassettes" and "cassettes") are compact analog tapes seated in plastic containers. They came in various sizes and were used for dictation and spoken-word and music recordings. Popular from the 1960s through the 1980s, they came in two forms: prerecorded or blank. Eight-track tapes were also manufactured in the 1960s, but were replaced by cassette tapes. In the 1980s, digital formats such as compact discs (CDs) started to overtake cassettes in the marketplace.

In addition to compact discs, digital formats include optical disc and digital audio files. Sam Brylawski, an authority on the preservation of recorded sound, has written a standard manual for the Association for Recorded Sound Collections, the *ARSC Guide to Audio Preservation.*[50] He observes that "digital file formats are independent of any specific physical carrier and are likely never to have a physical carrier. Most digital audio files are encoded representations of an analog sound wave."[51] Born-digital audio exists on such carriers as digital audio tape (DAT) as well as in computer files. Digital recording makes it possible to attain better control over sound reproduction than did earlier technologies. Digital also makes it possible to create exact copies, unlike analog processes.

Best Practices

Like film and photographs, sound recordings exist on many analog and digital file formats. Analog file formats, including cylinders, grooved discs, magnetic formats, compact audio cassettes, vinyl records, and open-reel tapes, present a significant preservation and access concern: they depend on physical carriers and playback equipment that must be maintained. As time goes by, the playback equipment becomes increasingly difficult to repair or replace. Although record players have made a comeback and cassette tape and eight-track players can be found at flea markets, a preservation manager cannot depend on this marketplace. Most likely, only institutions with significant audio collections will be able to maintain the original equipment needed to play these various formats. For most archives, digitizing audio media is the best strategy, though this can be expensive. For those who keep their audio materials and playback equipment, there are basic guidelines for the proper care of them:

- A/V materials must be stored in a stable environment.
- The environment should be as dust-free as possible.
- If materials are stored in a cool environment, they must acclimatize to room temperature before they are played.
- A/V materials must be handled with clean hands.
- The playing surfaces of A/V materials should not be touched.
- Playback equipment must be kept clean, and it should be well maintained.
- To enforce these guidelines, archivists should guide their patrons in proper use and handling.

In regard to storage and handling, open shelving should be used for discs, audiotapes, and grouped formats in boxes, and cabinets and drawers are recommended for cylinders, cartridges, CDs, and other small formats. Each format has its own handling requirements.[52] As with other tapes, audiotape should be stored in a cool, dry, clean environment. *The ARSC Guide* provides recommendations for short-term storage, defined as less than ten years, and long-term storage. Short-term storage temperatures should be kept cooler than room temperatures, and RH should be between 30% and 50%. For the long term, the temperature should be kept between 46 and 53 degrees F, but no lower than 46. Audio recordings should not be frozen. The RH should be kept between 25% and 35%.

In most instances, the original housing can be preserved unless it is harming the recording, for example, by off-gassing. Housing should also be replaced if it is torn or broken and exposes the playing area, or if it has been water damaged or contaminated with mold or pest droppings.[53]

If original storage materials are discarded, the metadata they contain, such as maker, date, and medium information, should be retained. Audio recordings should be cleaned regularly, as should playback machines. Recordings should never be placed on a playback machine without having been properly cleaned, as dust, dirt, and other foreign substances may further damage the recording and the playback equipment.[54]

Tapes with sticky-shed syndrome, except for acetate tape, can be baked.[55] Baking the tape temporarily restores it by driving the water molecules from the binder so that its contents can be safely copied to another tape.

Reformatting and imaging techniques are also useful preservation strategies, and, as already mentioned, carrier deterioration and technical obsolescence sometimes make digital reformatting necessary. When reformatting, three digital files should be produced: one preservation master, one access master, and one access copy.[56]

Imaging techniques such as the Image, Reconstruct, Erase Noise, Etc. (IRENE/3D) system can retrieve sound from discs and wax cylinders without damaging the original formats. IRENE is a specialized scanner developed by Carl Haber and others at the Lawrence Berkeley National Laboratory that uses optical scanning to preserve and restore sound recordings. The scanner "creates a high-resolution digital map of a disc or cylinder without touching the object's surface and processes the images into digital sound files. This 'touchless' technology allows damaged recordings, such as broken cylinders and records, to be digitally reassembled."[57]

In summary, to be seen and heard, audio recordings must be mediated through some system. Digitization is the best strategy to preserve audiovisual media. The degradation of audio media and the obsolescence of playback equipment make it nearly impossible to maintain legacy systems. Useful resources for managing sound collections include the National Recording Preservation Board of the Library of Congress,[58] the National Audio-Visual Conservation Center Blog,[59] and the Association for Recorded Sound Collections (ARSC).[60] Finally, several institutions have developed excellent tools for audio evaluations and surveys: the Field Audio Collection Evaluation Tool (FACET), Indiana University;[61] AVPreserve, Audio/Video Survey, Columbia University Libraries;[62] and the Audiovisual Self-Assessment Tool (AvSAP), University of Illinois, Urbana-Champaign.[63]

Digital Media: Email, Websites, and Tweets

Background and Challenges

Email has existed as a communication medium for some fifty years. It was used at the Massachusetts Institute of Technology in the 1960s, but in those early days, mail could be sent only to users of the same computer. It was further developed at the Advanced Research Projects Agency (ARPA) of the United States Department of Defense. ARPANET was the packet-switching network that made it possible to distribute emails. However, only with the popularity of the World Wide Web and the internet in the late 1990s did email became widespread and nearly ubiquitous. Before the web, only text messages could be exchanged. Now, emails have evolved into complex multimedia documents that may contain embedded sound and images, videos, and hyperlinks.

Email forms a significant part of our cultural record, and it has been the focus of various studies and projects. An early preservation initiative was the Collaborative Electronic Records Project (CERP), a joint venture of the Smithsonian Institution Archives and the Rockefeller

Archive Center, from 2005 to 2008. These partners devised recommendations for best practices, a workflow outline, and an evaluation of existing software. They were able to parse 89,000 email messages with a 99 percent success rate.[64] University of Illinois archivist Christopher Prom advocated for preservation actions for email throughout its life cycle as part of this project, from the creation of email, to its capture, to its migration to a stable format, to its storage, and to management of the files.[65]

Today, new tools such as ePADD and Archive-It help archivists address email issues. ePADD is an open-source software package developed by Stanford University's Special Collections and University Archives that supports archival processes around the appraisal, ingestion, processing, discovery, and delivery of email archives.[66] It allows repositories and users to interact with email archives before and after they have been transferred to a repository. In phase 2 of its development (2015–2018), Stanford partnered with Harvard University, the Metropolitan New York Library Council (METRO), the University of Illinois at Urbana-Champaign, and the University of California, Irvine. Two primary goals defined this collaboration: 1) to develop critical functional improvements to the Appraisal, Processing, Discovery, and Delivery modules developed in phase 1, and 2) to create broad and sustained community engagement. These goals have been taken up by a few institutions, but the many challenges of preserving email are still widespread and unresolved.

The Andrew W. Mellon Foundation Task Force on Technical Approaches to Email Archives has funded the BitCurator NLP project, which has also developed software for libraries and archives.[67] New tools will continue to be created, but it will be necessary for archivists to work with donors on pretransfer appraisal of emails.

Preserving websites presents additional challenges. Because they can change from minute to minute, the primary approach is to capture sites at regular intervals and times. The pioneer in website archiving remains the Internet Archive, which was launched in 2001.

Brewster Kahle, the philanthropic founder of this nonprofit entity, began this work in the 1990s with the "Wayback Machine" that allowed users to access previous versions and defunct websites. The Library of Congress (LC) has been archiving websites since 2000. The LC began its efforts by participating in two major projects: the 2000 US elections and 9/11. For the 9/11 Archive, the library had national and international partners, most prominently, the Center for History and New Media at George Mason and the Internet Archive.[68] This kind of theme- or events-based approach has proven a popular way for archives to harvest web pages.

Archive-It was developed in 2006 by the Internet Archive as a subscription web-archiving service. This tool allows institutional partners to harvest, build, and preserve collections of digital content and to catalog and manage those collections. Internet Archive data centers host and store content and provide for access 24/7.[69]

Efforts to preserve the massive amounts of digital information that exist on social media sites have proven especially challenging and yield no easy solutions. In 2010, the Library of Congress decided to try to comprehensively archive tweets. In December 2017, the institution modified this course and announced instead that it would archive them selectively.[70] Recently, the Welsh government's Information and Archive Service carried out a mini-pilot project to explore making tweets available via its Soutron Library Management System.[71]

The volume of e-generated communication is overwhelming. New forms of social networking will continue to present challenges, and everything cannot be preserved. In fact, the amount of electronic data produced in a single day is probably beyond any institution's capacity to preserve.

Selection and appraisal will continue to be critical components of preservation. But, as we have seen, much work is underway to create new open-source archiving tools to keep up with ever-increasing amounts of data and with evolving demands and threats to preservation.

Archivist Adrian Brown aptly summarizes the general threats to preserving digital media:

- Generic threats (technology obsolescence; inadequate skills and resources)
- Threats to reliability
- Threats to integrity (media decay, media damage, bit rot, media loss, hardware failure, disasters, etc.)
- Threats to usability
- Legal issues[72]

To his list we would add:

- The corporate ownership of a steadily increasing amount of information
- Cloud service providers

The for-profit sector has created a pervasive and pernicious threat to digital preservation. Corporations such as Google, Amazon, and Facebook own a significant amount of personal information and intellectual property. Publishers, subscription services, and aggregators are also aggressively controlling information. Subscription services cancel journals while libraries discard books and periodicals as they become available online. Subscribing to databases or open-access scholarly communication systems does not ensure long-term access to information, a point that may get lost when we consider the challenges of digital preservation. Also, the databases that we subscribe to are generally leased. It takes a long-term, ongoing expense to maintain continued access to them. Furthermore, commercial vendors do not want present technology to stagnate; it must continue to evolve for the vendors to continue to profit. And, evolving technology practically guarantees digital obsolescence. Until vendors are incentivized to stop constantly changing their products—basically to stop making profits—"digital preservation" will remain challenging.

We also add to the "threat list" the inadequacy of some cloud providers for preservation and access. Cloud providers enable ubiquitous on-demand network access to such resources as networks, servers, and storage. To deliver these services, cloud providers must have on-demand self-service, broad network access, resource pooling, rapid elasticity, and measured service. Cloud-based preservation services are scarce.[73] Approaches to cloud computing will depend on the size and resources of an archives. However, the monitoring of cloud services must be incorporated into any comprehensive preservation program.

Digital Media

(A Quest for) Best Practices

Digital preservation experts Ross Harvey and Jaye Weatherburn have called for a new plan for preserving digital media that takes into account the preponderance of digital information and the changing nature of preservation work. In the past, information professionals typically focused on acquiring, storing, and providing access to information resources from particular individuals and institutions. Now, an institution may lease rather own some of those resources, and digital resources require more active management than do most analog information. In fact, as mentioned in earlier chapters, the old life-cycle models are no longer adequate. Plans must be made for the preservation of digital resources even before they are born or ingested. When considering analog materials, passive preservation management appears a viable option if their storage conditions remain sound. With digital media, a plan for the ongoing and active refreshing or migrating of information it contains as well as more extensive security provisions must be made. Passive preservation has clear limitations in the digital age.

Harvey and Weatherburn contrast predigital and digital preservation principles as follows:

Predigital Preservation Principles:

- When materials are treated, the treatments must be as reversible as is possible.
- Whenever possible or appropriate, the originals should be preserved; only materials that are untreatable should be reformatted.
- Efforts should be put into preventive conservation and aimed at providing appropriate storage and handling of artifacts.
- Benign neglect [or passive preservation] may sometimes be the best practice.[74]

Digital Preservation Principals: The preservation of digital documents and objects is a series of managed activities for ensuring

- **Access** to records,
- their **authenticity**,
- the **accountability** of governments, organizations, and people,
- and the **sustainability** of the records
- for the **short-**, **medium-**, or **long-term**.

Differences clearly exist between the predigital and digital worlds. The digital world is dynamic; therefore, preservation must be incorporated into the initial design of systems and tailored to specific formats. Recognizing this need, the National Digital Stewardship Alliance (NDSA) developed a "Levels of Digital Preservation" matrix to help organizations establish targets appropriate for their specific collections.[75] NDSA identifies four levels of preservation (see Figure 7.2).

Within this context, several current digital preservation strategies are available to archivists. These include:

- **Migration:** the transferring of digital objects from one technology to another
- **Emulation:** the development of software that mimics an earlier, sometimes obsolete, software
- **Technology preservation** (also known as "digital archaeology"): the application of techniques to recover digital objects that have become damaged or inaccessible
- **Digital forensics:** the use of data-recovery techniques to recover data from storage media that have become damaged or inaccessible
- **Standardization of data formats** (also known as "normalization"): the conversion of digital data into accessible or open formats so that they are widely available
- **Encapsulation:** the packaging of a digital object with the means of viewing it in a wrapper, for example, the use of an XML document

Functional Area	LEVEL			
	LEVEL 1 (Know your content)	LEVEL 2 (Protect your content)	LEVEL 3 (Monitor your content)	LEVEL 4 (Sustain your content)
Storage	Have two complete copies in separate locations. Document all storage media where content is stored. Put content into stable storage.	Have three complete copies with at least one copy in a separate geographic location. Document storage and storage media indicating the resources and dependencies they require to function.	Have at least one copy in a geographic location with a different disaster threat than the other copies. Have at least one copy on a different storage media type. Track the obsolescence of storage and media.	Have at least three copies in geographic locations, each with a different disaster threat. Maximize storage diversification to avoid single points of failure. Have a plan and execute actions to address obsolescence of storage hardware, software, and media.
Integrity	Verify integrity information if it has been provided with the content. Generate integrity information if not provided with the content. Virus check all content; isolate content for quarantine as needed.	Verify integrity information when moving or copying content. Use write-blockers when working with original media. Back up integrity information and store copy in a separate location from the content.	Verify integrity information of content at fixed intervals. Document integrity information verification processes and outcomes. Perform audit of integrity information on demand.	Verify integrity information in response to specific events or activities. Replace or repair corrupted content as necessary.
Control	Determine the human and software agents that should be authorized to read, write, move, and delete content.	Document the human and software agents authorized to read, write, move, and delete content and apply these.	Maintain logs and identify the human and software agents that performed actions on content.	Perform periodic review of actions/access logs.
Metadata	Create inventory of content, also documenting current storage locations. Back up inventory and store at least one copy separately from content.	Store enough metadata to know what the content is (this might include some combination of administrative, technical, descriptive, preservation, and structural).	Determine what metadata standards to apply. Find and fill gaps in your metadata to meet those standards.	Record preservation actions associated with content and when those actions occur. Implement metadata standards chosen.
Content	Document file formats and other essential content characteristics including how and when these were identified.	Verify file formats and other essential content characteristics. Build relationships with content creators to encourage sustainable file choices.	Monitor for obsolescence and changes in technologies on which content depends.	Perform migrations, normalizations, emulation, and similar activities that ensure content can be accessed.

FIGURE 7.2. National Digital Stewardship Alliance, *Levels of Digital Preservation, Version 2.0 Matrix*

Clearly, archivists can incorporate the dynamism of the current digital environment into their preservation principals. One way is to acknowledge that the notion of "fixity" is rooted in the analog world. To embrace the dynamic nature of digital media, archivists must realize that as technology changes, their approaches must as well. For example, archivists may need to accept a certain amount of loss. And, perhaps more than that, they must also acknowledge that digital technology has changed the ways in which they will address preservation in the future, because the future of technology is out of their control.

Conclusion

This chapter has highlighted some of the many types of information objects and records that archivists must care for. All collections must be *managed*, and some must be more actively managed than others throughout the records' life cycle. While the particular methods used will vary by format, most preservation strategies are format-agnostic. These include risk assessment, environmental monitoring, emergency planning, and other approaches that can be used to protect entire collections. Archivists manage their collections by monitoring them so that their integrity is preserved, so that they are safely and securely stored, and so that they remain accessible for as long as they are needed. The preservation of analog and digital content depends on planning, creating effective policies, choosing appropriate technologies, and collaborating with professionals inside and outside the archives. The success of archival preservation programs can only be measured and assured through regular assessment.

NOTES

1 Matthew G. Kirschenbaum et al., *Digital Materiality: Preserving Access to Computers as Complete Environments*, in *Proceedings, iPres 2009: The Sixth International Conference on Preservation of Digital Objects, San Francisco: October 5, 2009*, https://escholarship.org/uc/item/7d3465vg.

2 Crystal Sanchez and Lauren Sorensen, "The Physical Nature of Digital and What It Means for Conservation," (paper presented at Material Matters: 46th Annual Meeting of the American Institute for Conservation of Historic and Artistic Works, Houston, TX, May 29–June 2, 2018), preprint, 19.

3 Christine Ward, "Preservation Program Planning for Archives and Historical Records Repositories," in *Preservation: Issues and Planning*, ed. Paul N. Banks and Roberta Pilette (Chicago: American Library Association, 2000), 44–45.

4 It is not possible to discuss every medium and format here, as new ones are constantly being created. Archivists should keep abreast of new trends by reading widely in professional and popular publications.

5 Among the many monographs and reports on digital preservation published just since 2017 are Edward M. Corrado and Heather Moulaison Sandy (2017), Ross Harvey and Jaye Weatherburn (2018), Trevor Owens (2018), Aaron D. Purcell (2019), Oya Y. Rieger (2018), and Nanna Bonde Thylstrup (2018).

6 Matthew Farrell, "Email," in *The Digital Archives Handbook: A Guide to Creation, Management, and Preservation*, ed. Aaron D. Purcell (Lanham, MD: Rowman & Littlefield, 2019), 226–27.

7 See https://siarchives.si.edu/about/smithsonian-pan-institutional-survey-audiovisual-collections, captured at https://perma.cc/QFA2-7HL9.

8 Pamela W. Darling, "Creativity v. Despair: The Challenge of Preservation Administration," *Library Trends* 30, no. 2 (1981): 179–88, http://hdl.handle.net/2142/7193; Ross Harvey and Martha R. Mahard, *The Preservation Management Handbook:*

A 21st-Century Guide for Libraries, Archives, and Museums (Lanham, MD: Rowman & Littlefield, 2014), 61. Darling was writing in the 1970s, but this article expands on her earlier ideas.

9 Caryn Anderson, "Technology 7 Framework" (unpublished framework that Anderson uses in her technology courses at Simmons University), modified here with Caryn Anderson's permission. The quote is from an email from Anderson to Michèle Cloonan, April 27, 2019.

10 POWRR, "Tool Grid," https://digitalpowrr.niu.edu/digital-preservation-101/tool-%20grid, captured at https://perma.cc/JT8P-MQA2, and POWRR, "About the POWRR Tool Grid," http://www.digipres.org/tools/about.

11 Ulla Bøgvad Kejser, Anders Bo Nielsen, and Alex Thirifays, "Cost Model for Digital Preservation: Cost of Digital Migration," *The International Journal of Digital Curation* 1, no. 6 (2011): 255–67, https://doi.org/10.2218/ijdc.v6i1.186.

12 Kejser et al., "Cost Model for Digital Preservation," 255.

13 Paul N. Banks, "Environment and Building Design for Preservation of Library Materials," in *Preservation: Issues and Planning*, 114.

14 InterPARES is a multinational, interdisciplinary research project that has explored issues of trust and trustworthiness of records and data in online environments. It was established by archival educator and theorist Luciana Duranti, and others, in 1998. The work of InterPARES is ongoing.

15 *The InterPARES Glossary* (2001), http://interpares.org/display_file.cfm?doc=ip1_glossary.pdf, captured at https://perma.cc/F4JM-K3CG. See also Terry Eastwood et al., *Chain of Preservation Model Diagrams and Definitions*, Appendix 14 (2008), interpares.org/ip2/ip2_terminology_db.cfm.

16 T. H. Tsien with Edward Shaughnessy, *Written on Bamboo and Silk: The Beginnings of Chinese Books and Inscriptions*, 2nd ed., rev. (Chicago: University of Chicago Press, 2013).

17 *Permanence of Paper for Publications and Documents in Libraries and Archives*, ANSI/NISO Z39.48-1992 (R2009) (Baltimore: National Information Standards Organization, 2010).

18 *Permanence of Paper for Publications and Documents in Libraries and Archives*, ANSI/NISO Z39.48-1992 (R2009).

19 American Booksellers Association, "Green Press Initiative: It's Better Being Green," (March 24, 2005), bookweb.org.

20 The website for the Image Permanence Institute contains detailed information on this topic, https://www.imagepermanenceinstitute.org.

21 Monique Fischer, "5.1 A Short Guide to Film Base Photographic Materials: Identification, Care, and Duplication," Northeast Document Conservation Center Preservation Leaflet series (2012), https://www.nedcc.org/assets/media/documents/Preservation%20Leaflets/5_1_FilmBaseGuide.pdf, captured at https://perma.cc/YN52-8GBK.

22 American Institute for Conservation of Historic and Artistic Works (AIC), "Photographic Processes," http://www.conservation-wiki.com/wiki/Category:Photographic_Processes.

23 Image Permanence Institute (IPI), "Graphics Atlas," http://www.graphicsatlas.org.

24 Image Permanence Institute (IPI), "Photographic Process Identification Webinars," https://www.imagepermanenceinstitute.org/process-id-webinars.

25 Daniel Burge, "IPI Guide to Preservation of Digitally-Printed Photographs," http://www.dp3project.org/webfm_send/739, captured at https://perma.cc/4QSS-2J5Q.

26 Northeast Document Conservation Center (NEDCC), "5.3 Care of Photographs," Preservation Leaflet series, https://www.nedcc.org/free-resources/preservation-leaflets/5.-photographs/5.3-care-of-photographs, captured at https://perma.cc/VNB8-ERTA.

27 Northeast Document Conservation Center, "Care of Photographs," Preservation Leaflet, 5.3. https://www.nedcc.org/free-resources/preservation-leaflets/5.-photographs/5.3-care-of-photographs, captured at https://perma.cc/VNB8-ERTA.

28 Burge, "IPI Guide to Preservation of Digitally-Printed Photographs."

29 Burge, "IPI Guide to Preservation of Digitally-Printed Photographs," 1.

30 Richard Pearce-Moses, *A Glossary of Archival and Records Terminology*, https://www2.archivists.org/glossary.

31 Edward M. Corrado and Heather Moulaison Sandy, *Digital Preservation for Libraries, Archives, and Museums*, 2nd ed. (London, UK: Rowman & Littlefield, 2017), 213.

32 Photographic Materials Group (PMG) of the American Institute for Historic and Artistic Works (AIC), https://www.conservation-us.org/specialty-topics/photographic-materials-group.

33 Image Permanence Institute at the Rochester Institute of Technology, https://www.imagepermanenceinstitute.org.

34 Craig Blaha, "Preserving Facebook Records: Subscriber Expectations and Behavior," *Preservation, Digital Technology & Culture* 42, no. 3 (2013): 115, 125, https://doi.org/10.1515/pdtc-2013-0017.

35 Liz Coffey and Elizabeth Walters, "Moving Image Materials," in *The Preservation Management Handbook*, ed. Ross Harvey and Martha R. Mahard, 260–61.

[36] Library of Congress, "Care, Handling, and Storage of Motion Picture Film," https://www.loc.gov/preservation/care/film.html, captured at https://perma.cc/HV8Z-VZJK.

[37] Kodak, "Storage and Handling of Processed Nitrate Film," https://www.kodak.com/motion/support/technical_information/storage/storage_and_handing_of_processed_nitrate_film/default.htm.

[38] NFPA, *Standard for the Storage and Handling of Cellulose Nitrate Film* (2016), https://catalog.nfpa.org/NFPA-40-Standard-for-the-Storage-and-Handling-of-Cellulose-Nitrate-Film-P1176.aspx?icid=D729.

[39] Coffey and Walters, "Moving Image Materials," 276–77; AMPEX website at http://www.ampex.com/ampex-history.

[40] The film was *Windhorse.* See Wikipedia, s.v. "digital cinematography," https://en.wikipedia.org/wiki/Digital_cinematography, captured at https://perma.cc/Z66Q-WPD6.

[41] Andy Maltz, "Will Today's Digital Movies Exist in 100 Years?," *IEEE Spectrum* (February 21, 2014), https://spectrum.ieee.org/consumer-electronics/standards/will-todays-digital-movies-exist-in-100-years.

[42] Annette Melville and Scott Simmon, *Film Preservation 1993: A Study of the Current State of American Film Preservation: Report of the Librarian of Congress* (Washington, DC: NFPB/LOC, 1993).

[43] Library of Congress, "Care, Handling."

[44] Coffey and Walters, "Moving Image Materials," 283.

[45] Coffey and Walters, "Moving Image Materials," 284.

[46] National Park Service, "Care of Archival Digital and Magnetic Media, *Conserve O Gram* 19/20 (September 1996), https://www.nps.gov/museum/publications/conserveogram/19-20.pdf, captured at https://perma.cc/22WK-BYDC.

[47] Library of Congress, Moving Image Resource Center, Motion Picture, Broadcasting, and Recorded Sound Division, https://www.loc.gov/rr/mopic.

[48] See Ampex history, http://www.ampex.com/ampex-history.

[49] Wikipedia, s.v. "vinyl revival," https://en.wikipedia.org/wiki/Vinyl_revival, captured at https://perma.cc/LD9P-PBG2.

[50] Sam Brylawski et al., eds., *ARSC Guide to Audio Preservation*, CLIR Publication 164 (Washington, DC: Council on Library and Information Resources, Association for Recorded Sound Collections, and the National Recording Preservation Board of the Library of Congress, May 2015), 32.

[51] Brylawski et al., eds., *ARSC Guide to Audio Preservation*, 32.

[52] Brylawski et al., eds., *ARSC Guide to Audio Preservation*, 52–54.

[53] Brylawski et al., eds., *ARSC Guide to Audio Preservation*, 62.

[54] Brylawski et al., eds., *ARSC Guide to Audio Preservation*, 58.

[55] Brylawski et al., eds., *ARSC Guide to Audio Preservation*, 61.

[56] Brylawski et al., eds., *ARSC Guide to Audio Preservation*, 111–12.

[57] Northeast Document Conservation Center (NEDCC), "Session 7: Reformatting Media Collections," https://www.nedcc.org/preservation101/session-7/7reformatting-media-collections, captured at https://perma.cc/Q8SN-6TT3.

[58] Library of Congress, "National Recording Preservation Board," https://www.loc.gov/programs/national-recording-preservation-board/about-this-program.

[59] Library of Congress, *Now See Hear!* (blog), National Audio-Visual Conservation Center, https://blogs.loc.gov/now-see-hear.

[60] Association for Recorded Sound Collections (ARSC), http://www.arsc-audio.org/index.php.

[61] Indiana University Digital Library Program, Sound Directions, "Field Audio Collection Evaluation Tool (FACET)," http://www.dlib.indiana.edu/projects/sounddirections/facet/index.shtml.

[62] Columbia University Libraries, Preservation and Digital Conversion, "Audio/Video Survey," https://library.columbia.edu/services/preservation/audiosurvey.html.

[63] University of Illinois at Urbana-Champaign, Audiovisual Self-Assessment Program, https://www.library.illinois.edu/avsap.

[64] *Collaborative Electronic Records Project: An Introduction and Overview* (Rockefeller Archive Center and Smithsonian Institution Archives, December 2008), http://siarchives.si.edu/cerp/CERP_Overview_CC.pdf, captured at https://perma.cc/SC9Y-SBV3.

[65] Christopher J. Prom, *Preserving Email* (Charles Beagrie Ltd. and the Digital Preservation Coalition, 2011), http://dx.doi.org/10.7207/twr11-01.

[66] Stanford Libraries, "ePADD," https://library.stanford.edu/projects/epadd.

[67] Farrell, "Email," 227–28.

[68] Abbie Grotke, "It Takes a Village . . . to Archive the Internet," *The Signal* (blog), Library of Congress (July 14, 2011), https://blogs.loc.gov/thesignal/2011/07/it-takes-a-village%E2%80%A6to-archive-the-internet, captured at https://perma.cc/UH4J-WV3U.

69 Howard Besser, "Archiving Websites Containing Streaming Media" (PowerPoint presented at Archiving Conference, Society for Imaging Science and Technology, May 16, 2017), http://besser.tsoa.nyu.edu/howard/Talks/17archiving-streaming-media.pdf, captured at https://perma.cc/YFG3-BNPL.

70 "The Library of Congress Will No Longer Archive Every Tweet," *The Two-Way* (blog), National Public Radio (December 26, 2017), https://www.npr.org/sections/thetwo-way/2017/12/26/573609499/library-of- congress-will-no-longer-archive-every-tweet, captured at https://perma.cc/95RX-EHJ3.

71 *Information Today Europe*, "Archiving and Preserving Tweets Using a Library Management System," https://www.infotoday.eu/Articles/Editorial/Featured-Articles/Archiving-and-preserving-tweets-using-a-Library-Management-System-126129.aspx, captured at https://perma.cc/4GTB-4JSF.

72 Adrian Brown, *Practical Digital Preservation: A How-To Guide for Organizations of Any Size* (Chicago: Neal-Schuman, 2013), 202.

73 Corrado and Moulaison Sandy, *Digital Preservation for Libraries, Archives, and Museums,* 154.

74 Ross Harvey and Jaye Weatherburn, *Preserving Digital Materials*, 3rd ed. (Lanham, MD: Rowman & Littlefield, 2018), 6–10.

75 National Digital Stewardship Program, Levels of Digital Preservation V2.0, https://ndsa.org/activities/levels-of-digital-preservation/, captured at https://perma.cc/79F6-S344.

8

Risk Management: A Programmatic Approach

Introduction

The previous three chapters focused on developing a preservation plan, managing a program, and caring for collections. This chapter focuses broadly on a programmatic approach to risk management, with examples of how it can be applied to disaster prevention planning and recovery, environmental controls in buildings, security, information technology (IT) systems, and digital collections.

Risk management is a strategy for minimizing risk or damage to collections, systems, and infrastructure. Although nearly every preservation action contributes to alleviating risk, risk must be considered in the context of all the threats and vulnerabilities the entire institution faces—as well as with respect to the broader administrative and legal infrastructure in which the institution exists. A successful preservation program is impossible unless one understands the risk tolerance of an institution. That is, to what degree will the institution accept, avoid, transfer, or limit risk?

In the information management field, risk constitutes the "net impact . . . of a vulnerability considering the probability and the impact of occurrence."[1] Thus, risk management involves assessing, planning for, and mitigating risk based on the probability that the damage will occur or recur. It is a preventive decision-making tool, and for risk management to succeed requires an organization-wide commitment to the program that involves staff at all levels and across departments.

Many threats exist to the longevity of collections: thefts, disasters, deterioration caused by poor storage or inherent vice, the obsolescence of hardware and software, the failure to back up systems, and inadequate cloud storage. In the institutional infrastructure, there also are specific risks to IT systems, sometimes referred to as "vulnerabilities." These are natural or environmental threats (long-term power failure, pollution, chemicals, global warming) and human threats

Environmental

- Fire
- Water
- Pests
- Contaminants
- Light and UV radiation
- Unacceptable temperature and humidity fluctuations
- Power outages

People

- Human errors (neglect, lack of training, lack of data security protocols)
- Criminal acts (theft, cyberattacks, terrorism)
- Staffing changes

Systems and Intrastructure

- Failure to preserve bits
- Obsolescence (software, storage media)
- Corrupted files
- Lack of redundancy of files
- Inadequate or inaccessible metadata
- Organizational changes
- Lack of resources (budget, staff, facilities)

FIGURE 8.1. Sources of risk

(sabotage, hacking, or accidental harm caused by staff without proper training or expertise) (see Figure 8.1). Pure, or absolute, risk is a threat beyond human control that results in a loss.[2] Examples are natural disasters, fires, terrorism, and the loss of critical personnel and their expertise. The aim of risk management is to understand these threats and to determine the appropriate procedures for preventing or minimizing them. Figure 8.1 lists many common sources of risk. It is not exhaustive, and most can be attributed to the lack of well-managed care.

Background and History

Modern risk management was developed during the late 1950s and early 1960s in the for-profit sector to manage corporate financial risk. It achieved special popularity among engineers, who developed technological risk-management models.[3] Before that time, risk management simply meant being insured, referred to today as "risk transference." However, with the rising costs of insurance and the complexities of managing a variety of hazards, corporations developed new strategies for dealing with risks. Typical approaches include contingency planning, training and safety programs, and self-insurance for some types of losses. Insurance came to be seen as an incomplete strategy for dealing with risk, because it neglects prevention. As the governance of risk management evolved, so too did staffing, as corporations hired specially trained managers for this purpose.[4]

While loss can be minimized, it cannot always be prevented. If original documents that are not backed up or reformatted are subjected to a natural disaster or a disaster caused by humans, a devastating and permanent loss could result. Insurance companies may offer financial compensation to an institution for "replacement costs," but many kinds of materials simply remain irreplaceable. Moreover, insurance does not cover many hazards, and this approach to managing risk must be balanced with preventive actions and risk mitigation.

Risk management was developed initially in the for-profit sector, however, it is equally applicable to nonprofit organizations, such as those engaged in the preservation of cultural heritage.[5] In recent years, many nonprofits have adopted business management models, with an increasing emphasis on accountability to stakeholders and constituencies, the introduction of standard business practices, and an emphasis on fiduciary responsibilities. For example, governing boards may expect their nonprofits to have business plans that include risk management. Directors of libraries, archives, and museums, in particular, better understand the vulnerability of their collections than do their boards; and natural disasters, thefts, terrorism, global warming, and the vulnerability of IT systems are increasingly on the minds of nonprofit administrators and boards of trustees.

Many resources are available for institutions that wish to implement risk-management programs. The Federal Emergency Management Agency (FEMA) and its Federal Insurance and Mitigation Administration (FIMA) have published guides that cover all kinds of risks. The United States Geological Survey (USGS) similarly issues many useful publications, some emanating from particular programs, such as the National Earthquake Information Center. Two organizations have created useful publications for risk management of IT systems: the Software Engineering Institute (SEI), a federally funded research and development center at Carnegie Mellon University, and the National Institute of Standards and Technology (NIST), part of the US Department of Commerce.[6]

Programmatic Approaches to Risk Management

Risk management involves assessing, planning for, and mitigating risk. Disaster planning and emergency response are related and integral aspects of risk management. Determining the risk level of a disaster at an institution is a key element in developing an effective plan for all materials, analog and digital. The NIST *Risk Management Guide for Information Technology Systems*[7] contains detailed procedures for assessment and mitigation according to the following general categories:

Assessment

- Threat identification
- Vulnerability identification
- Control analysis (for current and planned controls)
- Likelihood determination
- Impact analysis
- Risk determination

Mitigation

- Options (risk assumption, avoidance, limitation, planning, transference)
- Strategy
- Technical security controls
- Management controls
- Operational controls

Planning for risk management includes the assignment of risk levels to every threat. An assessment of previous and potential threats and disasters is critical to predicting future catastrophes. Determining the levels of institutional risk is the first step in applying a risk-management program. The results of an assessment, and the use of risk management strategies, will apply to planning for, limiting, and recovering from events that harm people, collections, and buildings and will preserve resources.

Thus, a risk assessment identifies internal and external threats. A typical assessment begins with a historical review of local emergencies and disasters, as well as those that have impacted the institution directly. In developing an event history, the assessment team identifies the type of hazards that have occurred and when and where they happened. For example: What are common (or uncommon) weather hazards? Are fires, floods, earthquakes, hurricanes, or tornadoes typical or even possible threats? Is a building's infrastructure outdated with water pipes or electrical wiring at risk? Has there been a history of flood, mold, pests, or leaks? What technological hazards might affect the institution?

When possible, those with knowledge of a prior event should be interviewed for information about previous disasters, and the responses should be documented and maintained with the assessment and other planning documents.

Another crucial step in an evaluation is determining the probability that a risk will occur or recur. This is referred to as a "likelihood determination." Risk-management specialist Robert Waller developed the "Cultural Property Risk Analysis" to assist in assessing risk at three levels: rare, sporadic, and continual. A rare level might occur once every hundred years, sporadic levels could take place once per decade, and continual risks plague institutions on a yearly basis.[8] In addition, he assigned numeric values to each risk to indicate the likelihood that an event will happen again. For example, assessment might show that items stored in a particular area of the stacks are prone to mold because five events have been documented in that area over a three-year period. Or, the analysis may determine a regular pattern of roof leaks during fall and winter over the last five years. Or, perhaps an information network was offline because a construction company cut a fiber cable, but it happened only once. Each incident would receive a probability number of 1 to 10, with 10 indicating the highest number of occurrences in the event-history period.

Consideration of the seasonality of these hazards is also important. An area (or external) history is a detailed list of the types of hazards—natural, human caused, and technological—that have occurred in the local area over the past five or more years. Once again, numbers can be assigned to each occurrence based on frequency. Once the probabilities have been calculated, the information can be used as a tool. Using the results of the assessment can help archivists to identify steps to manage hazards and threats. This type of risk assessment works well because it focuses on how probability factors may inform the selection and prioritization of mitigation strategies.

Once the risks are determined, the next step is to decide whether the institution will accept, avoid, transfer, or limit the risk. The four key approaches are:

1. **Risk Acceptance:** Disasters will happen, and one strategy is to acknowledge the inevitable and accept the risk. This strategy recognizes that the cost of other risk-management options such as avoidance or limitation may outweigh the cost of the risk itself. Any organization that cannot afford to address risks with a low possibility of occurrence may

choose a risk-acceptance strategy. Such an organization may mitigate some of the risk by being insured.

2. **Risk Avoidance:** Risk avoidance takes the opposite approach and aims to avoid all known exposure to the risk. Risk avoidance is usually the most expensive strategy. For example, an archives or museum in an earthquake area may employ basic protections mandated by building codes. However, to avoid additional risks to collections, the institution may also install structural building reinforcements and protective guards on shelves to prevent items from falling during earthquakes, or it may install seismic isolators underneath unstable objects. These are effective but potentially expensive and time-consuming strategies.[9]
3. **Risk Limitation:** Risk limitation, the most common strategy, limits an institution's exposure. It uses strategies associated with risk acceptance and avoidance. For example, most institutions back up their data to other locations to limit the impact of failed servers or disc drives. Others have a regular schedule for inspecting their building(s) for emerging hazards and attempt to address these threats before they occur.
4. **Risk Transference:** This simply means that an institution contracts some of its risk to a third party. A common example is maintaining an insurance policy on buildings and infrastructure, and, less frequently, on collections. Another is outsourcing certain operations such as customer service, payroll services, and collections storage. This can benefit an institution if addressing the transferred risk is not one of its core competencies. Most organizations, particularly small ones, rely on outside vendors for such services as cloud storage, disaster recovery, conservation, or digitization.

Planning for Risk Mitigation

Once the hazards are identified, the information gained from the risk-assessment report provides the preservation staff, and in the worst scenarios, a disaster team, with a number of options and plans of action that mitigate or respond to the damage. A plan of action does not reduce the frequency of events such as snowstorms and lightning strikes. However, the plan could address the repeated occurrences of mold and roof leaks, particularly in how to reduce the damage they cause. Generally, the plan should address any item with a risk probability of 80 percent or higher, though disasters with lower probabilities should also receive some attention. The event and area histories must be kept with the institutional disaster plan. They are dynamic documents that are never final, requiring periodic reviews and updates.

Those addressing risk mitigation should ensure that sufficient resources exist to implement the plan and that key stakeholders or their representatives are involved in the planning process. Sufficient resources to implement the plan are also critical. The plan should consider that one risk might have one or more causes and establish any underlying relationships across risks. The plan should also factor in the necessary resources and personnel. Some front-line and back-up staff may require additional training.

The plan of action should also include a strategy to guarantee that all critical information and essential records are identified and backed up and/or stored in alternate locations, possibly in multiple formats as well. As with all aspects of risk management, broader institutional involvement and buy-in are necessary for the plan to work. These considerations indicate the complexity of the planning and implementation processes.

Disaster Planning: Preparedness and Response

While risk management aims to reduce the probability of disaster, disasters do occur. As with the assessment of all risks, determining the likelihood of a disaster is a key element in developing an effective disaster plan for all materials, analog and digital. Thus, risk assessment informs disaster planning, because it focuses on how information derived from a risk assessment may affect the selection of mitigation strategies and preparation for disasters.

The Society of American Archivists maintains an excellent site devoted to disaster planning and prevention.[10] Many archives use SAA and other resources such as dPlan, which has a template that allows institutions of all sizes to develop customized plans.[11] Unfortunately, disaster recovery plans often exist as stand-alone documents created without the context of an overall program of risk management. While a number of staff members may have contributed to an archives' plan, and while the plan may have been regularly updated and tested, such plans may not be understood or applicable throughout the parent institution.

Successful disaster planning begins with the formation of a disaster planning team that should include the facility manager, a member of the IT department, a representative from preservation, collections managers, and representatives from other appropriate departments. It is important to make sure that one team member has the authority to activate a disaster recovery contractor's contract, initiate emergency response activities, sign contracts/work orders, and authorize expenditures, including permission for people to work overtime. Ad hoc members of the disaster team should include the spokesperson for the facility and representatives from human resources and legal counsel, along with a representative from the office of the institution's leadership. The team should meet regularly to write, and later, review the plan.

Another issue to consider in disaster planning is how risk-management principles are applied for analog and digital materials. For example, how will digital storage be addressed in disaster planning? For digital documents and records, all potential vulnerabilities identified in a risk assessment should be addressed in disaster planning. The disaster plan must also address the IT systems, including an inventory of hardware (e.g., servers, desktops, laptops, and wireless devices), software applications, data, and a list of vendors. Using standardized hardware will make it easy to replicate and reimage data in replacement hardware. The institution must make sure that copies of software are available to enable reinstallation of replacement equipment, and it must prioritize hardware and software restoration.[12] IT disaster recovery planning is an emerging field with a short history of response to disasters. Hence, the available information and research are provided mostly by businesses, not archives. Standards and best practices continue to be developed. One exception is the *Risk Management Guide for Information Technology Systems*, which was written for a variety of audiences.[13]

The emergence of cloud computing has also impacted disaster planning. In a sense, cloud computing transfers risk to external parties by using commercial vendors to outsource problems. Use of a commercial vendor for cloud storage, however, can itself constitute a potential vulnerability.

While cloud computing can be an open and flexible means of storing information, many users may share IT resources. Risk assessors may justifiably raise concerns about reliance on cloud storage without a practicable means for backing up data. What happens if the vendor relaxes its security procedures? What happens if the vendor goes out of business or is acquired by another company? Does the vendor have procedures in place for handling its own disasters?[14]

Once a plan is established and accepted by the institutional administration, the following seven considerations are critical to ongoing preparedness and should be assessed regularly.

1. Establish salvage priorities: compile a list of salvage priorities for each department, area, or office. On a floor plan, highlight the locations of items designated in the disaster plan as salvage priorities. Maintain copies of the floor plan in the disaster plan. Share the floor plans with first responders. Discussion questions include:
    - What is critical for the ongoing operations of the institution?
    - What can be replaced?
    - Would replacement cost be more/less than conservation?
2. Establish clear lines of authority as staff changes. Who is responsible for disaster planning and for implementing the plan of action? Who can sign contracts and authorize expenditures? Who will be responsible for disseminating information?
3. Develop and maintain a relationship with the fire department. Invite fire department personnel to regularly review the facility. Identify locations of rare materials; share salvage priorities and their locations; provide them with a floor plan.
4. Include the institution's essential records in the disaster-planning process. This is especially important when the institution's operations are centralized. Ensure that the IT department has a contingency plan to recover systems and essential records and to address IT security issues that might be compromised.
5. Maintain current information about all IT and systems and update the risk assessment for new and potential hazards.
6. Update and test the plan regularly.
    - Review, and if necessary, update it after a disaster or emergency.
    - Maintain multiple paper copies, in several locations. (If the plan is maintained only in electronic form, a power outage will eliminate access to the information.)
    - Require all key staffers to be familiar with the document.
7. Continually advocate for administrative support for disaster preparedness, mitigation, and response and recovery efforts.

Recovery and Reconstitution

Soon after a disaster, when the situation is stabilized, the long- and short-term activities of recovery begin. Reconstitution is the process of bringing back operations and services to predisaster levels, or to recognizing that a "new normal" exists. These efforts should be implemented concurrent with the response efforts, if possible. Recovery procedures are part of the disaster-planning process. For example, to facilitate a future recovery effort, the building's blueprints or architectural drawings might be designated as an essential record with copies safeguarded in several formats and locations. The same applies to personnel and payroll records, because access will facilitate recovery. Depending on the magnitude of the damage, determinations might be made about the gradual resumption of operations and services. A good reconstitution plan template is available on the FEMA website, and it can be customized for individual institutions.[15]

Recovery and reconstitution involve returning to normal operations and services. These activities are significant components of disaster planning, and procedures for accomplishing them remain key elements of planning for, and mitigating risk to, the institution. The essential records of the institution must always be the top priority in a recovery effort. These are not the holdings or collections, but rather the operational, organizational, financial, personnel, and legal records that the institution must maintain. These records must be identified, and their priority for recovery is an essential part of the disaster-planning and recovery strategies of any institution.

Staff Training and Responsibilities

It is not sufficient for only the disaster team to be privy to the disaster plan and response strategies. When a disaster strikes, it affects the entire institution and its staff. Therefore, every new employee orientation should include an overview of individual responsibilities relative to disaster planning and response. Periodic refresher courses should be available to staff. There should also be a regular training and drill schedule. The disaster plan and the IT disaster plan should be tested periodically to make sure they work. Afterward, the plans should be updated based on lessons learned.

Environmental Controls

Environmental controls are another method used by archivists to manage risks in their institutions. Beginning in the 1990s, the American Society of Heating, Refrigerating, and Air-Conditioning Engineers (ASHRAE) began incorporating risk-management principles into its recommendations for libraries, archives, and museums.[16]

For many years, climate experts offered simple advice: libraries, archives, and museums (LAMs) should maintain temperatures of 21 degrees C (70 F) and 50% RH. And it was widely accepted that even smaller and less-well-funded institutions could improve their building environments by focusing on the greatest risks to their collections: minimizing large temperature and humidity fluctuations, and preventing dampness.[17]

In recent years, conservators have been less likely to recommend rigid temperature and humidity levels, and institutions have begun to move away from set control points for temperature and RH to consider the building envelope, the local climate, and the specific needs of the collections. Chapter 9 will discuss the impact of climate control on the environment and the move toward more sustainable practices.

Risk management strategies influence current approaches based on scientific research, cost/benefit analysis, and sustainability to environmental monitoring. These strategies have also led to the development of a variety of risk-assessment tools by organizations such as the Canadian Conservation Institute and the Image Permanence Institute.[18]

Security

Security risks to collections involve such chronic problems as theft and vandalism. Effective strategies for combatting these problems include background checks on staff, security guards, security cameras, regular collection inspections, regular collection inventories, staff training, and securing the building. Constraints that handicap effective security programs include budget, staffing, policies, and ignorance. Managing organizational risk is critical to a successful security program. Implementing a program entails imposing controls, which must be implemented, assessed, and monitored. Preservation managers implementing security procedures must understand their institutions' approach to risk: acceptance, avoidance, limitation, or transference. No matter the approach, the security of collections and staff requires an organization-wide program.

Many strategies for developing effective security programs exist, and not all of them require a lot of money. Sidney E. Berger's chapter on security in *Rare Books and Special Collections* outlines some useful ways in which to address this issue.[19] In the security area, as with other risks to collections, effective solutions involve assessment, mitigation (when possible), and regular monitoring.

Security is often considered a technological issue. Indeed, IT security is a growing field that emphasizes controls for information systems. However, in archival settings, the security of both digital and analog collections deserves equal consideration. How can the invaluable assets of an institution's collections be protected, especially when the resources to safeguard them are modest? Can an institution afford not to protect its assets?

Information Systems and Digital Collections

Risk management must address the vulnerability of the systems in our institutions and associated threats to digital collections. These include hostile cyber or physical attacks, human errors of omission or commission, structural failures, and natural and human-caused disasters. The National Institute of Standards and Technology has published an extensive and daunting list of adversarial and nonadversarial threats. Adversarial threats include the illegal gathering of information online, the creation of attack tools such as phishing or counterfeiting websites, the installation of mechanisms such as malware, and forms of exploitation in mobile systems or cloud environments. Adversarial threats impact security; IT risk management must include security protocols. Nonadversarial threats include power outages, low performance of systems due to aging, and disc errors.[20]

If the archives is part of a large institution, risk management processes for digital collections and systems are likely in place, but probably remain outside the control or influence of archivists. Furthermore, many levels of bureaucracy may be in place relating to the management of information technology. At the same time, archivists must understand how their institution responds to and monitors risk. In a small archives, the archivist may be actively involved in risk-mitigation efforts for digital resources.

Risk management of digital collections should be integrated into preservation management. A survey of hardware and software along with an inventory of digital assets are useful in beginning to assess and monitor risk. Addressing risk will require acceptable answers to the following questions: Are resources adequate for migrating digital collections? Does the archives have policies in place? Does the institution favor open-source software? What is the interplay between proprietary versus nonproprietary systems? How often are systems upgraded? Who is responsible for licenses and licensing agreements? Is this a shared digital repository? Where is information about systems stored? If cloud storage is used, what are the vulnerabilities? The more documentation that exists about the collections and the environments in which they are accessed, the easier it will be to assess and mitigate risk.

Conclusion

This chapter has broadly examined risk management. We have shown how it can be used in disaster planning, preparedness, and recovery; environmental monitoring; security; and IT systems and digital collections. The old saying "failing to plan is planning to fail" remains a fitting reminder that risk management is an important aspect of preservation. As the authors of *Risk Management Guide for Information Technology Systems* accurately observe, "Every organization has a mission. In this digital era, as organizations use automated information technology (IT) systems to process their information for better support of their missions, risk management plays a critical role in protecting an organization's information assets, and therefore its mission, from IT-related risk."[21]

NOTES

Thanks to Shelby Sanett for her suggestions on early versions of this chapter.

1 Gary Stoneburner, Alice T. Goguen, and Alexis Ferrigan, *Risk Management Guide for Information Technology Systems*, NIST SP 800-30 (Washington, DC: National Institute of Standards & Technology, 2002), 1, http://delivery.acm.org/10.1145/2210000/2206240/sp800-30.pdf?ip=174.63.43.121&id=2206240&acc=OPEN&key=4D4702B0C3E38B35%2E4D4702B0C3E38B35%2E4D4702B0C3E38B35%2E6D218144511F3437&acm=1533156823_4bb66aed3d00f7cdf46449ed d8ce82bc.This version was replaced by a new one, Revision 1, in September 2012. However, some of the text removed from the 2002 version is useful, so it is cited here.

2 *Merriam-Webster* defines it as "a risk that can only result in a loss," https://www.merriam-webster.com/legal/pure%20risk, captured at https://perma.cc/4RLQ-PVDY.

3 Georges Dionne, *Risk Management: History, Definition and Critique*, CIRRELT-2013-56 (Montréal: Université de Montréal, September 2013), 2, https://www.cirrelt.ca/DocumentsTravail/CIRRELT-2013-56.pdf, captured at https://perma.cc/8GKW-E3KS. Dionne focuses on the financial industry and details the various hedges against risk. He points to successes and failures including the fall of Enron and the passage of Sarbanes-Oxley in 2002. But regulations and governance rules can be skirted, and he gives as an example the financial crisis that started in 2007.

4 Dionne, *Risk Management.*

5 Today, risk management is a profession that follows national standards and has its own journals.

6 The FEMA website contains information about applying for disaster assistance and for finding local resources, which are searchable by zip code. See fema.gov. Information about FIMA is on the FEMA website. The *Local Mitigation Planning Handbook* (March 2013) is available on the site. USGS: NIST runs a Computer Security Resource Center which includes information on risk management. See National Institute of Standards and Technology (NIST), nist.gov. The Software Engineering Institute (SEI) at Carnegie Mellon University has a comprehensive website that includes its many publications, podcasts, and blog posts, sei.cmu.edu.

7 Stoneburner et al., *Risk Management Guide for Information Technology Systems.*

8 Robert R. Waller, "Cultural Property Risk Analysis Model (CPRAM): A Very Brief Introduction to Key Concepts (Orléans, Ontario: Protect Heritage Corp., 2013) (handout from a workshop held at Trinity College, Dublin, November 18–19, 2013), https://www.iiconservation.org/sites/default/files/news/attachments/6652-iic-itcc_2015_notes_quick_summary_of_cpram_robert_waller.pdf, captured at https://perma.cc/C3K6-PPFW.

[9] For a description of seismic isolator technology, see Necdet Torunbalci, "Seismic Isolation and Energy Dissipating Systems in Earthquake Resistant Design" (Paper No. 3273 presented at 13th World Conference on Earthquake Engineering, Vancouver, BC, August 1–6, 2004), https://www.iitk.ac.in/nicee/wcee/article/13_3273.pdf, captured at https://perma.cc/U9FU-8W5K.

[10] Society of American Archivists, "Annotated Resources," https://www2.archivists.org/initiatives/mayday-saving-our-archives/annotated-resources, captured at https://perma.cc/XTF5-WF72.

[11] See dPlan: The Online Disaster-Planning Tool, "Welcome to dPlan," dplan.org. It is customizable.

[12] Department of Homeland Security, Ready, "IT Disaster Recovery Plan," https://www.ready.gov/business/implementation/IT, captured at https://perma.cc/RY9J-VNZF.

[13] Stoneburner et al., *Risk Management Guide for Information Technology Systems.*

[14] Xuan Zhang et al., "Information Security Risk Management Framework for the [*sic*] Cloud Computing Environments" (paper presented at the 10th IEEE International Conference on Computer and Information Technology, 2010), 1328–34, https://ieeexplore.ieee.org/document/5577860; and Robin Hastings, *Planning Cloud-Based Disaster Recovery for Digital Assets* (Santa Barbara, CA: Libraries Unlimited, 2017).

[15] See, for example, FEMA's "Reconstitution Template," https://www.fema.gov/media-library/assets/documents/86280.

[16] Stefan Michalski, "The Ideal Climate, Risk Management, the ASHRAE Chapter, Proofed Fluctuations, and toward a Full Risk Analysis Model" (paper presented at Experts Roundtable on Sustainable Climate Management Strategies, Tenerife, Spain: Getty Conservation Institute, April 2007), 2, http://www.getty.edu/conservation/our_projects/science/climate/paper_michalski.pdf, captured at https://perma.cc/V7SA-RPRE.

[17] Michalski, "The Ideal Climate," 5–6.

[18] For example, The Image Permanence Institute: eClimate Notebook, Dew Point Calculator; and Canadian Conservation Institute: Light Damage Calculator, Preventive Conservation Guidelines.

[19] Sidney E. Berger, *Rare Books and Special Collections* (Chicago: Neal Schuman, 2014), 187–210. See also the recent "Best Practice" issued by the Rare Books and Manuscripts Section of the Association of College and Research Libraries, of the American Library Association, and the Society of American Archivists, http://www.ala.org/acrl/standards/security_theft, captured at https://perma.cc/N7GA-639X.

[20] National Institute of Standards and Technology (NIST), Joint Task Force Transformation Initiative, *Guide for Conducting Risk Assessments: Information Security* NIST Special Publication 800-30, Revision 1 (US Department of Commerce, NIST, September 2012), 8–9; Appendixes E and F (this is the update of the 2002 version cited in note 2, by authors Stoneburner, Goguen, and Ferrigan), https://csrc.nist.gov/publications/detail/sp/800-30/rev-1/final.

[21] Stoneburner et al., *Risk Management Guide for Information Technology Systems*, 1.

Section III

The Ethics and Moral Implications of Contemporary Preservation Practices

9

Sustainable Preservation Practices

> Human Activity is putting such a strain on the natural functions of the Earth that the ability of the planet's ecosystems to sustain future generations can no longer be taken for granted.[1]
>
> —*United Nations Millennium Ecosystem Assessment, 2005*

> We stand now where two roads diverge. But unlike the roads in Robert Frost's familiar poem, they are not equally fair. The road we have long been traveling is deceptively easy, a smooth superhighway on which we progress with great speed, but at its end lies disaster. The other fork of the road—the one "less traveled by"—offers our last, our only chance to reach a destination that assures the preservation of our earth.[2]
>
> —*Rachel Carson, 1962*

Introduction

The impact of human activity on the environment has been a concern since the dawn of the industrial age. Prominent among early thinkers about this topic was John Ruskin, whose 1884 lecture "The Storm Cloud of the Nineteenth Century" warned of pollution's ill effects on nature and the built environment, as evidenced in the black clouds over parts of England during this period.[3] In the 1950s, Rachel Carson significantly advanced this debate in her seminal work, *Silent Spring*, by drawing attention to the environmental impacts of synthetic pesticides.[4] In 1987, the *Report of the World Commission on Environment and Development: Our Common Future* defined sustainable development for the first time and also set an international agenda for future action.[5] Motivated in part by this report, the United Nations Environmental Programme authorized the

Intergovernmental Panel on Climate Change and the Millennium Ecosystem Assessment to evaluate the most recent scientific, technical, and socioeconomic information relevant to our understanding of climate change and the degradation of the planet's environment. The four primary findings in the committee's 2005 final report are summarized here:

1. Over the past fifty years, humans have changed ecosystems more rapidly and extensively than in any comparable period of time in human history, largely to meet rapidly growing demands for food, fresh water, timber, fiber, and fuel. This has resulted in a substantial and largely irreversible loss in the diversity of life on earth.
2. The changes made to ecosystems contribute to substantial net gains in human well-being and economic development, but these gains have been achieved at growing costs in the form of the degradation of many ecosystem services and the exacerbation of poverty for some groups of people. These problems, unless addressed, will substantially diminish the benefits that future generations obtain from ecosystems.
3. The degradation of ecosystems could grow significantly worse during the first half of this century.
4. The challenge of reversing the degradation of ecosystems while meeting increasing demands for their resources will involve significant changes in policies, institutions, and practices that are not currently underway.[6]

In 2018, the International Panel on Climate Change (IPCC) issued a report, "Global Warming of 1.5°C," that evaluates the impact of global warming of 1.5°C above preindustrial levels and highlights the effects at various temperature levels that could be avoided by limiting global warming. The IPCC emerged from the Paris Agreement, which was adopted by 195 nations in December 2015 with the aim of strengthening the global response to the threat of climate change.[7] The report suggests that the planet is at a tipping point that may not be reversible if increases in global warming are not addressed in a timely manner.

The emerging evidence about climate change and global warming shows that museums, libraries, archives, and other institutions that care for the nation's cultural heritage will face complex challenges linked to changing climates, diminishing resources, and natural disasters. These uncertainties highlight the importance of creating sustainable preservation practices for collections. In response to these concerns, the major professional organizations and their allies have developed committees, such as American Library Association's Sustainability Roundtable, that exchange ideas about sustainable library practices. One of the first initiatives, sponsored by the University of Texas, Austin, in 2007, resulted in a symposium, *From Gray Areas to Green Areas: Developing Sustainable Practices in Preservation Environments*, which encouraged the integration of sustainable technologies with preservation activities.[8] Shortly after, in 2008, the International Federation of Library Associations and Institutions (IFLA) established its Sustainability, Environment, and Libraries Special Interest group to study the effects of climate change on libraries, increase awareness of environmental concerns, and promote environmentally friendly practices in libraries. Also in 2008, the International Institute for Conservation launched the first in a series of public roundtables titled Dialogues for the New Century, with an event specifically devoted to "Climate Change and Museum Collections."[9] In the same year, the American Institution for Conservation of Historic and Artistic Works (AIC) established the Green Task Force among American conservators to evaluate current awareness of sustainability. This group conducted a survey that confirms a strong commitment to green practices by conservation professionals.[10]

Efforts to promote sustainable conservation practices continue through AIC's current Sustainability Committee. Also in 2008, the American Alliance of Museums (AAM) established its PIC Green Committee to promote museum leadership in environmental sustainability. That same year, the National Endowment for the Humanities (NEH) and the Consiglio Nazionale delle Ricerche of Italy held a joint conference to explore sustainable strategies for the care of tangible cultural heritage. The panel focused on the impact of climate change on cultural heritage, methodologies for assessing the condition of collections and monuments, and strategic approaches to managing collection environments.[11] The conference proceedings supported the development of NEH's new grant program, Sustaining Cultural Heritage Collections, established in 2010, to assist cultural institutions with the complex challenge of preservation by supporting sustainable approaches that mitigate deterioration, prolong the useful life of collections, and support institutional resilience. The next year, the Society of American Archivists (SAA) took up the issue during its annual conference devoted to an exploration of "Sustainable Archives." In 2012, the United Nations Conference of Sustainable Development (commonly known as the *Rio+20*) took place in Brazil. The participants evaluated twenty years of activity in this area and published a report, *Sustainable Development for the 21st Century*, that set goals for the coming century. In 2013, AAM continued its focus on green practices, sponsoring a Summit on Sustainability Standards in Museums that resulted in published recommendations for shared museum standards.[12] That same year, National Digital Information Infrastructure and Preservation Program (NDIIP) partners addressed environmentally sustainable digital preservation strategies.[13] In 2015, the National Alliance for Digital Stewardship recommended an increase in interdisciplinary research and development on the environmental impact of digital collections.[14] In 2016, AAM devoted its annual meeting to the topic "Environmental Sustainability, Power, Influence and Responsibility."

This expanded international focus on the effects of climate change and sustainable practices has influenced how cultural institutions approach preservation. As stewards of our cultural heritage, archivists, librarians, and museum professionals are particularly adept at thinking about the long-term needs of the materials in their care and have much to contribute to this conversation. For example, archivist Heidi Abbey Moyer's "The Green Archivist" reviews the history of environmental, economic, and social sustainability across libraries, archives, and museums. Her research suggests that archives are not keeping pace with other professionals in addressing this concern.[15]

More recently, archivists Eira Tansey, Tara Mazurczyk, Nathan Piekielek, and Benjamin Goldman initiated important investigations into the long-term implications of climate change on archives. They observe that archivists must adapt their core archival practices, from appraisal and acquisition to outreach and advocacy, to make archives more resilient and less vulnerable to change that is beyond the control of any one institution.[16] In 2019, Keith L. Pendergrass, Walker Sampson, Tim Walsh, and Laura Alagna examined environmentally sustainable digital practices and the impact of the interconnected systems supporting information and communication technology (ICT).[17] They suggest several ways to reverse the negative environmental effects of the technology used for digital preservation. These recommendations include rethinking the emphasis on the digitization of large collections for access, as well as the current use of energy-intensive systems for access, storage, and delivery.[18] This work is an important beginning, but more archival research is needed in this area.

In an era of shrinking budgets and rising energy costs, it is imperative that the guardians of cultural heritage collections reconsider the impact of their traditional preservation practices and become more efficient and thoughtful stewards of the environment. Central to this conversation is the concept of *preventive conservation*, actions that avert or delay the deterioration of archival materials. These measures can reduce potential hazards through control of the environment and other conditions that damage collections. These efforts typically involve the use of passive measures to improve collection conditions that do not depend on mechanical processes, such as heating and cooling systems. Specifically, passive measures aim at reducing energy demand by increasing the use of natural heating, cooling, and lighting potentials, as well as reducing energy losses through the building envelope.

As archives, library, and museum staff endeavor to lower operation costs, achieve sustainability, and provide for preservation, they are confronted with an array of new strategies and standards that may include reducing energy consumption and limiting the electronic waste associated with managing digital collections. These efforts can lower costs and mitigate the impact of preservation practices on the environment, especially those that rely on stringent environmental controls and standards for storage conditions. As we have seen, the maintenance of digital formats, infrastructure, and networking services requires extensive technical, human, and financial support.

These new and growing challenges will certainly shape future preservation practices. And, for the first time in an SAA Fundamentals Series publication, this chapter considers the history and development of sustainable preservation. The research and subsequent recommendations presented here discuss how cultural institutions may meet the complex challenge of preserving large and diverse holdings for use by future generations. Responsible stewardship of our environment will require new approaches to managing energy consumption, rethinking the current approach to preservation, and anticipating and responding to natural and human-caused disasters.[19]

What Are Sustainable Preservation Strategies?

Establishing a commonly understood definition of "sustainability" and "sustainable development" is fundamental to the discussion of sustainable preservation. The *Oxford English Dictionary* defines "sustainable" as "able to be maintained at a certain rate or level," and also "conserving an ecological balance by avoiding depletion of natural resources."[20] For cultural heritage institutions, sustainability can also mean achieving long-term financial stability, or it can mean a long-term institutional commitment to "green" building practices and a reduction of the carbon footprint. The concept is also relevant with respect to the longevity of technology and information systems and their environmental impact, a topic in need of additional research, particularly in the context of archives and recordkeeping.[21] We will consider sustainability in the context of the commonly held definition for "sustainable development," established by the United Nations World Commission on Environment and Development in its 1987 report *Our Common Future:* "the ability to meet present needs, without compromising the ability of future generations to meet their own needs."[22]

When we apply the concept of sustainability to archival preservation practices, the focus is understandably on preservation strategies that balance effectiveness, cost, and environmental impact. This balance can contribute to an institution's financial health, reduce its fossil fuel consumption, and ensure that significant collections are well cared for and available for long-term access. At its root, the word "sustain" denotes that the activities will be lasting, and it implies that the sustaining resources will be in place for the future. In this sense, then, sustainability could be the institution's incentive to maintain long-term funding for preservation initiatives.

Just as the word "sustainability" has several meanings, a sustainable preservation strategy can take many forms depending on the nature of an institution, its collections, its resources, and its location and climate zone. Sustainable preservation requires several important considerations.[23] Those in charge of such programs must

- Establish preservation requirements based on the specific conditions and associated risks to collections, rather than on ideal and prescriptive targets, such as the long-held standards associated with temperature and humidity;
- Understand the characteristics and performance of the building in which collections are housed, the building envelope and systems, and how these factors influence the interior environment;
- Consider the impact of the local climate on managing the interior environment, including establishing relative humidity and temperature setpoints;
- Consider the potential effects of climate change on cultural property;
- Evaluate energy use, costs, and environmental impacts of existing and alternative preservation strategies;
- Prioritize passive, or nonmechanical, methods to improve and manage collection environments, optimizing the natural internal and external conditions when possible;
- Design and use mechanical systems, such as heating and cooling, only after implementing passive (nonmechanical) approaches for achieving desired conditions;
- Develop preservation solutions tailored to the capabilities of the organization and its staff and provide regular state-of-the-art training; and
- Evaluate and measure the effectiveness of alternate preservation strategies through the collection of data that goes beyond the simple monitoring of the environment by tracking energy use and costs.

The implementation of sustainable preservation may involve large-scale modifications to existing buildings and systems and the application of these strategies in the design of new buildings or spaces. Sustainable strategies require skills outside those of traditional archival practice and require the participation of collaborative teams with specialized expertise. This interdisciplinary activity may go beyond traditional workflows in most institutions. Often, at the outset of a building project, architects and facilities experts create designs for spaces and systems with little input from key stakeholders, such as collection managers or preservation staff. In the planning and design phase, the available budget, space requirements, and architectural guidelines that prioritize human comfort shape critical decisions. Planning for the needs of collections and storage often comes much later in the process when it is too late to address critical preservation concerns or incorporate sustainable practices. Thus, in planning for sustainable environments, an interdisciplinary team must be developed that includes staff knowledgeable about facilities, conservation, curation, education and interpretation, finance, and building design and construction. The team should be involved throughout the planning, design, construction, and approval of new preservation systems, building modifications, or construction. This collaboration should continue as new systems and facilities are evaluated and monitored. If appropriate expertise is not available through regular staffing, it may be necessary to use the services of expert consultants and contractors.[24] Of course, the personnel who will be working in and inhabiting the new space must contribute input from the very beginning of the planning.

A key element of sustainable preservation is disaster planning. This type of planning has become increasingly difficult as global warming and unpredictable weather patterns bring disasters to parts of the world where the weather was once relatively predictable. Projected climate trends indicate an increase in temperatures and temperature fluctuations, a surge in the frequency and intensity of rainfall, rising sea levels and coastal flooding, increasingly powerful tornadoes and hurricanes, and exceptional hot and cold spells.[25] Careful planning will allow archives to respond to the changing environment and remain functional after a disaster. "Resilience" is the ability to prepare and plan for, absorb, respond to, recover from, and adapt to emergencies and adverse events. As with all aspects of sustainable preservation, many measures should be considered as part of long-term, holistic, and interdisciplinary planning.

Such considerations might include[26]

- Performing a detailed risk assessment of collections, the building envelope, and the exterior environment
- Considering the effect of climate change on local or regional weather patterns
- Evaluating existing preventive measures, such as fire suppression, security, storage furniture, and pest control
- Identifying passive ways to control the interior environment to reduce reliance on mechanical and electrical systems
- Ensuring that sustainable measures consider current and future staff resources and abilities

In addition to human-created and natural disasters, a variety of factors threatens the sustainability of institutions and their ability to preserve their collections. Two of the primary challenges are the increasing costs to maintain facilities and digital systems and the rapidly changing technology needed to support digital collections. As Kevin Bradley of the National Library of Australia observes, digital sustainability entails a complex set of actions that can be understood as encompassing the wide range of issues and concerns that contribute to the longevity of digital information.[27] He notes that "it is not possible to preserve digital information without a sustainable organizational, economic, social, structural, and technical infrastructure."[28] Economic sustainability is the ability to marshal sufficient long-term resources to meet preservation objectives.[29] To be successful, the highest hierarchical levels in the organization must embrace these goals. Such support will require effective advocacy and marketing from archivists and librarians.

The Blue Ribbon Task Force on Sustainable Digital Preservation and Access was created in 2010 to explore the economic sustainability challenges of digital preservation and access. The project was funded by the National Science Foundation and the Andrew W. Mellon Foundation, in partnership with the Library of Congress, the Joint Information Systems Committee of the United

Kingdom, the Council on Library and Information Resources, and National Archives and Records Administration.

The final report of the task force, *Sustainable Economics for a Digital Planet: Ensuring Long-Term Access to Digital Information*, examines financial sustainability as a basic component of digital preservation. The authors identify three imperatives: articulating a compelling value proposition for preservation; offering clear incentives for the public interest in preservation; and defining roles and responsibilities among stakeholders for the allocation of resources throughout the digital life cycle.[30] Their recommendations emphasize human, technical, and financial resources as a framework for achieving financially sustainable digital preservation, and they ask their audience to consider three simple questions: What digital information should be preserved? Who should preserve it? And who should pay for it?

Sustainability also refers to the longevity of digital preservation programs. Several guidelines for managing digital preservation programs recommend the maintenance of specific actions over time. For example, the Digital Preservation Network and the UNESCO/PERSIST Content Task Force offer curriculum and advocacy that support the operational aspects of digital preservation.[31]

Considering new approaches to the management of technology and infrastructure is also critical in the development of sustainable preservation. As we have established throughout this book, digital preservation is the active management of digital content, driven by technological obsolescence and the need to migrate, emulate, or duplicate data. Rapid technological change necessitates the constant monitoring of data to guarantee access to, and the authenticity of, information over time. Sustainable digital preservation in archives is achieved with the audit and certification criteria used for trusted digital repositories[32] and formalized as an ISO standard, which many libraries and archives have implemented as common practice.[33] The application of the Open Archival Information Reference Model, along with advocacy and support for trusted institutional repositories, will be critical to establishing a common framework for sustainable digital preservation. Such efforts, however, contain substantial environmental costs. Toxic metals and plastics are used in the manufacture of computer hardware and systems. And, it is necessary to house and maintain the digital information produced with this technology in vast climate-controlled data centers often powered by fossil fuels. The carbon footprint and environmental impact of such facilities are significant and mounting. Research in this area will be critical in assisting archivists to develop sustainable approaches to digital preservation that are friendly to the atmosphere.

In 2013, the National Digital Information Infrastructure and Preservation Program (NDIIPP) convened a "Green Bytes" panel that examined how the cultural heritage professions might adopt innovations from the technology sector, including green approaches to managing data facilities.[34] The National Digital Stewardship Alliance has also examined environmental sustainability of digital collections and the operational costs of data centers.[35] Linda Tadic, a founding member and former president of the American Association of Moving Image Archivists, has also explored the connections between digital practices and sustainability. Her work evaluated the environmental impact of digitizing and disposing of large quantities of audio-video materials on obsolete and toxic media carriers and recommended a series of staff actions and technological changes that could reduce fossil fuel consumption and the negative impacts of e-waste, such as using cleaner energy sources, limiting digitization, and recycling.[36]

Research on Managing the Storage Environments for Preservation

As we have established, the rising cost of energy and the uncertainty of a changing environment will increasingly impact the ability of institutions to preserve their collections. For much of the latter half of the twentieth century, commonly accepted approaches to managing collections and their storage environments required the maintenance of stringent conditions, especially for temperature and humidity. These "ideal" conditions are achieved through the significant consumption of fossil fuels. Climate control became common practice in the 1970s, influenced by scientists such as Garry Thomson, whose work focused on the damaging effects of light, humidity, and air pollution on collections.[37] In hindsight, professionals were perhaps too rigid in implementing these guidelines. For most archival institutions, the commonly accepted ranges for temperature and humidity became standardized at 35% to 45% RH and 65 degrees F with fluctuation not to exceed 5% RH and 5 degrees for exhibition and storage spaces.[38] These widely accepted standards led collections managers to tighten their requirements for environmental conditions, especially with regard to humidity. As engineer and architect Michael Henry notes, when these measures were established, the cost of energy was comparatively cheap. This coincided with the emergence of sophisticated mechanical control systems and low-cost data-loggers that made the regulation of temperature and humidity possible and affordable.[39]

In 1996, architectural and conservation experts J. P. Brown and William Rose suggested that established environment standards were based on custom and practice rather than on well-designed research. They observed that as mechanical systems increased in sophistication, the general consensus grew that tighter and more stringent controls on the performance of mechanical systems and environmental control was necessary. For most institutions, any deviation from established environmental setpoints became a cause for alarm. Furthermore, the lack of quantitative research on the effects of environmental controls led to a "fundamental miscommunication between museum staff (conservators, curators) on the one hand, and mechanical engineers on the other."[40]

Marion Mecklenberg and his colleagues at the Smithsonian Museum Conservation Institute studied the history and development of environmental recommendations over the past several decades. Their research reveals that extremes of dryness and dampness pose the greatest risk of physical damage to collections. They also found that little scientific evidence supports the values and ranges in common use today, especially for relative humidity. They note that sharply increasing energy costs in museums directly correlate with stringent requirements for temperature and humidity.[41] As a result of this research, in 2004, the Smithsonian adopted new guidelines of 45% RH +/- 8% RH and 70°F +/- 4° for its facilities. The new guidelines allow for greater flexibility in temperature and humidity fluctuation in most collection and building spaces. These changes have resulted in dramatic energy cost savings (about 17% per year), less condensation on walls in the winter resulting in less wear and tear on the building envelope, and no known problems for any object, artifact, or collection.[42]

Many recent studies address sustainable preservation, the built environment, and cultural heritage institutions. For example, Sarah Brophy and Elizabeth Wylie address sustainable building design and operations in their work on green museums.[43] Richard Kershner has researched efficient preservation systems and collection storage that incorporate natural environmental conditions.[44]

Rebecca Meyer, Sarah Struble, and Phyllis Catskis review sustainable practices, such as minimal-impact building design, humidity and temperature controls, and energy efficiency.[45]

James Reilly of the Image Permanence Institute (IPI) has also researched sustainable preservation options and strategies. Originally interested in the preservation of image media, he subsequently investigated the effects of temperature and humidity on the decay of cultural heritage collections. His work explores the relationship between heating, ventilation, and air-conditioning (HVAC) systems and outdoor climate.[46] His research resulted in the development of environment-management tools and changes in practice designed to help preservation professionals document and understand the impact of the environment on collections over time. These include IPI's datalogger, the PEM2, and the eClimateNotebook, a data-management and analysis software program for the storage, organization, analysis, and sharing of temperature and humidity data.[47] IPI also developed the applied Preservation Metrics, computer-modeling algorithms that measure the effects of the storage environment on collections. These tools and analysis methods, based on laboratory research, field work, and data collection, encourage a management approach that balances the long-term preservation of collections with the efficient operation of mechanical systems. The company's recommendations include energy-saving approaches such as timed system shutdowns, modification of system setpoints on a seasonal schedule, light reduction in storage areas, and adjustment of air from outside the building to levels necessary to prevent the build-up of gases that can pose risks for collections.[48] More recently, Reilly partnered with researchers Peter Herzog and Jeremy Linden to prove that scheduled shutdowns of HVAC systems result in significant energy savings with no detrimental effect on collections.[49]

This section has evaluated the impact and value of commonly accepted environmental standards for the storage of analog collections, an area of significant research in the past several decades. The storage and delivery of digital content requires massive energy resources. These data centers and networks form the foundation of the internet and the basis for what is known as "cloud" storage. For many, mass digitization and storage in the cloud is the sustainable alternative to the traditional climate-controlled archival repository. However, these enormous data centers must also be kept constantly cool, using significant amounts of water and energy.

For example, Facebook reported using over 200 million gallons of fresh water to cool its data centers in 2015.[50] This represents a great loss of water, and, even if it is recycled, it must be re-cooled, thus requiring significant additional energy use. Establishing sustainable preservation environments is complicated because digitized content, whether born digital or digitized from analog sources, is growing at a rapid rate and will continue to grow worldwide for the foreseeable future. The application of energy-efficient approaches to digital storage and delivery centers is essential to developing sensible and sustainable digital preservation.

Passive Approaches to Preservation and Sustainable Climate Management

Based on current research, cultural heritage professionals are rethinking the rigid designs and performance requirements for buildings and systems. As James Reilly points out, "an optimal preservation environment is one that achieves the best preservation for collections, with the least consumption of energy, and that is sustainable over time."[51] This idea radically shifts our thinking about preservation practices and facilities standards with the added notion that no uniform or standard solution addresses all the preservation needs of every organization. Optimal conditions for one institution may not be ideal in a different context. In his presentation at the "Gray Areas to Green" conference, noted architect Michael Henry pointed out that preservation environments are a function of geography, the building, and the attributes or formats of the collections themselves and that no individual set of rigid requirements works for all environments or collections. Henry further observed that even in the same location or climate zone, differences exist in building construction and climate-control systems. To complicate matters further, even within the building envelope different types of spaces exist, such as reading rooms, processing areas, storage and exhibition areas, offices, and other secure or public spaces not devoted to collections. Within these discrete environments, each type of collection can have separate requirements for stability and preservation.[52] For example, photographs and audiovisual materials require more stringent environmental controls for long-term preservation than do other more stable formats, such as paper and most objects. Thus, the need for potentially multiple "optimal" environments for collections intensifies the problem. Clearly, institutions cannot support several HVAC systems for various areas in a single building. The best approach involves compromising with one optimally designed system that works adequately for all of these different collections.

Passive preservation strategies, also known as "preventative preservation," address the maintenance of storage areas, handling procedures, and the physical treatment (including digitization) of materials to make long-term access to them possible. Sustainability, in this context, focuses more on avoiding risk than on maintaining ideal conditions. Passive, or nonmechanical, measures, such as organizing collections by material type and placing only highly sensitive materials in tightly controlled environments, can improve conditions. Passive and active strategies, including digitization, maintain and ensure accessibility over time, though just how long digitization allows for long-term access remains under review.

Passive measures can improve collection conditions; however, no single solution exists for every situation, and strategies will depend on institutional type and capacity. But, several common approaches can be considered in most institutional situations:[53]

- Ensure that moisture is not entering the building due to improper site drainage, poorly functioning gutters, or problems with the building envelope.
- Assess the building conditions and features, and assign sensitive collections to spaces that are not inclined to fluctuations in environmental conditions.
- Use the buffering capacity of buildings, storage furniture, and document enclosures to moderate the effect of changes in relative humidity and temperature.
- Organize collections by material type, and specify tighter control of conditions only for collections that require them.
- Use microclimates and sealed-case environments for sensitive items rather than conditioning large spaces to meet the needs of a small number of objects.
- Reduce lighting, heating, cooling, and ventilation loads by storing collections centrally and separately from work spaces.

Some of these measures may not work for all facilities, and some may have significant initial costs. But the long-term savings should be worth the initial investment. And, for many institutions, the implementation of passive measures might eliminate or reduce the need for costly and inefficient mechanical systems. For others, employing more passive measures, often in combination with "active" mechanized systems, may enable institutions to achieve their preservation goals in cost-effective and energy-efficient ways. A growing literature on this topic exists, and some of the most important research in this area is currently being done in Europe. *Museum Microclimates*, the proceedings of a conference held in Denmark in 2007, offer an excellent overview of international research in the preservation of collections through manipulation of the environment. This conference included groundbreaking studies by Tim Padfield, Poul Klenz Larsen, James M. Reilly, Michael Højlund Rasmussen, and others on the long-term effect of energy-efficient climate control in archives and museums that deserve a wide American audience.[54] Jorgen Erik Christensen, a professor of civil engineering at the University of Denmark, has explored the intersection of climate and passive hygrothermal control of museum storage buildings.[55]

Applying passive approaches to digital preservation is uncharted territory. By its very nature, digital preservation is an active process requiring that digital resources be changed, transmitted, copied, and reconstituted in new contexts to ensure long-term durability.[56] A passive approach might include reconsideration of archival preservation theory and practice to align with current trends in archival appraisal, such as the MPLP approach suggested by Mark Greene and Dennis Meissner. At the center of this approach are decisions regarding what to save and what not to save, and accepting that the impermanence of some records is inevitable.[57] Archivist Ben Goldman, in writing about Greene's contributions to digital preservation theory, states that perhaps there is "no natural stability for digital objects, as much as we might want it." He says that archival theory should consider acceptable levels of mutability and notes that "lossiness" is a word with negative connotations in the digital preservation context, but perhaps loss can be a sustainability strategy if we account for the *environmental* impact of our work. He suggests that archivists can do this without sacrificing archival authenticity and integrity if they adapt digital preservation theory and practice to be transparent around a certain amount of acceptable loss.[58]

As we have emphasized, this constitutes a radical theoretical departure from past practices. Some digital archivists would no doubt argue that there is no such thing as passive preservation in a medium that is, by its very nature, active and constantly mutable. A book, left on a shelf, untouched, and in a good physical environment, may present a practicable preservation solution, because its rate of deterioration will be minimal. But electronic materials are not books. They deteriorate in ways that make access increasingly complex as technology changes over time. A floppy disc or even a thumb drive may retain its information for years or even possibly decades, but the hardware to access that information is evolving rapidly. It will remain to be seen if passive preservation is a practicable option for many digital texts. Nonetheless, the preservation of digital content will remain an active and labor-intensive process. Archivists must migrate files to different formats or create multiple derivatives as part of a digitization workflow, a practice that increases the volume of digital content to be maintained and monitored. Durable preservation and access require digital information to be stored on computer servers backed up to tape or remote data centers. In most instances, large numbers of servers are clustered into data farms that use large amounts of electricity to keep the machines running and accessible at all times. Despite popular opinion, mass digitization is not an environmentally friendly solution to energy-hungry preservation, and storage in the cloud is not a green alternative to the traditional climate-controlled archival repository.

Developing and Administering Sustainable Preservation Environments

Cost-efficient design and operation of buildings, storage areas, and information systems are critical elements in archival preservation. Using green or sustainable construction methods for storage facilities can yield good preservation outcomes. The Building Services Research and Information Association (BSRIA) defines "sustainable construction" as "the creation and responsible management of a healthy built environment based on resource efficient and ecological principles."[59] As digital technologist Sarah Kim asserts,

> Applying green construction to buildings means more than adding a couple of green elements to save on energy bills. Green construction reflects consideration of the impact of buildings on occupants and on the future of our global environment. Through building green archival structures, archives can respond to social concerns about climate change, global warming and harmoniously living with nature.[60]

Many federal, state, and local standards guide building practices that are informed by international standards. These include standards developed by the International Organization for Standardization (ISO), the National Information Standards Organization (NISO), and the National Archives. Archival facility experts Michele Pacifico and Thomas Wilsted contributed to the development of standards for archival buildings through their book, *Archives and Special Collections Facilities*. Their research emphasizes the need for an interdisciplinary team approach to designing sustainable archival structures. Their editor, Peter Wosh, observes that Pacifico and Wilsted intend their work as "a blueprint for a fully formed national standard."[61] And, in fact, the Society of American Archivists adopted their guidelines as a standard in 2009.

Several other relevant building and design standards exist for archival facilities. These incorporate sustainable strategies to varying degrees, but sustainability has emerged with increasing emphasis as they are updated:

- NARA 1571 is a policy directive from the National Archives and Records Administration establishing the internal NARA structural, environmental control, fire safety, preservation, and security standards for appropriate archival storage conditions in NARA archival facilities (2002), and the standard was supplemented by the Architectural and Design Standards for Presidential Libraries (2014).[62]
- ISO 11799:201, *Document Storage Requirements for Archive and Library Material*, specifies the characteristics of repositories used for the long-term storage of archival and library materials. It addresses the siting and construction and renovation of buildings, as well as the installation and equipment to be used within and around the facility. The standard applies to all archival and library materials in repositories where mixed media may be stored together with paper-based materials. It does not preclude the establishment of separate areas or compartments in individual repositories, where the environment can be controlled to create conditions suitable for the needs of specific archival materials, thereby encouraging cost-efficient energy use.[63]
- ASHRAE Chapter 23 applies to the application of HVAC systems for museums, libraries, and archives. The American Society of Heating, Refrigerating and Air-Conditioning

Engineers (ASHRAE), founded in 1894, is an international organization that provides technical and educational information regarding the use and control of a range of mechanical systems. The most commonly known publications produced by this professional association are the ASHRAE Handbooks, a four-volume publication that covers a wide range of standards for refrigeration and the application of HVAC systems, including standards relevant to the regulation of temperature and relative humidity in cultural institutions. In recent years, ASHRAE has begun to investigate sustainable approaches to heating, refrigeration, and cooling.[64] Currently, ASHRAE is updating its guidelines defined under Chapter 23 for museums, libraries, and archives. Observers anticipate that these changes will be flexible in ways that will allow for more sustainable approaches to climate control than in the past.

- PAS 198: 2012, *Specification for Managing Environmental Conditions for Cultural Collections*. PAS 198, developed in the United Kingdom, specifies requirements for environmental conditions for cultural collections in storage, on display, or on loan. The primary goal of this document involves minimizing the damage to items caused by inappropriate environmental conditions. PAS 198 differs from other specifications by its evidence-led approach that allows for risk-based decision-making in the management of environmental conditions and its emphasis on responsible use of energy.[65]

In addition to these standards and guidelines, several national and international sustainability standards focus specifically on the design and maintenance of green archival facilities. Many organizations concerned with sustainability have rating systems that offer assessment and grant credentials for those seeking to implement sustainable best practices. Most rate these practices across a continuum that considers social, economic, and environmental measurements. These ratings and assessment measures also address building design and operation. One of the best-known leaders in the development and administration of sustainable building practices is the US Green Building Council that administers the Leadership in Energy and Environmental Design program (LEED), the most widely used green-building rating system in the world. This system assesses the design, construction, operation, and maintenance of green buildings, homes, and neighborhoods, and assists building owners and managers in using resources efficiently while limiting environmental impact.[66]

Institutions of higher education also provide leadership in sustainable practices. The Association of University Leaders for a Sustainable Future (ULSF) promotes sustainable practices in teaching, research, operations, and outreach at colleges and universities worldwide through publications, research, and assessment. ULSF is the secretariat for signatories of the Talloires Declaration. Created in 1990 at an international conference in Talloires, France, this declaration is the first official statement made by university presidents, chancellors, and rectors of a commitment to environmental sustainability. It has been signed by over 500 university leaders in more than fifty countries.[67]

The Association for the Advancement of Sustainability in Higher Education (AASHE) sponsors the Sustainability Tracking, Assessment and Rating System (STARS), a self-reporting framework for colleges and universities to measure their sustainability performance. The rating system is based on performance indicators and criteria organized into four categories: Academics, Engagement, Operations, and Planning and Administration, with building designs and systems comprising an essential measuring element.[68]

The museum and conservation fields have also provided foundational work in the development of sustainable standards. Some of the most important include the joint International Council of Museums and the International Institute for Conservation Declaration on Environmental Guidelines, whose efforts have united the conservation profession behind environmental guidelines for the sustainable management of collections and conditions. The joint recommendations, some of the most forward-thinking in the field, are summarized here.[69]

- Museum sustainability is much broader than the discussion on environmental standards and needs to be an underlying criterion of future principles.
- Museums and other collecting institutions should reduce their environmental impact by reducing their energy consumption and use alternative renewable energy sources.
- Care of collections should be achieved in a way that, if possible, does not assume the requirement for air conditioning (HVAC). Passive methods, simple technology that is easy to maintain, air circulation, and lower energy solutions should be considered.
- Risk management should be embedded in museum management.

A reasonable strategy for sustainable digital preservation is not yet a reality. However, Keith Pendergrass and his colleagues undertook an exploration of environmentally sustainable digital preservation strategies that offer a common-sense approach to reducing the environmental impact of digital preservation through the use of technology. The authors suggest that organizations must "reduce the amount of digital content they produce while reducing the resource-intensity of its storage and delivery." They suggest that institutions implement new systems or change existing ones, alter scheduling so that high-energy and high-bandwidth tasks occur at off-peak times, and switch to clean-energy sources. They call for a "paradigm shift" in how archivists approach their work. They suggest that the environmental impact of preservation should inform the appraisal process, and archivists must accept that a certain amount of loss is inevitable. And, finally, they suggest that cultural heritage institutions should reexamine the justification for mass digitization, implement simplified on-demand digitization strategies, adjust storage technologies for frequency of access, and ensure timely rather than immediate delivery.[70]

Conclusion

Collecting institutions face a unique challenge. They must provide appropriate stewardship for the resources in their care; however, the cost of energy and the burden of maintaining sustainable information systems can often drain limited budgets and negatively impact the long-term capacity to care for materials. Merely allowing collections to deteriorate in poor environmental conditions, or allowing them to disappear due to obsolete technology would result in unacceptable loss. For this reason, when archivists address the long-term preservation of digital or analog materials, it is necessary to implement sustainable practices that account for challenging economic, technological, and environmental realities.[71]

Thus, environmental sustainability and climate change are among the most critical issues of our time. Former secretary of the Smithsonian G. Wayne Clough states, "We take our role as environmental stewards seriously, making sustainability a centerpiece of our preservation strategy. Sustainable approaches not only minimize the human impact of our activities on our environment but also reduce long-term costs and allow better use of scarce funds to serve collection needs."[72]

As heritage professionals, archivists should engage in preservation efforts that do not contribute to environmental problems or that will affect the ability of future generations to use the materials they are charged with preserving.

Yet, as archivist Mark Wolfe has pointed out, green technologies alone are not enough to ensure sustainability. Energy-efficient and cost-saving measures are necessary because of shrinking budgets and climate change, but transitioning to energy efficiency and environmental sustainability cannot be achieved simply through improvements to infrastructure. Archival theory and practice must also address the sustainability of repositories and collections.[73]

In addressing sustainability, archivists largely rely on research and standards that have emerged from allied professions, particularly in articulating and implementing passive approaches to storage and collections management. Additional research and development specific to sustainable archival practice is needed. This research must focus on different types of archival institutions that maintain both analog and digital materials. This calls for an interdisciplinary approach that draws on a broad range of expertise from both inside and outside the profession.

Climate change has accelerated the discussion of sustainable practices with significant implications for archival preservation. As stewards of our cultural heritage, archivists are particularly adept at thinking about long-term preservation. They have long understood that effective and sustainable preservation must be informed by the nature of an institution and its collections. As awareness of how traditional archival practices impact the environment and as energy prices escalate, the profession must consider new standards and practices. As Mark Wolfe notes, ultimately, the environmental sustainability of our cultural heritage is as much behavioral as it is technological. Until economic incentives and national policies and mandates favor choosing environmentally friendly technologies, archival institutions are unlikely to make deep long-term commitments to these choices.[74] All of these considerations are critical to long-term sustainability. Preservation, like other challenges, is a balancing act, weighing the needs and desires of the present day with those of the future.

NOTES

1 United Nations Millennium Ecosystem Assessment, 2005, http://www.sustainablescale.org/ConceptualFramework/UnderstandingScale/MeasuringScale/MillenniumEcosystemAssessment.aspx.

2 Rachel Carson, *Silent Spring* (Boston: Houghton Mifflin; Cambridge, MA: Riverside Press, 1962), 244.

3 Brian J. Day, "The Moral Intuition of Ruskin's 'Storm-Cloud,'" *Studies in English Literature, 1500–1900* 45, no. 4 (2005): 917–33. See also "Sustainable Preservation," chapter 9 in Michèle Valerie Cloonan, *The Monumental Challenge of Preservation: The Past in a Volatile World* (Cambridge, MA: MIT Press, 2018), 155–73.

4 Rachel Carson, *Silent Spring.*

5 United Nations, World Commission on Environment and Development, *Our Common Future* (Oxford, UK: Oxford University Press, 1987). Also known as the Brundtland Report, this document defines sustainable development as "development that meets the needs of the present without compromising the ability of future generations to meet their own needs."

6 *Ecosystems and Human Well-being: Synthesis,* Millennium Ecosystem Assessment (Washington, DC: Inland Press, 2005), 1, https://www.millenniumassessment.org/documents/document.356.aspx.pdf, captured at https://perma.cc/JY7L-UCE3.

7 Valerie Masson-Delmotte et al., eds., Intergovernmental Panel on Climate Change, "Global warming of 1.5°C," (Switzerland: IPCC, 2018), https://report.ipcc.ch/sr15/pdf/sr15_spm_final.pdf, captured at https://perma.cc/347F-BAJT.

8 *From Gray Areas to Green Areas: Developing Sustainable Practices in Preservation Environments Symposium Proceedings* (Austin: University of Texas, November 2007), https://www.ischool.utexas.edu/kilgarlin/gaga/proceedings.html, captured at https://perma.cc/L9U7-FWAZ.

[9] International Institute for Conservation of Historic and Artistic Works, *Climate Change and Museum Collections*, 3rd IIC Roundtable (London, UK: National Gallery of Art, September 17, 2008), http://www.iiconservation.org/docs/IIC_climate_change_transcript.pdf, captured at https://perma.cc/3FKN-HTLN.

[10] Patricia Silence, *Green Task Force Survey Summary Report* (presented at the Issue Session of AIC's 37th Annual Meeting, May 21, 2009, Los Angeles, CA), https://www.conservation-us.org/our-organizations/association-(aic)/initiatives/surveys/green-task-force#.WpHEtrOIaT8.

[11] National Endowment for the Humanities (NEH) and the Consiglio Nazionale delle Ricerche (CNR), *Sustainable Cultural Heritage Conference Proceedings* (Washington, DC: NEH, May 11, 2009), https://www.neh.gov/files/divisions/preservation/neh_cnr_conference_may_2009.pdf. See also NEH Staff, *NEH Sustainable Preservation Strategies* (blog), National Endowment for the Humanities (July 12, 2012), https://www.neh.gov/divisions/preservation/resource/sustainable-preservation-strategies, captured at https://perma.cc/P8FS-C4YJ.

[12] American Alliance of Museums (AAM), *Museums, Environmental Sustainability and Our Future: A Call to Action from the Summit on Sustainability Standards in Museums 2013* (Washington, DC: AAM, 2013) ww2.aam-us.org/docs/default-source/professional-networks/picgreenwhitepaperfinal.pdf, captured at https://perma.cc/RU6J-UWDP.

[13] David Rosenthal, Kris Carpenter, and Krishna Kant, "Green Bytes: Sustainable Approaches to Digital Stewardship" (Plenary, National Digital Information Infrastructure Meeting, Alexandria, VA, July, 2013), http://www.digitalpreservation.gov/meetings/documents/ndiipp13/Green_Bytes_Abstract_FINAL.pdf, captured athttps://perma.cc/938U-T59D.

[14] National Digital Stewardship Alliance, *2015 National Agenda for Digital Stewardship* (September 2014), http://www.digitalpreservation.gov/documents/2015NationalAgenda.pdf, captured at https://perma.cc/EA6S-DX2U.

[15] Heidi N. Abbey (now Heidi Abbey Moyer), "The Green Archivist: A Primer for Adopting Affordable, Environmentally Sustainable, and Socially Responsible Archival Management Practices," *Archival Issues* 34, no. 2 (2012): 91–115, https://www.jstor.org/stable/i40081871.

[16] Eira Tansey, "Archival Adaptation to Climate Change," *Sustainability: Science, Practice, & Policy* 11, no. 2 (2015): 45–56, https://doi.org/10.1080/15487733.2015.11908146; and Tara Mazurczyk, Nathan Piekielek, Eira Tansey, and Ben Goldman, "American Archives and Climate Change: Risks and Adaptation," *Climate Risk Management* 20 (2018): 111–25, https://doi.org/10.1016/j.crm.2018.03.005.

[17] Keith L. Pendergrass, Walker Sampson, Tim Walsh, and Laura Alagna, "Toward Environmentally Sustainable Digital Preservation," *American Archivist* 82, no. 1 (2019), 165–206, https://doi.org/10.17723/0360-9081-82.1.165.

[18] Pendergrass et al., "Toward Environmentally Sustainable Digital Preservation," 195.

[19] For an overview of publications about sustainability in LAMs, see Rebecca Meyer, Shannon Struble, and Phyllis Catsikis, "Sustainability: A Review," in *Preserving Our Heritage: Perspectives from Antiquity to the Digital Age*, ed. Michèle Valerie Cloonan (Chicago: Neal-Schuman/American Library Association, 2015), 637–56.

[20] *Oxford English Dictionary*, s.v. "sustainable" (Oxford: Oxford University Press, 2013).

[21] See Tracy A. Jenkins, Jane Webster, and Lindsay McShane, "An Agenda for 'Green' Information Technology and Systems Research," *Information and Organization* 21, no. 1 (2011): 17–40, https://doi.org/10.1016/j.infoandorg.2010.09.003, and *Sustainability of Scholarly Information* (London, UK: Facet Publishing, 2014).

[22] United Nations, World Commission on Environment and Development, *Our Common Future* (Oxford, UK: Oxford University Press, 1987).

[23] These considerations are modified from National Endowment for the Humanities, Division of Preservation and Access, "Sustaining Cultural Heritage Collections Guidelines, Frequently Asked Questions" (2018), https://www.neh.gov/sites/default/files/inline-files/sustaining-cultural-.heritage-faqs%2C%202019.pdf.

[24] Michael C. Henry, "What Will the Cultural Record Say About Us? The Stewardship of Culture and the Mandate for Environmental Sustainability," in *From Gray Areas to Green Areas: Developing Sustainable Practices in Preservation Environments.*

[25] Henry, "What Will the Cultural Record Say About Us?," in *From Gray Areas to Green Areas*, 1.

[26] These considerations are modified from "Sustaining Cultural Heritage Collections Guidelines, Frequently Asked Questions."

[27] Kevin Bradley, "Defining Digital Sustainability," *Library Trends* 56, no. 1 (2007): 148–63.

[28] Bradley, "Defining Digital Sustainability," 157.

[29] Brian Lavoie and Lorcan Dempsey, "Thirteen Ways of Looking at . . . Digital Preservation," *D-Lib Magazine* 10, nos. 7–8 (2004), 20, http://www.dlib.org/dlib/july04/lavoie/07lavoie.html20.

[30] Blue Ribbon Task Force on Sustainable Digital Preservation and Access, *Sustainable Economics for a Digital Planet: Ensuring Long Term Access to Digital Information* (February 2010), http://blueribbontaskforce.sdsc.edu/biblio/BRTF_Final_Report.pdf, captured at https://perma.cc/76P5-NJXF. See also Edward M. Corrado and Heather Moulaison Sandy, *Digital Preservation for Libraries, Archives, and Museums,* 2nd ed. (Lanham, MD: Rowman & Littlefield, 2017), 124.

[31] Digital Preservation Network, "Digital Preservation Workflow Curriculum" (March 2017), https://www.weareavp.com/wp-content/uploads/2017/10/Digital-Preservation-Workshop-Curriculum-%E2%80%94-2017-03-08.pdf, captured at https://perma.cc/PPT7-N34P; and UNESCO/PERSIST Content Task Force, *Guidelines for the Selection of Digital Heritage for Long-term Preservation* (March 2016), https://unescopersist.files.wordpress.com/2017/02/persist-content-guidelines

_en.pdf, captured at https://perma.cc/SU7R-PYNW. UNESCO.PERSIST project is a partnership with the International Council on Archives (ICA) and the International Federation of Library Associations and Institutions (IFLA) to create practical solutions in the area of sustainable digital preservation.

32 Robin Dale and Bruce Ambacher, "Trustworthy Repositories Audit & Certification (TRAC): Criteria and Checklist" (OCLC Online Computer Library Center, 2007), https://www.crl.edu/sites/default/files/d6/attachments/pages/trac_0.pdf, captured at https://perma.cc/QU3D-4VY7.

33 Center for Research Libraries, "ISO 16363 / TDR," https://www.crl.edu/archiving- preservation/digital-archives/metrics-assessing-and-certifying/iso16363, captured at https://perma.cc/U8MC-6LXG.

34 Rosenthal et al., "Green Bytes."

35 National Digital Stewardship Alliance (NDSA), "Levels of Digital Preservation," http://ndsa.org/activities/levels-of-digital-preservation, captured at https://perma.cc/J78D-KD2F.

36 Linda Tadic, "The Environmental Impact of Digital Preservation" (presentation, Association of Moving Image Archivists conference, Portland, OR, November 18–21, 2015, updated 2018), https://www.digitalbedrock.com/resources-2, captured at https://perma.cc/242T-EW3V.

37 Garry Thomson, *Museum Environment Control Preservation*, 2nd ed., Butterworth- Heinemann Series on Conservation and Museology (Oxford, UK: Butterworth-Heinemann, 1986).

38 Mary Lynn Ritzenthaler, *Preserving Archives & Manuscripts*, 2nd ed. (Chicago: Society of American Archivists, 2010), 115.

39 Henry, "What Will the Cultural Record Say About Us?," in *From Gray Areas to Green Areas*, 3.

40 J. P. Brown and William B. Rose, "Humidity and Moisture in Historic Buildings: The Origins of Building and Object Conservation," *APT Bulletin* 27, no. 3 (1996): 19.

41 Marion Mecklenburg, *Determining the Acceptable Ranges of Relative Humidity and Temperature in Museums and Galleries: Part 1, Structural Response to Relative Humidity* (Washington, DC: Smithsonian Museum Conservation Institute, 2007), https://www.si.edu/mci/downloads/reports/Mecklenburg-Part1-RH.pdf, captured at https://perma.cc/QJ8D-WH34; and Mecklenberg, *Determining the Acceptable Ranges of Relative Humidity and Temperature in Museums and Galleries, Part 2, Structural Response to Temperature*, https://www.si.edu/mci/downloads/reports/Mecklenburg-Part2-Temp.pdf, captured at https://perma.cc/BQ55-JVEC. See also David Erhardt and Marion Mecklenburg, "Relative Humidity Re-examined," *Studies in Conservation* 39, Issue supplement 2 (1994): 32–38, https://doi.org/10.1179/sic.1994.39.Supplement-2.32; David Erhardt, Charles S. Tumosa, and Marion F. Mecklenburg, "Applying Science to the Question of Museum Climate," in *Museum Microclimates: Contributions to the Conference in Copenhagen*, ed. Tim Padfield and Karen Borchersen (Copenhagen: National Museum of Denmark, November 19–23, 2007), 11–19, https://www.conservationphysics.org/mm/musmic/musmic150.pdf, captured at https://perma.cc/J34X-SYWR; and David John Artigas, "A Comparison of the Efficacy and Costs of Different Approaches to Climate Management in Historic Buildings and Museums" (master's thesis, University of Pennsylvania, January 2007), http://repository.upenn.edu/hp_theses/63.

42 Smithsonian Museum Conservation Institute, "Culmination of 20 Years of Green, Energy Savings Research," https://www.si.edu/mci/english/research/consulting/MuseumEnvironment.html, captured at https://perma.cc/VD5U-MHJZ.

43 Sarah Brophy and Elizabeth Wylie, *The Green Museum: A Primer on Environmental Practice* (Latham, MD: AltaMira Press, 2008).

44 Richard Kershner, "Providing Safe and Practical Environments for Cultural Property in Historic Buildings—and Beyond" (paper presented at Experts Roundtable on Sustainable Climate Management Strategies, Tenerife, Spain, April 2007), https://www.getty.edu/conservation/our_projects/science/climate/paper_kerschner.pdf, captured at https://perma.cc/UD2B-UKLP.

45 Meyer et al., "Sustainability: A Review," in *Preserving Our Heritage*, 637–56.

46 Image Permanence Institute, *Guide to Sustainable Preservation Practices for Managing Storage Environments* (Rochester, NY: Rochester Institute of Technology, 2012), 96–137. See also eClimateNotebook, "Fundamentals: Preservation Metrics," https://www.eclimatenotebook.com/fundamentals_nl.php, captured at https://perma.cc/7YQZ-BJ7D.

47 For an overview of IPI tools for environmental management, see Image Permanence Institute, "Collections Environmental Monitoring," https://www.imagepermanenceinstitute.org/environmental/overview, captured at https://perma.cc/TE9D-NTCB.

48 Image Permanence Institute, *Guide to Sustainable Preservation Practices for Managing Storage Environments*, 96–137.

49 Jeremy Linden, James Reilly, and Peter Herzog, "Research on Energy Savings Opportunities in University Libraries," *Library Hi Tech* 30, no. 3 (2012): 384–96, DOI:10.1108/07378831211266537.

50 Facebook, "Our Footprint" (2015), https://sustainability.fb.com/our-footprint.

51 Image Permanence Institute, *Guide to Sustainable Preservation Practices for Managing Storage Environments*, 1.

52 Henry, *"What Will the Cultural Record Say About Us?,"* in *From Gray Areas to Green Areas*, 3.

53 These considerations are modified from National Endowment for the Humanities, "Sustaining Cultural Heritage Collections Guidelines, Frequently Asked Questions."

54 Tim Padfield and Karen Borchersen, eds., *Museum Microclimates: Contributions to the Copenhagen Conference* (Copenhagen: National Museum of Denmark, November 19–23, 2007), https://www.conservationphysics.org/mm/musmic/musmic150.pdf, captured at https://perma.cc/J34X-SYWR.

55 Jorgen Eric Christensen and Hans Janssen, "Passive Hygrothermal Control of a Museum Storage Building in Vejle," in *Proceedings of Building Simulation 2010: 12th Conference of International Building Performance Simulation Association*, Report R-220 (Kongens Lyngens, DK: November 2010), 7, http://orbit.dtu.dk/en/publications/passive- hygrothermal-control-of-a-museum-storage-building-in-vejle(1f014358-53e5-4697-8109- 2550844623a6).html, captured at https://perma.cc/G9QH-LV8N.

56 Heather Marie MacNeil and Bonnie Mak, "Constructions of Authenticity," *Library Trends* 56, no. 1 (2007): 26–52, https://doi.org/10.1353/lib.2007.0054.

57 Mark Greene, "The Power of Archives: Archivists' Values and Value in the Postmodern Age," *American Archivist* 72, no. 1 (2009): 13–41, https://doi.org/10.17723/aarc.72.1.k0322x0p38v44l53.

58 Ben Goldman, "It's Not Easy Being Green(e): Digital Preservation in the Age of Climate Change," in *Archival Values: Essays in Honor of Mark Greene,* ed. Christine Weideman and Mary A. Caldera (Chicago: Society of American Archivists, 2019), 182.

59 Building Services Research and Information Association (BSRIA) is a consultancy and research organization for construction industries based in the United Kingdom.

60 Sarah Kim, "Green Archives: Applications of Green Construction to Archival Facilities," *The Primary Source* 28, no. 1 (2009), https://doi.org/10.18785/ps.2801.03.

61 Peter Wosh, in *Archives and Special Collections Facilities: Guidelines for Archivists, Librarians, Architects and Engineers,* ed. Michele F. Pacifico and Thomas R. Wilsted (Chicago: Society of American Archivists, 2009), viii.

62 National Archives and Records Administration (NARA), "Digitization at the National Archives: Relevant NARA Guidance," https://www.archives.gov/digitization/guidance, captured at https://perma.cc/3PHE-KAPD. NARA's recommended setpoints for temperature and relative humidity currently do not take into account recent research on sustainable practices.

63 International Organization for Standardization (ISO), *Standards Catalog*, "ISO 11799:2015 Document Storage Requirements for Archive and Library Materials" (2015), https://www.iso.org/standard/63810.html, captured at https://perma.cc/8KT4-YCVS.

64 The American Society of Heating, Refrigerating and Air-Conditioning Engineers (ASHRAE), *ASHRAE Handbook Online*, "Industrial Applications for Museums, Galleries, Libraries and Archives" (Atlanta: ASHRAE, 2016), Chapter 23, https://www.ashrae.org/technical-resources/ashrae-handbook, captured at https://perma.cc/5EX9-BLSB.

65 British Standards Institution (BSI), PAS 198: *2012 Specification for Managing Environmental Conditions for Cultural Collections* (London: BSI Standards Limited, 2012). See also "International Federation of Library Associations and Institutions (IFLA), "Energy Savings and Preservation in Libraries and Archives," *International Preservation News*, no. 55 (December 2011), http://www.ifla.org/files/assets/pac/ipn/IPN%2055%20web%206%20megas.pdf, captured at https://perma.cc/823B-JZQD.

66 United States Green Building Council, "LEED Rating System," https://new.usgbc.org/leed.

67 Association of University Leaders for a Sustainable Future (ULSF), "Talloires Declaration" (1990), http://ulsf.org/talloires-declaration, captured at https://perma.cc/8PHB-BBBW.

68 The Association for the Advancement of Sustainability in Higher Education (AASHE) sponsors the Sustainability Tracking, Assessment & Rating System (STARS), "About STARS," https://stars.aashe.org/pages/about/stars-overview.html, captured at https://perma.cc/W4KU-XFXQ.

69 International Council of Museums and the Institute for Conservation Declaration on Environmental Guidelines, "Declaration on Environmental Guidelines" (2014), http://www.icom-cc.org/332/-icom-cc-documents/declaration-on-environmental-guidelines/#.WsJooNT4-T8, https://perma.cc/4CLG-WN7F.

70 Pendergrass et al., "Toward Environmentally Sustainable Digital Preservation,"177–94.

71 Image Permanence Institute, *Guide to Sustainable Preservation Practices for Managing Storage Environments* (Rochester, NY: Rochester Institute of Technology, 2012), 2.

72 G. Wayne Clough, "Letter from the Secretary" in *Proceedings of the Smithsonian Institution Summit on the Museum Preservation Environment,* ed. Sarah Stauderman and William G. Tompkins (Washington, DC: Smithsonian Institution Scholarly Press, 2016), v.

73 Mark Wolfe, "Beyond 'Green Buildings': Exploring the Effects of Jevons' Paradox on the Sustainability of Archival Practices," *Archival Science* 12, no. 1 (2012), 35, 47, https://doi.org/10.1007/s10502-011-9143-4.

74 Wolfe, "Beyond 'Green Buildings,'" 50.

10

The Right to Preserve: Who Decides?

> When we try to pick anything out by itself, we find that it is hitched to everything else in the universe.
>
> —*John Muir, 1911*[1]

Introduction

Archivists preserve the past. This critical work depends on relationships with the people, institutions, and communities that create documents essential to understanding the history and meaning of our cultural heritage. Archivists build the cultural record through selection and appraisal. These decisions shape the documentation preserved for future generations.

Thus, through their collecting efforts, archivists have enormous power to define and refine the context for cultural memory. As archivist Elisabeth Kaplan presciently observed two decades ago, "the archival record does not just happen. It is created by individuals and organizations, and used, in turn, to support their values and missions, all of which comprise a practice that is certainly not politically and culturally neutral."[2]

Thus, archivists may control future interpretations of the past by privileging certain historical and personal narratives while marginalizing others. The cultural record is often biased toward the activities and interests of the wealthy and powerful, leaving significant portions of society either undocumented or underdocumented, and potentially lost to history. To address this inequity, archivists have become increasingly inclusive in the selection and appraisal of materials. In fact, a good deal of recent archival literature focuses on the power of archives to shape public memory, and an emerging professional imperative encourages all archivists to collect and document the records of marginalized and underrepresented communities.[3] As democratic principles evolve and the world grows increasingly interconnected, the archivist's desire to leave a representative and inclusive record to future generations is becoming a commonly accepted value. It constitutes a natural outcome of a broader scholarly reevaluation of the meaning and power of the archival record. As archivists reconsider their role in selection, documentation, acquisition, and appraisal, they must also rethink their prerogative to preserve. Preservation has been viewed as a central archival ethic that serves the public good.[4] The acquisition of archival materials is linked to an ethical obligation to make them permanently accessible. However, some groups view this claim to ownership of the archival record as theft. Others demand control over the interpretation of their heritage and legacy through repatriation, shared stewardship, or community-based archiving. Still others demand the right to be forgotten. In fact, in 2014, Google claimed it had received more than 650,000 requests to remove certain websites from its search results since a European court ordered the company to allow Europeans the "right to be forgotten."[5]

Documenting society on equitable and inclusive terms requires that archivists build trusting and respectful relationships with many constituencies. It also requires rethinking the ethics of long-term stewardship. This chapter will consider a variety of ethical problems in archival preservation with respect to underrepresented and marginalized communities.

Cultural Ownership and Memory

Archives are collected and maintained to ensure that important documents are preserved, used, and made accessible over time. Collecting historical materials, though, is not the same as preserving historical memory. Archives exist so that society can interpret and reinterpret the impact of human activities. Archived documents are stable and trustworthy sources of information over time, but memory is fluid. Clearly, only a small fraction of the human record can be collected. Due to the vast abundance of information, the decision to preserve specific documents is a statement of what society values at a particular point in time, as well as a statement about what collectors value. Over fifty years ago, University of Wisconsin archivist F. Gerald Ham suggested in his influential article "The Archival Edge" that our most important and intellectually demanding task as archivists is to make informed selections of information that will provide the future with a representative record of human experience. And, he asked, "Why must we do it so badly?"[6] Ham understood that the massive societal changes of his times, coupled with innovations in information technology, would have a huge impact on the nature of the archival record and the archival profession. He said that "the process of institutionalizing and nationalizing decision-making . . . has had a profound impact on documentation, making the archives of associations, pressure groups, protest organizations, and institutions of all sorts relatively more important than the papers of individuals and families."[7] Ham focused on the failures of archival custody and worried about the amassing of large quantities of documentation into single archival repositories, insisting that alternative strategies and actions were necessary to ensure that the work of archivists would remain relevant in an era of information abundance. He urged archivists to set aside their custodial mindset and to think critically and collaboratively about selection and strategies for documentation across institutions and repositories.[8] His work remains relevant and unfinished, as a new generation of archivists struggles with questions of custody, ownership, power, memory, justice, and the preservation of today's archival record.

Within this framework, a close examination of archival custodial theory is central to this discussion, offering important context for sections of this chapter. The legal and physical ownership of records has long been recognized as a fundamental principle of archival management.[9] Redefining archival appraisal and selection, as suggested by Ham and archivists of his generation, helped to reframe the future of preservation. Innovative approaches to archival custody and evolving technologies give archivists a chance to reconsider the ethical principles of preservation, particularly as a public good. For most archivists, custody means assuming responsibility for the care and control of documentation, especially for its security and preservation. This guardianship ensures an unbroken chain of custody with a guarantee of the authenticity of records and other resources. The newer archival concept of post-custody implies that archivists may no longer physically acquire and maintain records; rather, they will offer management oversight for information remaining in the custody of the records creators. This role change for archivists responded initially to the challenge of digital records, recognizing that, in some instances, preservation can be best managed if records are linked to the IT systems that produce and store them. This post-custodial (or perhaps more accurately noncustodial) method of archiving has called into question a long-held belief that archives are the best venues for keeping documentation of our cultural heritage. More important, the post-custodial model allows for the oversight of information where the materials are created and used, with an emphasis away from ownership and toward one of shared stewardship instead. This shift influences the decisions that archivists make about what to acquire and preserve and how to manage relationships with those creating and holding vital cultural materials, especially documentation of underrepresented and marginalized groups.

The post-custodial approach involves its own subset of challenges. First, the creators of the content are usually not trained archivists, librarians, historians, or researchers. They may have a limited perspective about the materials worth keeping and those that can be jettisoned. Second, archivists generally do not have the resources and time to identify all the content worth preserving. And, even if they do identify these creators of content, they certainly do not have the time to educate all of them about archival preservation principles and practices. Third, the creators of the content that needs to be preserved may not have the resources to create adequate preservation environments. This may be especially true for underrepresented and marginalized groups. A fourth consideration involves guaranteeing the sustainability of content. Who is responsible for preservation and for how long? The creators may feel strong social obligation to the records that they generate and maintain, but once they pass on, it appears legitimate to question whether information will be properly stewarded by subsequent generations.

Community Archiving

These challenges are especially profound for marginalized and underrepresented groups who have political interest in the creation, preservation, and curation of their documentation. For many communities, these resources reflect their experience and verify a shared history of repression and struggle for civil rights and equal protection. They understand the value of the records documenting their historical and social progress; however, controlling the use and interpretation of them remains central to their empowerment and identity. For these communities, the emerging archival theory and practice of post-custodianship aligns with their goals for the stewardship of community-based collections, or community archiving.

"Community" can be defined by geographic place, cultural identity, gender, socioeconomic status, or ethnicity. "Community archives" is a fluid and evolving term in archival literature.[10] Mary Stevens, Andrew Flinn, and Elizabeth Shepard define it "as collections of material gathered primarily by members of a given community and over whose use community members exercise some level of control."[11] Central to this consideration is control, and, more specifically, who has the right to control these records. The records of marginalized and repressed communities, such as Indigenous peoples and those historically subjected to colonization, are often in the custody and control of governmental or academic institutions.[12] In other instances, these materials may remain in the communities that created them. The desire to retain custody of materials documenting a shared history is understandable for communities engaged in civil and political activism, such as lesbian, gay, bisexual, transgender, and queer (LGBTQ) groups and tribal organizations that represent Native peoples. Marginalized communities understand that limited or biased documentation impedes political activism and that by ensuring an accurate archival record, the group can establish its meaning for both its members and the broader society. This documentation, defined and collected by a community, shapes and promotes a shared identity that counterbalances its marginalization.

When documentation is removed from its community context and deposited in a mainstream repository, it becomes less accessible to the communities that value it the most. For this reason, a community-based archives is often administered by dedicated volunteer activists who recognize the significance of the collections, as well as the importance of a secure community venue for research, discussion, and education. As the collections expand, these untrained volunteers or employees can become overwhelmed by increased research interest and user expectations for reasonable access to underused historical records, while effectively managing such preservation concerns as security, storage, and handling during use. Furthermore, individuals who manage the materials may not be trained in proper archival practices.

To meet these demands, organizations must commit resources to train their staffs in appropriate access and preservation, including the development of the proper facilities for research and storage. The cost of implementing archival best practices and investing in professional development, however, can strain already limited resources. More important, securing the funding required to sustain community archives can conflict with the broader goals and objectives of the organization. At this point in their development, many organizations first contact a funding agency or mainstream institution to seek advice and assistance relating to preservation and access. Organizations at this juncture are typically struggling with critical questions related to their vision and strategic priorities. A commitment to long-term archival administration essentially expands the organization's mission beyond political activism and social justice to service and scholarship. Rather than taking this step, an organization may donate its records to an established and trusted archival repository, or may seek collaborative relationships with outside entities to assist in processing and digitizing collections. This transition can be difficult for many organizations that recognize that mainstream archives have, in some instances, misrepresented, neglected, or completely omitted their past from the historical record. And, for many people involved in community archives, a tension exists between a desire for sustainability and deeply held values of autonomy, independence, and self-sufficiency associated with participation in social movements. Joan Nestle, founder of the Lesbian Herstory Archives of New York, clearly articulated these issues three decades ago:

> To survive in America as an archives we have had to call ourselves a not-for-profit information resource center because the New York State Board of Regents maintains control over educational institutions and could therefore confiscate the collection for "just cause." We take no money from the government, believing that such an action would be an exercise in neocolonialism, believing that the society that ruled us out of history should never be relied upon to make it possible for us to exist. All the technology the archives has—the computer, the xeroxing machine—comes from lesbian, gay, feminist and radical funding sources.[13]

Researcher expectations have changed dramatically since Nestle wrote these words in 1990. Increasingly, users of archives expect access to digitized content, further straining the balance between sustainability and mission. Although the availability of online access to collections may reduce staff effort, developing and maintaining the necessary digital infrastructure is often beyond the means of community archives. Many turn to outside organizations for assistance with basic areas of archival practice, including collection development, custody, preservation, access, education, and training.

For example, the UCLA Center for the Study of Women, the June L. Mazer Lesbian Archives, and the UCLA Library have partnered in outreach and collection development activities. Leveraging their shared expertise, staff at these organizations arranged, described, and digitized papers of lesbian writers and activists; the records of cultural, political, and professional organizations; and oral histories chronicling the lives and personal stories of West Coast lesbian feminist activists. The collections are now permanently housed in the UCLA Library, accessible through its Special Collections and online through the California Digital Library. Moreover, the relationship with UCLA inspired the confidence of potential donors and enhanced the collecting efforts of these resources by the Mazer Archives.

This partnership was influenced by an earlier project based at the ONE Institute's National Gay and Lesbian Archives. Founded in 1952, the ONE Institute houses the largest library dedicated to lesbian, gay, bisexual, and transgender history in the United States, including over 250 archival collections and two million items. *ONE* originated as the earliest national gay publication and evolved into a learning institute that conferred the first academic certificates in gay studies. The ONE archives, an independent nonprofit organization, deposited its collections with the University of Southern California, and USC supports a research facility on the campus for the archives, including building services. In addition, the ONE archives sponsors campus-related events, specialized student research, and internships.

These two successful examples of shared stewardship prove that collaboration between community archives and mainstream institutions has many advantages. Partnerships between two or more organizations can enhance opportunities for outside funding, offer a means for shared expertise and perspective, and leverage resources to support sustainable infrastructure and preservation.[14]

Another way that community archives can address preservation and access challenges, without the transfer of legal and physical custodianship, is through digitization. Cyndi Shein and Emily Lapworth examined what they have termed the "scan-and-return" approach to digitization partnerships, claiming that this method is really a form of "distributed custody," meaning that digitized materials are distributed among a repository and other individuals or groups. Their work describes how distributed custody builds digital collections in academic institutions, including Virginia Commonwealth University's MultiCultural Archives, Washington State University's Plateau Peoples' Web Portal, Utah Academic Library Consortium's Pioneers in Your Attic, and the University of Texas at Austin Libraries' Genocide Archive of Rwanda and Guatemalan National Police Historical Archive.[15] Shein and Lapworth argue that "by leveraging the latest technologies, cooperating on documentation strategies, supporting communities in the preservation of their own cultural patrimony, and elevating access above custody, these projects are variations on the themes found in Ham's strategies for the post-custodial era."[16] The authors recognize that sustainable preservation of the digital surrogates is a challenge, but not one limited to the scan-and-return method. The authors point out that the creation of digital collections provides "an opportunity to build a relationship of mutual understanding, respect, and trust between repository and an individual, family, or community."[17] This method is also a means of ensuring the long-term preservation of cultural heritage in shared-custody environments.[18]

Collaborative digitization, like the scan-and-return model, supports trust-building in communities, increases access to archives, and assists established institutions in building their digital collections. This and other approaches to community archives depend upon the archivist's ability to balance the philosophical and social justice concerns for independence and control with practical approaches that ensure sustainable outcomes, including a long-term commitment to preservation. While engaging in community archiving offers many advantages, the long-term sustainability of these projects requires ongoing financial resources and a strategy for digital preservation.

Native American Materials

The preservation and management of Indigenous materials deserves special consideration in this discussion regarding the right to preserve. In fact, no area of cultural stewardship raises more ethical and moral questions than the preservation of Native American collections and who makes decisions regarding collection care. As Miriam Jorgensen notes in her groundbreaking 2012 report on the status and needs of American Indian, Alaska Native, and Native Hawaiian cultural organizations, "sovereignty, self-determination, and self-governance are primary goals of Indigenous nations worldwide—and they take important steps toward those goals by renewing control over their stories, documents and artifacts. In the U.S. the last 30 years have been a remarkable period of reasserted and reaffirmed authority over such cultural patrimony through the creation of tribal archives, libraries and museums."[19]

The dispensation of Indigenous materials is often decided through law, policy, and international declarations that have huge implications for cultural heritage organizations.[20] The Native American Graves Protection and Repatriation Act (NAGPRA), a critical law that impacts most cultural organizations, became effective on November 16, 1990. This watershed legislation describes the rights of Native American descendants, Indian tribes, and Native Hawaiian organizations with respect to the treatment, repatriation, and disposition of Native American human remains, funerary objects, sacred objects, and objects of cultural patrimony. These resources are referred to collectively in the statute as "cultural items" with which interested parties can show a relationship of lineal descent or cultural affiliation.[21] The passage of NAGPRA empowered Indigenous nations to take steps toward reaffirming their heritage and patrimony through the legal and rightful transfer of cultural resources from outside institutions to community-based organizations. It established who had the "right" to preserve certain aspects of Native American heritage.[22]

Long before the passage of NAGPRA, tribal organizations were interested in locating, acquiring, and providing context for their cultural and historical documents, many of which were housed in non-Native institutions. In their quest for sovereignty, many tribes first contacted non-tribal organizations to research, and possibly repatriate, documents and artifacts. These nontribal institutions were often unfamiliar with the traditional knowledge associated with such materials, or with the culturally sensitive nature of the resources in their care.

Although NAGPRA creates context for respectful collaboration and the return of many items, the legislation does not address the disposition of rights associated with archival materials. This left staff at many institutions scrambling for guidance on the ethical management of Indigenous materials, including records, manuscripts, photographs, and audio and video recordings. In 2006, a group of Native and non-Native professionals created the *Protocols for Native American Archival Materials*, a set of best practices developed for the culturally responsive care and use of Native American materials.[23] The *Protocols* were developed by the First Archivist Circle, a group of archivists, librarians, museum curators, historians, and anthropologists representing fifteen Native American, First Nations, Indigenous, and Aboriginal communities. Their work has helped archivists to understand and manage the preservation of, and access to, Native knowledge and traditional cultural expressions of the materials in their repositories. The principles articulated in the *Protocols* offer guidance in understanding Indigenous values and perspectives, as well as important policy and legal considerations related to the management and care of Native American materials. The *Protocols* focus on

- The importance of consultation with and concurrence of tribal communities in decisions and policies
- The need to recognize and provide special treatment for culturally sensitive materials;
- Rethinking public accessibility to and use of some materials
- The role of intellectual and cultural property rights
- The need to consider copying, sharing, and/or repatriation of certain materials
- The recognition of community-based research protocols and contracts
- Reciprocal education and training for Native and non-Native communities
- Raising awareness of these issues in the profession

When presented with the *Protocols* in 2008, the Society of American Archivists Council declined to endorse them, opting instead to solicit feedback and discussion over several years. The Council again declined to endorse the *Protocols* in 2012.[24] SAA has acknowledged that many of the original criticisms of the document were based "in the language of cultural insensitivity and white supremacy" and that the archival profession was divided regarding the intent and purpose of the guidelines.[25] Some of the main objections focused on whether Native Americans have special rights pertaining to traditional cultural expressions and knowledge, and whether these rights transcend American legal traditions supporting open access and scholarship.[26] Despite the lack of support by some professional organizations, and in the absence of any sanctioned guidelines, many institutions began to use the best practices recommended by the *Protocols* in the structures and agreements supporting collaboration between tribal and nontribal organizations.[27]

At the 2018 meeting of the Society of American Archivists, the SAA Council finally endorsed the *Protocols* as an external standard of the organization. The Council recognized that the *Protocols* provide a necessary foundation for archival practice in caring for culturally sensitive records and acknowledged the role of Native American communities in the preservation of, and access to, their own materials. The SAA Council further acknowledged that its validation of the *Protocols* was long overdue and stated that "we regret and apologize that SAA did not take action to endorse the Protocols sooner and engage in more appropriate discussion."[28]

The endorsement of the *Protocols* accepts that cultural sensitivity and differing claims of ownership influence the conditions under which knowledge can be ethically and legally acquired, archived, preserved, accessed, published, and used. Thus, the best practices emerging from the *Protocols* also have implications for archival preservation. Organizations with significant holdings of Native American materials must develop policies and procedures for the ethical stewardship of these resources. These policies should include tribal expertise and traditional knowledge in the selection and management of content, and they should explain the arrangement, description, interpretation, and preservation of Indigenous cultural materials. In this way, the creators can explain where important or sensitive information exists in the materials. This shared stewardship may culminate in special treatment for sensitive cultural materials, including the removal of works, reclassification and revised description, or the decision not to preserve certain items.

The museum field also grapples with protocols that promote community-based collaboration. The *Museum + Communities Guidelines*, published in 2017 by the School for Advanced Research, Indian Arts Research Center, were developed in a three-year effort involving Native and non-Native museum professionals, cultural leaders, and artists. The guidelines are a resource for community members who collaborate with museums. They provide advice on building community relationships through collaboration in areas such as community-based arts programming, descriptive practices, collection stewardship, loans and exhibition development, and collaborative conservation and preservation.[29]

Canadian museum professionals and archivists are also responding to changing perspectives concerning the preservation of Indigenous cultural heritage. As museum conservator Miriam Clavir points out, many First Nations view the preservation of an item of cultural significance as inseparable from the preservation of traditions, identity, and community. Preservationists focus on the physical nature of the object. Members of First Nations groups, in contrast, believe that the decision to preserve is derived from the context in which an object originates. In *Preserving What Is Valued*, Clavir compares the perspectives of two groups: museum conservators and First Nation representatives, mainly from British Columbia. These voices offer important insights into the tensions surrounding the preservation of cultural heritage within and outside of the communities that created them.[30]

Digital repatriation is another collaborative method that museums, archives, and other cultural heritage institutions use in the ethical management of Native and First Nation collections. This approach uses technology to return expressions of cultural heritage to Indigenous communities. Such collaboration can also assist the communities in refining and developing descriptive metadata that incorporates Native knowledge, language, and names. It also helps those processing the materials to identify culturally sensitive materials that may require limited access and research restrictions.

Collaborations between tribal and nontribal organizations bring diverse communities together, often for the first time, to educate and learn, to address misinterpretations, and to share resources and knowledge. To collaborate, Native and non-Native organizations must develop sustainable partnerships based on respect and an understanding of differing cultural traditions. This is particularly challenging when core beliefs such as freedom of information and the ownership of cultural heritage differ. As the national conversation on these issues progresses, openness to learn from diverse perspectives that recognize historical differences in power and privilege increases. When attempting to resolve past inequities, archivists must engage in reciprocal partnerships that value knowledge and expertise equally. They should also acknowledge that preservation is ongoing and that it remains the responsibility of all partners. As with community archiving, the sustainability of these partnerships requires committed financial resources and a strategy for digital preservation.

Technology and the Business of Preservation

In previous chapters, we discussed the "business of digital obsolescence" and the impact of this business model on sustainable digital preservation. Today's software and hardware will eventually be obsolete. Because of the rapid evolution and proliferation of software and hardware, modes of digital encoding, and operating systems, digital obsolescence will remain a challenge. As archivists address inequities in the cultural record, they must also be aware of the moral and ethical issues associated with planned obsolescence and the commitments made to marginalized and underrepresented communities to preserve their materials. Such commitment must be realistic and sustainable, and archivists must consider the business practices of the technology industry and how those practices impact archival preservation.

Moreover, cultural and political communities and groups use social media networks to share and preserve documentation of their activities. Today, most areas of business and society rely on social media, big data analysis, algorithms, machine learning, and artificial intelligence to connect with the universe of information and to make daily decisions. These new tools at the intersection between technology and culture are transferring the authority for the preservation of information stored and maintained on social networks from traditional repositories to private businesses such as Facebook and Twitter.

As Clifford Lynch of the Coalition for Networked Information points out, we live in the "age of algorithms."[31] "Algorithms" are sets of rules and calculations that capture historical data and influence decision-making. Computer algorithms affect our world in profound and mostly invisible ways, giving social media networks great power to shape the cultural record.

The algorithms used by social networks identify newsworthy trends, identify consumer preferences, and filter what we see on social media. In fact, everything on the web is a product of algorithms. And their use is expanding as massive amounts of data are being created, captured, and analyzed by businesses and governments. Lynch claims that we can no longer pretend that it is possible to document the behavior of the large, complex, sociotechnical systems that power social media.[32] Archivists simply cannot preserve this information or the systems that produce it. In reality, these business networks are already deciding what to discard and what to preserve. Such decisions do not value archival preservation of physical and digital objects or the accompanying systems used to create them. For example, on August 21, 2018, Facebook announced that it removed 652 accounts and pages originating in Iran and Russia for "coordinated inauthentic behavior" that targeted people in the Middle East, Latin America, the United Kingdom, and the

United States.[33] Facebook's vigilance on this issue was prompted by a congressional investigation of Facebook's data practices that revealed its entanglement with Cambridge Analytica, a political consultancy group that improperly accessed 87 million Facebook users' names, "likes," and other personal information.

Recognizing this threat, the European Union enacted the General Data Protection Regulation (GDPR), a comprehensive law that requires US organizations to properly secure all information collected from European Union (EU) citizens. Specifically, it dictates how organizations must handle any personally identifiable information. The purpose of the legislation is to ensure that individuals have control over their personal information, including the right to actively consent to the use of personal data, the right to limit that use, the right to be forgotten, the right to have their data portable, and the right to seek damages should they suffer from misuse and/or breach of their data.[34]

Current legislative and legal trends such as these indicate that the removal of personal or controversial information from social media networks will become increasingly common. As a result, some cultural and historical information will be unavailable to archivists or librarians and will be lost to history. It may be appropriate to remove information and to restrict its misuse, but such actions will also remove data to which researchers may wish access to in the future. The removal of web-based information that could lead to a dangerous political or personal attack may be prudent, but such a removal may have the unintended side effect of hindering future scholars who wish to study such attacks.

Further highlighting this reality was the recent announcement by the Library of Congress (LC) of its intention to amend its collection strategy for its Twitter Archive by acquiring tweets only selectively. In retreating from its previous more comprehensive collecting strategy, the LC explained that the changes in volume and format make the comprehensive archiving of tweets unsustainable.[35] This is especially concerning as elected officials, such as Donald Trump, increasingly use Twitter as a primary mechanism for official communication. Certainly, tweets from someone as prominent as the US president should be preserved. But at what level of prominence should tweets be saved, or selectively saved? Who will decide whose tweets to retain and whose to ignore? It is true that the volume of tweets, to name only one social medium, makes it impracticable to save them all. But the scope and scale of the twitterverse constitutes a monumental challenge for archivists who wish to responsibly document contemporary culture.

Conclusion

Preservation is a political act—one that must consider the autonomy, expectations, and demands of the people and communities represented in archival collections. Archives are collected to be used, accessed, preserved, and interpreted. Historically, this work has been the responsibility of the archivist who decides what to acquire and what to preserve. Many archives hold documents that some communities wish to be forgotten or would like to have returned or repatriated. Other communities seek partnerships for the sustainable management of resources that document the experience of marginalized or underrepresented groups. These records may contain evidence of social progress while simultaneously revealing human rights abuses and the impact of colonization and repression.

Moreover, archival collections may contain privileged and sensitive information that some groups believe should be interpreted by, and accessible only to, the cultures documented in those records. In many cases, these resources are housed in institutions with little or no connection to the communities and cultural perspectives they represent. As we have asked several times in this book, how do we ethically select, preserve, and make accessible these complex resources—and who decides what to preserve?

Gerald Ham predicted over five decades ago that two forces will continue to influence the archival endeavor: the evolving nature of information technology and the need to address inequities in the archival record. Collaboration, community archiving, and other methods of preservation that entail shared stewardship or post-custodial relationships may provide a partial answer for many communities. Advances in technology enable and simplify the sharing and repatriation of cultural materials. But collaborative digitization and shared metadata arrangements are not sufficient to accomplish the broader goal of creating an inclusive and just archival record. To accomplish this, archivists must engage in research and promote education and training to help them understand the perspectives of groups that live in their communities and that are represented in their archives. These cultural competencies will assist archivists in building trusting and sustainable relationships with diverse and underserved communities. The resulting partnerships will expand the archival record through shared documentation and interpretation of cultural resources. This work must be supported by shared and mutually beneficial protocols, standards, and best practices for preservation and access. Success will depend on archivists' ability to effectively document society on equitable and inclusive terms. This requires cultural sensitivity and mutual respect. It also requires rethinking the ethics of archival custody, stewardship, and the impact of social media on preservation practices.

NOTES

1 John Muir, *My First Summer in the Sierra* (Boston: Houghton Mifflin, 1911).

2 Elisabeth Kaplan, "We Are What We Collect, We Collect What We Are: Archives and the Construction of Identity," *American Archivist* 63, no. 1 (2000): 147, https://doi.org/10.17723/aarc.63.1.h554377531233l05.

3 Works in the area include Jeannette A. Bastian and Ben Alexander, eds., *Community Archives, The Shaping of Memory* (London, UK: Facet Publishing, 2009); Randall C. Jimerson, *Archives Power: Memory, Accountability, and Social Justice* (Chicago: Society of American Archivists, 2009); Dominique Daniel and Amalia Levi, *Identity Palimpsests: Archiving Ethnicity in the U.S and Canada* (Sacramento: Litwin Press, 2013); Mary A. Caldera and Kathryn M. Neal, *Through the Archival Looking Glass: A Reader on Diversity and Inclusion* (Chicago: Society of American Archivists, 2014); Terry Cook, "Evidence, Memory, Identity, and Community: Four Shifting Archival Paradigms," *Archival Science* 13, nos. 2–3 (2013): 95–120, DOI:10.1007/s10502-012-9180-7; Michelle Caswell, "Defining Human Rights Archives: Introduction to the Special Double Issue on Archives and Human Rights," *Archival Science* 14, nos. 3–4 (2014): 207–13, https://doi.org/10.1007/s10502-014-9226-0. Most of the articles in the double issue were originally presented at the 2013 symposium "The Antonym of Forgetting: Global Perspectives on Human Rights Archives," hosted by the University of California, Los Angeles. Joan Schwartz has also written extensively on these topics.

4 Paul Conway, "Archival Preservation Practice in a Nationwide Context," *American Archivist* 53, no. 2 (1990): 204–22, https://doi.org/10.17723/aarc.53.2.d0gt78p562832655.

5 James Doubek, "Google Has Received 650,000 'Right To Be Forgotten' Requests Since 2014," *The Two-Way* (blog), National Public Radio (February 28, 2018), https://www.npr.org/sections/thetwo-way/2018/02/28/589411543/google-received-650-000-right-to-be-forgotten-requests-since-2014, captured at https://perma.cc/PY4T-859U. See also "IFLA Statement on the "Right to Be Forgotten" (2016), https://www.ifla.org/publications/node/10320, captured at https://

perma.cc/9ET9-43MR; Leticia Bode and Meg Leta Jones, "Ready to Forget: American Attitudes toward the Right to be Forgotten," *The Information Society: An International Journal* 33, no. 2 (2017): 76–85, https://doiorg/10.1080/01972243.2016.1271071; and Virginia Dressler, "The Right to Be Forgotten and Implications on Digital Collections: A Survey of ARL Member Institutions on Practice and Policy," *College & Research Libraries* 79, no. 7 (2018), https://crl.acrl.org/index.php/crl/article/view/16890.

6 F. Gerald Ham, "The Archival Edge," *American Archivist* 38, no. 1 (1975): 5, https://doi.org/10.17723/aarc.38.1.7400r86481128424.

7 Ham, "The Archival Edge," 8.

8 For Ham's key works, see Ham, "The Archival Edge," 5–13; F. Gerald Ham, "Archival Choices: Managing the Historical Record in an Age of Abundance," *American Archivist* 47, no. 1 (1984): 11–22, https://doi.org/10.17723/aarc.47.1.v382727652114521; and F. Gerald Ham, "Archival Strategies for the Post-Custodial Era," *American Archivist* 44, no. 3 (1981): 207–16, https://doi.org/10.17723/aarc.44.3.6228121p01m8k376.

9 Jeannette A. Bastian, "A Question of Custody: The Colonial Archives of the United States Virgin Islands," *American Archivist* 64, no. 1 (2001): 97, https://doi.org/10.17723/aarc.64.1.h6k872252u2gr377.

10 This definition was provided by Cathleen Tefft, NEH program officer, whose advice helped us shape this section on community archives.

11 Mary Stevens, Andrew Flinn, and Elizabeth Shepherd, "New Frameworks for Community Engagement in the Archives Sector: From Handing Over to Handing On," *International Journal of Heritage Studies* 16, nos. 1–2 (2010): 59, https://doi.org/10.1080/13527250903441770.

12 For an example of competing custody claims on the archival record, see Jeannette A. Bastian, "A Question of Custody: The Colonial Archives of the United States Virgin Islands," *American Archivist* 64, no. 1 (2001): 96–114, https://doi.org/10.17723/aarc.64.1.h6k872252u2gr377.

13 Joan Nestle, "The Will to Remember: The Lesbian Herstory Archives of New York," *Feminist Review* 34 (1990): 92, https://doi.org/10.1057/fr.1990.12.

14 This discussion of the ONE Archive and the Mazer collaboration with UCLA is elaborated in Elizabeth Joffrion, "The Will to Collaborate," in *June L. Mazer Lesbian Archives: Making Invisible Histories Visible: A Resource Guide to the Collections*, ed. Kathleen Anne McHugh, Brenda Johnson-Grau, and Ben Raphael Sher (Los Angeles: UCLA Center for the Study of Women, 2014), 29–32.

15 Cyndi Shein and Emily Lapworth, "Say Yes to Digital Surrogates: Strengthening the Archival Record in the Postcustodial Era," *Journal of Western Archives* 7, no. 1 (2016): 1–50, https://digitalcommons.usu.edu/westernarchives/vol7/iss1/9.

16 Shein and Lapworth, "Say Yes to Digital Surrogates," 17–18.

17 Shein and Lapworth, "Say Yes to Digital Surrogates," 27.

18 Independent community archives also use the scan-and-return approach to build their collections. For further discussion of these efforts in Southern California, see Jimmy Zavala et al., "'A Process Where We're All at the Table': Community Archives Challenging Dominant Modes of Archival Practice," *Archives & Manuscripts* 45, no. 3 (2017): 202–15, https://doi.org/10.1080/01576895.2017.1377088.

19 Miriam Jorgensen, *Sustaining Indigenous Culture: The Structure, Activities and Needs of Tribal Archives, Libraries and Museums* (Oklahoma City: Association of Tribal Archives, Libraries, and Museums, 2012).

20 See Walter Echo-Hawk, *In the Light of Justice: The Rise of Human Rights in Native America and the UN Declaration of the Rights of Indigenous Peoples* (Golden, CO: Fulcrum Publishers, 2013) and *In the Courts of the Conqueror: The 10 Worst Indian Law Cases Ever Decided* (Golden, CO: Fulcrum Publishers, 2010).

21 Native American Graves Protections and Repatriation Act (NAGARA), 25 U.S.C 3001-3013 (2006). See also Jack F. Trope and Walter R. Echo-Hawk, "The Native American Graves Protection and Repatriation Act, Background and Legislation," in *Repatriation Reader: Who Owns American Indian Remains?*, ed. Devon A. Mihesuah (Lincoln: University of Nebraska Press, 2000), 123–68.

22 For more on the establishment of tribal cultural centers and their needs, see Miriam Jorgensen, *Sustaining Indigenous Culture: The Structure, Activities and Needs of Tribal Archives, Libraries and Museums* (Oklahoma City: Association of Tribal Archives, Libraries, and Museums, 2012).

23 *Protocols for Native American Archival Materials*, http://www2.nau.edu/libnap-p, captured at https://perma.cc/J4S2-Z3ZU. See also Jennifer O'Neal, "Respect, Recognition and Reciprocity: The Protocols for Native American Archival Materials," in *Identity Palimpsests: Archiving Ethnicity in the U.S. and Canada,* eds. Dominque Daniel and Amelia Levi (Sacramento: Litwin Books, 2014), 125–42.

24 Additional information about past discussions can be found at Society of American Archivists, "Protocols for Native American Materials Information and Resources," https://www2.archivists.org/groups/native-american-archives-section/protocols-for-native-american-archival-materials-information-and-resources-page, captured at https://perma.cc/N3VN-87DF.

[25] Society of American Archivists, "SAA Council Endorsement of Protocols for Native American Materials," https://www2.archivists.org/statements/saa-council-endorsement-of-protocols-for-native-american-archival-materials, captured at https://perma.cc/CS8V-WFJG.

[26] For debates surrounding the protocols, see John Bolcer, "The Protocols for Native American Archival Materials: Considerations and Concerns from the Perspective of a Non-Tribal Archivist," *Easy Access* 34, no. 4 (2009): 3–6; Society of American Archivists Council, *Report: Task Force to Review Protocols for Native American Archival Materials,* prepared by Frank Boles, David George-Shongo, and Christine Weideman (2008), http://files.archivists.org/governance/taskforces/0208-NativeAmProtocols-IIIA.pdf, captured at https://perma.cc/5CJL-MZGF; Karen J. Underhill, "Protocols for Native American Archival Materials," *RBM: A Journal of Rare Books, Manuscripts, and Cultural Heritage* 7, no. 2 (2006): 134–14, https://doi.org/10.5860/rbm.7.2.267.

[27] Elizabeth Joffrion and Natalia Fernandez, "Collaboration between Tribal and Nontribal Organizations: Suggested Best Practices for Sharing Expertise, Knowledge, and Cultural Resources," *American Archivist* 78, no. 1 (2015): 191–236, https://doi.org/10.17723/0360-9081.78.1.192.

[28] Society of American Archivists, "SAA Council Endorsement of Protocols for Native American Materials" (August 13, 2018), https://www2.archivists.org/statements/saa-council-endorsement-of-protocols-for-native-american-archival-materials, captured at https://perma.cc/CS8V-WFJG.

[29] School for Advanced Research, Indian Arts Research Center, "Guidelines for Collaboration" (2017), http://sarweb.org/guidelinesforcollaboration, captured at https://perma.cc/3SJT-589T.

[30] Miriam Clavir, *Preserving What Is Valued: Museums, Conservation and First Nations* (Vancouver, BC: University of British Columbia Press, 2002).

[31] Clifford Lynch, "Stewardship in the 'Age of Algorithms,'" *First Monday* 22, no. 12 (2017), http://firstmonday.org/article/view/8097/6583, captured at https://perma.cc/6SCK-VHVX.

[32] Lynch, "Stewardship in the 'Age of Algorithms.'"

[33] Facebook Newsroom, "Taking Down More Coordinated Inauthentic Behavior" (August 21, 2018), https://newsroom.fb.com/news/2018/08/more-coordinated-inauthentic-behavior, captured at https://perma.cc/CK7J-QTTT. See also Ari Levy, "Facebook Says It Removed Content from Iran and Russia," CNBC (August 21, 2018), https://www.cnbc.com/2018/08/21/facebook-says-it-removed-content-from-iran-and-russia.html, captured at https://perma.cc/E52P-TTLM.

[34] "Regulation (EU) 2016/679 of the European Parliament and of the Council of April 27, 2016, on the protection of natural persons with regard to the processing of personal data and on the free movement of such data, and repealing Directive 95/46/EC (General Data Protection Regulation)," *Official Journal of the European Union* (May 4, 2016), https://eur-lex.europa.eu/legal-content/EN/TXT/PDF/?uri=CELEX:32016R0679, captured at https://perma.cc/63SY-C4P7.

[35] Library of Congress, "Update on the Library of Congress Twitter Archive" (December 2017), https://blogs.loc.gov/loc/files/2017/12/2017dec_twitter_white-paper.pdf, captured at https://perma.cc/ZF6A-SPDJ.

11

Final Remarks

Introduction

The issues we have dealt with in this book cover a wide range of concerns, all of which are critical for the long-term access to information. Archives inherently involve the acquisition, analysis, description, and sharing of information, with an eye to long-term accessibility. At the center of this endeavor is selection and appraisal, which form the foundation for all preservation activities. Our ability to advance preservation depends on our placing it in a complex future context in which users will have even greater expectations concerning professional service. Records are no longer simply carriers of information; they are dynamic and generative as well.

In chapters 1, 3, 4, 6, and 7, we showed that preservation has evolved from a distinct archival specialization in an analog world to a field transformed by rapid technological change. Several developments have fueled this change:

- New technologies allow the capture of analog records through digitization, and digital technology can even be employed to control the environment, a central element of preservation. At the same time, digital applications make it possible for archivists to monitor the environment with new tools, such as programmable data-loggers, that can measure, record, and analyze data. Once the records have been captured, archivists can manipulate them in various ways and make them accessible to anyone in the world who has the requisite hardware and software. Access to information, after all, is archivists' primary mandate.
- Conservators can examine artifacts using applications that have recently emerged from the medical field, such as 3-D scanning and tomographic imaging. New technologies

will continue to be discovered that will change the ways in which archivists can "read" documents.

- Many records are now born digital. This means that archivists must develop preservation strategies for records from their creation, rather than later in their life cycles. And even the notion of the life cycle has changed and now seems static as preservation is a continual process with ever-increasing numbers of stakeholders. The life cycle ends only if records are destroyed or inadvertently disappear.
- Now users can access records in a physical archives or remotely on their personal computers, laptops, notebooks, or telephones. Access to records, published materials, and objects is ubiquitous, and this ubiquity is changing the way that we teach, learn, and do research.

Along the way, we recognize that the digital realm of modern archives still runs parallel to the analog realm, which remains at the core of most collections. Thus, archivists must consider digital and analog formats in a holistic manner and not lose sight of their responsibilities in either realm. In fact, the analog component of traditional archives may be useful as the model for the design of new strategies for the growing scale and abundance of digital materials. For example, the ability to stabilize analog records must be incorporated into the dynamic nature of digital migration and software and hardware updates. Digital preservation cannot be conquered merely by perfecting new technologies. As with analog preservation, it is about people and politics.

Other key considerations were delineated in chapters 9, "Sustainable Preservation Practices," and 10, "The Right to Preserve: Who Decides?" Sustainability has three meanings. First, preservation programs must be created with institutional commitment and long-term support. Second, the deleterious impact of human activity on the environment must be considered. As ecosystems continue to change as the result of global warming and other generally human-produced phenomena, archivists must carefully nurture their collections and preserve their resources. The move toward sustainability in cultural heritage institutions has led them to reconsider former approaches to controlling the environments in which artifacts are stored. Archivists must study current weather patterns and global warming to understand future risks. Third, the profession must develop and standardize practices that truly preserve digital information. To ensure sustainable long-term access to archival materials, archivists must influence hardware and software decisions in the commercial world where these two components of digital infrastructure are constantly changing.

But changes in the physical and technological environment are not alone in impacting the field. Social changes are transforming archival practices as well. The profession's custodial model is evolving from giving archivists complete control of the records in their care to one in which communities play a strong role as well. We introduced the idea that preservation is a political act—one that must consider the autonomy, expectations, and demands of the people and communities represented in archival collections. Chapter 2, "History of Archival Preservation," introduced developments that have led to post-custodial practices. Chapter 10 discussed, among other examples, the 2006 *Protocols for Native American Archival Materials,* adopted by the Society of American Archivists only in August 2018, after considerable debate.

In the past, archival preservation focused on specific risks to collections, and most commonly on planning for disasters. Today, as we discussed in chapter 8, cultural heritage institutions must approach risk systematically, following practices of the for-profit sector. Thus, archivists now manage risk in a more comprehensive way. For example, in the past, they examined hazards to collections brought about by poor building conditions. Today they use data about broad climate conditions (and changes) to factor in geographical risks to collections. The availability of new data about climate risks makes it possible for archivists to conduct more systematic procedures for protecting collections than they could before such data were available.

Chapter 5, "Planning and Developing a Preservation Program," described the process for determining programmatic objectives and strategic priorities. It also discussed resources available for preservation initiatives, which are important for establishing, maintaining, and continually assessing a program. Strategic priorities will likely shift more rapidly than ever before, given the profound and rapid changes that new technologies have brought about.

Some of the topics that we considered include the impact of new technologies on the creation, use, and preservation of information; new ways of teaching and learning that will place new demands on the online availability of paper-based historical records; new areas of research that are increasingly interdisciplinary and depend on the availability of big data. We also considered the fact that many federal granting agencies now mandate the preservation of data created through their grants. New demands are being placed on archives as resources in many institutions continue to shrink. And community archiving initiatives and outreach are increasing.

Chapters 3 and 4, "Principles of Archival Preservation" and "Context for Archival Preservation" offered critical new definitions and frameworks for the holistic preservation of analog and digital content. In these chapters, we acknowledged that many social or technological changes have taken place. However, the premise of preservation remains the same: archivists steward their shared heritage for themselves and for the future, aiming that stewardship at long-term, wide access to their collections.

Emerging Trends

The prospects of advancing preservation are exciting and daunting, but one thing is clear: preservation must be a dynamic enterprise. It must not just respond to changes; it must anticipate them. Emerging trends that may seem farfetched today will have direct and indirect impacts on the future of preservation. For example, Forrester, a market research company that studies emerging trends and forecasts innovations, puts out an annual list of "The Top Emerging Technologies to Watch." The 2018 list includes four areas already of interest to libraries, archives, and museums: computer vision, 3-D printing, augmented reality, and virtual reality.

Computer vision is a type of artificial intelligence for the analysis of digital images and videos that will change our relationship to surrogates. Future users will seek new information and knowledge from visual information. The Brooklyn Museum is already engaged in research in image matching. This area has an impact on how people learn, and, ultimately, how they will engage with cultural objects.

3-D printing is widely available at archives, libraries, and museums. As such objects enter collections, what will be preserved and how will archivists preserve it? And do archivists wish to offer to patrons the opportunity to create 3-D objects from their collections?

Augmented reality is changing the way we understand built heritage and collections. How can archivists capture and preserve these experiences? Do they wish to create augmented reality experiences for their patrons?

Museums have been using the immersive, computer-generated experiences of *Virtual reality* (VR) for nearly a decade. The Museum of Contemporary Art in Chicago recently held an exhibition called *I Was Raised on the Internet.*[1] Here is an excerpt from the museum's website describing it:

> *I Was Raised on the Internet* focuses on how the internet has changed the way we experience the world. Due to new types of gaming and entertainment and the rise of social media and alternative modes of representation, the everyday is no longer what it used to be. The ways we interact with each other have shifted through the connected nature of telecommunications devices across the internet, including mobile applications, social media platforms, and large search engines that have become everyday tools for individuals from all walks of life. New modes, not only of seeing but also of feeling, have emerged in response to this.

The exhibition was divided into five sections, each describing a different mode of interaction between a viewer and an art object. Three of them have direct connections to preservation: "Look at Me," which considers social media; "Control Me," which addresses the pervasive culture of surveillance and data collection that network technology enables; and "Play with Me," which illustrates immersive and interactive technologies—including VR. The very act of creating such an exhibition is a way of creating a record and thus preserving the phenomenon of whatever is being exhibited. This also raises the issue for archivists of ways to appraise and preserve the experiences of users.

The number of social media users in the world was estimated in 2017 to be 2.46 billion; in 2019, as we write this, it is projected to be 2.77 billion.[2] Therefore, the relationship between people and computers is important to monitor because it will continue to have an impact on how information is created, used, and shared—and for us, captured, preserved, and disseminated. The method of and impact on how archivists will preserve information are not yet fully understood. User experience must be a part of advancing archival preservation.

Research

Archivists need to engage in an active agenda of research to back up these trends. Studies in three areas would be particularly useful: 1) user studies; 2) impact of digital culture; and 3) analyses of gaps in digital preservation initiatives. A recent article by archivist Jessica Tai and several colleagues on records as agents in community archives notes that "little empirical data has been collected to assess how users of community archives conceive of the agency of records."[3] More fundamentally, as archival scholar Elizabeth Yakel points out, most of the voluminous literature on information-seeking behavior focuses on how users approach published works rather than primary sources.[4] Her model on archival intelligence includes "the ability to understand the connection between representations of documents, activities, and processes with the actual object or process being represented."[5] Research on the information needs of those who use archives could be expanded to account for how preservation facilitates—or impedes—the use of primary sources.

What is behind the staggering numbers of social media users? What will the impact of digital culture be on our institutions? How will this new culture influence demands for access to primary source materials? It might be useful for researchers to gather comparative statistics among a host of archives to determine the online and face-to-face use of archives. Are trends already emerging that archivists are not yet cognizant of? Once again, the answers may have ramifications for preservation as well as access.

In a 2018 research report on digital preservation,[6] expert Oya Rieger examined advances, challenges, and research opportunities. In a section on research, she observed that "it is difficult to study user experience without also looking at the contextual issues such as the software needed to make sense of preserved data. . . ."[7] She makes a good point, but robust data about user experience in archives, or about how users today work with primary source materials, are still lacking.

She also addresses the lack of a "cohesive and compelling roadmap" to guide the international community in further advancing digital preservation.[8] Developing a roadmap would greatly facilitate international initiatives while advancing digital preservation worldwide.

Not all future preservation research will be in the realm of the digital. As this book goes to press in the spring of 2020, the COVID 19 pandemic is ravaging the globe. Archivists and librarians are struggling with unprecedented challenges regarding the transmission of communicable diseases with scant data upon which to base decisions on pandemic prevention and preparedness. Future research will inform emerging standards and best practices needed to guide institutions in managing staff and services in future health crises, including methods for handling, disinfecting, and quarantining collections to mitigate risk.

How do we characterize the future of preservation specialists? Will they merely be stewards? Will they be Sherpa guides? Teachers? Facilitators? Or, a combination of all of these things? Their future will depend on their ability to embrace new roles and to respect a variety of approaches to preservation. As we have shown, preservation is an evolving field, with a future that is, in some respects, foreordained, and in others, unpredictable. Preservation is daunting, challenging, and stimulating (and advancing in promising ways).

NOTES

1 Museum of Contemporary Art, Chicago, *I Was Raised on the Internet* (June 23–October 14, 2018), https://mcachicago.org/Exhibitions/2018/I-Was-Raised-On-The-Internet, captured at https://perma.cc/33AY-32NN.

2 Statista: The Statistics Portal, "Number of Social Media Users Worldwide from 2010 to 2021 (in Billions)," https://www.statista.com/statistics/278414/number-of-worldwide-social-network-users, captured at https://perma.cc/9KSL-5ZHR.

3 Jessica Tai et al., "Summoning the Ghosts: Records as Agents in Community Archives," *Journal of Contemporary Archival Studies* 6, no. 1 (2019), https://elischolar.library.yale.edu/jcas/vol6/iss1/18.

4 Elizabeth Yakel, "Archival Intelligence," in *Theories of Information Behavior*, ed. Karen E. Fisher, Sanda Erdelez, and Lynne E. F. McKechnie (Medford, NJ: Information Today, 2005), 49–57.

5 Yakel, "Archival Intelligence," in *Theories of Information Behavior*, 50.

6 Oya Y. Rieger, *The State of Digital Preservation in 2018*, Issue Brief (October 29, 2018), Ithaka S&R, https:doi.org/10.18665/sr.310626.

7 Rieger, *The State of Digital Preservation in 2018*, 12.

8 Rieger, *The State of Digital Preservation in 2018*, 13.

APPENDIX A

Example Collection Development Policy

Yale University, Archives and Manuscripts, Understanding the Collection Development Policies, 2014

The University Archives' collection development policies specify what types of records should be transferred to the University Archives after the period of their active administrative use ends. The policies are organized according to the activities performed at Yale, rather than by the offices that perform those activities.

Each policy defines specific topics of interest and a list of the types of records that the University Archives wishes to document that activity. It is important to note that these listings of record types are not exhaustive. Any records may be considered archival if they document the topics of interest listed in the collection development policy. For questions about the topics of interest or record types, please contact the University Archives at archives@yale.edu.

Record Formats

The collection development policies apply to records of all formats, including paper records, computer files (e-mail, word-processed documents, spreadsheets, databases, and materials in imaging systems), photographs, audiovisual materials, and publications (e.g., newsletters, calendars of events, books, newspapers, websites, etc.). While the nature of different formats may require different methods of transfer and long-term care, the value of a given record is based on the information and evidence it provides, not on its format. When arranging a record transfer, University Archives staff will indicate how records of varying formats should be transferred.

Official Record Copy

Each policy has a section explaining who has primary responsibility for the records documenting that function. Very often, copies of the same records will be located in numerous offices on campus, although the official record copy only exists in one office. Each collection development policy identifies which office holds the official record copies. The office or individual responsible for maintaining these records is called the office of record (i.e., the holder of the official records copies). All other copies used by other university offices are not of permanent archival value and should not be transferred to the University Archives. If they are no longer of use to that office, they can be destroyed, provided there is no legal or administrative reason for their retention. If an office has any questions about the disposition of any non-permanent records, visit the Office of General Counsel and review the University's record retention schedule: http://ogc.yale.edu/yale-records-retention-schedule.

APPENDIX B

Example Preservation Policy

University of Texas Libraries Preservation Policy, 2020

Philosophy

The collections of the University of Texas Libraries, in addition to their intellectual and aesthetic value, represent an enormous economic investment. The University of Texas Libraries is committed to providing a comprehensive preservation program for these collections, consistent with the goals and objectives of the Library and the University and with the Library's stature as a major national research collection.

A comprehensive preservation program encompasses a system of plans, policies, procedures, and resources required to properly care for and prolong the life of these collection for the use of the educational and research community. An active preservation program encourages respect for the library and its collections, reduces the loss of materials through neglect or carelessness, and conserves resources through the application of preventive and corrective measures. Preservation, in fact, is an essential component in any activity involving introduction of library materials into collections (selection, acquisition, and cataloging) and handling by library staff and users.

The success of the University of Texas Libraries preservation program to a large extent depends on staff understanding and observance of good preservation practices. Because library materials are handled extensively by library staff, and because library users look to staff as exemplars in library matters, the observance of good preservation practice is extremely important. Active participation and leadership in the preservation program is the responsibility of all staff.

Definitions

"Preservation" is the set of actions taken to prevent, stop or retard deterioration of library materials through the management of: storage environment; housing materials and techniques; security; handling practices; as well as through user and staff education. Replacement is a form of preservation, as is changing the format of materials in order to preserve the intellectual content. "Conservation" implies the actions taken to prevent, stop, or retard deterioration of individual items through treatment level intervention into the physical state of the item. "Preservation" is used here as the broader term encompassing both preservation and conservation. A forthcoming revision of the Preservation Policy will address the UT Libraries' digital preservation efforts as part of a comprehensive preservation program for both physical and digital collection material.

Administration

Responsibility for directing the preservation program rests with the Assistant Director of Stewardship, who, with appropriate consultation, formulates, implements, and coordinates preservation policies and activities on a library-wide basis. The Assistant Director of Stewardship also maintains active liaison with the preservation programs of other campus agencies.

Program Objectives

Within the limitations imposed by budget and staffing levels, the University of Texas Libraries strives to provide a comprehensive preservation program that includes the following elements:

I. Adheres to internationally accepted preservation standards and techniques. This includes limited conservation treatment of library materials using permanent, nondestructive materials.

II. Evaluates and improves the physical care of library materials. This includes handling and storage, environmental conditions, collections security, and up-to-date disaster prevention and preparedness planning.

III. Ensures that the most effective preservation options are implemented. Present options include commercial binding and rebinding, in-house repair and binding, protective enclosures, replacement, limited preservation photoduplication and microfilming and, in rare instances, conservation.

IV. Identifies materials requiring preservation measures. Items in poor condition are identified through general stack maintenance, circulation, and physical surveys of collections. In cases of non-routine treatment, bibliographers recommend preservation options appropriate to the material under review.

V. Conducts an on-going program of staff training and awareness.

APPENDIX C

Example Digital Preservation Policy

Indiana University Libraries Digital Preservation Policy, 2017

Purpose

This policy statement formalizes Indiana University Libraries' commitment to meeting the challenges of long-term stewardship, preservation, and access to digital content. The policy framework comprises a set of guidelines from which procedures can be developed that meet accepted standards, use resources effectively, and support the mission and goals of the Libraries. The policy framework establishes guiding principles, identifies the scope of digital preservation activities and content to be preserved, cites institutional commitments and obligations that depend on effective stewardship, identifies stakeholders and responsibilities, describes guidelines for deposit, and establishes a basis and time frame for ongoing review.

Guiding Principles

In undertaking digital preservation activities, Indiana University Libraries will operate in accordance with the following principles:

Access

Indiana University is dedicated to providing current and future access to scholarly and historically significant digital objects that are within the purview of this policy, as broadly and openly as possible. Digital Preservation is only one piece of the digital curation lifecycle; access is fundamental both to ensuring the success of preservation activities and to providing avenues for the creation of new knowledge.

Authenticity and Integrity

The ability to maintain trust of scholarly outputs is paramount to long-term preservation efforts. Indiana University Libraries will take every step possible to ensure the authenticity and integrity of all digital objects. Provenance and fixity information will be maintained alongside every object.

Collaboration

Digital preservation is a campus- and university-wide endeavor that requires partnerships and input from various stakeholders. Where possible, Indiana University Libraries will act as a leader in digital preservation efforts across both the Bloomington campus and the entire university. To support this mission, Indiana University Libraries further commits to participating in local, national, and international efforts related to digital preservation.

Compliance with Standards and Best Practices

Indiana University Libraries will comply with current community-developed standards and best practices where they exist related to the creation, maintenance, storage, and delivery of digital objects and corresponding metadata.

Open Access

Providing open access to digital objects, when appropriate, is especially crucial to the scholarly record, as it allows future students, scholars, and the general public to freely use, and often re-use, past scholarly outputs and historically significant artifacts.

Outreach and Education

Indiana University Libraries will provide regular training for its faculty and staff working in areas related to digital preservation. Indiana University Libraries will also provide outreach to the university community in order to educate staff, faculty, and students about best practices in digital curation.

Rights and Privacy

Indiana University Libraries will provide access to digital objects while also respecting and upholding the intellectual property rights of authors and privacy concerns of donors. Rights management actions will be documented and rights information will be preserved with digital content. Indiana University Libraries will provide education to authors and donors in regards to their rights, and will obtain prior consent whenever possible. The Indiana University Libraries will also ensure that its infrastructure supports necessary access control settings in order to support content with various rights.

Sustainability

Indiana University Libraries is fully committed to providing staff, training, and equipment, as well as funding and additional resources as needed, to ensure the long-term sustainability of digital objects that fall within the scope of this policy.

Technology

Indiana University Libraries will ensure that the necessary hardware, software, and expertise are procured and maintained in order to support the long-term sustainability of digital objects. The Libraries will work with its partners to monitor technological advancements to ensure that the local technical infrastructure is maintained in accordance with current best practices.

Transparency

Indiana University Libraries strives to consistently document practices, procedures, policies, and strategies related to digital preservation efforts on a regular basis and to make this documentation publicly accessible wherever possible.

Mandate

Indiana University Libraries is responsible for the sustainability of digital objects and aims to provide long-term access to usable versions that we are committed to preserving for our community. The Libraries' mandate for digital preservation, however, is multifaceted, as the unique needs of various content types require different preservation actions and allow for different provisions of access. Although content in the Indiana University Libraries digital infrastructure is primarily intended to be made publicly available for the broadest possible dissemination, some content will be restricted for a limited period of time in accordance with state and federal laws, to prevent unauthorized access to content of a sensitive or confidential nature, and in accordance with submission agreements as stipulated by the donor of the content. Access and use of content will be in compliance with applicable laws and Indiana University policies relating to intellectual property, copyright, and ownership rights.

Scope

The scope of the Indiana University Libraries' responsibility for digital preservation derives from a variety of factors, including source, ownership and content type.

Libraries Content

Indiana University Libraries is responsible for the ongoing curation and management of all content owned by internal units. Indiana University Libraries is responsible for digital content generated from analog and digital reformatting projects as well as content that is born-digital.

University Content

Indiana University Libraries is responsible for the long-term preservation of all content owned by the Trustees of Indiana University once it is deposited into a digital repository or physical collection managed by the Libraries. The Libraries is responsible for working with other units to determine whether and how items should be transferred to and maintained by the Libraries.

Faculty and Student Content

Indiana University Libraries has a strong stake in ensuring the persistence of scholarship and educational resources created by the university's faculty and students. While the Libraries are best able to ensure the sustainability of such content when it is deposited into the university's institutional repository, IUScholarWorks, this is not always ideal or possible. In such cases, Indiana University Libraries is responsible for assisting faculty and students in identifying appropriate field-specific repositories and ensuring that such external repositories have a mandate for long-term preservation as well as documented preservation policies and procedures.

Open Access and Public Domain Content

Indiana University Libraries is committed to providing the highest level of access to digital objects as possible, and as such, promotes the principle of open access. Further, Indiana University Libraries is committed to ensuring the long-term viability of content in the public domain that has been determined to fit within the collecting scope of the Libraries.

Licensed Content

Indiana University Libraries aims to ensure that all licensed content vendors participate in community preservation programs such as LOCKSS, CLOCKSS, or Portico or have a robust, independent preservation plan in place. In lieu of this, Indiana Universities Libraries will endeavor to negotiate licenses with vendors that will enable the Libraries to maintain a local copy for preservation of content licensed in perpetuity.

Content Originating Elsewhere

Indiana University Libraries often works with affiliated faculty or units outside of Indiana University to curate digital objects identified as fitting within the Libraries' collecting scope. Where possible, Indiana University Libraries is responsible for ensuring that the appropriate intellectual property licensing is in place to ensure long-term preservation capabilities when content is ingested into its repositories. When this is not possible, the Libraries will provide guidance for content owners to ensure the appropriate curation measures are in place to meet the unique needs of the content.

Roles and Responsibilities

All Indiana University Libraries staff assist in the implementation of this policy as appropriate to their roles and responsibilities. The Dean of the Libraries is responsible for appointing the appropriate staff to ensure the maintenance and review of this policy. Library Administration is responsible for ensuring that every digital object is maintained within a collection that has a corresponding collection owner. The supervisor of the collection owner is responsible for ensuring that a new owner is designated should the incumbent vacate their role. All Indiana University Libraries staff are accountable to their managers for compliance with this policy and related policies, standards, and guidelines.

The Indiana University Libraries has primary responsibility for digital preservation at Indiana University, but it is also a shared responsibility across the organization. All responsible units, content creators, and curators with a custodial role for digital objects identified for long-term preservation have a responsibility to actively contribute to the intent and priorities necessary to fulfill this policy.

Guidelines for Ingest

In order to ensure long-term preservation of digital objects, Indiana University Libraries will ensure that specific steps are taken to align with best practices as part of the ingest process. This includes replication across multiple storage infrastructures and regular fixity checking within the repository and storage environments to ensure bit-level preservation. This also includes maintaining minimum necessary metadata with all objects.

Prior to ingest into the Indiana University Libraries digital infrastructure, content managers, with assistance from members of Library Technologies, are required to:

- Provide contact information for the content manager, including departmental affiliation, and a contingency contact in the event that the originally assigned content manager is unable to serve in this role
- Provide adequate documentation (donor agreement, memorandums of agreement, etc.) that states terms of use, with an emphasis whenever possible on use/re-use for teaching or research purposes; ensure alignment with repository-level policies related to descriptive metadata, recommended metadata standards, and minimum descriptive metadata requirements that captures the objects' provenance, aboutness, and context
- Ensure alignment with repository-level policies related to file formats, recommended format standards, and minimal technical metadata requirements that captures the objects' authenticity, integrity, and reliability
- Ensure alignment with university policies for sensitive, private, and restricted data (see Guiding Principles and Appendix II: Related Indiana University Policies and Standards)

In addition to the requirements above, the content managers and members of Library Technologies should verify that there are no proprietary licenses or encumbrances which may restrict the Libraries' ability to store, manipulate, or migrate data from one format or standard to another. In the event that the Libraries accepts proprietary content, the content managers should assist in identifying sufficient non-proprietary tools to manipulate and provide access to the content in a standard format.

Policy Review

This policy will be reviewed on an ongoing basis, with a review occurring no more than once per year and no less than once per three years.

Bibliography

Abbey, Heidi N. "The Green Archivist: A Primer for Adopting Affordable, Environmentally Sustainable, and Socially Responsible Archival Management Practices." *Archival Issues: Journal of the Midwest Archives Conference* 34, no. 2 (2012): 91–115, https://www.jstor.org/stable/i40081871.

Alberts, Christopher J., and Audrey J. Dorofee. *Risk Management Framework.* Technical Report CMU/SEI-2010-TR-017. Pittsburgh: Software Engineering Institute, Carnegie Mellon, August 2010. https://resources.sei.cmu.edu/asset_files/TechnicalReport/2010_005_001_15245.pdf, captured at https://perma.cc/TE8F-GASA.

Allen, Stephanie, Sofía Becerra-Licha, Kenn Bicknell, Jacqueline E. Chapman, Genna Duplisea, M. Alison Eisendrath, Joe Filapek, Jan Levinson Hebbard, James Himphill, Jeffrey Inscho, Susan M. Irwin, Elizabeth Joffrion, Stephanie Baltzer Kom, Melissa Levine, Christina E. Newton, Mega Subramaniam, Gina Watkinson, and Darla Wegener. *Collective Wisdom: An Exploration of Library, Archives and Museum Cultures.* Dublin, Ohio: OCLC Research, 2017. http://www.oclc.org/content/dam/research/publications/2017/collective-wisdom-white-paper.pdf, captured at https://perma.cc/A54X-D7EY.

American Alliance of Museums. *Museums, Environmental Sustainability and Our Future: A Call to Action from the Summit on Sustainability Standards in Museums 2013.* Washington, DC: AAM, 2013. ww2.aam-us.org/docs/default-source/professional-networks/picgreenwhitepaperfinal.pdf, captured at https://perma.cc/RU6J-UWDP.

American Association for State and Local History. "Statement of Professional Standards and Ethics," revised 2017. https://d221a1e908576484595f-1f424f9e28cc684c8a6264aa2ad33a9d.ssl.cf2.rackcdn.com/aaslh_f3b127c7bc6e406a8ae1829095a08c49.pdf, captured at https://perma.cc/Y9T7-96P3.

American Institute for Conservation of Historic and Artistic Works. Ethics and Standards Committee. "Code of Ethics and Guidelines for Practice," www.conservation-us.org/ethics, captured at https://perma.cc/VF85-38SD.

______. Green Task Force. *Summary Report.* Presented by Patricia Silence, Chair. Los Angeles: AIC 37th Annual Meeting, May 21, 2009. https://www.culturalheritage.org/docs/default-source/reports/aic-green-task-force-survey-report.pdf?sfvrsn=2.

______. "Photographic Processes." http://www.conservation-wiki.com/wikiCategory:Photographic_Processes.

American Library Association. "Frontline Fundraising Toolkit," April 5, 2011, 2.

______. Committee on Professional Ethics. "Professional Ethics." http://www.ala.org/tools/ethics, captured at https://perma.cc/9YEQ-42YT.

Anderson, Ian. "Archival Digitization: Breaking Out of the Strong Box." In *Record Keeping in a Hybrid Environment: Managing the Creation, Use, Preservation and Disposal of Unpublished Information Objects in Context.* Edited by Alistair Tough and Michael Moss. Oxford, UK: Chandos, 2006, 203–25.

Artigas, David John. "A Comparison of the Efficacy and Costs of Different Approaches to Climate Management in Historic Buildings and Museums." Master's thesis, University of Pennsylvania, January 2007. http://repository.upenn.edu/hp_theses/63.

Ashley-Smith, Jonathan. "Challenges of Managing Collection Environments." *Conservation Perspectives: The Getty Conservation Institute Newsletter* 33, no. 2 (2018): 4–9.

______. *Risk Assessment for Object Conservation.* Oxford, UK: Butterworth-Heinemann, 1999.

Association of the American Society of Heating, Refrigerating and Air-Conditioning Engineers. *ASHRAE Handbook Online.* Chapter 23, "Industrial Applications for Museums, Galleries, Libraries and Archives." Atlanta: ASHRAE, 2016. https://www.ashrae.org/technical-resources/ashrae-handbook, captured at https://perma.cc/5EX9-BLSB.

Association of University Leaders for a Sustainable Future (ULSF). "Talloires Declaration." N.p.: 1990. http://ulsf.org/talloires-declaration, captured at https://perma.cc/8PHB-BBBW.

Baca, Murtha, ed. *Introduction to Metadata.* 3rd ed. Los Angeles: Getty Publications, 2016. http://www.getty.edu/publications/intrometadata.

Bailey, Jefferson. "Disrespect des Fonds: Rethinking Arrangement and Description in Born-Digital Archives." *Archive Journal* 3 (June 2013). http://www.archivejournal.net/essays/disrespect-des-fonds-rethinking-arrangement-and-description-in-born-digital-archives, captured at https://perma.cc/EKT5-QQ38.

Baker, Cathleen, A., and Randy Silverman. "Misperceptions about White Gloves." *International Preservation News: A Newsletter of the IFLA Core Activity on Preservation and Conservation,* no. 37 (2005): 4–9. https://www.ifla.org/files/assets/pac/ipn/ipnn37.pdf, captured at https://perma.cc/M889-WK5L.

Baker, Nicholson. *Double Fold: Libraries and the Assault on Paper.* New York: Random House, 2001.

Ball, Alex. "Web Archiving." Edinburgh: Digital Curation Centre, 2010. https://www.era.lib.ed.ac.uk/bitstream/handle/1842/3327/Ball%20sarwa-https://www.era.lib.ed.ac.uk/bitstream/handle/1842/3327/Ball%20sarwa-v1.1.pdf, captured at https://perma.cc/5CYH-QNJV.

Banks, Paul N. "Environment and Building Design for Preservation of Library Materials." In *Preservation: Issues and Planning.* Edited by Paul N. Banks and Roberta Pilette. Chicago: American Library Association, 2000, 114–44.

______. "The Laws of Conservation." In *Preserving Our Heritage: Perspectives from Antiquity to the Digital Age.* Edited by Michèle Valerie Cloonan. Chicago: Neal-Schuman/American Library Association, 2015, 328.

Bastian, Jeannette A. "A Question of Custody: The Colonial Archives of the United States Virgin Islands." *American Archivist* 64, no. 1 (2001): 96–114. https://doi.org/10.17723/aarc.64.1.h6k872252u2gr377.

______, and Ben Alexander, eds. *Community Archives: The Shaping of Memory.* London, UK: Facet Publishing, 2009.

Bates, Marcia J., and Mary Niles Maack, eds. *Encyclopedia of Library and Information Sciences.* 3rd ed. N.p.: Taylor & Francis Group, 2009.

Baynes-Cope, A. D. *Caring for Books and Documents.* 2nd ed. London, UK: British Library, 1989.

Beagrie, Neil, Najla Semple, Peter Williams, and Richard Wright. *Digital Preservation Policies Study.* Technical Report. N.p.: Charles Beagrie Limited, October 2008.

______, Maggie Jones, and the Digital Preservation Centre (DPC). *Preservation Management of Digital Material: The Handbook.* Glasgow: DPC, 2008. www.beagrie.com.

Becker, Christoph et al. "Systematic Planning for Digital Preservation: Evaluating Potential Strategies and Building Preservation Plans." *International Journal of Digital Libraries* 10, no. 4 (2009): 133–57. https://doi.org/10.1007/s00799-009-0057-1.

Becker, Christoph, Luis Faria, and Kresimir Duretec. "Scalable Decision Support for Digital Preservation: An Assessment." *OCLC Systems & Services: International Digital Library Perspectives* 31, no. 1 (2015): 11–34. http://dx.doi.org/10.1108/OCLC-06-2014-0026.

Bee, Robert. "The Importance of Preserving Paper-Based Artifacts in a Digital Age." *The Library Quarterly* 78, no. 2 (April 2008): 179–94. https://doi.org/10.1086/528888.

Berger, Sherri, "The Evolving Ethics of Preservation: Redefining Practices and Responsibilities in the 21st Century." *The Serials Librarian* 57, nos. 1–2 (2009): 57–68. https://doi.org/10.1080/03615260802669086.

Berger, Sidney E. *Rare Books and Special Collections.* Chicago: Neal-Schuman/American Library Association, 2014.

Besser, Howard. "Archiving Websites Containing Streaming Media." PowerPoint presentation. Archiving Conference, Society for Imaging Science and Technology, 2017. http://netpreserve.org/ga2018/wp-content/uploads/2018/11/IIPC_WAC2018-Howard_Besser-Archiving_websites_containing_streaming_media.pdf, captured at https://perma.cc/YFG3-BNPL.

Bishoff, Liz. "Digital Preservation Plan: Ensuring Long-Term Access and Authenticity of Digital Collections." *Information and Standards Quarterly* 22, no. 2 (2010): 21–22. https://doi.org/10.3789/isqv22n2.2010.03

_______, the Bishoff Group, and Erin Rhodes. "Planning for Digital Preservation: A Self-Assessment Tool." Andover, MA: Northeast Document Conservation Center, n.d. https://www.nedcc.org/assets/media/documents/DigitalPreservationSelfAssessmentfinal.pdf, captured at https://perma.cc/RP4S-MY4G.

Blaha, Craig. "Preserving Facebook Records: Subscriber Expectations and Behavior." *Preservation, Digital Technology & Culture* 42, no. 3 (2013): 115–28. https://doi.org/10.1515/pdtc-2013-0017.

Blue Ribbon Task Force on Sustainable Digital Preservation and Access. *Sustainable Economics for a Digital Planet: Ensuring Access to Long-term Digital Information*. Final Report. La Jolla, CA: OCLC, February 2010.

Bode, Leticia, and Meg Leta Jones. "Ready to Forget: American Attitudes toward the Right to Be Forgotten." *The Information Society: An International Journal* 33, no. 2 (2017): 76–85. https://doi.org/10.1080/01972243.2016.1271071.

Bolcer, John. "The Protocols for Native American Archival Materials: Considerations and Concerns from the Perspective of a Non-Tribal Archivist." *Easy Access* 34, no. 4 (2009): 3–6.

Boles, Frank, David George-Shongo Jr., and Christine Weideman. *Report: Task Force to Review Protocols for Native American Archival Materials.* Society of American Archivists Council Meeting, February 7–10, 2008. Washington, DC: Society of American Archivists, January 2009.

Bonn, Maria, Lori Kendall, and Jerome McDonough. *Libraries and Archives and the Preservation of Intangible Cultural Heritage: Defining a Research Agenda.* A White Paper of the School of Information Sciences, University of Illinois at Urbana-Champaign. Champaign: University of Illinois, July 2017.

Bradley, Kevin. "Defining Digital Sustainability." *Library Trends* 56, no. 1 (2007): 148–63. http://hdl.handle.net/2142/3772.

Briston, Heather. "Understanding Copyright Law." In *Rights in the Digital Era*, Module 4 in the Trends in Archives Practice series. Chicago: Society of American Archivists, 2015. https://www2.archivists.org/sites/all/files/Module_4_CaseStudy_HeatherBriston.pdf, captured at https://perma.cc/DCF9-HHQE.

British Standards Institute (BSI). *Specification for Managing Environmental Conditions for Cultural Collections*. PAS 198: 2012. N.p.: March 28, 2012. https://shop.bsigroup.com/ProductDetail/?pid=000000000030219669.

Brophy, Sarah, and Elizabeth Wylie. *The Green Museum: A Primer on Environmental Practice.* Latham, MD: AltaMira Press, 2008.

Brown, Adrian. *Practical Digital Preservation: A How-To Guide for Organizations of Any Size.* Chicago: Neal-Schuman, 2013.

Brown, J. P., and William B. Rose. "Humidity and Moisture in Historic Buildings: The Origins of Building and Object Conservation." *APT Bulletin* 27, no. 3 (1996): 12–23.

Brylawski, Sam et al., eds. *ARSC Guide to Audio Preservation.* CLIR Publication 164. Washington, DC: Council on Library and Information Resources, Association for Recorded Sound Collections, and the National Recording Preservation Board of the Library of Congress, May 2015.

Bülow, Anna E. "Collection Management Using Preservation Risk Assessment." *Journal of the Institute of Conservation* 33, no. 1 (2010): 65–78. https://doi.org/10.1080/19455220903509960.

Burge, Daniel. "IPI Guide to Preservation of Digitally-Printed Photographs." http://www.dp3project.org/webfm_send/739, captured at https://perma.cc/4QSS-2J5Q.

Caldera, Mary A., and Kathryn M. Neal. *Through the Archival Looking Glass: A Reader on Diversity and Inclusion.* Chicago: Society of American Archivists, 2014.

Caplan, Priscilla. *Metadata Fundamentals for All Librarians.* Chicago: American Library Association, 2003.

______. *Understanding PREMIS.* Washington, DC: Library of Congress, 2017. http://www.loc.gov/standards/premis/understanding-premis-rev2017.pdf, captured at https://perma.cc/ZE8E-GFQJ.

Cappon, Lester J. Quoted in Randall C. Jimerson, ed. *American Archival Studies: Readings in Theory and Practice.* Chicago: The Society of American Archivists, 2000.

Carson, Rachel. *Silent Spring.* Boston: Houghton Mifflin; Cambridge, MA: Riverside Press, 1962.

Casey, Mike. *Format Characteristics and Preservation Problems.* Version 1.0. FACET: The Field Audio Collection Evaluation Tool. Bloomington: Indiana University, 2007. http://www.dlib.indiana.edu/projects/sounddirections/facet/facet_formats.pdf, captured at https://perma.cc/6BTX-G7TU.

Caswell, Michelle. "Defining Human Rights Archives: Introduction to the Special Double Issue on Archives and Human Rights." In *Archives and Human Rights.* Edited by Michelle Caswell. *Archival Science* 14, nos. 3–4 (2014): 207–13. https://doi. org/10.1007/s10502-014-9226-0.

Center for Research Libraries. *Space Data and Information Transfer Systems: Audit and Certification of Trustworthy Digital Repositories.* ISO16363/2012/TDR. Chicago: CRL, 2012. https://webstore.ansi.org/Standards/ISO/ISO163632012?gclid=EAIaIQobChMI0P3axsS76AIVCtVkCh0OcA1vEAAYASAAEgK6l_D_BwE.

Charles Beagrie Ltd. "Keeping Research Data Safe (KRDS)." N.P.: July 2011. https://www.beagrie.com/krds.php.

Child, Margaret. "Planning and Prioritizing. 1.5 Collection Policies and Preservation." Andover, MA: NEDCC Preservation Leaflet Series, n.d. https://www.nedcc.org/free-resources/preservation-leaflets/1.-planning-and-prioritizing/1.5-collections-policies-and-preservation, captured at https://perma.cc/2U58-7BDY.

Chowdhury, G. G. *Sustainability of Scholarly Information.* London, UK: Facet Publishing, 2014.

Christensen, Jørgen Erik, and Hans Janssen. "Passive Hygrothermal Control of a Museum Storage Building in Vejle." In *Proceedings of Building Simulation 2010: 12th Conference of International Building Performance Simulation Association.* Kongens Lyngens, DK: November 2010. (Report R-220). http://orbit.dtu.dk/en/publications/passive-hygrothermal-control-of-a-museum-storage-building-in-vejle(1f014358-53e5-4697-8109-2550844623a6).html, captured at https://perma.cc/G9QH -LV8N.

Clapp, Verner W. "The Story of Permanent/Durable Paper, 1115-1970." *Restaurator* Supplement, no. 3 (1972): 1–58. https://doi.org/10.1515/rest.1972.1.s3.1.

Clavir, Miriam. *Preserving What Is Valued: Museums, Conservation and First Nations.* Vancouver, BC: University of British Columbia Press, 2002.

Cloonan, Michèle Valerie. "Conservation and Preservation of Library and Archival Materials." *Encyclopedia of Library and Information Sciences.* 3rd ed. New York: Francis & Taylor, 2010, 1–19.

______. *The Monumental Challenge of Preservation: The Past in a Volatile World.* Cambridge, MA: MIT Press, 2018.

______. "The Pedagogy of Preservation." Unpublished paper given at SAA, San Diego, August 8, 2012.

______, ed. *Preserving Our Heritage: Perspectives from Antiquity to the Digital Age.* Chicago: Neal-Schuman/American Library Association, 2015.

______, and Patricia Norcott. "The Evolution of Preservation Librarianship as Reflected in Job Descriptions from 1975 through 1987." *College & Research Libraries* 50, no. 6 (1989): 646–56. https://doi.org/10.5860/crl_50_06_646.

Cocciolo, Anthony. *Moving Image and Sound Collections for Archivists.* Chicago: Society of American Archivists, 2017.

Coffey, Liz, and Elizabeth Walters. "Moving Image Materials." In *The Preservation Management Handbook.* Edited by Ross Harvey and Martha R. Mahard, 276–77. Lanham, MD: Rowman & Littlefield, 2014.

Collaborative Electronic Records Project. *Collaborative Electronic Records Project: An Introduction and Overview.* N.p.: Rockefeller Archive Center and Smithsonian Institution Archives, December 2008. http://siarchives.si.edu/cerp/CERP_Overview_CC.pdf, captured at https://perma.cc/SC9Y-SBV3.

Colwell, Chip. *Plundered Skulls and Stolen Spirits: Inside the Fight to Reclaim Native America's Culture.* Chicago: University of Chicago Press, 2017.

Consultative Committee for Space Data Systems. *Reference Model for an Open Archival Information System (OAIS): Recommended Practice CCSDS 650.0M-2: Recommendation for Space Data System Practices.* Magenta Book, Recommended Practice 2. Washington, DC: CCSDS Secretariat, June 2012, 19. https://public.ccsds.org/pubs/650x0m2.pdf, captured at https://perma.cc/9S3L-Y83M.

Conway, Paul. "Archival Preservation Practice in a Nationwide Context." *American Archivist* 53, no. 2 (1990): 204–22. https://doi.org/10.17723/aarc.53.2.d0gt78p562832655.

______. "Perspectives on Archival Resources: The 1985 Census of Archival Institutions." *American Archivist* 50, no. 2 (1987): 174–91. https://doi.org/10.17723/aarc.50.2.l211240g46238078.

______. *Preservation in the Digital World.* Washington, DC: Council of Library and Information Resources, March 1996.

______, and Devan Ray Donaldson. "Implementing PREMIS: A Case Study at the Florida Digital Archive." *Library Hi Tech* 28, no. 2 (2010): 273–89. https://doi:10.1108/07378831011047677.

Cook, Terry. "Evidence, Memory, Identity, and Community: Four Shifting Archival Paradigms." *Archival Science* 13, nos. 2–3 (2013): 95–120. https://doi.org/10.1007/s10502-012-9180-7.

______. "What Is Past Is Prologue: A History of Archival Ideas since 1898 and the Future of the Paradigm Shift." *Archivaria* 43 (Spring 1997): 17–63. https://archivaria.ca/index.php/archivaria/article/view/12175/13184.

Corrado, Edward M., and Heather Moulaison Sandy. *Digital Preservation for Libraries, Archives, and Museums.* 2nd ed. Lanham, MD: Rowman & Littlefield, 2017.

Cox, Richard, and James M. O'Toole. *Understanding Archives & Manuscripts*, Archival Fundamentals Series II. Chicago: Society of American Archivists, 2006.

Cox, Robert S. "Maximal Processing, or, Archivist on a Pale Horse." *Journal of Archival Organization* 8, no. 2 (2010): 134–48. https://doi.org/10.1080/15332748.2010.526086.

Cunningham, Adrian. "Digital Curation/Digital Archiving: A View from the National Archives of Australia." *American Archivist* 71, no. 2 (2008): 530–43. https://doi.org/10.17723/aarc.71.2.p0h0t68547385507.

Currall, James, Michael Moss, and Susan Stuart. "What Is a Collection?" *Archivaria* 58 (2004): 131–46. https://archivaria.ca/index.php/archivaria/article/view/12480.

Dale, Robin, and Bruce Ambacher. "Trustworthy Repositories Audit and Certification (TRAC): Criteria and Checklist." Dublin, OH: Online Computer Library Center, 2007.

Daniel, Dominique, and Amalia Levi, eds. *Identity Palimpsests: Archiving Ethnicity in the U.S. and Canada.* Sacramento: Litwin Press, 2014.

Dappert, Angela, Rebecca Squire Guenther, and Sébastien Peyrard, eds. "Digital Preservation Metadata for Practitioners, Implementing PREMIS." 2016. https://doi.org/10.1007/978-3-319-43763-7.

Darling, Pamela W. "Creativity v. Despair: The Challenge of Preservation Administration." *Library Trends* 30, no. 2 (1981): 179–88. http://hdl.handle.net/2142/7193.

______, and Duane E. Webster. *Preservation Planning Program: An Assisted Self-Study Manual for Libraries*. Expanded 1987 edition. Washington, DC: Association of Research Libraries, Office of Management Studies, 1987.

Dawson, Alex, and Nick Poole. *Benchmarks in Collections Care 2.1.* London, UK: Collections Trust, 2018. https://326gtd123dbk1xdkdm489u1q-wpengine.netdna-ssl.com/wp-content/uploads/2016/11/BENCHMARKS-Case_Studies_FINAL_03.pdf, captured at https://perma.cc/9RLK-7QAJ.

Day, Brian J. "The Moral Intuition of Ruskin's 'Storm Cloud.'" *Studies in English Literature, 1500–1900* 45, no. 4 (2005): 917–33.

Department of Homeland Security. Ready. "IT Disaster Recovery Plan." https://www.ready.gov/business/implementation/IT, captured at https://perma.cc/RY9J-VNZF.

de Tocqueville, Alexis. *Democracy in America.* Published as *De la démocratie en Amérique*. Paris: Librairie de Charles Gosselin 1835;1840; English version, Philadelphia: J. & H. Langley, 1841; rpt. New York: Library of America. Distributed to the trade in the U.S. by Penguin Putnam, 2004. The Library of America, 147.

Dessem, Matthew. "Film Preservation 2.0." *The Dissolve* (blog), February 24, 2014. https://thedissolve.com/features/exposition/429-film-preservation-20, captured at https://perma.cc/8XP2-8KBT.

"Digital Archive Software." N.p.: Preservica, n.d. https://preservica.com/digital-archive-software.

Digital Curation Centre. "DCC Lifecycle Model." Edinburgh: DCC, 2007. http://www.dcc.ac.uk/resources/curation-lifecycle-model, captured at https://perma.cc/Q23Z-SE4W.

______. "What Is Digital Curation?" http://www.dcc.ac.uk/digital-curation/what-digital-curation, captured at https://perma.cc/A97K-EAAH.

Digital Preservation Coalition. *Digital Preservation Handbook*. 2nd ed. 2015. https://www.dpconline.org/handbook.

Digital Preservation Network, "Digital Preservation Workflow Curriculum," March 2017. https://www.weareavp.com/wp-content/uploads/2017/10/Digital-Preservation-Workshop-Curriculum-%E2%80%94-2017-03-08.pdf, captured at https:// perma.cc/PPT7-N34P.

Dionne, Georges. *Risk Management: History, Definition and Critique*. CIRRELT-2013-56. Montréal: Université de Montréal, September 2013. https://www.cirrelt.ca/DocumentsTravail/CIRRELT-2013-56.pdf, captured at https://perma.cc/8GKW-E3KS.

Donaldson, Devan Ray, and Elizabeth Yakel. "Secondary Adoption of Technical Standards: The Case of PREMIS." *Archival Science* 13, no. 1 (2013): 55–83. http://hdl.handle.net/2022/22472.

Dooley, Jackie M., and Katherine Luce. *Taking Our Pulse: The OCLC Research Survey of Special Collections and Archives.* Report of OCLC Research. Dublin, Ohio: OCLC, 2010. http://www.oclc.org/research/publications/library/2010/2010-11.pdf, captured at https://perma.cc/8Q9E-BQEZ.

Doubek, James. "Google Has Received 650,000 'Right To Be Forgotten' Requests Since 2014." *The Two-Way* (blog). National Public Radio, February 28, 2018. https://www.npr.org/sections/thetwo-way/2018/02/28/589411543/google-received-650-000-right-to-be-forgotten-requests-since-2014, captured at https://perma.cc/PY4T-859U.

dPlan: The Online Disaster-Planning Tool for Cultural and Civic Institutions. "Welcome to dPlan." Northeast Document Conservation Center, 2006. dPlan.org.

Dressler, Virginia, and Cindy Kristof. "The Right to Be Forgotten and Implications on Digital Collections: A Survey of ARL Member Institutions on Practice and Policy." *College & Research Libraries* 79, no. 7 (2018): 972–90. https://crl.acrl.org/index.php/crl/article/view/16890.

Duranti, Luciana. "Diplomatics: New Uses for an Old Science." *Archivaria* 28 (1989): 7–27. https://archivaria.ca/index.php /archivaria/article/view/11567/12513, captured at https://perma.cc/8UV7-CGVC.

______, and Giovanni Michetti. "The Archival Method." In *Research in the Archival Multiverse.* Edited by Anne Gilliland, Sue McKemmish, and Andrew J. Lau, 84–85. Clayton, Victoria: Monash University Publishing, 2017.

______, and Patricia C. Franks, eds. *Encyclopedia of Archival Science.* Lanham, MD: Rowman & Littlefield, 2015.

Eastwood, Terry, Bart Ballaux, Rachel Mills, and Randy Preston. "Appendix 14. The InterPARES Chain of Preservation Model Diagrams and Definitions." In *International Research on Permanent Authentic Records in Electronic Systems (InterPARES) 2: Experiential, Interactive and Dynamic Records.* Edited by Luciana Duranti and Randy Preston. Rome, Italy: Associazione Nazionale Archivistica Italiana, 2008. http://www.interpares.org/display_file.cfm?doc=ip2_COP_diagrams(complete).pdf, captured at https://perma.cc/AH7L-SFYP.

Echo-Hawk, Walter R. *In the Courts of the Conqueror: The 10 Worst Indian Law Cases Ever Decided.* Golden, CO: Fulcrum Publishers, 2010.

______. *In the Light of Justice: The Rise of Human Rights in Native America and the UN Declaration on the Rights of Indigenous Peoples.* Golden, CO: Fulcrum Publishers, 2013.

Ecosystems and Human Well-being: Synthesis. Millennium Ecosystem Assessment. The Millennium Ecosystems Series. Washington, DC: Island Press, 2005.

Ellis, Roger H., and Peter Walne, eds. *Selected Writings of Sir Hilary Jenkinson.* Chicago: Society of American Archivists, 2003.

Ercegovac, Zorana, ed. "Integrating Multiple Overlapping Metadata Standards." Special issue, *Journal of the American Society for Information Science* 50, no. 13 (1999): 1165–1223.

Erhardt, David, Charles S. Tumosa, and Marion F. Mecklenburg. "Applying Science to the Question of Museum Climate." In *Conference on Microclimates in Museums*. Edited by Tim Padfield and Karen Borchersen. Copenhagen: National Museum of Denmark, 2007. https://repository.si.edu/handle/10088/8131.

______, and Marion Mecklenburg. "Relative Humidity Re-examined." *Studies in Conservation* 39, Issue supplement 2 (1994): 32–38. https://doi.org/10.1179/sic.1994.39.Supplement-2.32.

Erway, Ricky. "Defining 'Born Digital': An Essay." Dublin, OH: Online Computer Library Center, 2010. http://www.oclc.org/content/dam/research/activities/hiddencollections/borndigital.pdf, captured at https://perma.cc/TZ8A-HYYT.

Farquhar, A. Adam, and Helen Hockx-Yu. "Planets: Integrated Services for Digital Preservation." *International Journal of Digital Curation* 2, no. 2 (2007): 88–99.

Farrell, Matthew. "Email." In *The Digital Archives Handbook: A Guide to Creation, Management, and Preservation*. Edited by Aaron D. Purcell. Lanham, MD: Rowman & Littlefield, 2019, 215–29.

Federal Emergency Management Agency (FEMA). "Hazard Identification and Risk Assessment." https://www.fema.gov/hazard-identification-and-risk-assessment.

______. "Reconstitution Template." https://www.fema.gov/media-library/assets/documents/86280.

Fischer, Monique. *A Short Guide to Film-Based Photographic Materials: Identification, Care, and Duplication*. Andover, MA: Northeast Document Conservation Center, 2012.

Flynn, Sarah J. A. "The Records Continuum Model in Context and Its Implications for Archival Practice." *Journal of the Society of Archivists* 22, no. 1 (2001): 79–93. https://doi.org/10.1080/00379810120037522.

Foot, Mirjam M. *Building a Preservation Policy*. London, UK: British Library Preservation Advisory Centre, 2013.

______. "Preservation Policy and Planning." In *Preservation Management for Libraries, Archives and Museums*. Edited by G. E. Gorman and Sydney J. Shep. London, UK: Facet Publishing, 2006, 19–41.

Franklin, Phyllis. "Scholars, Librarians, and the Future of Primary Records." *College & Research Libraries* 54, no. 5 (1993): 397–406. http://hdl.handle.net/2142/41619.

Frey, William H. "The U.S. Will Become 'Minority White' in 2045." In *Census Projects: Youthful Minorities*. https://www.brookings.edu/blog/the-avenue/2018/03/14/the-us-will-become-minority-white-in-2045-census-projects, captured at https://perma.cc/33A9-UCXA.

Frick, Caroline. *Saving Cinema: The Politics of Preservation*. New York: Oxford University Press, 2011.

Geiger, A. W. "Most Americans—Especially Millennials—Say Libraries Can Help Them Find Reliable, Trustworthy Information." *Fact Tank* (blog). Pew Research Center, August 30, 2017. http://www.pewresearch.org/fact-tank/2017/08/30/most-americans-especially-millennials-say-libraries-can-help-them-find-reliable-trustworthy-information, captured at https://perma.cc/N6D7-4J6L.

Gilliland, Anne. J. "Archival and Recordkeeping Traditions in the Multiverse and Their Importance for Researching Situations and Situating Research." In *Research in the Archival Multiverse*. Edited by Anne J. Gilliland, Sue McKemmish, and Andrew J. Lau. Clayton, Victoria: Monash University, 2017, 31–73.

______. "Setting the Stage." In *Introduction to Metadata*. 3rd ed. Edited by Murtha Baca. Los Angeles: Getty Publications, 2016. http://www.getty.edu/publications/intrometadata.

______, Sue McKemmish, and Andrew J. Lau, eds. *Research in the Archival Multiverse*. Victoria, Australia: *Monash University Press*, 2016.

Goldman, Ben. "It's Not Easy Being Green(e): Digital Preservation in the Age of Climate Change." In *Archival Values: Essays in Honor of Mark Greene*. Edited by Christine Weideman and Mary A. Caldera. Chicago: Society of American Archivists, 2019, 174–87.

Government of Canada. Canadian Heritage Information Network. *Digital Preservation Policy Framework: Development Guidelines*, version 2.1. https://www.canada.ca/en/heritage-information-network/services/digital-preservation/policy-framework-development-guideline.html#a1, captured at https://perma.cc/ZB7D-HUHF.

Greene, Mark A. "MPLP: It's Not Just for Processing Anymore." *American Archivist* 73, no. 1 (2010): 175–203. https://doi.org/10.17723/aarc.73.1.m577353w31675348.

______. "The Power of Archives: Archivists' Values and Value in the Postmodern Age." *American Archivist* 72, no. 1 (2009): 13–41. https://doi.org/10.17723/aarc.72.1.k0322x0p38v44l53.

______, and Dennis Meissner. "More Product, Less Process: Revamping Traditional Archival Processing." *American Archivist* 68, no. 2 (2005): 208–63. https://doi.org/10.17723/aarc.68.2.c741823776k65863.

Grotke, Abbie. "It Takes a Village . . . to Archive the Internet." *The Signal* (blog). Library of Congress. https://blogs.loc.gov/thesignal/2011/07/it-takes-a-village%E2%80%A6to-archive-the-internet, captured at https://perma.cc/UH4J-WV3U.

Ham, F. Gerald. "Archival Choices: Managing the Historical Record in an Age of Abundance." *American Archivist* 47, no. 1 (1984): 11–22. https://doi.org/10.17723/aarc.47.1.v382727652114521.

______. "The Archival Edge." *American Archivist* 38, no. 1 (1975): 5–13. https://doi.org/10.17723/aarc.38.1 .7400r86481128424.

______. "Archival Strategies for the Post-Custodial Era." *American Archivist* 44, no. 3 (1981): 207–16. https://doi.org/10.17723/aarc.44.3.6228121p01m8k376.

Harpring, Patricia. "Metadata Standards Crosswalk." Los Angeles: Getty Vocabulary Program, Getty Research Institute. Last modified October 24, 2017. http://www.getty.edu/research/publications/electronic_publications/intrometadata/crosswalks.html, captured at https://perma.cc/26QT-TKV9.

Harrison, Rodney. "Forgetting to Remember, Remembering to Forget: Late Modern Heritage Practices, Sustainability and the 'Crisis' of Accumulation of the Past." *International Journal of Heritage Studies* 19, no. 6 (2013): 579–95. https://doi.org/10.1080/13527258.2012.678371.

Harvey, Ross, and Jaye Weatherburn. *Preserving Digital Materials.* 3rd ed. Lanham, MD: Rowman & Littlefield, 2018.

______, and Martha R. Mahard. *The Preservation Management Handbook: A 21st-Century Guide for Libraries, Archives, and Museums.* Lanham, MD: Rowman & Littlefield, 2014.

Hastings, Robin. *Planning Cloud-Based Disaster Recovery for Digital Assets.* Santa Barbara, CA: Libraries Unlimited, 2017.

Hedstrom, Margaret. "Digital Preservation: A Time Bomb for Digital Libraries." *Computers and the Humanities* 31, no. 3 (1997): 189–202. https://www.jstor.org/stable/30200423.

______. *Digital Preservation: Problems and Prospects.* Ann Arbor: School of Information, University of Michigan, 2001. http://www.dl.slis.tsukuba.ac.jp/DLjournal/No_20/1-hedstrom/1-hedstrom.html, captured at https://perma.cc/U568-NV3X.

______, and Sheon Montgomery. *Digital Preservation Needs and Requirements in RLG Member Institutions.* Mountain View, CA: Research Libraries Group, 1998.

Henderson, Jane. *Environment.* London, UK: British Library, 2007; rev. June 2013. Library-archive-environment-guide.pdf.

Henry, Michael C. "What Will the Cultural Record Say About Us? The Stewardship of Culture and the Mandate for Environmental Sustainability." In *From Gray Areas to Green Areas: Developing Sustainable Practices in Preservation Environments Symposium Proceedings.* Edited by Melissa Tedone. Austin: University of Texas, November 1–2, 2007. https://www.ischool.utexas.edu/kilgarlin/gaga/proceedings.html, captured at https:// perma.cc/L9U7-FWAZ.

Heritage Preservation. *A Public Trust at Risk: The Heritage Health Index Report on the State of America's Collections.* Washington, DC: Heritage Preservation, 2005.

Higginbotham, Barbra Buckner, and Judith W. Wild. *The Preservation Program Blueprint.* Chicago: American Library Association, 2001.

Hirsh, Sandra. *Information Services Today: An Introduction.* 2nd ed. Lanham, MD: Rowman & Littlefield, 2018.

Hirtle, Peter. *Copyright Term and the Public Domain in the United States.* Ithaca, NY: Cornell University Library, 2018. https://copyright.cornell.edu/sites/default/files/2018-01/copyright_term_and_the_public_domain2018.pdf, captured at https://perma.cc/5BCH-CX75.

Hoad, T. F. *Online Etymology Dictionary* and *The Concise Oxford Dictionary of English Etymology.* Oxford, UK: Oxford University Press, 2003. https://www.etymonline.com.

Horsman, Peter. "The Last Dance of the Phoenix, or the De-discovery of the Archival Fonds." *Archivaria* 54 (Fall 2002): 1–23. https://archivaria.ca/index.php/archivaria/article/view/12853.

Hubbles, Chris. "No Country for Old Media." PhD diss., University of Washington, 2018.

Humanities Advanced Technology and Information Institute. *The NINCH Guide to Good Practice in the Digital Representation and Management of Cultural Heritage Materials*. Washington, DC: National Initiative for a Networked Cultural Heritage, 2002.

Hunter, Gregory S. *Developing and Maintaining Practical Archives: A How-To Manual*. New York: Neal Schuman, 2003.

Hyry, Thomas. "More for Less in Archives." *Annotation* 33, no. 2 (2007): 7–10. https://www.archives.gov/files/nhprc/annotation/2007/2007-spring.pdf, captured at https://perma.cc/HF3G-VRTC.

______. "More for Less in Archives: The Greene/Meissner Approach at Work at Yale." Paper presented at Washington, DC: RLG Members Forum: More, Better, Faster, Cheaper: The Economics of Descriptive Practice, Washington, DC, August 8, 2006. http://www.worldcat.org/arcviewer/1/OCC/2007/08/08/0000070504/viewer/file209.pdf, captured at https://perma.cc/R392-W2M3.

______. "Reassessing Backlogs: Extensible Processing Is a Better Way to Make Materials Available." *Library Journal* 132, no. 7 (2007): S8.

Image Permanence Institute. "Graphics Atlas." http://www.graphicsatlas.org.

______. *Guide to Sustainable Preservation Practices for Managing Storage Environments*. Rochester, NY: Rochester Institute of Technology, 2012.

______. "Photographic Process Identification Webinars." https://www.imagepermanenceinstitute.org/process-id-webinars.

______. *The Preservation of Magnetic Tape Collections: A Perspective*. Rochester, NY: Image Permanence Institute, December 22, 2006. https://studylib.net/doc/11115658/the-preservation-of-magnetic-tape-collections-a-perspective.

Institute of Library and Museum Services. *Protecting America's Collections: Results from the Heritage Health Information Survey*. Washington, DC: IMLS, February 2019. https://www.imls.gov/sites/default/files/publications/documents/imls-hhis-report.pdf, captured at https://perma.cc/8CGC-7BPT.

International Council of Museums and the Institute for Conservation Declaration on Environmental Guidelines, "Declaration on Environmental Guidelines" (2014). http://www.icom-cc.org/332/-icom-cc-documents/declaration-on-environmental-guidelines/#.W39FQNhKhAY, captured at https://perma.cc/4CLG-WN7F.

International Institute for Conservation of Historic and Artistic Works. *Climate Change and Museum Collections*. Papers presented at the 3rd IIC Roundtable, London, UK, National Gallery of Art, September 17, 2008. http://www.iiconservation.org/docs/IIC_climate_change_transcript.pdf, captured at https://perma.cc/3FKN-HTLN.

International Standards Organization (ISO). *ISO 11799:2015 Information and Documentation: Document Storage Requirements for Archive and Library Materials*. https://www.iso.org/standard/63810.html, captured at https:// perma.cc/8KT4-YCVS.

______. "Technical Committee 46: Information and Documentation." (ISO/TC46). https://www.iso.org/committee/48750.html.

InterPARES Glossary, 2001. http://interpares.org/display_file.cfm?doc=ip1_glossary.pdf, captured at https://perma.cc/F4JM-K3CG.

iPres 2009: The Sixth International Conference on Preservation of Digital Objects. San Francisco: iPres, October 5–6, 2009. https://escholarship.org/uc/cdl_ipres09.

Jenkins, Tracy A., Jane Webster, and Lindsay McShane. "An Agenda for 'Green' Information Technology and Systems Research." *Information and Organization* 21, no. 1 (2011): 17–40. https://doi.org/10.1016/j.infoandorg.2010.09.003.

Jenkinson, Hilary. *A Manual of Archive Administration.* London, UK: Percy Lund, Humphries & Co., 1937.

Jimerson, Randall C., ed. *American Archival Studies: Readings in Theory and Practice.* Chicago: Society of American Archivists, 2000.

______. *Archives Power: Memory, Accountability, and Social Justice.* Chicago: Society of American Archivists, 2009.

Joffrion, Elizabeth et al. "Advice for Grant Seeking in Cultural Heritage Communities." Washington, DC: Council on Library and Information Resources, 2012. https://www.clir.org/hiddencollections/applicants/advice-for-grant-seekers-in-the-cultural-heritage-communities.

______. "The Will to Collaborate." In *June L. Mazer Lesbian Archives: Making Invisible Histories Visible: A Resource Guide to the Collections.* Edited by Kathleen Anne McHugh, Brenda Johnson-Grau, and Ben Raphael Sher. Los Angeles: UCLA Center for the Study of Women, 2014, 29–32.

______, and Natalia Fernández. "Collaboration between Tribal and Nontribal Organizations: Suggested Best Practices for Sharing Expertise, Cultural Resources, and Knowledge." *American Archivist* 78, no. 1 (2015): 192–237.

______, and Lexie Tom. "Broken Promises: A Case Study in Reconciliation." *Archival Issues* 37, no. 2 (2016): 7–22.

Jorgensen, Miriam. *Sustaining Indigenous Culture: The Structure, Activities and Needs of Tribal Archives, Libraries and Museums.* Oklahoma City, OK: Association of Tribal Archives, Libraries, and Museums, 2012.

Kaplan, Elisabeth. "We Are What We Collect, We Collect What We Are: Archives and the Construction of Identity." *American Archivist* 63, no. 1 (2000): 126–51.

Kaplan, Hilary A., and Brenda S. Banks. "Archival Preservation: The Teaming of the Crew." *American Archivist* 53 (1990): 266–73.

Kejser, Ulla Bøgvad, Anders Bo Nielsen, and Alex Thirifays. "Cost Model for Digital Preservation: Cost of Digital Migration," *The International Journal of Digital Curation* 6, no. 1 (2011): 255–67.

Kenney, Anne R., and Nancy Y. McGovern. "The Five Organizational Stages of Digital Preservation." In *Digital Libraries: A Vision for the Twenty-first Century, A Festschrift to Honor Wendy Lougee*, Ann Arbor, MI: Scholarly Publishing Office, University of Michigan, 2003. http://dx.doi.org/10.3998/spobooks.bbv9812.0001.001.

______, Oya Y. Rieger, and Research Libraries Group. *Moving Theory into Practice: Digital Imaging for Libraries and Archives*. Mountain View, CA: Research Libraries Group, 2000.

______ et al. *Trusted Digital Repositories: Attributes and Responsibilities*. Mountain View, CA: Research Libraries Group, May 2002. http://www.oclc.org/content/dam/research/activities/trustedrep/repositories.pdf, captured at https://perma.cc/45U5-3ALK.

Kerschner, Richard. "Providing Safe and Practical Environments for Cultural Property in Historic Buildings—and Beyond." Paper presented at Getty Conservation Institute Experts Roundtable on Sustainable Climate Management Strategies, Tenerife, Spain, April 2007. https://www.getty.edu/conservation/our_projects/science/climate/paper_kerschner.pdf, captured at https://perma.cc/UD2B-UKLP.

Ketelaar, Eric. "Archival Turns and Returns." In *Research in the Archival Multiverse*. Edited by Anne J. Gilliland, Sue McKemmish, and Andrew J. Lau, 228–268. Victoria, Australia: Monash University Press, 2016.

Kim, Sarah. "Green Archives: Applications of Green Construction to Archival Facilities." *The Primary Source* 28, no. 1 (2009). https://doi.org/10.18785/ps.2801.03.

Kirschenbaum, Matthew G. et al. "Digital Materiality: Preserving Access to Computers as Complete Environments." In *The Sixth International Conference on Preservation of Digital Objects*. San Francisco: iPres, October 5, 2009. https://escholarship.org/uc/item/7d3465vg.

Kodak. "Storage and Handling of Processed Nitrate Film." https://www.kodak.com/motion/support/technical_information/storage/storage_and_handing_of_processed_nitrate_film/default.htm.

Kozlowski, Roman. "Collection Environments and Evidence-Based Decision-Making." *Conservation Perspectives: The Getty Conservation Institute Newsletter* 33, no. 2 (2018): 13–15.

Krummel, D. W. *Fiat Lux, Fiat Latebra: A Celebration of Historical Library Functions*. Occasional Papers. Champaign: Graduate School of Library and Information Science, University of Illinois, 1999, 2.

Kurtz, Michael J. "Archival Management." In *Managing Archives and Archival Institutions*. Edited by James Gregory Bradsher. Chicago: University of Chicago Press, 1988, 241–53.

______. *Managing Archival & Manuscript Repositories*, Chicago: Society of American Archivists, 2004.

Lafferty-Hess, Sophia, and Thu-Mai Christian. "More Data, Less Process? The Application of MPLP to Research Data." *IASSIST Quarterly* 40, no. 4 (2016): 6–13.https://doi.org/10.29173/iq907.

Laise, Kristen Overbeck. "The Heritage Health Index Findings on Digital Collections." *First Monday* 12, no. 7 (2007). http://dx.doi.org/10.5210/fm.v12i7.1920.

Lavoie, Brian, and Lorcan Dempsey. "Thirteen Ways of Looking at . . . Digital Preservation." *D-Lib Magazine* 10, nos. 7–8 (2004). http://www.dlib.org/dlib/july04/lavoie/07lavoie.html.

______, and Digital Preservation Coalition. *The Open Archival Information System (OAIS) Reference Model: Introductory Guide.* 2nd ed. N.p.: Digital Preservation Coalition Technology Watch Report 14-02, 2014.

______, and Richard Gartner. *Preservation Metadata.* 2nd ed. N.p.: Digital Preservation Coalition Technology Watch Report, No. 13-03, May 2013. https://doi.org/10.7207/twr13-03.

Lee, Christopher A., and Helen R. Tibbo. "Digital Curation and Trusted Repositories: Steps toward Success." *Journal of Digital Information* 8, no. 2 (2007). https://journals.tdl.org/jodi/index.php/jodi/article/view/229/183.

Library of Congress. "About. What Is Digital Preservation?" http://www.digitalpreservation.gov/about.

______. Blogs. *Now See Hear!* https://blogs.loc.gov/now-see-hear.

______. "Care Handling, and Storage of Motion Picture Film." https://www.loc.gov/preservation/care/film.html, captured at https://perma.cc/HV8Z-VZJK.

______. "The Deterioration and Preservation of Paper: Some Essential Facts." http://www.loc.gov/preservation/care/deterioratebrochure.html.

______. "National Recording Preservation Board." https://www.loc.gov/programs/national-recording-preservation-board/about-this-program.

______. "PREMIS Resources." https://www.loc.gov/standards/premis/bibliography.html.

______. "Publications by Preservation Directorate Staff." https://www.loc.gov/preservation/resources/staffpubs/index.html.

______. "Section 108 Study Group Report." 2008. http://www.section108.gov/docs/Sec108StudyGroupReport.pdf.

______. "Standards." https://www.loc.gov/librarians/standards.

Linden, Jeremy, James Reilly, and Peter Herzog. "Research on Energy Savings Opportunities in University Libraries." *Library Hi Tech* 30, no. 3 (2012): 384–96. https://doi.org/10.1108/07378831211266537.

Lipinski, Tomas A. *The Librarian's Legal Companion for Licensing and Information Resources and Services.* New York: Neal-Schuman, 2012.

Lor, Peter Johan, and Johannes J. Britz. "An Ethical Perspective on Political-Economic Issues in the Long-Term Preservation of Digital Heritage." *Journal of the American Society for Information Science and Technology* 63, no. 11 (2012): 2153–64. https://doi.org/10.1002/asi.22725.

Lowenthal, David. "Natural and Cultural Heritage." *International Journal of Heritage Studies* 11, no. 1 (2005): 81–92. https://doi.org/10.1080/13527250500037088.

Lynch, Clifford. "Stewardship in the 'Age of Algorithms.'" *First Monday* 22, no. 12 (2017). http://firstmonday.org/article/view/8097/6583, captured at https://perma.cc/6SCK-VHVX.

Maceli, Monica G., and Anthony Cocciolo. "Monitoring Environmental Conditions with Low-Cost Single-Board Computers." *Preservation, Digital Technology & Culture* 46, no. 4 (2017): 124–31. https://doi.org/10.1515/pdtc-2017-0008.

Mabillon, Jean. *De Re Diplomatica.* Luteciae Parisionum, 1681.

MacNeil, Heather Marie, and Bonnie Mak. "Constructions of Authenticity." *Library Trends* 56, no. 1 (2007): 26–52. https://doi.org/10.1353/lib.2007.0054.

Maemura, Emily, Nathan Moles, and Christoph Becker. "Organizational Assessment Frameworks for Digital Preservation: A Literature Review and Mapping." *Journal of the Association for Information Science and Technology* 68 (2017): 1619–37. https://doi.org/10.1002/asi.23807.

Maltz, Andy. "Will Today's Digital Movies Exist in 100 Years?" *IEEE Spectrum* (February 21, 2014). https://spectrum.ieee.org/consumer-electronics/standards/will-todays-digital-movies-exist-in-100-years.

Marcum, Deanna. "Libraries, Archives and Museums, Coming Back Together?" *Information & Culture: A Journal of History* 49, no. 1 (2014): 74–89. https://doi.org/10.1353/lac.2014.0001.

Marks, Steve. "Module 8: Becoming a Trusted Repository." In *Digital Preservation Essentials.* Edited by Michael Shallcross. Chicago: Society of American Archivists, 2016.

Marshall, Peter. "Life Cycle Versus Continuum—What's the Difference?" *Informational Quarterly* 16, no. 2 (2000): 20–25.

Marty, Paul F. "Digital Convergence and the Information Profession in Cultural Heritage Organizations: Reconciling Internal and External Demands." *Library Trends* 62, no. 3 (2014): 613–27. https:// www.ideals.illinois.edu/bitstream/handle/2142/89728/62.3.marty.pdf.

______. "An Introduction to Digital Convergence: Libraries, Archives, and Museums in the Information Age." *Library Quarterly* 80, no. 1 (2010): 1–5. https://doi.org/10.1086/648549.

______, ed. "Libraries, Archives and Museums, Intersecting Missions and Converging Futures." Special issue, *RBM: A Journal of Rare Books, Manuscripts and Cultural Heritage* 8, no. 1 (2007). https://doi.org/10.5860/rbm.8.1.281.

Marwick, Claire S. "An Historic Study of Paper Document Restoration Methods." Master's thesis, American University, Washington, DC, 1964.

Masson-Delmotte, Valerie et al., eds. *Global Warming of 1.5°C. An IPCC Special Report on the impacts of global warming of 1.5°C above pre-industrial levels and related global greenhouse gas emission pathways, in the context of strengthening the global response to the threat of climate change, sustainable development, and efforts to eradicate poverty.* Switzerland: Intergovernmental Panel on Climate Change, 2018. https://report.ipcc.ch/sr15/pdf/sr15_spm_final.pdf, captured at https://perma.cc/347F-BAJT.

Mazurczyk, Tara, Nathan Piekielek, Eira Tansey, and Ben Goldman. "American Archives and Climate Change: Risks and Adaptation." *Climate Risk Management* 20 (2018): 111–25. https://doi.org/10.1016/j.crm.2018.03.005.

McAlister, Sheila. "Designing a Preservation Survey: The Digital Library of Georgia." *Provenance, Journal of the Society of Georgia Archivists* 25, no. 1 (2007). http://digitalcommons.kennesaw.edu/provenance/vol25/iss1/3.

McCann, Laura. "Preservation as Obstacle or Opportunity? Rethinking the Preservation-Access Model in the Age of MPLP." *Journal of Archival Organization* 11, nos. 1–2 (2013): 23–48. https://doi.org/10.1080/15332748.2013.871972.

McGovern, Nancy. "Current Status of Trustworthy Systems." In *Building Trustworthy Digital Repositories: Theory and Implementation.* Edited by Philip C. Bantin. Lanham, MD: Rowman & Littlefield, 2016, 325–36.

_______. *The Digital Preservation Policy Framework: Development Guidelines.* Version 2.1. Ottawa: Canadian Heritage Information Network, October 2012.

McKemmish, Sue, Frank Herbert Upward, and Barbara Reed. "Records Continuum Model." *Encyclopedia of Library and Information Sciences.* 3rd ed. (2010), 4447–48.

Mecklenburg, Marion. *Determining the Acceptable Ranges of Relative Humidity and Temperature in Museums and Galleries: Part 1, Structural Response to Relative Humidity.* Washington, DC: Smithsonian Museum Conservation Institute, 2007. https://www.si.edu/mci/downloads/reports/Mecklenburg-Part1-RH.pdf, captured at https://perma.cc/QJ8D-WH34.

_______. *Determining the Acceptable Ranges of Relative Humidity and Temperature in Museums and Galleries, Part 2, Structural Response to Temperature.* Washington, DC: Smithsonian Museum Conservation Institute, 2007. https://www.si.edu/mci/downloads/reports/Mecklenburg-Part2-Temp.pdf, captured at https://perma.cc/BQ55-JVEC.

Meissner, Dennis, and Mark A. Greene. "More Application While Less Appreciation: The Adopters and Antagonists of MPLP." *Journal of Archival Organization* 8, nos. 3–4 (2010): 174–226. https://doi.org/10.1080/15332748.2010.554069.

Melville, Annette, and Scott Simmon. *Film Preservation 1993: A Study of the Current State of American Film Preservation: Report of the Librarian of Congress.* Washington, DC: NFPB/LOC, 1993.

Meyer, Rebecca, Shannon Struble, and Phyllis Catsikis. "Sustainability: A Review." In *Preserving Our Heritage: Perspectives from Antiquity to the Digital Age.* Edited by Michèle Valerie Cloonan. Chicago: Neal-Schuman/American Library Association, 2015, 637–56.

Michalski, Stefan. "The Ideal Climate, Risk Management, the ASHRAE Chapter, Proofed Fluctuations, and toward a Full Risk Analysis Model." Paper presented at Getty Conservation Institute Experts Roundtable on Sustainable Climate Management Strategies, Tenerife, Spain, April 2007. http://www.getty.edu/conservation/our_projects/science/climate/paper_michalski.pdf, captured at https://perma.cc/V7SA-RPRE.

Mink, Meridith Beck. *Keepers of Our Digital Future: An Assessment of the National Digital Stewardship Residencies, 2013–16.* Washington, DC: Council on Library and Information Resources, December 2016.

Minow, Mary, and Tomas A. Lipinski. *The Library's Legal Answers Book.* Chicago: American Library Association, 2003.

Mossberger, Karen, Caroline J. Tolbert, and Mary Stansbury. *Virtual Inequality: Beyond the Digital Divide.* Washington, DC: Georgetown University Press, 2003.

Muller, Samuel, J. A. Feith, and R. Fruin, *Manual for the Arrangement and Description of Archives.* 2nd ed. Translated by Arthur Leavitt. New York: H.W. Wilson, 1940.

Museum of Contemporary Art, Chicago. *I Was Raised on the Internet.* Exhibition. Chicago: MCA, June 23–October 14, 2018. https://mcachicago.org/Exhibitions/2018/I-Was-Raised-On-The-Internet, captured at https://perma.cc/33AY-32NN.

Museum of Fine Arts, Boston. *Conservation and Art Materials Encyclopedia Online* (CAMEO). http://cameo.mfa.org/wiki/Main_Page.

National Archives. "National Archives Announces a New Model for the Preservation and Accessibility of Presidential Records." Press release, May 3, 2017. Washington, DC: NARA, 2017. https://www.archives.gov/press/press-releases/2017/nr17-54, captured at https://perma.cc/6DQW-VTTK.

National Archives of Australia. "Storing Information." https://www.naa.gov.au/information-management/store-and-preserve-information/storing-information, captured at https://perma.cc/L9LA-NDZQ.

National Association of Government Archives and Records Administrators (NAGARA). *Preservation Needs in State Archives.* Albany: NAGARA, 1986.

National Digital Stewardship Alliance (NDSA). *2015 National Agenda for Digital Stewardship.* Washington DC: NDSA, 2014. http://www.digitalpreservation.gov/documents/2015NationalAgenda.pdf, captured at https://perma.cc/EA6S-DX2U.

______. "Levels of Digital Preservation." http://ndsa.org/activities/levels-of-digital-preservation, captured at https://perma.cc/CTB6-ZPDS.

National Endowment for the Humanities (NEH) and the Consiglio Nazionale delle Ricerche (CNR). *Sustainable Cultural Heritage Conference Proceedings.* Washington, DC: NEH, May 11, 2009.

National Film Preservation Foundation. *The Film Preservation Guide: The Basics for Archives, Libraries and Museums.* San Francisco: National Film Preservation Foundation, 2004.

National Fire Protection Association (NFPA). *NFPA 40 Standard for the Storage and Handling of Cellulose Nitrate Film.* Quincy, MA: NFPA 2019. https://catalog.nfpa.org/NFPA-40-Standard-for-the-Storage-and-Handling-of-Cellulose-Nitrate-Film-P1176.aspx?icid=D729.

National Information Standards Organization (NISO). ANSI/NISO Z39.48-1992 (R2009), *Permanence of Paper for Publications and Documents in Libraries and Archives.* Baltimore: NISO, 2010.

National Institute of Standards and Technology (NIST), Joint Task Force Transformation Initiative. *Guide for Conducting Risk Assessments: Information Security.* NIST Special Publication 800-30, Revision 1. Washington, DC: US Department of Commerce, NIST, September 2012), 8–9; Appendixes E and F.

National Library of New Zealand. *Metadata Standards Framework—Preservation Metadata.* Rev. ed. Wellington: National Library of New Zealand, June 2003. https://natlib.govt.nz/records/20714436?tab=cart&text=METADATA, captured at https://perma.cc/NJ2U-2XPP.

National Park Service. "Care of Archival Digital and Magnetic Media." *Conserve O Gram* 19/20, September 1996. https://www.nps.gov/museum/publications/conserveogram/19-20.pdf, captured at https://perma.cc/22WK-BYDC.

Nestle, Joan. "The Will to Remember: The Lesbian Herstory Archives of New York." *Feminist Review* 34, no. 1 (1990): 86–94. https://doi.org/10.1057/fr.1990.12.

Nichols, Stephen G., and Abby Smith. *The Evidence in Hand: Report of the Task Force on the Artifact in Library Collections. Optimizing Collections and Services for Scholarly Use.* Washington, DC: CLIR, 2001.

Nora, Pierre. *Rethinking France: Les Lieux de Mémoire,* Vol. 4 of *Histories and Memories.* Translation edited by David P. Jordan. Chicago: University of Chicago Press, 2010.

Norris, Debra Hess, and Jennifer Jae Gutierrez, eds. *Issues in the Conservation of Photographs: Readings in Conservation.* Los Angeles: Getty Conservation Institute, 2010.

Northeast Document Conservation Center (NEDCC). "5.3 Care of Photographs," Preservation Leaflet Series, Andover, MA: NEDCC, n.d. https://www.nedcc.org/free-resources/preservation-leaflets/5.-photographs/5.3-care-of-photographs, captured at https://perma.cc/VNB8-ERTA.

______. "Digital Preservation." Andover, MA: NEDCC, n.d. https://www.nedcc.org/free-resources/digital-preservation.

______. "Funding Opportunities." Andover, MA: NEDCC, n.d. https://www.nedcc.org/free-resources/funding-opportunities/overview.

______. "Preservation 101, Session 7. Reformatting Media Collections." Andover, MA: NEDCC, n.d. https://www.nedcc.org/preservation101/session-7/7reformatting-media-collections, captured at https://perma.cc/Q8SN-6TT3.

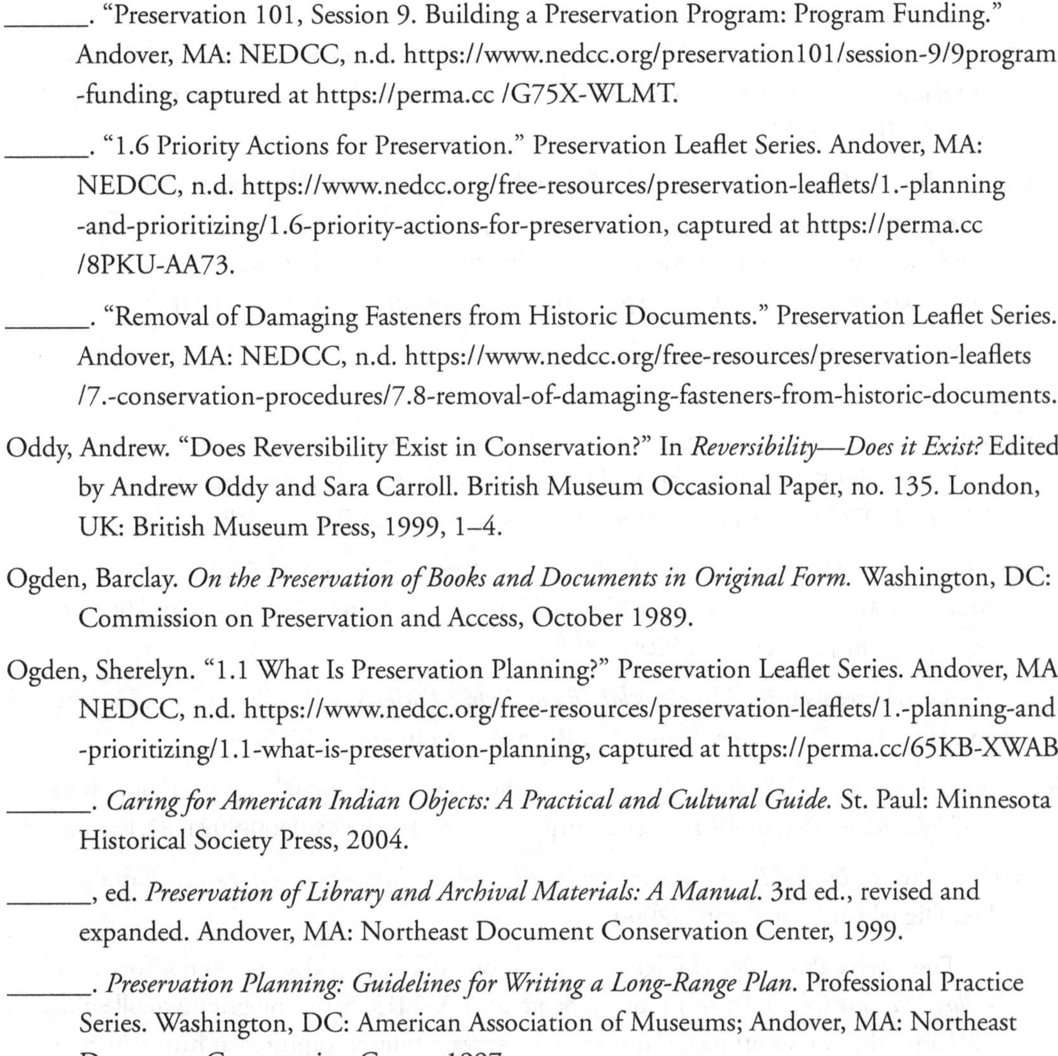

______. "Preservation 101, Session 9. Building a Preservation Program: Program Funding." Andover, MA: NEDCC, n.d. https://www.nedcc.org/preservation101/session-9/9program-funding, captured at https://perma.cc/G75X-WLMT.

______. "1.6 Priority Actions for Preservation." Preservation Leaflet Series. Andover, MA: NEDCC, n.d. https://www.nedcc.org/free-resources/preservation-leaflets/1.-planning-and-prioritizing/1.6-priority-actions-for-preservation, captured at https://perma.cc/8PKU-AA73.

______. "Removal of Damaging Fasteners from Historic Documents." Preservation Leaflet Series. Andover, MA: NEDCC, n.d. https://www.nedcc.org/free-resources/preservation-leaflets/7.-conservation-procedures/7.8-removal-of-damaging-fasteners-from-historic-documents.

Oddy, Andrew. "Does Reversibility Exist in Conservation?" In *Reversibility—Does it Exist?* Edited by Andrew Oddy and Sara Carroll. British Museum Occasional Paper, no. 135. London, UK: British Museum Press, 1999, 1–4.

Ogden, Barclay. *On the Preservation of Books and Documents in Original Form.* Washington, DC: Commission on Preservation and Access, October 1989.

Ogden, Sherelyn. "1.1 What Is Preservation Planning?" Preservation Leaflet Series. Andover, MA: NEDCC, n.d. https://www.nedcc.org/free-resources/preservation-leaflets/1.-planning-and-prioritizing/1.1-what-is-preservation-planning, captured at https://perma.cc/65KB-XWAB.

______. *Caring for American Indian Objects: A Practical and Cultural Guide.* St. Paul: Minnesota Historical Society Press, 2004.

______, ed. *Preservation of Library and Archival Materials: A Manual.* 3rd ed., revised and expanded. Andover, MA: Northeast Document Conservation Center, 1999.

______. *Preservation Planning: Guidelines for Writing a Long-Range Plan.* Professional Practice Series. Washington, DC: American Association of Museums; Andover, MA: Northeast Document Conservation Center, 1997.

Oliver, Gillian, and Ross Harvey. *Digital Curation.* 2nd ed. London, UK: Facet Publishing, 2016.

O'Meara, Erin, and Kate Stratton. "Module 12: Preserving Digital Objects." In *Digital Preservation Essentials*. Edited by Christopher J. Prom. Chicago: Society of American Archivists, 2016.

O'Neal, Jennifer R. "Respect, Recognition and Reciprocity: The Protocols for Native American Archival Materials." In *Identity Palimpsests: Archiving Ethnicity in the U.S. and Canada.* Edited by Dominique Daniel and Amalia Levi. Sacramento: Litwin Books, 2014, 125–42.

Owens, Trevor. *The Theory and Craft of Digital Preservation.* Baltimore: Johns Hopkins University Press, 2018.

Pacifico, Michele F., and Thomas R. Wilsted, eds. *Archives and Special Collections Facilities: Guidelines for Archivists, Librarians, Architects and Engineers.* Chicago: Society of American Archivists, 2009.

Padfield, Timothy, and Karen Borchersen, eds. *Museum Microclimates*. Contributions to the conference in Copenhagen, November 19–23, 2007. Copenhagen: National Museum of Denmark. conservationphysics.org/mm/musmic/musmic150.pdf, captured at https://perma.cc/J34X-SYWR.

Palmer, Marlize, and James Dawes. "Archiving and Preserving Tweets Using a Library Management System." *Information Today Europe*. (July 6, 2018). https://www.infotoday.eu/Articles/Editorial/Featured-Articles/Archiving-and-preserving-tweets-using-a-Library-Management-System-126129.aspx, captured at https://perma.cc/4GTB-4JSF.

Patkus, Beth. *Assessing Preservation Needs: A Self-Study Guide*. Andover, MA: Northeast Document Conservation Center, n.d.

Payne, Lizanne. *Library Storage Facilities and the Future of Print Collections in North America.* Dublin, OH: OCLC, 2007. https://www.oclc.org/content/dam/research/publications/library/2007/2007-01.pdf, captured at https://perma.cc/VR8Q-LEVB.

Pearce-Moses, Richard, ed. *A Glossary of Archival and Records Terminology*. Chicago: Society of American Archivists, 2005. http://files.archivists.org/pubs/free/SAA-Glossary-2005.pdf, captured at https://perma.cc/9RAQ-36E4.

_____. "Archival Preservation." In *Encyclopedia of Archival Science*, edited by Luciana Duranti and Patricia C. Franks. Lanham, MD: Rowman & Littlefield, 2015.

Pendergrass, Keith L. et al. "Toward Environmentally Sustainable Digital Preservation." *American Archivist*, 82 no. 1 (2019): 165–206. https://doi.org/10.17723/0360-9081-82.1.165.

Pennock, Maureen. *Digital Preservation: Continued Access to Authentic Digital Assets*. Edinburgh: ISC Digital Curation Centre, 2006.

______. "The Twelve Principles of Digital Preservation (and a Cartridge in a Repository . . .)." *Collection Care* (blog). British Library, September 3, 2013. http://blogs.bl.uk/collectioncare/2013/09/the-twelve-principles-of-digital-preservation.html, captured at https://perma.cc/2V76-BJS9.

Peterson, Annie, Holly Robertson et al. "Do You Count? The Revitalization of a National Preservation Statistics Survey." *Library Resources and Technical Services* 60, no. 1 (2016). http://doi.org/10.5860/lrts.60n1http://doi.org/10.5860/lrts.60n1.

_______, Holly Robertson, Nick Szydlowski, and Joshua Ranger. *Preservation Statistics Survey: FY2015 Report*. Chicago: Preservation and Reformatting Section (PARS), Association of Library Collections and Technical Services (ALCTS), and the American Library Association (ALA), December 2016. http://www.ala.org/alcts/sites/ala.org.alcts/files/content/resources/preserv/presstats/FY2015/FY2015PreservationStatistics.pdf, captured at https://perma.cc/MNQ4-JGW4.

Philadelphia Area Consortium of Special Collections Libraries. Consortial Survey Initiative, 2006. http://archive.pacscl.org/pacsclsurvey/about.html.

Phillips, Jessica. "A Defense of Preservation in the Age of MPLP." *American Archivist* 78, no. 2 (2015): 470–87. https://americanarchivist.org/doi/abs/10.17723/0360-9081.78.2.470.

Phillips, Megan, Jefferson Bailey, Andrea Goethals, and Trevor Owens. "The NDSA Levels of Digital Preservation: An Explanation and Uses." *Proceedings of the Archiving (IS&T) Conference.* Washington, DC: NDSA, April 2013. http://ndsa.org/documents/NDSA_Levels_Archiving_2013.pdf, captured at https://perma.cc/QKX8-M62K.

Pomian, Krzysztof. "The Archives: From the *Trésor des Chartes* to the CARAN." In *Rethinking France: Les Lieux de Mémoire,* Vol. 4 of *Histories and Memories*, 47–49. Chicago: University of Chicago Press, 2010.

Poole, Frazer G. "Current Lamination Policies of the Library of Congress." *American Archivist* 39, no. 2 (1976): 157–59. https://doi.org/10.17723/aarc.39.2.vg627658l7421233.

Posner, Ernst. *Archives and the Public Interest: Selected Essays.* Edited by Ken Munden. Chicago: Society of American Archivists, 2006.

PREMIS. *Data Dictionary for Preservation Metadata.* Rev. ed. 3.0. Dublin, Ohio: OCLC and RLG, 2015. http://www.loc.gov/standards/premis/v3/premis-3-0-final.pdf, captured at https://perma.cc/T5JU-SXRB.

______. "Home." www.loc.gov/standards/premis.

Preservica. "Digital Archive Software." https://preservica.com/digital-archive-software.

"Preservation Metadata: Implementation Strategies (PREMIS)." In *Data Dictionary for Preservation Metadata: Final Report of the PREMIS Working Group.* Dublin, OH: OCLC and RLG, May 2005. http://www.oclc.org/research/projects/pmwg/premis-final.pdf, captured at https://perma.cc/G5K9-EQNT.

Priddle, Charlotte, and Laura McCann. "Off-Site Storage and Special Collections: A Study in Use and Impact in ARL Libraries in the United States." *College & Research Libraries* 76, no. 5 (2015): 652–70. https://doi.org/10.5860/crl.76.5.652.

Prom, Christopher J., ed. *Digital Preservation Essentials.* Chicago: Society of American Archivists, 2016.

______. "Optimum Access? Processing in College and University Archives." *American Archivist* 73, no. 1 (2010): 146–74. https://doi.org/10.17723/aarc.73.1.519m6003k7110760.

______. *Preserving Email.* Technical Watch Report 11-01 December 2011. N.p.: Charles Beagrie Ltd. and the Digital Preservation Coalition, 2011.

Protocols for Native American Archival Materials. 2006. www2.nau.edu/libnap-p, captured at https://perma.cc/J4S2-Z3ZU.

Public Safety Canada. "About Disaster Mitigation." Modified December 22, 2015. https://www.publicsafety.gc.ca/cnt/mrgnc-mngmnt/dsstr-prvntn-mtgtn/bt-dsstr-mtgtn-en.aspx.

Purcell, Aaron D., ed. *The Digital Archives Handbook: A Guide to Creation, Management, and Preservation.* Lanham, MD: Rowman & Littlefield, 2019.

Reilly, Bernard. "Planning for Digital Preservation: 20 Questions for Providers of Digital Storage Services." Andover, MA: NEDCC, n.d. https://www.nedcc.org/free-resources/nedcc-publications. https://www.nedcc.org/assets/media/documents/QuestionstoAskProvidersofDigitalStoragefinal.pdf, captured at https://perma.cc/5BHE-FLR5.

Reilly, James M. "Specifying Storage Environments in Libraries and Archives." In *From Gray Areas to Green Areas: Developing Sustainable Practices in Preservation Environments*, 2007, *Symposium Proceedings*. Edited by Melissa Tedone. Austin: Kilgarlin Center for Preservation of the Cultural Record, 2008. University of Texas. https://www.ischool.utexas.edu/kilgarlin/gaga/proceedings.html, captured at https://perma.cc/L9U7-FWAZ.

______. *Care and Identification of 19th Century Photographic Prints*. Rochester, NY: Eastman Kodak, 2009.

Research Libraries Group, and National Archives and Records Administration, Task Force on Digital Repository. *Trustworthy Repositories Audit and Certification: Criteria and Checklist*. Chicago: Center for Research Libraries, February 2007. https://www.crl.edu/sites/default/files/attachments/pages/trac_0.pdf, captured at https://perma.cc/9PK6-N6YU.

Rieger, Oya Y. "The State of Digital Preservation in 2018: A Snapshot of Challenges and Gaps." October 29, 2018. Issue Brief. Ithaka S&R, October 29, 2018. https:doi.org/10.18665/sr.310626.

Riley, Jenn. *Understanding Metadata*. Baltimore: National Information Standards Organization, 2004.

______. *Understanding Metadata, What Is Metadata, and What Is It For? A Primer Publication of the National Information Standards Organization*. Baltimore: N.p.: NISO Primer Series, 2017. https://www.niso.org/publications/understanding-metadata-2017, captured at https://perma.cc/8SYL-QU5L.

Ritzenthaler, Mary Lynn. *Preserving Archives & Manuscripts*. 2nd ed. Chicago: Society of American Archivists, 2010.

______, and Diane L. Vogt-O'Connor et al. *Photographs: Archival Care and Management*. Chicago: Society of American Archivists, 2006.

Roggia, Sally. "William James Barrow: A Biographical Study of His Formative Years and His Role in the History of Library and Archives Conservation from 1931–1941." PhD diss., Columbia University, School of Library Service, 1999.

Rosenthal, David, Kris Carpenter, and Krishna Kant. "Green Bytes: Sustainable Approaches to Digital Stewardship." Plenary Session, National Digital Information Infrastructure Meeting, Alexandria, VA, July, 2013. http://www.digitalpreservation.gov/meetings/documents/ndiipp13/Green_Bytes_Abstract_FINAL.pdf, captured at https://perma.cc/938U-T59D.

Rubin, Richard E. *Foundations of Library and Information Science*. 4th ed. Chicago: American Library Association, 2016.

Sanchez, Crystal, and Lauren Sorensen. "The Physical Nature of Digital and What It Means for Conservation." In *Material Matters: 46th Annual Meeting of the American Institute for Conservation of Historic and Artistic Works, Houston, TX, May 29–June 2, 2018*. Preprint. Washington, DC: AIC, 2018.

Sanett, Shelby et al. "Holdings Protection." In *The Preservation Management Handbook A 21st-Century Guide for Libraries, Archives, and Museums*. Edited by Ross Harvey and Martha R. Mahard. Lanham, MD: Rowman & Littlefield, 2014, 133–46.

Schellenberg, Theodore R. "The Appraisal of Modern Public Records." In *A Modern Archives Reader: Basic Readings on Archival Theory and Practice*. Edited by Maygene F. Daniels and Timothy Walch. Washington, DC: National Archives and Records Service, 1984, 57–70.

______. *Modern Archives: Principles and Techniques*. Chicago: University of Chicago Press, 1956; rpt. Society of American Archivists, 1975.

School for Advanced Research, Indian Arts Research Center. "Guidelines for Collaboration." https://sarweb.org/tag/guidelines-for-collaboration, captured at https://perma.cc/3SJT-589T.

Schwartz, Joan M. "The Photograph in the Archive: Concept, Principles, and Practices." In *Encyclopedia of Archival Science*. Lanham, MD: Rowman & Littlefield, 2015, 272–74.

Sheffield, Rebecka T. "More Than Acid-Free Folders: Extending the Concept of Preservation to Include the Stewardship of Unexplored Histories." *Library Trends* 64, no. 3 (2016): 572–84. https://perma.cc/M94J-N7CC.

Shein, Cyndi, and Emily Lapworth. "Say Yes to Digital Surrogates: Strengthening the Archival Record in the Postcustodial Era." *Journal of Western Archives* 7, no. 1 (2016): 1–50. https://digitalcommons.usu.edu/westernarchives/vol7/iss1/9.

Sheldon, Madeline. "Analysis of Current Digital Preservation Policies: Archives, Libraries and Museums." *The Signal* (blog). Library of Congress, August 13, 2013. https://blogs.loc.gov/thesignal/2013/08/analysis-of-current-digital-preservation-policies-archives-libraries-and-museums, captured at https://perma.cc/KNE2-JNS5.

Silverman, Randy. "Surely, We'll Need Backups." *Preservation, Digital Technology & Culture* 45, no. 3 (2016): 102–21. https//doi:10.1515/pdtc-2016-0013.

Sinclair, Pauline. *The Digital Divide: Assessing Organisations' Preparations for Digital Preservation*. Planets: A Planets White Paper. N.p.: Planets, March 2010. http://www.planets-project.eu/docs/reports/planets-market-survey-white-paper.pdf, captured at https://perma.cc/4RJC-88GS.

Sitts, Maxine K., and Northeast Document Conservation Center (NEDCC). *Handbook for Digital Projects: A Management Tool for Preservation and Access*. Andover, MA: Northeast Document Conservation Center, 2000.

Smithsonian Museum Conservation Institute. "Culmination of 20 Years of Green Energy Savings Research." https://www.si.edu/mci/english/research/consulting/MuseumEnvironment.html, captured at https://perma.cc/VD5U-MHJZ.

Society of American Archivists. "Annotated Resources." https://www2.archivists.org/initiatives/mayday-saving-our-archives/annotated-resources, captured at https://perma.cc/XTF5-WF72.

______. "SAA Core Values Statement and Code of Ethics." https://www2.archivists.org/statements/saa-core-values-statement-and-code-of-ethics, captured at https://perma.cc/BF9K-HSJR.

______. "SAA Council Endorsement of Protocols for Native American Materials," August 13, 2018. https://www2.archivists.org/statements/saa-council-endorsement-of-protocols-for-native-american-archival-materials, captured at https://perma.cc/CS8V-WFJG.

______. *Report: Task Force to Review Protocols for Native American Archival Materials*. Chicago: SAA, 2008. http://files.archivists.org/governance/taskforces/0208-NativeAmProtocols-IIIA.pdf, captured at https://perma.cc/5CJL-MZGF.

Stauderman, Sarah, and William G. Tompkins, eds. *Proceedings of the Smithsonian Institution Summit on the Museum Preservation Environment*. Washington, DC: Smithsonian Institution Scholarly Press, 2016.

Stevens, Mary, Andrew Flinn, and Elizabeth Shepherd. "New Frameworks for Community Engagement in the Archives Sector: From Handing Over to Handing On." *International Journal of Heritage Studies* 16, nos. 1–2 (2010): 59–76. https://doi.org/10.1080/13527250903441770.

Stoneburner, Gary, Alice T. Goguen, and Alexis Ferriga. *Risk Management Guide for Information Technology Systems*, NIST SP 800-30. Washington, DC: National Institute of Standards & Technology, 2002. http://delivery.acm.org/10.1145/2210000/2206240/sp800-30.pdf?ip=174.63.43.121&id=2206240&acc=OPEN&key=4D4702B0C3E38B35%2E4D4702B0C3E38B35%2E4D4702B0C3E38B35%2E6D218144511F3437&acm=1533156823_4bb66aed3d00f7cdf46449edd8ce82bc.

Sutton, Shan C. "Balancing Boutique-Level Quality and Large Scale Production: The Impact of 'More Product, Less Process' on Digitization in Archives and Special Collections." *RBM: A Journal of Rare Books, Manuscripts, & Cultural Heritage* 13, no. 1 (2012). https://doi.org/10.5860/rbm.13.1.369.

Tadic, Linda. "The Environmental Impact of Digital Preservation." Paper presented at the Association of Moving Image Archivists conference, Portland OR, November 18–21, 2015, updated 2018. https://www.digitalbedrock.com/resources-2, captured at https://perma.cc/242T-EW3V.

Tai, Jessica et al. "Summoning the Ghosts: Records as Agents in Community Archives." *Journal of Contemporary Archival Studies* 6, no. 1 (2019). https://elischolar.library.yale.edu/jcas/vol6/iss1/18.

Tammaro, Anna Maria, Melody Madrid, and Vittore Casarosa. "Digital Curators' Education: Professional Identity vs. Convergence of LAM [*sic*] (Libraries, Archives, Museums)." In *Digital Libraries and Archives. IRCDL 2012.* Edited by Maristella Communications in Computer & Information Science 354. Berlin: Springer, 2013, 184–94. https://doi.org/10.1007/978-3-642-35834-0_19.

Tanselle, G. Thomas. "Introduction: Statement on the Significance of Primary Records." In *Significance of Primary Records*, first published in *Profession 95* (New York: Modern Language Association, 1995): 27–50. https://apps.mla.org/pdf/spr_print.pdf, captured at https://perma.cc/MQ6H-HQGM.

Tansey, Eira. "Archival Adaptation to Climate Change." *Sustainability: Science, Practice, & Policy* 11, no. 2 (2015): 45–56. https://doi.org/10.1080/15487733.2015.11908146.

Task Force on Technical Approaches for Email Archives. "Email Archiving Tools." March 2019. http://www.emailarchivestaskforce.org/documents/email-tools, caputured at https://perma.cc/A48L-J9U2.

______. "The Future of Email Archives: A Report from the Task Force on Technical Approaches for Email Archives." August 2018. clir.org/wp-content/uploads/sites/6/2018/08/CLIR-pub175.pdf, captured at https://perma.cc/FM3J-3CSM.

Task Force on the Archiving of Digital Information. *Report of the Task Force on Archiving of Digital Information.* Washington, DC: Commission for Preservation and Access and Research Libraries Group, 1996. https://clir.wordpress.clir.org/wp-content/uploads/sites/6/pub63watersgarrett.pdf, captured at https://perma.cc/N959-SE6J.

Tedone, Melissa, ed. *From Gray Areas to Green Areas: Developing Sustainable Practices in Preservation Environments Symposium Proceedings.* Austin: Kilgarlin Center for Preservation of the Cultural Record, 2008. University of Texas, 2007. https://www.ischool.utexas.edu/kilgarlin/gaga/proceedings.html, captured at https:// perma.cc/L9U7-FWAZ.

Thomson, Garry. *The Museum Environment.* 2nd ed. Butterworth-Heinemann Series on Conservation and Museology. Oxford, UK: Butterworth-Heinemann, 1986.

Thylstrup, Nanna Bonde. *The Politics of Mass Digitization.* Cambridge, MA: MIT Press, 2018.

Torunbalci, Necdet. "Seismic Isolation and Energy Dissipating Systems in Earthquake Resistant Design." Paper No. 3273 presented at the 13th World Conference on Earthquake Engineering, Vancouver, BC, Canada, August 1–6, 2004. https://www.iitk.ac.in/nicee/wcee/article/13_3273.pdf, captured at https://perma.cc/U9FU-8W5K.

Tough, Alistair, and Michael Moss, eds. *Record Keeping in a Hybrid Environment: Managing the Creation, Use, Preservation and Disposal of Unpublished Information Objects in Context.* Oxford, UK: Chandos, 2006.

Trope, Jack F., and Walter R. Echo-Hawk. "The Native American Graves Protection and Repatriation Act, Background and Legislation." In *Repatriation Reader: Who Owns American Indian Remains?* Edited by Devon A. Mihesuah. Lincoln: University of Nebraska Press, 2000, 123–68.

Tschan, Reto. "A Comparison of Jenkinson and Schellenberg on Appraisal." *American Archivist* 65, no. 2 (2002): 176–95. https://doi.org/10.17723/aarc.65.2.920w65g3217706l1.

Tsien, T. H. *Written on Bamboo and Silk: The Beginnings of Chinese Books and Inscriptions.* 2nd rev. ed., with Edward Shaughnessy. Chicago: University of Chicago Press, 2013.

Underhill, Karen J. "Protocols for Native American Archival Materials." *RBM: A Journal of Rare Books, Manuscripts, and Cultural Heritage* 7, no. 2 (2006): 134–14. https://doi.org/10.5860/rbm.7.2.267.

United Nations. *Millennium Ecosystem Assessment.* 2005. https://www.millenniumassessment.org/ConceptualFramework/UnderstandingScale/measuringScale/MillenniumEcosystemAssessment.aspx.

______. World Commission on Environment and Development. *Our Common Future.* Oxford, UK: Oxford University Press, 1987.

United Nations Educational, Scientific and Cultural Organization. UNESCO/PERSIST Programme. Content Task Force. *Guidelines for the Selection of Digital Heritage for Long-term Preservation.* N.p.: United Nations Educational, Scientific and Cultural Organization, March 2016. Captured at https://perma.cc/SU7R-PYNW.

United States Green Building Council (USGBC). "LEED Rating System." https://www.usgbc.org/leed.

University of Illinois at Champaign-Urbana. The Preservation Self-Assessment Program (PSAP), 2016. https://psap.library.illinois.edu.

Vaidhyanathan, Siva. *The Googlization of Everything.* Berkeley: University of California Press, 2012.

Vermaaten, Sally, Brian Lavoie, and Priscilla Caplan. "Identifying Threats to Successful Digital Preservation: The SPOT Model for Risk Assessment." *D-Lib Magazine* 18, nos. 9–10 (2012). http://www.dlib.org/dlib/september12/vermaaten/09vermaaten.html.

Waibel, Günter, and Ricky Erway, "Think Global, Act Local—Library, Archive and Museum Collaboration." *Museum Management and Curatorship* 24, no. 4 (2009): 323–35. https://doi.org/10.1080/09647770903314704.

Walker, R. Gay, Jane Greenfield, John Fox, and Jeffrey Simonoff. "The Yale Survey: A Large-Scale Study of Book Deterioration in the Yale University Library." *College & Research Libraries* 46 (1985): 111–32. https://doi.org/10.5860/crl_46_02_111.

Waller, Martin, Robert Sharpe, and the Digital Preservation Coalition (DPC). *Mind the Gap: Assessing Digital Preservation Needs in the UK.* York, UK: DPC, 2006.

Waller, Robert R. "Cultural Property Risk Analysis Model (CPRAM): A Very Brief Introduction to Key Concepts." https://www.iiconservation.org/sites/default/files/news/attachments/6652-iic-itcc_2015_notes_quick_summary_of_cpram_robert_waller.pdf, captured at https://perma.cc/C3K6-PPFW.

Walters, Tyler et al. "Distributed Digital Preservation: Technical, Sustainability, and Organizational Developments." In *iPRES 2009 Proceedings, The Sixth International Conference of Digital Objects October 5–7 2009, San Francisco.* https://services.phaidra.univie.ac.at/api/object/o:294025/diss/Content/get, captured at https://perma.cc/QF8M-WNLT.

Wamsley, Laurel. "The Library of Congress Will No Longer Archive Every Tweet." *The Two-Way* (blog). National Public Radio, December 26, 2017. https://www.npr.org/sections/thetwo-way/2017/12/26/573609499/library-of-congress-will-no-longer-archive-every-tweet, captured at https://perma.cc/95RX-EHJ3.

Ward, Christine. "Preservation Program Planning for Archives and Historical Records Repositories." In *Preservation: Issues and Planning*. Edited by Paul N. Banks and Roberta Pilette. Chicago: American Library Association, 2000, 43–62.

Waters, Donald J., and John Garrett. *Preserving Digital Information: Report of the Task Force on Archiving of Digital Information.* CLIR Publication 63. Washington, DC: Council on Library and Information Resources, 1996. See The Commission on Preservation and Access and the Research Libraries Group.

Webb, Colin, David Pearson, and Paul Koerbin. "'Oh, You Wanted Us to Preserve That?!': Statements of Preservation Intent for the National Library of Australia's Digital Collections." *D- Lib Magazine* 19, nos. 1–2 (2013). http://www.dlib.org/dlib/january13/webb/01webb.html.

White, Kelvin. "Race and Culture: An Ethnic Studies Approach to Archival and Recordkeeping Research in the United States." In *Research in the Archival Multiverse*. Edited by Anne J. Gilliland, Sue McKemmish, and Andrew J. Lau, 352–81. Victoria, Australia: Monash University Press, 2016.

Wolfe, Mark D. "Beyond 'Green Buildings': Exploring the Effects of Jevons' Paradox on the Sustainability of Archival Practices." *Archival Science* 12, no. 1 (2012): 35–50. https://doi.org/10.1007/s10502-011-9143-4.

Wong, Patty, Miguel Figueroa, and Melissa Cardenas-Bow. "Diversity, Equity of Access, and Social Justice." In *Information Services Today: An Introduction*. Edited by Sandra Hirsh, 52–68. Lanham, MD: Rowman & Littlefield, 2018.

Woodyard-Robinson, Deborah. *Implementing the PREMIS Data Dictionary: A Survey of Approaches*. Washington, DC: Library of Congress, June 2007. http://www.loc.gov/standards/premis/implementation-report-woodyard.pdf, captured at https://perma.cc/7FUT-VZ6D.

Yakel, Elizabeth. "Archival Intelligence." In *Theories of Information Behavior*, edited by Karen E. Fisher, Sanda Erdelez, and Lynne E.F. McKechnie, 49–57. Medford, NJ: Information Today, 2005.

Yarrow, Alexandra, Barbara Clubb, and Jennifer-Lynn Draper. *Public Libraries, Archives and Museums: Trends in Collaboration and Cooperation*. IFLA Professional Reports, no. 108. The Hague: International Federation of Library Associations and Institutions, 2008.

Yeo, Geoffrey. "Concept of Record (1): Evidence, Information, and Persistent Representations." *American Archivist* 70, no. 2 (2007): 315–43. https://doi.org/10.17723/aarc.70.2.u327764v1036756q.

Zavala, Jimmy et al. "'A Process Where We're All at the Table': Community Archives Challenging Dominant Modes of Archival Practice." *Archives & Manuscripts* 45, no. 3 (2017): 202–15. https://doi.org/10 .1080/01576895.2017.1377088.

Zeng, Marcia Lei, and Jian Qin. *Metadata.* New York: Neal-Schuman, 2008.

Zhang, Xuan et al. "Information Security Risk Management Framework for the [*sic*] Cloud Computing Environments." Paper presented at the 2010 10th IEEE International Conference on Computer and Information Technology (2010), 1328–34. https://ieeexplore.ieee.org/document/5577860.

Zorich, Diane M. *Charting the Digital Landscape of the Conservation Profession: A Report to the Profession.* Report of the Foundation of the American Institute for Conservation of Historic and Artistic Works, Washington, DC, 2016, 1. https://www.culturalheritage.org/docs/default-source/publications/reports/digital-landscape-report.pdf?sfvrsn=4, captured at https://perma.cc/X2QY-T548.

______. *Report of the Summit on Digital Curation in Art Museums.* Washington, DC: Krieger School of Arts & Sciences, Johns Hopkins University, 2015.

______, Günter Waibel, and Ricky Erway. *Beyond the Silos of the LAMs: Collaboration among Libraries, Archives and Museums.* Dublin, OH: OCLC Programs and Research, 2008.

Acknowledgments

Writing is a collaborative process, and this book would not have been possible without a network of supportive colleagues. We are deeply indebted to Peter Wosh, Teresa Brinati, Christopher Prom, the SAA Publication's Board, SAA copyeditors, and our three peer reviewers for their encouragement and insight. Numerous individuals offered suggestions on the initial outline and structure for the book and commented on various drafts of the manuscript. Special thanks go to Jeannie Drewes, Rachel Onuf, Richard Pearce-Moses, Ellen Cunningham-Kruppa, Michele Pacifico, Waverly Lowell, Mary Lynn Ritzenthaler, Howard Besser, Anne J. Gilliland, Tom Clareson, Joel Wurl, Cathleen Tefft, Ben Goldman, Jennifer Waxman, Rand Jimerson, Jamie Ganzel, Diana Shenk, and the staff of WWU's Heritage Resources Division: Ruth Steele, Michael Taylor, Tony Kurtz, Roz Koester, Tamara Belts, Rachel Thompson, David Schlitt, and Eric Mastor for their unflagging support. And, finally, we are deeply indebted to Sidney Berger, an extraordinary editor who brings art to his craft.

Elizabeth is deeply appreciative of the fellowship and wisdom that Michèle Cloonan brought to the project. Her preservation expertise and deep network in the preservation field were central to framing the structure for *Advancing Preservation*. In particular, Michèle's knowledge of preservation history and practice supported chapters 6 through 8 in the second section of the book, freeing Elizabeth to focus on defining principles and context for the first section of the book and the final chapters in the third section regarding the ethics and moral implications of contemporary preservation practice, as well as the opportunity to examine the intersection of preservation and MPLP. Michèle is appreciative of Beth's deep knowledge about archives. Themes that she has been writing about for years are now placed in a preservation context.

In closing, we would like to acknowledge Gregor Trinkaus-Randall for his contributions to this book and to the field of archival preservation. His passing is a loss to us all.

ELIZABETH JOFFRION and MICHÈLE CLOONAN

Acknowledgments

About the Authors

Michèle Valerie Cloonan is a professor in the School of Library and Information Science, College of Organizational, Computational, and Information Sciences, and Dean Emerita of the Graduate School of Library and Information Science at Simmons University. She studied humanities at Bennington College (AB) and the University of Chicago (AM) and has an MS and a PhD in library and information science from the University of Illinois. She was a conservator at the Newberry Library, a preservation administrator at Brown University libraries, and a rare book curator at Smith College. At UCLA she was associate professor and chair of Information Studies. In 2010, she was awarded the Paul Banks-Carolyn Harris Preservation Award from the American Library Association. Her book, *Preserving Our Heritage: Perspectives from Antiquity to the Digital Age* (ALA/Neal Schuman), received the 2016 Society of American Archivists' Preservation Publication Award. In 2018, she published *The Monumental Challenge of Preservation: The Past in a Volatile World* (MIT Press), winner of the University of Mary Washington Center for Historic Preservation Book Prize. More recently, a case study book that she coauthored with Peter Botticelli, Martha Mahard, and Simmons students, *Libraries, Archives, and Museums Today: Insights from the Field*, was published by Rowman & Littlefield.

Elizabeth Joffrion is the director of Heritage Resources and associate professor at Western Washington University where she leads the Libraries' Special Collections, University Archives and Record Center, and the Center for Pacific Northwest Studies. Prior to this position, she was a senior program officer at the National Endowment for the Humanities, Division of Preservation and Access where she coordinated the Preservation Assistance Grants Program. She has held professional positions at the Smithsonian Institution's Archives of American Art and the National Portrait Gallery, the North Carolina State Archives and the Historic New Orleans Collection, and has also taught courses on archives and special collections at Catholic University and Western Washington University. She received an MA in history from the University of New Orleans and a MLIS from the University of Maryland.

Index

R